THE LOEB CLASSICAL LIBRARY

FOUNDED BY JAMES LOEB, LL.D.

EDITED BY

G. P. GOOLD, PH.D.

PREVIOUS EDITORS

† T. E. PAGE, C.H., LITT.D.   † E. CAPPS, PH.D., LL.D.

† W. H. D. ROUSE, LITT.D.   † L. A. POST, L.H.D.

E. H. WARMINGTON, M.A., F.R.HIST.SOC.

SENECA
III

MORAL ESSAYS
III

310

SENECA

IN TEN VOLUMES

III

MORAL ESSAYS

WITH AN ENGLISH TRANSLATION BY

JOHN W. BASORE, Ph.D.

IN THREE VOLUMES

III

CAMBRIDGE, MASSACHUSETTS

HARVARD UNIVERSITY PRESS

LONDON

WILLIAM HEINEMANN LTD

MCMLXXV

American
ISBN 0-674-99343-8

British
ISBN 0 434 99310 7

First printed 1935
Reprinted 1958, 1964, 1975

Printed in Great Britain

CONTENTS OF VOLUME III

	PAGE
INTRODUCTION	vii
DE BENEFICIIS:	
BOOK I	2
BOOK II	50
BOOK III	126
BOOK IV	204
BOOK V	290
BOOK VI	364
BOOK VII	454
INDEX OF NAMES	527

INTRODUCTION

THE seven books *On Benefits*, addressed to Aebutius
Liberalis of Lyons, are a discursive and repetitious
treatment of the morality of giving and receiving—
the casuistry of benefaction and gratitude. The gist
of the matter is given more briefly in one of the
Epistles,[a] written in A.D. 64 after the publication of a
part or the whole of the *De Beneficiis.* The theme
was not new, but the lengthy elaboration of it is surprising. Some apology for this may be found in the
necessities of the ancient social order, in which, by
reason of many of its relations, benefaction and gratitude were counted, not private graces, but social
virtues.

Seneca's chief source was Hecaton, a Stoic philosopher of Rhodes, who had studied under Panaetius
and written numerous treatises now lost.

The date of the work is variously conjectured on
the basis of internal evidence, but there can be no
doubt that it belongs to the closing years of Seneca's
life.[b] Books I.-IV., from their essentially technical
character, form a unit, and probably appeared several
years after the death of Claudius (A.D. 54). That he

[a] lxxxi.
[b] Waltz, *Vie de Sénique*, p. 7, n. 2, places it between
A.D. 58 and 62.

was no longer living becomes evident from the sneer revealed at the end of Book I. The later books, which are supplementary and informal, are perhaps the most interesting. Books V. and VI. are placed by Duff[a] before Seneca's retirement in A.D. 62, and Book VII. still later, very near the end of his life (A.D. 65).

The best manuscript of the treatise is the *Codex Nazarianus*, of the eighth or ninth century, in the Palatine collection of the Vatican. Others of importance are R (*Codex Reginensis*), G (*Codex Guelferbytanus*), M (*Codex Monacensis*), and P (*Codex Parisinus*). In the critical notes O is used to designate a consensus of all or of most of these.

The Latin text, except for some matters of punctuation and orthography and the divergencies noted, is that of Hosius (second edition), Leipzig, 1914.

In general, for the elucidation of proper names the reader is referred to the Index.

<hr>

[a] *Literary Hist. of Rome in the Silver Age*, p. 218.

J. W. B.

ROME, *September*, 1935

SENECA
MORAL ESSAYS

L. ANNAEI SENECAE

AD AEBUTIUM LIBERALEM

DE BENEFICIIS

LIBER I

1 1. Inter multos ac varios errores temere incon-
sulteque viventium nihil propemodum indignius,[1]
vir optime Liberalis, dixerim, quam quod[2] beneficia
nec dare scimus nec accipere. Sequitur enim, ut
male collocata male debeantur ; de quibus non
redditis sero querimur ; ista enim perierunt, cum
2 darentur. Nec mirum est inter plurima maximaque vitia nullum esse frequentius quam ingrati animi.
Id evenire ex causis pluribus video.

Prima illa est, quod non eligimus dignos, quibus
tribuamus. Sed nomina facturi diligenter in patrimonium et vitam debitoris inquirimus, semina in
solum effetum et sterile non spargimus ; beneficia
sine ullo dilectu magis proicimus quam damus.

3 Nec facile dixerim, utrum turpius sit infitiari an
repetere beneficium ; id enim genus huius crediti

---

[1] indignius *commonly supplied* ; diffusius dixerim quam
quod *Bourgery* ; discerni haec duo dixerim quod *Préchac*.
[2] quam quod *MG*[2] : quod *N, Hosius after a lacuna.*

LUCIUS ANNAEUS SENECA

ON BENEFITS

BOOK I

AMONG the many and diverse errors of those who live
reckless and thoughtless lives, almost nothing that I
can mention, excellent Liberalis, is more disgraceful
than the fact that we do not know how either to give
or to receive benefits. For it follows that, if they are
ill placed, they are ill acknowledged, and, when we
complain of their not being returned, it is too late ;
for they were lost at the time they were given. Nor is
it surprising that among all our many and great vices,
none is so common as ingratitude. This I observe
results from several causes.

The first is, that we do not pick out those who are
worthy of receiving our gifts. Yet when we are about
to open an account with anyone, we are careful to
inquire into the means and manner of life of our
debtor ; we do not sow seed in worn-out and un-
productive soil ; but our benefits we give, or rather
throw, away without any discrimination.

Nor would it be easy to say whether it is more
shameful to repudiate a benefit, or to ask the repayment of it ; for from the nature of such a trust, we

3

est, ex quo tantum recipiendum sit, quantum ultro
refertur. Decoquere vero foedissimum ob hoc
ipsum, quia non opus est ad liberandam fidem facul-
tatibus sed animo ; reddit enim beneficium, qui
4 debet. Sed cum sit in ipsis crimen, qui ne confes-
sione quidem grati sunt, in nobis quoque est. Multos
experimur ingratos, plures facimus, quia alias graves
exprobratores exactoresque sumus, alias leves et quos
paulo post muneris sui paeniteat, alias queruli et
minima momenta calumniantes. Gratiam omnem
corrumpimus non tantum postquam dedimus bene-
5 ficia, sed dum damus. Quis nostrum contentus fuit
aut leviter rogari aut semel ? Quis non, cum aliquid
a se peti suspicatus est, frontem adduxit, vultum
avertit, occupationes simulavit, longis sermonibus et
de industria non invenientibus exitum occasionem
petendi abstulit et variis artibus necessitates prope-
6 rantes elusit ; in angusto vero comprensus aut distulit,
id est timide negavit, aut promisit, sed difficulter,
sed subductis superciliis, sed malignis et vix exeunti-
7 bus verbis ? Nemo autem libenter debet, quod non
accepit, sed expressit. Gratus adversus eum esse
quisquam potest, qui beneficium aut superbe abiecit
aut iratus impegit aut fatigatus, ut molestia careret,
dedit ? Errat, si quis sperat responsurum sibi, quem
8 dilatione lassavit, expectatione torsit. Eodem animo

have a right to receive back only what is voluntarily returned. To plead bankruptcy is, surely, most disgraceful, just for the reason that, in order to perform the promised payment, what is needed is, not wealth, but the desire; for, if a benefit is acknowledged, it is returned. But, while those who do not even profess to be grateful are blameworthy, so also are we. Many men we find ungrateful, but more we make so, because at one time we are harsh in our reproaches and demands, at another, are fickle and repent of our gift as soon as we have made it, at another, are fault-finding and misrepresent the importance of trifles. Thus we destroy all sense of gratitude, not only after we have given our benefits, but even while we are in the act of giving them. Who of us has been content to have a request made lightly, or but once? Who, when he suspected that something was being sought from him, has not knit his brows, turned away his face, pretended to be busy, by long-drawn conversation, which he purposely kept from ending, deprived another of the opportunity of making a request, and by various tricks baffled his pressing needs? Who, when actually caught in a corner, has not either deferred the favour, that is, been too cowardly to refuse it, or promised it with ungraciousness, with frowning brows, and with grudging words that were scarcely audible? Yet no one is glad to be indebted for what he had, not received, but extorted. Can anyone be grateful to another for a benefit that has been haughtily flung to him, or thrust at him in anger, or given out of sheer weariness in order to save further trouble? Whoever expects that a man whom he has wearied by delay and tortured by hope will feel any indebtedness

beneficium debetur, quo datur, et ideo non est neclegenter dandum ; sibi enim quisque debet, quod a
nesciente accepit ; ne tarde quidem, quia, cum omni
in officio magni aestimetur dantis voluntas, qui tarde
fecit, diu noluit ; utique non contumeliose ; nam cum
ita natura comparatum sit, ut altius iniuriae quam
merita descendant et illa cito defluant, has tenax
memoria custodiat, quid expectat, qui offendit, dum
obligat ? Satis adversus illum gratus est, si quis
beneficio eius ignoscit.

9 Non est autem, quod tardiores faciat ad bene
merendum turba ingratorum. Nam primum, ut dixi,
nos illam augemus ; deinde ne deos quidem immortales ab hac tam effusa nec cessante benignitate[1]
sacrilegi neclegentesque eorum deterrent. Utuntur
natura sua et cuncta interque illa ipsos munerum
suorum malos interpretes iuvant. Hos sequamur
duces, quantum humana imbecillitas patitur ; demus
beneficia, non feneremur. Dignus est decipi, qui de
recipiendo cogitavit, cum daret. At male cesserit.

10 Et liberi et coniuges spem fefellerunt, tamen et
educamus et ducimus, adeoque adversus experimenta
pertinaces sumus, ut bella victi et naufragi maria
repetamus. Quanto magis permanere in dandis

---

[1] nec cessante benignitate *corrected by Lipsius* : necessitate *O*.

deceives himself. A benefit is acknowledged in the same spirit in which it is bestowed, and for that reason it ought not to be bestowed carelessly ; for a man thanks only himself for what he receives from an unwitting giver. Nor should it be given tardily, since, seeing that in every service the willingness of the giver counts for much, he who acts tardily has for a long time been unwilling. And, above all, it should not be given insultingly ; for, since human nature is so constituted that injuries sink deeper than kindnesses, and that, while the latter pass quickly from the mind, the former are kept persistently in memory, what can he expect who, while doing a favour, offers an affront ? If you pardon such a man for giving a benefit, you show gratitude enough.

There is no reason, however, why the multitude of ingrates should make us more reluctant to be generous. For, in the first place, as I have said, we ourselves increase their number ; and, in the second place, not even the immortal gods are deterred from showing lavish and unceasing kindness to those who are sacrilegious and indifferent to them. For they follow their own nature, and in their universal bounty include even those who are ill interpreters of their gifts. Let us follow these as our guides in so far as human weakness permits ; let us make our benefits, not investments, but gifts. The man who, when he gives, has any thought of repayment deserves to be deceived. But suppose it has turned out ill. Both children and wives have disappointed our hopes, yet we marry and rear children, and so persistent are we in the face of experience that, after being conquered, we go back to war and, after being shipwrecked, we go back to sea. How much more fitting

7

beneficiis decet! Quae si quis non dat, quia non recepit, dedit, ut reciperet, bonamque ingratorum facit causam, quibus turpe est non reddere, si licet.

11 Quam multi indigni luce sunt! Tamen dies oritur. Quam multi, quod nati sunt, queruntur! Tamen natura subolem novam gignit ipsosque, qui non fuisse 12 mallent, esse patitur. Hoc et magni animi et boni proprium est, non fructum beneficiorum sequi, sed ipsa et post malos quoque bonum quaerere. Quid magnifici erat multis prodesse, si nemo deceperit? Nunc est virtus dare beneficia non utique reditura, quorum a viro egregio statim fructus perceptus est.

13 Adeo quidem ista res fugare nos et pigriores ad rem pulcherrimam facere non debet, ut, si spes mihi praecidatur gratum hominem reperiendi, malim non recipere beneficia quam non dare, quia, qui non dat, vitium ingrati antecedit. Dicam, quod sentio. Qui beneficium non reddit, magis peccat; qui non dat, citius.

1 2. Beneficia in volgus cum largiri institueris,
perdenda sunt multa, ut semel ponas bene.

In priore versu utrumque reprehendas; nam nec in vulgum effundenda sunt, et nullius rei, minime beneficiorum, honesta largitio est; quibus si detraxeris

---

a From an unknown author.

to persevere in bestowing benefits ! For if a man stops giving them because they were not returned, his purpose in giving them was to have them returned, and he supplies a just excuse to the ingrate, whose disgrace lies in not making a return if it is permissible. How many are unworthy of seeing the light ! Yet the day dawns. How many complain because they have been born ! Yet Nature begets new progeny, and even those who would rather not have been, she suffers to be. To seek, not the fruit of benefits, but the mere doing of them, and to search for a good man even after the discovery of bad men—this is the mark of a soul that is truly great and good. What glory would there be in doing good to many if none ever deceived you ? But as it is, it is a virtue to give benefits that have no surety of being returned, whose fruit is at once enjoyed by the noble mind. So true is it that we ought not to allow such a consideration to rout us from our purpose and make us less prone to do a very beautiful thing, that, even were I deprived of the hope of finding a grateful man, I should prefer not recovering benefits to not giving them, because he who does not give them merely forestalls the fault of the ungrateful man. I will explain what I mean. He who does not return a benefit, sins more, he who does not give one, sins earlier.

> To shower bounties on the mob should you delight,
> Full many must you lose, for one you place aright.[a]

In the first verse two points are open to criticism ; for, on the one hand, benefits ought not to be showered upon the mob, and, on the other, it is not right to be wasteful of any thing, least of all of benefits ; for, if you eliminate discernment in giving them, they cease

9

iudicium, desinunt esse beneficia, in aliud quodlibet
2 incident nomen. Sequens sensus mirificus est, qui uno
bene posito beneficio multorum amissorum damna
solatur. Vide, oro te, ne hoc et verius sit et magni-
tudini bene facientis aptius, ut illum hortemur ad
danda, etiam si nullum bene positurus est. Illud enim
falsum est " perdenda sunt multa " ; nullum perit,
3 quia, qui perdit, computaverat. Beneficiorum simplex
ratio est : tantum erogatur ; si reddet aliquid, lucrum
est, si non reddet, damnum non est. Ego illud dedi,
ut darem. Nemo beneficia in calendario scribit nec
avarus exactor ad horam et diem appellat. Numquam
illa vir bonus cogitat nisi admonitus a reddente ; alioqui in formam crediti transeunt. Turpis feneratio est
4 beneficium expensum ferre. Qualiscumque priorum
eventus est, persevera in alios conferre ; melius
apud ingratos iacebunt, quos aut pudor aut occasio
aut imitatio aliquando gratos poterit efficere. Ne
cessaveris, opus tuum perage et partes boni viri
exsequere. Alium re, alium fide, alium gratia,
alium consilio, alium praeceptis salubribus adiuva.
5 Officia etiam ferae sentiunt, nec ullum tam imman-
suetum animal est, quod non cura mitiget et in
amorem sui vertat. Leonum ora a magistris impune

10

to be benefits, and will fall under any other name you please. The sentiment of the second is admirable, for it allows a solitary benefit that is well placed to compensate for the loss of many that have been wasted. But consider, I beg of you, whether it may not be truer doctrine and more in accord with the generous spirit of the benefactor to urge him to give even though not one of his benefits is likely to be well placed. For " many must you lose " is a false sentiment ; not one is lost, because a loser is one who had kept an account. In benefits the book-keeping is simple—so much is paid out ; if anything comes back, it is gain, if nothing comes back, there is no loss. I made the gift for the sake of giving. No one enters his benefactions in his account-book, or like a greedy tax-collector calls for payment upon a set day, at a set hour. The good man never thinks of them unless he is reminded of them by having them returned ; otherwise, they transform themselves into a loan. To regard a benefit as an amount advanced is putting it out at shameful interest. No matter what the issue of former benefits has been, still persist in conferring them upon others ; this will be better even if they fall unheeded into the hands of the un-grateful, for it may be that either shame or opportunity or example will some day make these grateful. Do not falter, finish your task, and complete the rôle of the good man. Help one man with money, another with credit, another with influence, another with advice, another with sound precepts. Even wild beasts are sensible of good offices, and no creature is so savage that it will not be softened by kindness and made to love the hand that gives it. The lion will let a keeper handle his mouth with impunity,

11

tractantur, elephantorum feritatem usque in servile
obsequium demeretur cibus ; adeo etiam, quae extra
intellectum atque aestimationem beneficii posita sunt,
adsiduitas tamen meriti pertinacis evincit. Ingratus
est adversus unum beneficium ? Adversus alterum
non erit. Duorum oblitus est ? Tertium etiam in
eorum, quae exciderunt, memoriam reducet.

1　3. Is perdet beneficia, qui cito se perdidisse
credit ; at qui instat et onerat priora sequentibus,
etiam ex duro et immemori pectore gratiam ex-
tundit. Non audebit adversus multa oculos attol-
lere ; quocumque se convertit memoriam suam
fugiens, ibi te videat : beneficiis illum tuis cinge.

2　Quorum quae vis quaeve proprietas sit, dicam, si
prius illa, quae ad rem non pertinent, transilire mihi
permiseris, quare tres Gratiae et quare sorores sint,
et quare manibus implexis, et quare ridentes et
iuvenes[1] et virgines solutaque ac perlucida veste.

3 Alii quidem videri volunt unam esse, quae det beneficium, alteram, quae accipiat, tertiam, quae reddat ;
alii tria beneficorum[2] esse genera, promerentium,

4 reddentium, simul accipientium reddentiumque. Sed
utrumlibet ex istis iudica verum ; quid ista nos
scientia iuvat ? Quid ille consertis manibus in se
redeuntium chorus ? Ob hoc, quia ordo beneficii

---

[1] et iuvenes *added by Gertz.*
[2] beneficorum *corrected by Madvig* : beneficiorum *O.*

---

a Excuse for the digression is to be found in the fact
that the Latin name of the goddesses is associated with
gratus.

b Apparently, by bestowing them.

the elephant, for all his fierceness, is reduced to the docility of a slave by food; so true is it that even creatures whose condition excludes the comprehension and appraisement of a benefit, are nevertheless won over by persistent and steadfast kindness. Is a man ungrateful for one benefit? Perhaps he will not be so for a second. Has he forgotten two benefits? Perhaps a third will recall to memory the others also that have dropped from his mind.

That man will waste his benefits who is quick to believe that he has wasted them; but he who presses on, and heaps new benefits upon the old, draws forth gratitude even from a heart that is hard and unmindful. In the presence of multiplied benefits the ingrate will not dare to lift his eyes; wherever he turns, fleeing his memory of them, there let him see you—encircle him with your benefits.

Of the nature and property of these I shall speak later if you will permit me first to digress upon questions that are foreign to the subject—why the Graces [a] are three in number and why they are sisters, why they have their hands interlocked, and why they are smiling and youthful and virginal, and are clad in loose and transparent garb. Some would have it appear that there is one for bestowing a benefit, another for receiving it, and a third for returning it; others hold that there are three classes of benefactors—those who earn benefits,[b] those who return them, those who receive and return them at the same time. But of the two explanations do you accept as true whichever you like; yet what profit is there in such knowledge? Why do the sisters hand in hand dance in a ring which returns upon itself? For the reason that a benefit passing

13

per manus transeuntis nihilo minus ad dantem re-
vertitur et totius speciem perdit, si usquam inter-
ruptus est, pulcherrimus, si cohaeret et vices servat.
In eo est aliqua tamen maioris dignatio, sicut pro-
5 merentium. Vultus hilari sunt, quales solent esse,
qui dant vel accipiunt beneficia ; iuvenes, quia non
debet beneficiorum memoria senescere ; virgines,
quia incorrupta sunt et sincera et omnibus sancta ; in
quibus nihil esse adligati decet nec adstricti ; solutis
itaque tunicis utuntur ; perlucidis autem, quia beneficia conspici volunt.
6 Sit aliquis usque eo Graecis emancipatus, ut haec
dicat necessaria ; nemo tamen erit, qui etiam illud ad
rem iudicet pertinere, quae nomina illis Hesiodus imposuerit. Aglaien maximam natu appellavit, mediam
Euphrosynen, tertiam Thaliam. Horum nominum
interpretationem, prout cuique visum est, deflectit
et ad rationem aliquam conatur perducere, cum
Hesiodus puellis suis, quod voluit, nomen imposuerit.
7 Itaque Homerus uni mutavit, Pasithean appellavit et
in matrimonium promisit, ut scias non esse illas
virgines Vestales. Inveniam alium poetam, apud
quem praecingantur et spissis aut Phryxianis prod-
eant. Ergo et Mercurius una stat, non quia beneficia ratio commendat vel oratio, sed quia pictori ita
visum est.

---

a i.e., committed to virginity.
b i.e., of superior quality. The phrase is reminiscent of
the famous story of Phrixus and the Golden Fleece.
14

in its course from hand to hand returns nevertheless to the giver ; the beauty of the whole is destroyed if the course is anywhere broken, and it has most beauty if it is continuous and maintains an uninterrupted succession. In the dance, nevertheless, an older sister has especial honour, as do those who earn benefits. Their faces are cheerful, as are ordinarily the faces of those who bestow or receive benefits. They are young because the memory of benefits ought not to grow old. They are maidens because benefits are pure and undefiled and holy in the eyes of all ; and it is fitting that there should be nothing to bind or restrict them, and so the maidens wear flowing robes, and these, too, are transparent because benefits desire to be seen.

There may be someone who follows the Greeks so slavishly as to say that considerations of this sort are necessary ; but surely no one will believe also that the names which Hesiod assigned to the Graces have any bearing upon the subject. He called the eldest Aglaia, the next younger Euphrosyne, the third Thalia. Each one twists the significance of these names to suit himself, and tries to make them fit some theory although Hesiod simply bestowed on the maidens the name that suited his fancy. And so Homer changed the name of one of them, calling her Pasithea, and promised her in marriage in order that it might be clear that, if they were maidens, they were not Vestals.[a] I could find another poet in whose writings they are girdled and appear in robes of thick texture or of Phryxian wool.[b] And the reason that Mercury stands with them is, not that argument or eloquence commends benefits, but simply that the painter chose to picture them so.

15

8 Chrysippus quoque, penes quem subtile illud
acumen est et in imam penetrans veritatem, qui
rei agendae causa loquitur et verbis non ultra, quam
ad intellectum satis est, utitur, totum librum suum
his ineptiis replet, ita ut de ipso officio dandi, accipi-
endi, reddendi beneficii pauca admodum dicat ; nec
9 his fabulas, sed haec fabulis inserit. Nam praeter
ista, quae Hecaton transcribit, tres Chrysippus
Gratias ait Iovis et Eurynomes filias esse, aetate
autem minores quam Horas, sed meliuscula facie et
ideo Veneri datas comites. Matris quoque nomen
ad rem iudicat pertinere : Eurynomen enim dictam,
quia late patentis patrimonii sit beneficia dividere ;
tamquam matri post filias soleat nomen imponi
10 aut poetae vera nomina reddant ! Quemadmodum
nomenclatori memoriae loco audacia est et, cuicum-
que nomen non potest reddere, imponit, ita poetae
non putant ad rem pertinere verum dicere, sed aut
necessitate coacti aut decore corrupti id quemque
vocari iubent, quod belle facit ad versum. Nec illis
fraudi est, si aliud in censum detulerunt ; proximus
enim poeta suum illas ferre nomen iubet. Hoc ut
scias ita esse, ecce Thalia, de qua cum maxime
agitur, apud Hesiodum Charis est, apud Homerum
Musa.
1 4. Sed ne faciam, quod reprehendo, omnia ista,

---

a As the daughter of Ocean, she was the " Wide-Spreading
One."
b *i.e.*, a Grace.

Chrysippus, too, whose famous acumen is so keen and pierces to the very core of truth, who speaks in order to accomplish results, and uses no more words than are necessary to make himself intelligible—he fills the whole of his book with these puerilities, insomuch that he has very little to say about the duty itself of giving, receiving, and returning a benefit ; and his fictions are not grafted upon his teachings, but his teachings upon his fictions. For, not to mention what Hecaton copies from him, Chrysippus says that the three Graces are daughters of Jupiter and Eurynome, also that, while they are younger than the Hours, they are somewhat more beautiful, and therefore have been assigned as companions to Venus. In his opinion, too, the name of their mother has some significance, for he says that she was called Eurynome [a] because the distribution of benefits is the mark of an extensive fortune ; just as if a mother usually received her name after her daughters, or as if the names that poets bestow were genuine ! As a nomenclator lets audacity supply the place of memory, and every time that he is unable to call anyone by his true name, he invents one, so poets do not think that it is of any importance to speak the truth, but, either forced by necessity or beguiled by beauty, they impose upon each person the name that works neatly into the verse. Nor is it counted against them if they introduce a new name into the list ; for the next poet orders the maidens to take the name that he devises. And to prove to you that this is so, observe that Thalia, with whom we are especially concerned, appears in Hesiod as Charis,[b] in Homer as a Muse.

But for fear that I shall be guilty of the fault that

17

quae ita extra rem sunt, ut ne circa rem quidem sint,
relinquam. Tu modo nos tuere, si quis mihi obiciet,
quod Chrysippum in ordinem coegerim, magnum
mehercules virum, sed tamen Graecum, cuius acumen
nimis tenue retunditur et in se saepe replicatur;
etiam cum agere aliquid videtur, pungit, non per-
2 forat. Hic vero quod acumen est? De beneficiis dicendum est et ordinanda res, quae maxime humanam
societatem alligat; danda lex vitae, ne sub specie
benignitatis inconsulta facilitas placeat, ne liberalitatem, quam nec deesse oportet nec superfluere, haec
3 ipsa observatio restringat, dum temperat; docendi
sunt libenter dare, libenter accipere, libenter reddere
et magnum ipsis certamen proponere, eos, quibus
obligati sunt, re animoque non tantum aequare sed
vincere, quia, qui referre gratiam debet, numquam
consequitur, nisi praecessit; hi docendi sunt nihil
4 imputare, illi plus debere. Ad hanc honestissimam
contentionem beneficiis beneficia vincendi sic nos ad-
hortatur Chrysippus, ut dicat verendum esse, ne, quia
Charites Iovis filiae sunt, parum se grate gerere sacri-
5 legium sit et tam bellis puellis fiat iniuria! Tu me
aliquid eorum doce, per quae beneficentior gratiorque
adversus bene merentes fiam, per quae obligantium

I am criticizing, I shall abandon all these questions, which are so remote that they do not even touch the subject. Only do you defend me if anyone shall blame me for having put Chrysippus in his place—a great man, no doubt, but yet a Greek, one whose acumen is so finely pointed that it gets blunted and often folds back upon itself ; even when it seems to be accomplishing something, it does not pierce, but only pricks. But what has acumen to do here ? What we need is a discussion of benefits and the rules for a practice that constitutes the chief bond of human society ; we need to be given a law of conduct in order that we may not be inclined to the thoughtless indulgence that masquerades as generosity, in order, too, that this very vigilance, while it tempers, may not check our liberality, of which there ought to be neither any lack nor any excess ; we need to be taught to give willingly, to receive willingly, to return willingly, and to set before us the high aim of striving, not merely to equal, but to surpass in deed and spirit those who have placed us under obligation, for he who has a debt of gratitude to pay never catches up with the favour unless he outstrips it ; the one should be taught to make no record of the amount, the other to feel indebted for more than the amount. To this most honourable rivalry in outdoing benefits by benefits Chrysippus urges us by saying that, in view of the fact that the Graces are the daughters of Jupiter, we should fear that by showing a lack of gratitude we might become guilty of sacrilege and do an injustice to such beautiful maidens ! But teach thou me the secret of becoming more beneficent and more grateful to those who do me a service, the secret of the rivalry that is born in the hearts of the obligers

19

obligatorumque animi certent, ut, qui praestiterunt,
obliviscantur, pertinax sit memoria debentium.   Istae
vero ineptiae poetis relinquantur, quibus aures oblec-
6 tare propositum est et dulcem fabulam nectere.   At
qui ingenia sanare et fidem in rebus humanis retinere,
memoriam officiorum ingerere animis volunt, serio
loquantur et magnis viribus agant ; nisi forte existimas levi ac fabuloso sermone et anilibus argumentis
prohiberi posse rem perniciosissimam, beneficiorum
novas tabulas.

1   5. Sed quemadmodum supervacua transcurram,
ita exponam necesse est hoc primum nobis esse di-
scendum, quid accepto beneficio debeamus.   Debere
enim se ait[1] alius pecuniam, quam accepit, alius con-
2 sulatum, alius sacerdotium, alius provinciam.   Ista
autem sunt meritorum signa, non merita.   Non
potest beneficium manu tangi ; res animo geritur.
Multum interest inter materiam beneficii et beneficium ; itaque nec aurum nec argentum nec quicquam eorum, quae pro maximis accipiuntur, beneficium est, sed ipsa tribuentis voluntas.   Imperiti
autem id, quod oculis incurrit et quod traditur
possideturque, solum notant, cum contra illud, quod
in re carum atque pretiosum est, parvi pendunt.
3 Haec, quae tenemus, quae aspicimus, in quibus
cupiditas nostra haeret, caduca sunt, auferre nobis
et fortuna et iniuria potest.   Beneficium etiam amisso

---

[1] ait *added by Madvig.*

and the obliged so that those who have bestowed forget, those who owe persistently remember. As for those absurdities, let them be left to the poets, whose purpose it is to charm the ear and to weave a pleasing tale. But those who wish to heal the human soul, to maintain faith in the dealings of men, and to engrave upon their minds the memory of services— let these speak with earnestness and plead with all their power ; unless, perchance, you think that by light talk and fables and old wives' reasonings it is possible to prevent a most disastrous thing—the abolishment of benefits.

But, just as I am forced to touch lightly upon irrelevant questions, so I must now explain that the first thing we have to learn is what it is that we owe when a benefit has been received. For one man says that he owes the money which he has received, another the consulship, another the priesthood, another the administration of a province. But these things are the marks of services rendered, not the services themselves. A benefit cannot possibly be touched by the hand ; its province is the mind. There is a great difference between the matter of a benefit and the benefit itself ; and so it is neither gold nor silver nor any of the gifts which are held to be most valuable that constitutes a benefit, but merely the goodwill of him who bestows it. But the ignorant regard only that which meets the eye, that which passes from hand to hand and is laid hold of, while they attach little value to that which is really rare and precious. The gifts that we take in our hands, that we gaze upon, that in our covetousness we cling to, are perishable ; for fortune or injustice may take them from us. But a benefit endures even after that through which it

eo, per quod datum est, durat; est enim recte factum, quod irritum nulla vis efficit.

4 Amicum a piratis redemi, hunc alius hostis excepit et in carcerem condidit; non beneficium, sed usum beneficii mei sustulit. Ex naufragio alicui raptos vel ex incendio liberos reddidi, hos vel morbus vel aliqua fortuita iniuria eripuit; manet etiam sine illis, quod

5 in illis datum est. Omnia itaque, quae falsum beneficii nomen usurpant, ministeria sunt, per quae se voluntas amica explicat. Hoc in aliis quoque rebus

6 evenit, ut aliubi sit species rei, aliubi ipsa res. Imperator aliquem torquibus, murali et civica donat. Quid habet per se corona pretiosum? Quid praetexta? Quid fasces? Quid tribunal et currus? Nihil horum honor est, sed honoris insigne. Sic non est beneficium id, quod sub oculos venit, sed beneficii vestigium et nota.

1 6. Quid est ergo beneficium? Benevola actio tribuens gaudium capiensque tribuendo in id, quod facit, prona et sponte sua parata. Itaque non, quid fiat aut quid detur, refert, sed qua mente, quia beneficium non in eo, quod fit aut datur, consistit, sed in

2 ipso dantis aut facientis animo. Magnum autem esse inter ista discrimen vel ex hoc intellegas licet, quod

---

a *i.e.*, the true benefit lies in the intention; the service is but the manifestation of it.

was manifested has been lost ; for it is a virtuous act, and no power can undo it.

If I have rescued a friend from pirates, and afterwards a different enemy seized him and shut him up in prison, he has been robbed, not of my benefit, but of the enjoyment of my benefit. If I have saved a man's children from shipwreck or a fire and restored them to him, and afterwards they were snatched from him either by sickness or some injustice of fortune, yet, even when they are no more, the benefit that was manifested in their persons endures. All those things, therefore, which falsely assume the name of benefits, are but the services through which the goodwill *a* of a friend reveals itself. The same thing is true also of other bestowals—the form of the bestowal is one thing, the bestowal itself another. The general presents a soldier with a breast-chain or with a mural and civic crown. But what value has the crown in itself ? What the purple-bordered robe ? What the fasces ? What the tribunal and the chariot ? No one of these things is an honour, they are the badges of honour. In like manner that which falls beneath the eye is not a benefit—it is but the trace and mark of a benefit.

What then is a benefit ? It is the act of a well-wisher who bestows joy and derives joy from the bestowal of it, and is inclined to do what he does from the prompting of his own will. And so what counts is, not what is done or what is given, but the spirit of the action, because a benefit consists, not in what is done or given, but in the intention of the giver or doer. The great distinction that exists between these things, moreover, may be grasped from the simple statement that a benefit is un-

beneficium utique bonum est, id autem, quod fit aut
datur, nec bonum nec malum est. Animus est, qui
parva extollit, sordida illustrat, magna et in pretio
habita dehonestat ; ipsa, quae appetuntur, neutram
naturam habent, nec boni nec mali ; refert, quo illa
3 rector impellat, a quo forma rebus datur. Non est
beneficium ipsum, quod numeratur aut traditur, sicut
ne in victimis quidem, licet opimae sint auroque
praefulgeant, deorum est honor sed recta ac pia
voluntate venerantium. Itaque boni etiam farre ac
fitilla religiosi sunt ; mali rursus non effugiunt im-
pietatem, quamvis aras sanguine multo cruentaverint.
1 7. Si beneficia in rebus, non in ipsa bene-
faciendi voluntate consisterent, eo maiora essent,
quo maiora sunt, quae accipimus. Id autem falsum
est ; non numquam enim magis nos obligat, qui dedit
parva magnifice, qui " regum aequavit opes animo,"
qui exiguum tribuit sed libenter, qui paupertatis suae
oblitus est, dum meam respicit, qui non voluntatem
tantum iuvandi habuit sed cupiditatem, qui accipere
se putavit beneficium, cum daret, qui dedit tamquam
numquam[1] recepturus, recepit, tamquam non dedisset, qui occasionem, qua prodesset, et occupavit et
2 quaesiit. Contra ingrata sunt, ut dixi, licet re ac

[1] numquam *added by Préchac* : non *Hosius with inferior
MSS.*

---

[a] The thought follows the Stoic dogma that good and
evil are terms to be applied only to virtue and its opposite.
[b] *i.e.*, man's mind is part of the Universal Mind, the
creative principle of the world—God.
[c] Adapted from Virgil's description of the old man of
Corycus who lived upon his few acres with the contentment
of a king (*Georgics*, iv. 132).

doubtedly a good, while what is done or given is neither a good nor an evil. It is the intention that exalts small gifts, gives lustre to those that are mean, and discredits those that are great and considered of value; the things themselves that men desire have a neutral nature, which is neither good nor evil [a]; all depends upon the end toward which these are directed by the Ruling Principle [b] that gives to things their form. The benefit itself is not something that is counted out and handed over, just as, likewise, the honour that is paid to the gods lies, not in the victims for sacrifice, though they be fat and glitter with gold, but in the upright and holy desire of the worshippers. Good men, therefore, are pleasing to the gods with an offering of meal and gruel; the bad, on the other hand, do not escape impiety although they dye the altars with streams of blood.

If benefits consisted, not in the very desire to benefit, but in things, then the greater the gifts are which we have received, the greater would be the benefits. But this is not true; for sometimes we feel under greater obligations to one who has given small gifts out of a great heart, who " by his spirit matched the wealth of kings," [c] who bestowed his little, but gave it gladly, who beholding my poverty forgot his own, who had, not merely the willingness, but a desire to help, who counted a benefit given as a benefit received, who gave it with no thought of having it returned, who, when it was returned, had no thought of having given it, who not only sought, but seized, the opportunity of being useful. On the other hand, as I have said before, those benefits win no thanks, which, though they seem great

specie magna videantur, quae danti aut extorquentur
aut excidunt, multoque gratius venit, quod facili quam
3 quod plena manu datur. Exiguum est, quod in me
contulit, sed amplius non potuit ; at hic quod dedit,
magnum est, sed dubitavit, sed distulit, sed, cum
daret, gemuit, sed superbe dedit, sed circumtulit et
placere non ei, cui praestabat, voluit ; ambitioni
dedit, non mihi.

1 8. Socrati cum multa pro suis quisque facul-
tatibus offerrent, Aeschines, pauper auditor:
" Nihil," inquit, " dignum te, quod dare tibi possim,
invenio et hoc uno modo pauperem esse me sentio.
Itaque dono tibi, quod unum habeo, me ipsum.
Hoc munus rogo, qualecumque est, boni consulas
cogitesque alios, cum multum tibi darent, plus
2 sibi reliquisse." Cui Socrates : " Quidni tu," inquit,
" magnum munus mihi dederis, nisi forte te parvo
aestimas ? Habebo itaque curae, ut te meliorem
tibi reddam, quam accepi." Vicit Aeschines hoc
munere Alcibiadis parem divitiis animum et omnem
iuvenum opulentorum munificentiam.

1 9. Vides, quomodo animus inveniat liberalitatis
materiam etiam inter angustias. Videtur mihi
dixisse : " Nihil egisti, fortuna, quod me pauperem
esse voluisti ; expediam dignum nihilo minus huic viro

---

^a *i.e.*, he had great wealth and no less devotion.

from their substance and show, are either forced
from the giver or are carelessly dropped, and
that comes much more gratefully which is given
by a willing rather than by a full hand. The
benefit which one man bestowed upon me is small,
but he was not able to give more ; that which
another gave me is great, but he hesitated, he put
it off, he grumbled when he gave it, he gave it
haughtily, he published it abroad, and the person
he tried to please was not the one on whom he
bestowed his gift—he made an offering, not to me,
but to his pride.

Once when many gifts were being presented to
Socrates by his pupils, each one bringing according
to his means, Aeschines, who was poor, said to him :
" Nothing that I am able to give to you do I find
worthy of you, and only in this way do I discover that
I am a poor man. And so I give to you the only
thing that I possess—myself. This gift, such as it is,
I beg you to take in good part, and bear in mind that
the others, though they gave to you much, have left
more for themselves." " And how," said Socrates,
" could it have been anything but a great gift—unless maybe you set small value upon yourself ? And
so I shall make it my care to return you to yourself
a better man than when I received you." By this
present Aeschines surpassed Alcibiades, whose heart
matched his riches,[a] and the wealthy youths with all
their splendid gifts.

You see how even in pinching poverty the heart
finds the means for generosity. These, it seems to
me, were the words of Aeschines : " You, O Fortune,
have accomplished nothing by wishing to make me
poor ; I shall none the less find for this great man a

munus, et quia de tuo non possum, de meo dabo."
Neque est, quod existimes illum vilem sibi fuisse :
pretium se sui fecit. Ingeniosus adulescens invenit,
quemadmodum Socraten sibi daret. Non quanta
quaeque sint, sed a quali profecta, prospiciendum.[1]

2 Callidus[2] non difficilem aditum praebuit immodica
cupientibus spesque improbas nihil re adiuturus verbis
fovit ; at peior opinio, si lingua asper, vultu gravis
cum invidia fortunam suam explicuit. Colunt enim
detestanturque felicem et, si potuerint, eadem facturi
odere facientem.[3]

3 Coniugibus alienis ne clam quidem sed aperte
ludibrio habitis suas aliis permisere. Rusticus, inhumanus ac mali moris et inter matronas abominanda
condicio est, si quis coniugem suam in sella prostare
vetuit et vulgo admissis inspectoribus vehi perspicuam
4 undique. Si quis nulla se amica fecit insignem nec
alienae uxori annuum praestat, hunc matronae
humilem et sordidae libidinis et ancillariolum vocant.
Inde decentissimum sponsaliorum genus est adulterium et in consensu vidui caelibatus, quoniam nemo

---

[1] quali profecta prospiciendum *Hosius before a lacuna*:
quali proficiendum *NRP*; quali profecta scire proficit
Préchac.

[2] *Before* callidus *Préchac supplies* En dominus *and for*
opinio *below reads* Opimio (*cf. Hor.* Sat. ii. 3. 142).

[3] *After* facientem *Hosius indicates a lacuna.*

---

[a] The harshness of the transition here and at the following
paragraph points to losses in the text. From a consideration
of the character of benefactors the author was led, apparently,
into a digression upon the degeneracy of the times.

gift that is worthy of him, and, since I cannot give
to him from your store, I shall give from my own."
Nor is there any reason for you to suppose that he
counted himself cheap : the value he set upon himself
was himself. And so clever a young man was he that
he discovered a way of giving to himself—Socrates !
It is not the size of our respective benefits, but the
character of the one from whom they come that
should be our concern.

ᵃA man is shrewd if he does not make himself
difficult of access to those who come with immoderate
desires, and encourages their wild expectations by
his words although in reality he intends to give them
no help ; but his reputation suffers if he is sharp
of tongue, stern in countenance, and arouses their
jealousy by flaunting his own good fortune. For they
court, and yet loathe, the prosperous man, and they
hate him for doing the same things that they would
do if they could.

They make a laughing-stock of other men's wives,
not even secretly, but openly, and then surrender
their own wives to others. If a man forbids his wife
to appear in public in a sedan-chair and to ride exposed on every side to the view of observers who
everywhere approach her, he is boorish and unman-
nerly and guilty of bad form, and the married women
count him a detestable mate. If a man makes
himself conspicuous by not having a mistress, and
does not supply an allowance to another man's wife,
the married women say that he is a poor sort and
is addicted to low pleasures and affairs with maidservants. The result of this is that adultery has
become the most seemly sort of betrothal, and
the bachelor is in accord with the widower, since

29

5 uxorem duxit, nisi qui abduxit. Iam rapta spargere,
sparsa fera et acri avaritia recolligere certant; nihil
pensi habere, paupertatem alienam contemnere,
suam magis[1] quam ullum aliud vereri malum, pacem
iniuriis perturbare, imbecilliores vi ac metu premere.
Nam provincias spoliari et nummarium tribunal
audita utrimque licitatione alteri addici non mirum,
quoniam, quae emeris, vendere gentium ius est!

1 10. Sed longius nos impetus evehit provocante
materia; itaque sic finiamus, ne in nostro saeculo
culpa subsidat. Hoc maiores nostri questi sunt, hoc
nos querimur, hoc posteri nostri querentur, eversos
mores, regnare nequitiam, in deterius res humanas
et omne nefas labi. At ista eodem stant loco
stabuntque, paulum dumtaxat ultra aut citra mota,
ut fluctus, quos aestus accedens longius extulit,
2 recedens interiore litorum vestigio tenuit. Nunc in
adulteria magis quam in alia peccabitur, abrumpetque
frenos pudicitia; nunc conviviorum vigebit furor et
foedissimum patrimoniorum exitium, culina; nunc
cultus corporum nimius et formae cura prae se ferens
animi deformitatem; nunc in petulantiam et auda-
ciam erumpet male dispensata libertas; nunc in

---

[1] magis *added by Gertz; omitted by Hosius.*

30

the only man who takes a wife is one who takes away a wife. Now men vie in squandering what they have stolen and then in regaining by fierce and sharp greed what they have squandered; they have no scruples; they esteem lightly the poverty of others and fear poverty for themselves more than any other evil; they upset peace with their injustices, and hard press the weaker with violence and fear. That the provinces are plundered, that the judgement-seat is for sale, and, when two bids have been made, is knocked down to one of the bidders is of course not surprising, since it is the law of nations that you can sell what you have bought!

But, because the subject is alluring, my ardour has carried me too far; and so let me close by showing that it is not our generation only that is beset by this fault. The complaint our ancestors made, the complaint we make, the complaint our posterity will make, is that morality is overturned, that wickedness holds sway, and that human affairs and every sin are tending toward the worse. Yet these things remain and will continue to remain in the same position, with only a slight movement now in this direction, now in that, like that of the waves, which a rising tide carries far inland, and a receding tide restrains within the limits of the shoreline. Now adultery will be more common than other sins, and chastity will tear off its reins; now a furore for feasting and the most shameful scourge that assails fortunes, the kitchen, will prevail, and now excessive adornment of the body and the concern for its beauty that displays an unbeauteous mind; now ill-controlled liberty will burst forth into wantonness and presumption; and now the progress will be toward

31

crudelitatem privatam ac publicam ibitur bellorum-
que civilium insaniam, qua omne sanctum ac sacrum
profanetur ; habebitur aliquando ebrietati honor, et
plurimum meri cepisse virtus erit.

3 Non expectant uno loco vitia, sed mobilia et inter
se dissidentia tumultuantur, pellunt in vicem fugan-
turque ; ceterum idem semper de nobis pronuntiare
debebimus, malos esse nos, malos fuisse, — invitus
4 adiciam, et futuros esse. Erunt homicidae, tyranni,
fures, adulteri, raptores, sacrilegi, proditores ; infra
omnia ista ingratus est, nisi quod omnia ista ab
ingrato sunt, sine quo vix ullum magnum facinus
adcrevit.

Hoc tu cave tamquam maximum crimen ne
admittas ; ignosce tamquam levissimo, si admissum
est. Haec est enim iniuriae summa : beneficium
perdidisti. Salvum est enim tibi ex illo, quod est
5 optimum : dedisti. Quemadmodum autem cu-
randum est, ut in eos potissimum beneficia con-
feramus, qui grate responsuri erunt, ita quaedam,
etiam si male de illis sperabitur, faciemus tribue-
musque, non solum si iudicabimus ingratos fore, sed
si sciemus fuisse. Tamquam si filios alicui restituere
potero magno periculo liberatos sine ullo meo, non
dubitabo. Dignum etiam impendio sanguinis mei
tuebor et in partem discriminis veniam ; indignum

cruelty, on the part both of the state and of the individual, and to the insanity of civil war, which desecrates all that is holy and sacred; sometimes it will be drunkenness on which honour is bestowed, and he who can hold the most wine will be a hero.

Vices do not wait expectantly in just one spot, but are always in movement and, being at variance with each other, are in constant turmoil, they rout and in turn are routed; but the verdict we are obliged to pronounce upon ourselves will always be the same: wicked we are, wicked we have been, and, I regret to add, always shall be. Homicides, tyrants, thieves, adulterers, robbers, sacrilegious men, and traitors there always will be; but worse than all these is the crime of ingratitude, unless it be that all these spring from ingratitude, without which hardly any sin has grown to great size.

Do you beware of committing this crime as being the greatest there is; if another commits it, pardon it as being the most trivial. For the sum of your injury is this—you have wasted a benefit. For you have the best part of it still unharmed—the fact that you gave it. But, although we ought to be careful to confer benefits by preference upon those who will be likely to respond with gratitude, yet there are some that we shall do even if we expect from them poor results, and we shall bestow benefits upon those who, we not only think will be, but we know have been, ungrateful. For example, if I shall be able to restore to someone his sons by rescuing them from great danger without any risk to myself, I shall not hesitate to do so. If a man is a worthy one, I shall defend him even at the cost of my own blood, and share his peril; if he is unworthy, and I shall be able

si eripere latronibus potero clamore sublato, salutarem vocem homini non pigebit emittere.

1   11. Sequitur, ut dicamus, quae beneficia danda sint et quemadmodum. Primum demus necessaria, deinde utilia, deinde iucunda, utique mansura. Incipiendum est autem a necessariis ; aliter enim ad animum pervenit, quod vitam continet, aliter, quod exornat aut instruit. Potest in eo aliquis fastidiosus esse aestimator, quo facile cariturus est, de quo dicere licet : " Recipe, non desidero ; meo contentus sum." Interim non reddere tantum libet, quod acceperis, sed abicere.

2   Ex his, quae necessaria sunt, quaedam primum obtinent locum, sine quibus non possumus vivere, quaedam secundum, sine quibus non debemus, 3 quaedam tertium, sine quibus nolumus. Prima huius notae sunt : hostium manibus eripi et tyrannicae irae et proscriptioni et aliis periculis, quae varia et incerta humanam vitam obsident. Quidquid horum discusserimus, quo maius ac terribilius erit, hoc maiorem inibimus gratiam ; subit enim cogitatio, quantis sint liberati malis, et lenocinium est muneris antecedens metus. Nec tamen ideo debemus tardius quemquam servare, quam possumus, ut muneri 4 nostro timor imponat pondus. Proxima ab his sunt,

to rescue him from robbers by raising an outcry, I shall not be slow to utter the cry that will save a human being.

I pass next to the discussion of what benefits ought to be given and the manner of their bestowal. Let us give what is necessary first, then what is useful, then what is pleasurable, particularly things that will endure. But we should begin with necessities; for that which supports life impresses the mind in one way, that which adorns or equips life, in quite another. It is possible for a man to be scornful in his estimate of a gift which he can easily do without, of which he may say : " Take it back, I do not want it ; I am content with what I have." Sometimes it is a pleasure, not merely to give back, but to hurl from you, what you have received.

Of the benefits that are necessary, some, those without which we are not able to live, have the first place, others, those without which we ought not to live, the second, and still others, those without which we are not willing to live, the third. The first are of this stamp—to be snatched from the hands of the enemy, from the wrath of a tyrant, from proscription, and the other perils which in diverse and uncertain forms beset human life. The greater and the more formidable the danger from any one of these, the greater will be the gratitude that we shall receive when we have banished it ; for the thought of the greatness of the ills from which they have been freed will linger in men's minds, and their earlier fear will enhance the value of our service. And yet we ought not to be slower in saving a man than we might be solely in order that his fear may add weight to our service. Next to these come the blessings without

sine quibus possumus quidem vivere, sed ut mors
potior sit, tamquam libertas et pudicitia et mens
bona. Post haec habebimus coniunctione ac sanguine
usuque et consuetudine longa cara, ut liberos, coniuges, penates, cetera, quae usque eo animus sibi
applicuit, ut ab illis quam vita divelli gravius
existimet.

5   Subsecuntur utilia, quorum varia et lata materia
est ; hic erit pecunia non superfluens sed ad sanum
modum habendi parata ; hic erit honor et processus
ad altiora tendentium ; nec enim utilius quicquam
est quam sibi utilem fieri.

Iam cetera ex abundanti veniunt delicatos factura.
In his sequemur, ut opportunitate grata sint, ut non
vulgaria, quaeque aut pauci habuerint aut pauci intra
hanc aetatem aut hoc modo, quae, etiam si natura
6 pretiosa non sunt, tempore aut loco fiant. Videamus,
quid oblatum maxime voluptati futurum sit, quid
frequenter occursurum habenti, ut totiens nobiscum
quotiens cum illo sit. Utique cavebimus, ne munera
supervacua mittamus, ut feminae aut seni arma
venatoria, ut rustico libros, ut studiis ac litteris
dedito retia. Aeque ex contrario circumspiciemus,

---

^a Used in hunting.

which, indeed, we are able to live, yet death becomes preferable, such as liberty and chastity and a good conscience. After these will be the objects that we hold dear by reason of kinship and blood and experience and long habit, such as children, wives, household gods, and all the other things to which the mind becomes so attached that to be robbed of them seems to it more serious than to be robbed of life.

Next in order are the useful benefits, the matter of which is wide and varied ; here will be money, not in excess, but enough to provide for a reasonable standard of living ; here will be public office and advancement for those who are striving for the higher positions, for nothing is more useful than to be made useful to oneself.

All benefits beyond these come as superfluities and tend to pamper a man. In the case of these, our aim shall be to make them acceptable by reason of their timeliness, to keep them from being common-place, and to give the sort of things that either few, or few in our own time or in this fashion, have possessed, the sort of things that, even if they are not intrinsically valuable, may become valuable by reason of the time and place. Let us consider what will be likely to give the greatest pleasure after it has been bestowed, what is likely to meet the eyes of the owner over and over so that every time he thinks of it he may think of us. In every case we shall be careful not to send gifts that are superfluous, for example, the arms of the chase to a woman or to an old man, books to a bumpkin, or nets *a* to one who is devoted to study and letters. On the other hand we shall be equally careful, while wishing to

ne, dum grata mittere volumus, suum cuique morbum exprobratura mittamus, sicut ebrioso vina
et valetudinario medicamenta. Maledictum enim
incipit esse, non munus, in quo vitium accipientis
adgnoscitur.

1   12. Si arbitrium dandi penes nos est, praecipue
mansura quaeremus, ut quam minime mortale munus
sit. Pauci enim sunt tam grati, ut, quid acceperint,
etiam si non vident, cogitent. Ingratos quoque
memoria cum ipso munere incurrit, ubi ante oculos
est et oblivisci sui non sinit, sed auctorem suum
ingerit et inculcat. Eo quidem magis duratura
quaeramus, quia numquam admonere debemus; ipsa
2 res evanescentem memoriam excitet. Libentius
donabo argentum factum quam signatum; libentius
statuas quam vestem et quod usus brevis deterat.
Apud paucos post rem manet gratia; plures sunt,
apud quos non diutius in animo sunt donata, quam
in usu. Ego, si fieri potest, consumi munus meum
nolo; extet, haereat amico meo, convivat.

3   Nemo tam stultus est, ut monendus sit, ne cui
gladiatores aut venationem iam munere edito mittat
et vestimenta aestiva bruma, hiberna solstitio. Sit
in beneficio sensus communis; tempus, locum ob-

send what will be acceptable, not to send gifts that will reproach a man with his weakness, as for example wines to a drunkard and medicines to a valetudinarian. For a gift that recognizes a vice of the recipient tends to be, not a boon, but a bane.

If the choice of what is to be given is in our own hands, we shall seek especially for things that will last, in order that our gift may be as imperishable as possible. For they are few indeed who are so grateful that they think of what they have received even if they do not see it. Yet even the ungrateful have their memory aroused when they encounter the gift itself, when it is actually before their eyes and does not let them forget it, but instead brings up the thought of its giver and impresses it upon their mind. And let us all the more seek to make gifts that will endure because we ought never to remind anyone of them ; let the object itself revive the memory that is fading. I shall be more willing to give wrought than coined silver ; more willing to give statues than clothing or something that will wear out after brief usage. Few there are whose gratitude survives longer than the object given ; there are more who keep gifts in mind only so long as they are in use. For my part, if it is possible, I do not want my gift to perish ; let it survive, let it cling fast to my friend, let it live with him.

No one is so stupid as to need the warning that he should not send gladiators or wild beasts to a man who has just given a public spectacle, or send a present of summer clothing in midwinter and winter clothing in midsummer. Social tact should be used in bestowing a benefit ; there must be regard

servet, personas, quia momentis quaedam grata et ingrata sunt. Quanto acceptius est, si id damus, quod quis non habet, quam cuius copia abundat, quod diu quaerit nec invenit, quam quod ubique visurus

4 est! Munera non tam pretiosa quam rara et exquisita sint, quae etiam apud divitem sui locum faciant, sicut gregalia quoque poma et post paucos dies itura in fastidium delectant, si provenere maturius. Illa quoque non erunt sine honore, quae aut nemo illis alius dedit aut nos nulli alii.

1 13. Alexandro Macedoni, cum victor Orientis animos supra humana tolleret, Corinthii per legatos gratulati sunt et civitate illum sua donaverunt. Cum risisset hoc Alexander officii genus, unus ex legatis: "Nulli," inquit, "civitatem umquam dedimus alii

2 quam tibi et Herculi." Libens accepit non dilutum honorem et legatos invitatione aliaque humanitate prosecutus cogitavit, non qui sibi civitatem darent, sed cui dedissent; et homo gloriae deditus, cuius nec naturam nec modum noverat, Herculis Liberique vestigia sequens ac ne ibi quidem resistens, ubi illa defecerant, ad socium honoris sui respexit a dantibus, tamquam caelum, quod mente vanissima complecte-

for time, place, and the person, for some gifts are acceptable or unacceptable according to circumstances. How much more welcome the gift will be if we give something that a man does not have, rather than something with which he is abundantly supplied, something that he has long searched for and has not yet found, rather than something which he is likely to see everywhere ! Presents should be, not so much costly, as rare and choice—the sort which even a rich man will make a place for ; just as the common fruits, of which we shall grow tired after a few days, give us pleasure if they have ripened out of season. And, too, people will not fail to appreciate the gifts which either no one else has given to them, or which we have given to no one else.

When Alexander of Macedonia, being victorious over the East, was puffed up with more than human pride, the Corinthians sent their congratulations by an embassy, and bestowed upon him the right of citizenship in their state. This sort of courtesy made Alexander smile, whereupon one of the ambassadors said to him : " To no one besides Hercules and yourself have we ever given the right of citizenship." Alexander gladly accepted so marked an honour, and bestowed hospitality and other courtesy upon the ambassadors, reflecting, not who they were who had given him the privilege of citizenship, but to whom they had given it ; and, slave as he was to glory, of which he knew neither the true nature nor the limitations, following the footsteps of Hercules and of Bacchus, and not even halting his course where they ceased, he turned his eyes from the givers of the honour to his partner in it, just as if heaven, to which in supreme vanity he aspired, were now his because

3 batur, teneret, quia Herculi aequabatur! Quid enim
illi simile habebat vesanus adulescens, cui pro virtute
erat felix temeritas? Hercules nihil sibi vicit;
orbem terrarum transivit non concupiscendo, sed
iudicando, quid vinceret, malorum hostis, bonorum
vindex, terrarum marisque pacator. At hic a pueritia
latro gentiumque vastator, tam hostium pernicies
quam amicorum, qui summum bonum duceret terrori
esse cunctis mortalibus, oblitus non ferocissima
tantum, sed ignavissima quoque animalia timeri ob
malum virus.

1 **14.** Ad propositum nunc revertamur. Beneficium
si qui quibuslibet dat, nulli gratum est; nemo se
stabularii aut cauponis hospitem iudicat nec convivam dantis epulum, ubi dici potest: " Quid enim
in me contulit? Nempe hoc, quod et in illum vix
bene notum sibi et in illum etiam inimicum ac
turpissimum hominem. Numquid enim me dignum
iudicavit? Morbo suo morem gessit!" Quod voles
gratum esse, rarum effice; quivis[1] patitur sibi imputari.

2 Nemo haec ita interpretetur, tamquam reducam
liberalitatem et frenis artioribus reprimam; illa vero,
in quantum libet, exeat, sed eat, non erret. Licet ita
largiri, ut unusquisque, etiam si cum multis accepit,

[1] quivis *Préchac*: quis *N*; *so Hosius adding* volgaria
after imputari.

---

[a] This pitting of Alexander's fortune against his virtue is
the theme of an essay by Plutarch (Περὶ τῆς Ἀλεξάνδρου
τύχης ἢ ἀρετῆς).

[b] *i.e.*, his own vanity.

he was put on a level with Hercules! Yet what resemblance to him had that mad youth who instead of virtue showed fortunate [a] rashness? Hercules conquered nothing for himself; he traversed the world, not in coveting, but in deciding what to conquer, a foe of the wicked, a defender of the good, a peacemaker on land and sea. But this other was from his boyhood a robber and a plunderer of nations, a scourge alike to his friends and to his foes, one who found his highest happiness in terrorizing all mortals, forgetting that it is not merely the fiercest creatures, but also the most cowardly, that are feared on account of their deadly venom.

But let me return now to my subject. Whoever gives a benefit to anyone you please, has gratitude from no one; in an inn or a hotel no one regards himself as the guest of the landlord, or at a public feast as the intimate friend of the man who is giving it, for one may well say: "What favour, pray, has he conferred upon me? The same, to be sure, that he has conferred on that other fellow, whom he scarcely knows, and on that one over there, who is his enemy and a most disreputable man. Did he consider that I was worthy of it? He merely indulged a personal weakness [b]!" If you want to give what will be acceptable, make the gift a rare one—anyone can endure being indebted for that!

Let no one gather from my words that I desire to restrain liberality, to bridle it in with tighter reins; let it indeed go forth as far as it likes, but let it go by a path, and not wander. It is possible to distribute bounty in such a way that each person, even if he has received his gift in company with others, will not

3 in populo se esse non putet. Nemo non habeat
aliquam familiarem notam, per quam speret se propius admissum. Dicat : " Accepi idem, quod ille,
sed ultro. Accepi, quod ille, sed ego intra breve
tempus, cum ille diu meruisset. Sunt, qui idem
habeant, sed non eisdem verbis datum, non eadem
comitate tribuentis. Ille accepit, cum rogasset ; ego
non rogaram. Ille accepit, sed facile redditurus, sed
cuius senectus et libera orbitas magna promittebat ;
mihi plus dedit, quamvis idem dederit, quia sine
4 spe recipiendi dedit." Quemadmodum meretrix ita
inter multos se dividet, ut nemo non aliquod signum
familiaris animi ferat, ita, qui beneficia sua amabilia
esse vult, excogitet, quomodo et multi obligentur et
tamen singuli habeant aliquid, quo se ceteris prae-
ferant.

1   15. Ego vero beneficiis non obicio moras ; quo
plura maioraque fuerint, plus adferent laudis. At sit
iudicium ; neque enim cordi esse cuiquam possunt
2 forte ac temere data. Quare si quis existimat nos,
cum ista praecipimus, benignitatis fines introrsus referre et illi minus laxum limitem aperire, ne perperam
monitiones nostras exaudivit.[1] Quam enim virtutem

----

[1] exaudivit *Préchac* : exaudiat *O* : exaudit *Hosius*.

----

[a] *i.e.*, the giver might expect a legacy.

think that he is simply one of a crowd. Let everyone have some mark of intimacy which permits him to hope that he has been admitted to greater favour than others. He may say : " I received the same thing that So-and-so did, but without asking for it. I received the same thing that So-and-so did, but at the end of a short time, whereas he had long since earned it. There are those who have the same thing, but it was not given to them with the same words, with the same friendliness, on the part of the bestower. So-and-so received his gift after he had asked for it ; I did not ask for mine. So-and-so received a gift, but he could easily make return, but his old age and his irresponsible childlessness [a] afforded great expectations ; to me more was given although the same thing was given, because it was given without expectation of any return." A courtesan will distribute her favours among her many lovers in such a way that each one of them will get some sign of her intimate regard ; just so the man who wishes his benefactions to be appreciated should contrive both to place many under obligation, and yet to see that each one of them gets something that will make him think he is preferred above all the others.

In truth, I place no obstacles in the way of benefits ; the more there are and the greater they are, the more honour will they have. But let judgement be used ; for what is given in a haphazard and thoughtless manner will be prized by no one. Wherefore, if anyone supposes that in laying down these rules we mean to narrow the bounds of liberality, and to open to it a less extensive field, he really has heard my admonitions incorrectly. For what virtue do we

45

magis veneramur? Cui magis stimulos addimus?
Quibusve tam convenit haec adhortatio quam nobis
3 societatem generis humani sancientibus? Quid ergo
est? Cum sit nulla honesta vis animi, etiam si a
recta voluntate incepit, nisi quam virtutem modus
fecit, veto liberalitatem nepotari. Tunc iuvat accepisse beneficium et supinis quidem manibus, ubi
illud ratio ad dignos perducit, non quolibet casus
et consilii indigens impetus defert; quod ostentare
4 libet et inscribere sibi. Beneficia tu vocas, quorum
auctorem fateri pudet? At illa quanto gratiora sunt
quantoque in partem interiorem animi numquam
exitura descendunt, cum delectant cogitantem magis
a quo, quam quid acceperis?

5 Crispus Passienus solebat dicere quorundam se
iudicium malle quam beneficium, quorundam beneficium malle quam iudicium, et subiciebat exempla.
" Malo," aiebat, " divi Augusti iudicium, malo
6 Claudii beneficium." Ego vero nullius puto expetendum esse beneficium, cuius vile iudicium est.
Quid ergo? Non erat accipiendum a Claudio, quod
dabatur? Erat, sed sicut a fortuna, quam scires
posse statim malam fieri. Quid ista inter se mixta

Stoics venerate more ? What virtue do we try more to encourage ? Who are so fitted to give such admonition as ourselves—we who would establish the fellowship of the whole human race ? What, then, is the case ? Since no effort of the mind is praiseworthy, even if it springs from right desire, unless moderation turns it into some virtue, I protest against the squandering of liberality. The benefit that it is a delight to have received, yea, with outstretched hands, is the one that reason delivers to those who are worthy, not the one that chance and irrational impulse carry no matter where—one that it is a pleasure to display and to claim as one's own. Do you give the name of benefits to the gifts whose author you are ashamed to admit ? But how much more acceptable are benefits, how much deeper do they sink into the mind, never to leave it, when the pleasure of them comes from thinking, not so much of what has been received, as of him from whom it was received !

Crispus Passienus used often to say that from some men he would rather have their esteem than their bounty, and that from others he would rather have their bounty than their esteem ; and he would add examples. "In the case of the deified Augustus," he would say, " I prefer his esteem, in the case of Claudius, his bounty." I, for my part, think that we should never seek a benefit from a man whose esteem is not valued. What, then, is the case ? Should not the gift that was offered by Claudius have been accepted ? It should, but as it would have been accepted from Fortune, who you were well aware might the next moment become unkind. And why do we differentiate the two cases that thus have

dividimus? Non est beneficium, cui deest pars optima, datum esse iudicio : alioqui pecunia ingens, si non ratione nec recta voluntate donata est, non magis beneficium est quam thesaurus. Multa sunt autem, quae oportet accipere nec debere.

merged ? A gift is not a benefit if the best part of it is lacking—the fact that it was given as a mark of esteem. Moreover the gift of a huge sum of money, if neither reason nor rightness of choice has prompted it, is no more a benefit than is a treasure-trove. There are many gifts that ought to be accepted, and yet impose no obligation.

LIBER II

1 1. Inspiciamus, Liberalis virorum optime, id quod ex priore parte adhuc superest, quemadmodum dandum sit beneficium ; cuius rei expeditissimam videor monstraturus viam : sic demus, quomodo 2 vellemus accipere. Ante omnia libenter, cito, sine ulla dubitatione.

Ingratum est beneficium, quod diu inter dantis manus haesit, quod quis aegre dimittere visus est et sic dare, tamquam sibi eriperet. Etiam si quid intervenit morae, evitemus omni modo, ne deliberasse videamur ; proximus est a negante, qui dubitavit, nullamque iniit gratiam. Nam cum in beneficio iucundissima sit tribuentis voluntas, quia nolentem se tribuisse ipsa cunctatione testatus est, non dedit sed adversus ducentem male retinuit ; multi autem sunt, quos liberales facit frontis infirmitas. Gratissima sunt 3 beneficia parata, facilia, occurrentia, ubi nulla mora fuit nisi in accipientis verecundia. Optimum est

BOOK II

Now let us examine, most excellent Liberalis, what still remains from the first part of the subject—the question of the way in which a benefit should be given. And in this matter I think that I can point out a very easy course—let us give in the manner that would have been acceptable if we were receiving. Above all let us give willingly, promptly, and without any hesitation.

No gratitude is felt for a benefit when it has lingered long in the hands of him who gives it, when the giver has seemed sorry to let it go, and has given it with the air of one who was robbing himself. Even though some delay should intervene, let us avoid in every way the appearance of having deliberately delayed ; hesitation is the next thing to refusing, and gains no gratitude. For, since in the case of a benefit the chief pleasure of it comes from the intention of the bestower, he who by his very hesitation has shown that he made his bestowal unwillingly has not "given," but has failed to withstand the effort to extract it ; there are many indeed who become generous only from a lack of courage. The benefits that stir most gratitude are those which are readily and easily obtainable and rush to our hands, where, if there is any delay, it has come only from the delicacy of the

51

antecedere desiderium cuiusque, proximum sequi.
Illud melius, occupare ante quam rogemur, quia, cum
homini probo ad rogandum os concurrat et suffun-
datur rubor, qui hoc tormentum remittit, multiplicat
4 munus suum.   Non tulit gratis, qui, cum rogasset,
accepit, quoniam quidem, ut maioribus nostris
gravissimis viris visum est, nulla res carius constat,
quam quae precibus empta est.   Vota homines parcius
facerent, si palam facienda essent ; adeo etiam deos,
quibus honestissime supplicamus, tacite malumus et
intra nosmet ipsos precari.

1   2. Molestum verbum est, onerosum, demisso vultu
dicendum, rogo.   Huius facienda est gratia amico
et quemcumque amicum sis promerendo facturus ;
properet licet, sero beneficium dedit, qui roganti
dedit.   Ideo divinanda cuiusque voluntas et, cum
intellecta est, necessitate gravissima rogandi libe-
randa est ; illud beneficium iucundum victurum in
2 animo scias, quod obviam venit.   Si non contigit
praevenire, plura rogantis verba intercidamus ; ne
rogati videamur sed certiores facti, statim promit-
tamus facturosque nos, etiam antequam interpelle-
mur, ipsa festinatione approbemus.   Quemadmodum
in aegris opportunitas cibi salutaris est et aqua

recipient. The best course is to anticipate each one's desire ; the next best, to indulge it. The first is the better—to forestall the request before it is put ; for, since a respectable man seals his lips and is covered with blushes if he has to beg, he who spares him this torture multiplies the value of his gift. The man who receives a benefit because he asked for it, does not get it for nothing, since in truth, as our forefathers, those most venerable men, discerned, no other thing costs so dear as the one that entreaty buys. If men had to make their vows to the gods openly, they would be more sparing of them ; so true is it that even to the gods, to whom we most rightly make supplication, we would rather pray in silence and in the secrecy of our hearts.

It is unpleasant and burdensome to have to say, " I ask," and as a man utters the words he is forced to lower his eyes. A friend and every one whom you hope to make a friend by doing him a service must be excused from saying them ; though a man gives promptly, his benefit has been given too late if it has been given upon request. Therefore we ought to divine each man's desire, and, when we have discovered it, he ought to be freed from the grievous necessity of making a request ; the benefit that takes the initiative, you may be sure, will be one that is agreeable and destined to live in the heart. If we are not so fortunate as to anticipate the asker, let us cut him off from using many words ; in order that we may appear to have been, not asked, but merely informed, let us promise at once and prove by our very haste that we were about to act even before we were solicited. Just as in the case of the sick suitability of food aids recovery, and plain water given at the

tempestive data remedii locum obtinuit, ita, quamvis leve et vulgare beneficium est, si praesto fuit, si proximam quamque horam non perdidit, multum sibi adicit gratiamque pretiosi sed lenti et diu cogitati muneris vincit. Qui tam parate facit, non est dubium, quin libenter faciat; itaque laetus facit et induit sibi animi sui vultum.

1   3. Ingentia quorundam beneficia silentium aut loquendi tarditas imitata gravitatem et tristitiam corrupit, cum promitterent vultu negantium. Quanto melius adicere bona verba rebus bonis et praedicatione humana benignaque commendare, quae 2 praestes! Ut ille se castiget, quod tardior in rogando fuit, adicias licet familiarem querellam: " Irascor tibi, quod, cum aliquid desiderasses, non olim scire me voluisti, quod tam diligenter rogasti, quod quemquam adhibuisti. Ego vero gratulor mihi, quod experiri animum meum libuit; postea, quidquid desiderabis, tuo iure exiges; semel rusticitati tuae 3 ignoscitur." Sic efficies, ut animum tuum pluris aestimet quam illud, quidquid est, ad quod petendum venerat. Tunc est summa virtus tribuentis, tunc benignitas, ubi ille, qui discessit, dicet sibi: " Magnum hodie lucrum feci; malo, quod illum talem inveni, quam si multiplicatum hoc ad me, de quo

right time serves as a remedy, so a benefit, no matter how trivial and commonplace it may be, if it has been given promptly, if not an hour has been wasted, gains much in value and wins more gratitude than a gift that, though costly, has been laggard and long considered. One who acts thus readily leaves no doubt that he acts willingly ; and so he acts gladly, and his face is clothed with the joy he feels.

Some who bestow immense benefits spoil them by their silence or reluctant words, which give the impression of austerity and sternness, and, though they promise a gift, have the air of refusing it. How much better to add kindly words to kindly actions, and grace the gifts you bestow with humane and generous speech ! In order that the recipient may reproach himself because he was slow to ask, you might add the familiar rebuke : " I am angry with you because, when you needed something, you were not willing to let me know long ago, because you took so much pains in putting your request, because you invited a witness to the transaction. Truly I congratulate myself because you were moved to put my friendliness to the test ; next time you will demand by your own right whatever you need—this once I pardon your bashfulness." The result of this will be that he will value your friendliness more than your gift, no matter what it was that he had come to seek. The bestower attains the highest degree of merit, the highest degree of generosity, only when it will be possible for the man who has left him to say : " Great is the gain that I have made to-day ; but I would rather have found the giver to be the sort of man he was than to have had many times the amount that

loquebar, alia via pervenisset; huic eius animo numquam parem gratiam referam."

1 4. At plerique sunt, qui beneficia asperitate verborum et supercilio in odium adducunt eo sermone usi, ea superbia, ut impetrasse paeniteat. Aliae deinde post rem promissam secuntur morae; nihil autem est acerbius, quam ubi quoque, quod[1] im-
2 petrasti, rogandum est. Repraesentanda sunt beneficia, quae a quibusdam accipere difficilius est quam impetrare. Hic rogandus est, ut admoneat, ille, ut consummet; sic unum munus per multorum manus teritur, ex quo gratiae minimum apud promittentem remanet, quia auctori detrahit, quisquis post illum
3 rogandus est. Hoc itaque curae habebis, si grate aestimari, quae praestabis, voles, ut beneficia tua inlibata, ut integra ad eos, quibus promissa sunt, perveniant, sine ulla, quod aiunt, deductione. Nemo illa intercipiat, nemo detineat; nemo in eo, quod daturus es, gratiam suam facere potest, ut non tuam minuat.

1 5. Nihil aeque amarum quam diu pendere; aequiore quidam animo ferunt praecidi spem suam quam trahi. Plerisque autem hoc vitium est ambitione prava differendi promissa, ne minor sit rogantium turba, quales regiae potentiae ministri sunt,

---

[1] quod *commonly added.*

we were talking about come to me in some other way; for the spirit he has shown I can never return enough gratitude.

Yet there are very many who by the harshness of their words and by their arrogance make their benefits hateful, so that, after being subjected to such language and such disdain, we regret that we have obtained them. And then, after the matter has been promised, a series of delays ensues ; but nothing is more painful than when you have to beg even for what you have been promised. Benefits should be bestowed on the spot, but there are some from whom it is more difficult to get them than to get the promise of them. You have to beg one man to act as a reminder, another to finish the transaction ; so a single gift is worn down by passing through many men's hands, and as a result very little gratitude is left for the giver of the promise, for every later person whose help must be asked reduces the sum due to him. And so, if you wish the benefactions that you bestow to be rewarded with gratitude, you will be concerned to have them come undiminished to those to whom they were promised, to have them come entire and, as the saying is, " without deduction." Let no one intercept them, let no one retard them ; for in the case of a benefit that you are going to give, no one can appropriate gratitude to himself without reducing what is due to you.

Nothing is so bitter as long suspense ; some can endure more calmly to have their expectation cut off than deferred. Yet very many are led into this fault of postponing promised benefits by a perverted ambition to keep the crowd of their petitioners from becoming smaller ; such are the tools of royal power,

quos delectat superbiae suae longum spectaculum,
minusque se iudicant posse, nisi diu multumque
singulis, quid possint, ostenderint. Nihil confestim,
nihil semel faciunt ; iniuriae illorum praecipites,
2 lenta beneficia sunt. Quare verissimum existima,
quod ille comicus dixit :

> Quid ? tu non intellegis
> tantum te gratiae demere, quantum morae adicis ?

Inde illae voces, quas ingenuus dolor exprimit :
" Fac, si quid facis " et : " Nihil tanti est ; malo
mihi iam neges." Ubi in taedium adductus animus
incipit beneficium odisse, dum expectat, potest ob id
3 gratus esse ? Quemadmodum acerbissima crudelitas
est, quae trahit poenam, et misericordiae genus est
cito occidere, quia tormentum ultimum finem sui
secum adfert, quod antecedit tempus, maxima venturi supplicii pars est, ita maior est muneris gratia,
quo minus diu pependit. Est enim etiam bonarum
rerum sollicita expectatio, et cum plurima beneficia remedium alicuius rei adferant, qui aut diutius
torqueri patitur, quem protinus potest liberare, aut
4 tardius gaudere, beneficio suo manus adfert. Omnis
benignitas properat, et proprium est libenter facientis
cito facere ; qui tarde et diem de die extrahens
profuit, non ex animo fecit. Ita duas res maximas
perdidit, et tempus et argumentum amicae voluntatis ; tarde velle nolentis est.

---

^a From an unknown author.

who delight in prolonging a display of arrogance, and deem themselves to be robbed of power unless they show long and often, to one after another, how much power they have. They do nothing promptly, nothing once for all; their injuries are swift, their benefits slow. And therefore the words of the comic poet, you are to believe, are absolutely true :

> Know you not this—the more delay you make,
> The less of gratitude from me you take ? [a]

And so a man cries out in an outburst of noble anger : " If you are going to do anything, do it ; " and : " Nothing is worth such a price ; I would rather have you say no at once." When the mind has been reduced to a state of weariness, and, while waiting for a benefit, begins to loathe it, can one possibly feel grateful for it ? Just as the sharpest cruelty is that which prolongs punishment, and there is a sort of mercy in killing swiftly because the supreme torture brings with it its own end, whereas the worst part of the execution that is sure to come is the interval that precedes it, so, in the case of a gift, gratitude for it will be the greater, the less long it has hung in the balance. For it is disquieting to have to wait even for blessings, and, since most benefits afford relief from some trouble, if a man leaves another to long torture when he might release him at once, or to tardy rejoicing, he has done violence to the benefit he confers. All generosity moves swiftly, and he who acts willingly is prone to act quickly ; if a man gives help tardily, deferring it from day to day, he has not given it heartily. Thus he has lost two invaluable things—time and the proof of his friendly intent ; tardy goodwill smacks of ill-will.

1 6: In omni negotio, Liberalis, non minima portio
est, quomodo quidque aut dicatur aut fiat. Multum
celeritas adiecit, multum abstulit mora. Sicut in telis
eadem ferri vis est, sed infinitum interest, utrum ex-
cusso lacerto torqueantur an remissa manu effluant,
gladius idem et stringit et transforat, quam presso
articulo venerit, refert, ita[1] idem est, quod datur, sed
2 interest, quomodo detur. Quam dulce, quam pretiosum est, si gratias sibi agi non est passus, qui dedit, si
dedisse, dum dat, oblitus est! Nam corripere eum,
cui cum maxime aliquid praestes, dementia est et
inserere contumeliam meritis. Itaque non sunt
exasperanda beneficia nec quicquam illis triste
miscendum. Etiam si quid erit, de quo velis admonere, aliud tempus eligito.

1 7. Fabius Verrucosus beneficium ab homine
duro aspere datum panem lapidosum vocabat, quem
esurienti accipere necessarium sit, esse acerbum.

2 Ti. Caesar rogatus a Nepote Mario praetorio, ut
aeri alieno eius succurreret, edere illum sibi nomina
creditorum iussit; hoc non est donare sed creditores
convocare. Cum edita essent, scripsit Nepoti iussisse
se pecuniam solvi adiecta contumeliosa admonitione.
Effecit, ut Nepos nec aes alienum haberet nec bene-

---

[1] ita *added by Haase; omitted by Hosius.*

In every transaction, Liberalis, not the least important part is the manner in which things are either said or done. Much is gained by swiftness, much is lost by delay. Just as, in the case of javelins, while all may have the same weight of iron, it makes an infinite difference whether they are hurled with a swing of the arm, or slip from a slackened hand, and just as the same sword will both scratch and deeply wound—the tightness of the grasp which directs it makes the difference—so, while the thing that is given may be just the same, the manner of the giving is all important. How sweet, how precious is a gift, for which the giver will not suffer us to pay even our thanks, which he forgot that he had given even while he was giving it! For to reprimand a man at the very moment that you are bestowing something upon him is madness, it is grafting insult upon an act of kindness. Benefits, therefore, must not be made irritating, they must not be accompanied by anything that is unpleasant. Even if there should be something upon which you would like to offer advice, choose a different time.

Fabius Verrucosus used to say that a benefit rudely given by a hard-hearted man is like a loaf of gritty bread, which a starving man needs must accept, but which is bitter to eat.

When Marius Nepos, a praetorian, being in deb , asked Tiberius Caesar to come to his rescue, Tiberius ordered him to supply him with the names of his creditors ; but this is really, not making a gift, but assembling creditors. When the names had been supplied, he wrote to Nepos that he had ordered the money to be paid, adding at the same time some offensive admonition. The result was that Nepos had

61

ficium; liberavit illum a creditoribus, sibi non
3 obligavit. Aliquid Tiberius secutus est; puto, noluit
plures esse, qui idem rogaturi concurrerent. Ista
fortasse efficax ratio fuerit ad hominum improbas
cupiditates pudore reprimendas, beneficium vero
danti tota alia sequenda est via. Omni genere, quod
des, quo sit acceptatius, adornandum est. Hoc vero
non est beneficium dare, deprehendere est.

1 8. Et ut in transitu de hac quoque parte dicam,
quid sentiam, ne principi quidem satis decorum
est donare ignominiae causa. "Tamen," inquit,
" effugere Tiberius ne hoc quidem modo, quod
vitabat, potuit; nam aliquot postea, qui idem
rogarent, inventi sunt, quos omnes iussit reddere in
senatu aeris alieni causas, et ita illis certas summas
2 dedit." Non est illud liberalitas, censura est.
Auxilium est, principale tributum est; beneficium
non est, cuius sine rubore meminisse non possum.
Ad iudicem missus sum; ut impetrarem, causam
dixi.

1 9. Praecipiunt itaque omnes auctores sapientiae quaedam beneficia palam danda, quaedam
secreto. Palam, quae consequi gloriosum, ut militaria dona, ut honores et quidquid aliud notitia
2 pulchrius fit; rursus, quae non producunt nec
honestiorem faciunt, sed succurrunt infirmitati,

neither a debt nor a true benefit ; Tiberius freed him from his creditors, but failed to attach him to himself. Yet Tiberius had his purpose ; he wished to prevent others, I suppose, from rushing to him in order to make the same request. That, perhaps, may have been an effective way to check, through a sense of shame, the extravagant desires of men, but a wholly different method must be followed by one who is giving a benefit. In order that what you give may become the more acceptable, you should enhance its value by every possible means. Tiberius was really not giving a benefit—he was finding fault.

And—to say in passing what I think about this other point—it is not quite proper even for a prince to bestow a gift in order to humiliate. " Yet," it may be said, " Tiberius was not able even in this way to escape what he was trying to avoid ; for after this a goodly number were found to make the same request, and he ordered them all to explain to the senate why they were in debt, and under this condition he granted to them specific sums." But liberality that is not, it is censorship ; I get succour, I get a subsidy from the prince—that is no benefit which I am not able to think of without a blush. It was a judge before whom I was summoned ; I had to plead a case in order to obtain my request.

And so all moralists are united upon the principle that it is necessary to give certain benefits openly, others without witnesses—openly, those that it is glorious to obtain, such as military decorations or official honours and any other distinction that becomes more attractive by reason of publicity ; on the other hand, those that do not give promotion or prestige, yet come to the rescue of bodily infirmity,

egestati, ignominiae, tacite danda sunt, ut nota
sint solis, quibus prosunt.

1 10. Interdum etiam ipse, qui iuvatur, vel[1] fallendus[2] est, ut habeat nec, a quo acceperit, sciat.
Arcesilan aiunt amico pauperi et paupertatem suam
dissimulanti, aegro autem et ne hoc quidem con-
fitenti deesse sibi in sumptum ad necessarios usus,
clam succurrendum iudicasse ; pulvino eius ignorantis
sacculum subiecit, ut homo inutiliter verecundus,
quod desiderabat, inveniret potius quam acciperet.

2 " Quid ergo ? ille nesciet, a quo acceperit ? "
Primum nesciat, si hoc ipsum beneficii pars est ;
deinde multa alia faciam, multa tribuam, per quae
intellegat et illius auctorem ; denique ille nesciet
accepisse se, ego sciam me dedisse. " Parum est,"
inquis. Parum, si fenerare cogitas ; sed si dare,
quo genere accipienti maxime profuturum erit, dabis.
Contentus eris te teste ; alioqui non bene facere

3 delectat sed videri bene fecisse. " Volo utique
sciat." Debitorem quaeris. " Volo utique sciat."
Quid ? si illi utilius est nescire, si honestius, si
gratius, non in aliam partem abibis ? " Volo sciat."

---

[1] vel *added by Préchac.*
[2] favellendus *N*[1] : fallendus *Hosius.*

of poverty, of disgrace — these should be given quietly, so that they will be known only to those who receive the benefit.

Sometimes, too, the very man who is helped must even be deceived in order that he may have assistance, and yet not know from whom he has received it. There is a story that Arcesilaus had a friend who, though he was poor, concealed his poverty ; when, however, the man fell ill and, being unwilling to reveal even this, lacked money for the necessities of life, Arcesilaus decided that he must assist him in secret ; and so, without the other's knowledge, he slipped a purse under his pillow in order that the fellow who was so uselessly reserved might find, rather than receive, what he needed. "What, then ? —shall a man not know from whom he has received ? " In the first place, he must not know, if an element of the benefit is just that fact ; then, again, I shall do much else for him, I shall bestow upon him many gifts, and from these he may guess the author of the first one ; lastly, while he will not know that he has received a gift, I shall know that I have given one. "That is not enough," you say. That is not enough if you are thinking of making an investment ; but if a gift, you will give in the manner that will bring most advantage to the recipient. You will be content to have yourself your witness ; otherwise your pleasure comes, not from doing a favour, but from being seen to do a favour. "I want the man at least to know ! " Then it is a debtor that you are looking for. "I want the man at least to know ! " What ?— if it is more to his advantage, more to his honour, more to his pleasure not to know, will you not shift your position ? "I want him to know ! " So, then,

4 Ita tu hominem non servabis in tenebris? Non
nego, quotiens patitur res, respiciendum gaudium ex
accipientis voluntate; sin adiuvari illum et oportet
et pudet, si, quod praestamus, offendit, nisi abscon-
ditur, beneficium in acta non mitto. Quidni? ego
illi non sum indicaturus me dedisse, cum inter prima
praecepta ac maxime necessaria sit, ne umquam
exprobrem, immo ne admoneam quidem. Haec enim
beneficii inter duos lex est: alter statim oblivisci
debet dati, alter accepti numquam.

1   11. Lacerat animum et premit frequens meritorum commemoratio. Libet exclamare, quod ille
triumvirali proscriptione servatus a quodam Caesaris
amico exclamavit, cum superbiam eius ferre non
posset: " Redde me Caesari! " Quousque dices:
" Ego te servavi, ego eripui morti " ? Istud, si meo
arbitrio memini, vita est; si tuo, mors est. Nihil tibi
debeo, si me servasti, ut haberes, quem ostenderes.
Quousque me circumducis? Quousque oblivisci fortunae meae non sinis? Semel in triumpho ductus
2 essem! Non est dicendum, quid tribuerimus; qui
admonet, repetit. Non est instandum, non est
memoria renovanda, nisi ut aliud dando prioris
admoneas.

ᵃ Published daily at Rome by the authority of the government, it corresponded in some measure to our newspapers.

you will not save a man's life in the dark ? I do not
deny that, whenever circumstances permit, we should
have regard for the pleasure we get from the willingness of the recipient ; but, if he needs, and yet is
ashamed, to be helped, if what we bestow gives
offence unless it is concealed—then I do not put
my good deed into the gazette [a] ! Of course I am
careful not to reveal to him that the gift came from
me, since it is a first and indispensable requirement, never to reproach a man with a benefit,
nay, even to remind him of it. For, in the case of
a benefit, this is a binding rule for the two who
are concerned—the one should straightway forget
that it was given, the other should never forget that
it was received.

Repeated reference to our services wounds and
crushes the spirit of the other. He wants to cry out
like the man who, after being saved from the proscription of the triumvirs by one of Caesar's friends,
because he could not endure his benefactor's arrogance, cried " Give me back to Caesar ! " How long
will you keep repeating : " It is I who saved you, it
is I who snatched you from death " ? Your service,
if I remember it of my own will, is truly life ; if I
remember it at yours, it is death. I owe nothing to
you if you saved me in order that you might have
someone to exhibit. How long will you parade me ?
How long will you refuse to let me forget my misfortune ? In a triumph, I should have had to march
but once ! No mention should be made of what we
have bestowed ; to remind a man of it is to ask him
to return it. It must not be dwelt upon, it must not
be recalled to memory—the only way to remind a
man of an earlier gift is to give him another.

Ne aliis quidem narrare debemus ; qui dedit beneficium, taceat, narret, qui accepit. Dicetur enim,
quod illi ubique iactanti beneficium suum. " Non
negabis," inquit, " te recepisse " ; et cum respon-
disset : " Quando ? " " Saepe quidem," inquit, " et
multis locis, id est, quotiens et ubicumque narrasti."
3 Quid opus est eloqui, quid alienum occupare officium ? Est, qui istud facere honestius possit, quo
narrante et hoc laudabitur, quod ipse non narras.
Ingratum me iudicas, si istud te tacente nemo
sciturus est ! Quod adeo non est committendum, ut
etiam, si quis coram nobis narrabit, respondendum
sit : " Dignissimus quidem ille est maioribus beneficiis, sed ego magis velle me scio omnia illi praestare
quam adhuc praestitisse " ; et haec ipsa non verni-
liter nec ea figura, qua quidam reiciunt, quae magis
ad se volunt adtrahere.

4 Deinde adicienda omnis humanitas. Perdet agricola, quod sparsit, si labores suos destituit in semine;
multa cura sata perducuntur ad segetem ; nihil in
fructum pervenit, quod non a primo usque ad ex-
5 tremum aequalis cultura prosequitur. Eadem beneficiorum condicio est. Numquid ulla maiora possunt

And we must not tell others of it, either. Let the giver of a benefit hold his tongue ; let the recipient talk. For the same thing that was said to another man when he was boasting of a benefit he had conferred will be said to you. " You will not deny," said the beneficiary, " that you have had full return." " When ? " inquired the other. " Many times," was the reply, " and in many places—that is, every time and everywhere you have told of it ! " But what need is there to speak of a benefit, what need to pre-empt the right that belongs to another ? There is someone else who can do more creditably what you are doing, someone who in telling of your deed will laud even your part in not telling of it. You must adjudge me ungrateful if you suppose that no one will know of your deed if you yourself are silent ! But so far from its being permissible for us to speak of it, even if anyone tells of our benefits in our presence, it is our duty to reply : " While this man is in the highest degree worthy to receive even greater benefits, yet I am more conscious of being willing to bestow all possible benefits upon him than of having actually bestowed them hitherto." And in saying even this there must be no show of currying favour, nor of that air with which some reject the compliments that they would rather appropriate.

Besides, we must add to generosity every possible kindness. The farmer will lose all that he has sown if he ends his labours with putting in the seed ; it is only after much care that crops are brought to their yield ; nothing that is not encouraged by constant cultivation from the first day to the last ever reaches the stage of fruit. In the case of benefits the same rule holds. Can there possibly be any greater

esse, quam quae in liberos patres conferunt ? Haec
tamen irrita sunt, si in infantia deserantur, nisi
longa pietas munus suum nutrit. Eadem ceterorum
beneficiorum condicio est : nisi illa adiuveris, perdes;
parum est dedisse, fovenda sunt. Si gratos vis habere,
quos obligas, non tantum des oportet beneficia, sed
6 ames. Praecipue, ut dixi, parcamus auribus ; admonitio taedium facit, exprobratio odium. Nihil
aeque in beneficio dando vitandum est quam superbia.
Quid opus arrogantia vultus, quid tumore verborum ?
Ipsa res te extollit. Detrahenda est inanis iactatio;
res loquentur nobis tacentibus. Non tantum ingratum, sed invisum est beneficium superbe datum.

1 12. C. Caesar dedit vitam Pompeio Penno, si dat,
qui non aufert ; deinde absoluto et agenti gratias
porrexit osculandum sinistrum pedem. Qui excusant
et negant id insolentiae causa factum, aiunt socculum
auratum, immo aureum, margaritis distinctum ostendere eum voluisse. Ita prorsus : quid hic contume-
liosum est, si vir consularis aurum et margaritas
osculatus est alioquin nullam partem in corpore eius
2 electurus, quam purius oscularetur ? Homo natus in
hoc, ut mores liberae civitatis Persica servitute
mutaret, parum iudicavit, si senator, senex, summis
usus honoribus in conspectu principum supplex sibi

---

a Caligula's unconventional taste in footgear is often
censured.

benefits than those that a father bestows upon his children ? Yet they are all in vain if they are discontinued in the child's infancy—unless long-lasting devotion nurses its first gift. And the same rule holds for all other benefits—you will lose them unless you assist them ; it is not enough that they were given, they must be tended. If you wish to have gratitude from those whom you lay under an obligation, you must, not merely give, but love, your benefits. Above all, as I have said, let us spare the ears ; a reminder stirs annoyance, a reproach hatred. In giving a benefit nothing ought to be avoided so much as haughtiness. Why need your face show disdain, your words assumption ? The act itself exalts you. Empty boasting must be banished ; our deeds will speak even if we are silent. The benefit that is haughtily bestowed wins, not only ingratitude, but ill-will.

Gaius Caesar granted life to Pompeius Pennus, that is, if failure to take it away is granting it ; then, when Pompeius after his acquittal was expressing his thanks, Caesar extended his left foot to be kissed. Those who excuse the action, and say that it was not meant to be insolent, declare that he wanted to display his gilded—no, his golden—slipper studded with pearls.[a] Yes, precisely—what insult to the consular if he kissed gold and pearls, since otherwise he could have found no spot on Caesar's person that would be less defiling to kiss ? But this creature, born for the express purpose of changing the manners of a free state into a servitude like Persia's, thought it was not enough if a senator, an old man, a man who had held the highest public offices, bent the knee and prostrated himself before him in full sight of the

eo more iacuisset, quo hostes victi hostibus iacuere ;
invenit aliquid infra genua, quo libertatem detru-
deret ! Non hoc est rem publicam calcare, et quidem,
licet id aliquis non putet ad rem pertinere, sinistro
pede ? Parum enim foede furioseque insolens fuerat,
qui de capite consularis viri soccatus audiebat, nisi in
os senatoris ingessisset imperator epigros suos !

1 13. O superbia, magnae fortunae stultissimum
malum ! Ut a te nihil accipere iuvat ! Ut omne
beneficium in iniuriam convertis [1] ! Ut te omnia de-
decent ! Quoque altius te sublevasti, hoc depressior
es ostendisque tibi non datum adgnoscere ista bona,
quibus tantum inflaris ; quidquid das, corrumpis.

2 Libet itaque interrogare, quid se tanto opere re-
supinet, quid vultum habitumque oris pervertat, ut
malit personam habere quam faciem ? Iucunda sunt,
quae humana fronte, certe leni placidaque tribuuntur,
quae cum daret mihi superior, non exultavit supra
me, sed quam potuit benignissimus fuit descenditque
in aequum et detraxit muneri suo pompam, sic [2]
observavit idoneum tempus, ut in occasione potius

3 quam in necessitate succurreret. Uno modo istis
persuadebimus, ne beneficia sua insolentia perdant,
si ostenderimus non ideo videri maiora, quod tumul-

---

[1] *Hosius adds* ut te omnia nimia delectant.
[2] sic *Préchac* : si *N, Hosius.*

---

a The *soccus* belonged to comic actors, and was informal
and womanish.
b The obscure Latin word probably hides a sneer at the
studded pearls.

nobles, just as the conquered prostrate themselves before their conquerors ; he found a way of thrusting Liberty down even lower than the knees ! Is not this a trampling upon the commonwealth, and too—although the detail may not seem to some of any importance—with the left foot ? For he would have made too little display of shameful and crazy insolence in wearing slippers *a* when he was trying a consular for his life unless he had thrust his imperial hobnails *b* in the face of a senator !

O Pride, the bane of great fortune and its highest folly ! How glad we are to receive nothing from thee ! How thou dost turn every sort of benefit into an injury ! How ill all thy acts become thee ! The higher thou hast lifted thyself, the lower thou dost sink, and provest that thou hast no right to lay claim to those blessings that cause thee to be so greatly puffed up ; thou dost spoil all that thou givest. And so I like to ask her why she is so fond of swelling out her chest, of marring her expression and the appearance of her face to the extent of actually preferring to wear a mask instead of human visage. The gifts that please are those that are bestowed by one who wears the countenance of a human being, all gentle and kindly, by one who, though he was my superior when he gave them, did not exalt himself above me, but, with all the generosity in his power, descended to my own level, and banished all display from his giving, who thus watched for the suitable moment for the purpose of coming to my rescue with timely, rather than with necessary, aid. The only way in which we shall ever convince these arrogant creatures that they are ruining their benefits by their insolence is to show them that benefits do not appear more important

tuosius data sunt ; ne ipsos quidem ob id cuiquam
posse maiores videri ; vanam esse superbiae magnitudinem et quae in odium etiam amanda perducat.

1   14. Sunt quaedam nocitura impetrantibus, quae
non dare sed negare beneficium est ; aestimabimus
itaque utilitatem potius quam voluntatem petentium.
Saepe enim noxia concupiscimus, nec dispicere, quam
perniciosa sunt, licet, quia iudicium interpellat adfectus ; sed cum subsedit cupiditas, cum impetus ille
flagrantis animi, qui consilium fugat, cecidit, detes-
2 tamur perniciosos malorum munerum auctores.   Ut
frigidam aegris negamus et lugentibus ac sibi iratis
ferrum, ut amentibus, quidquid contra se usurus
ardor petit, sic omnino,[1] quae nocitura sunt, impense
ac summisse, non numquam etiam miserabiliter rogan-
tibus perseverabimus non dare.   Cum initia beneficiorum suorum spectare tum etiam exitus decet et
ea dare, quae non tantum accipere, sed etiam acce-
3 pisse delectet.   Multi sunt, qui dicant : " Scio hoc
illi non profuturum, sed quid faciam ?   Rogat, re-
sistere precibus eius non possum ; viderit : de se, non
de me queretur."   Falsum est : immo de te et merito
quidem ; cum ad mentem bonam redierit, cum
accessio illa, quae animum inflammabat, remiserit,

---

[1] omnino *Préchac after Gertz* : omnium *N,* *Hosius* : omnia
most editors.

simply because they were given with much noise; and, too, that they themselves do not appear more important in anyone's eyes because of that; that the importance of pride is an illusion, and tends to cause hatred for actions that ought to be loved.

There are certain gifts that are likely to harm those who obtain them, and, in the case of these, the benefit consists, not in giving, but in withholding, them; we shall therefore consider the advantage rather than the desire of the petitioner. For we often crave things that are harmful, and we are not able to discern how destructive they are because our judgement is hampered by passion; but, when the desire has subsided, when that frenzied impulse, which puts prudence to rout, has passed, we loathe the givers of the evil gifts for the destruction they have wrought. As we withhold cold water from the sick, and the sword from those who are stricken with grief and the rage of self-destruction, as we withhold from the insane everything that they could use against themselves in a fit of frenzy, so, in general, to those who petition for gifts that will be harmful we shall persistently refuse them although they make earnest and humble, sometimes even piteous, request. It is right to keep in view, not merely the first effects, but the outcome, of our benefits, and to give those that it is a pleasure, not merely to receive, but to have received. For there are many who say : " I know that this will not be to his advantage, but what can I do ? He begs for it, and I cannot resist his entreaties. It is his own look-out—he will blame himself, not me." No, you are wrong—you are the one he will blame, and rightly so. When he comes to his right mind, when the frenzy that inflamed his soul has subsided,

quidni eum oderit, a quo in damnum ac periculum
4 suum adiutus est ? Exorari in perniciem rogantium
saeva bonitas est. Quemadmodum pulcherrimum
opus est etiam invitos nolentesque servare, ita roganti-
bus pestifera largiri blandum et adfabile odium est.
Beneficium demus, quod in usu magis ac magis placeat,
quod numquam in malum vertat. Pecuniam non
dabo, quam numeraturum adulterae sciam, nec in
societate turpis facti aut consilii inveniar ; si potero,
5 revocabo, si minus, non adiuvabo scelus. Sive illum
ira, quo non debebit, impellet, sive ambitionis calor
abducet a tutis, in nullum malum vires a me sumere
ipso[1] patiar nec committam, ut possit quandoque
dicere : " Ille amando me occidit." Saepe nihil interest inter amicorum munera et hostium vota ;
quidquid illi accidere optant, in id horum intem-
pestiva indulgentia impellit atque instruit. Quid
autem turpius quam quod evenit frequentissime, ut
nihil intersit inter odium et beneficium ?

1 15. Numquam in turpitudinem nostram reditura
tribuamus. Cum summa amicitiae sit amicum sibi
aequare, utrique simul consulendum est. Dabo
egenti, sed ut ipse non egeam ; succurram perituro,

---

[1] vires a me sumere ipso patiar *Basore after Hosius who
reads* ipsas *for* ipso : vires a semet ipsa (ipso *M*) patiar *O* :
vires nisi a semet ipso peti patiar *Madvig* : vires asserere
sibi nisi a semet ipso patiar *Préchac*.

how can he help hating the one who helped to put him in the way of harm and danger? It is cruel kindness to yield to requests that work the destruction of those who make them. Just as it is a very noble act to save the life of a man, even against his will and desire, so to lavish upon him what is harmful, even though he begs for it, is but hatred cloaked by courtesy and civility. Let the benefit that we give be one that will become more and more satisfying by use, one that will never change into an evil. I will not give a man money if I know that it will be handed over to an adulteress, nor will I allow myself to become a partner in dishonour, actual or planned; if I can, I will restrain crime, if not, I will not aid it. Whether a man is being driven by anger in a direction that he ought not to take, or is being turned from the safe course by a burning ambition, I shall not permit him to draw from me myself the power to work any harm, nor allow it to be possible for him to say at any future time: "That man has ruined me by his love." Often there is no difference between the favours of our friends and the prayers of our enemies; into the ills that the latter desire may befall us, the former by their inopportune kindness drive us, and provide the means. Yet, often as it happens, what can be more disgraceful than that there should be no difference between beneficence and hatred?

Let us never bestow benefits that can redound to our shame. Since the sum total of friendship consists in putting a friend on an equality with ourselves, consideration must be given at the same time to the interests of both. I shall give to him if he is in need, yet not to the extent of bringing need upon myself; I shall come to his aid if he is at the point of ruin, yet

sed ut ipse non peream, nisi si futurus ero magn
2 hominis aut magnae rei merces. Nullum beneficiun
dabo, quod turpiter peterem. Nec exiguum dilatab
nec magna pro parvis accipi patiar ; nam ut qui, quo
dedit,[1] imputat, gratiam destruit, ita qui, quantun
det, ostendit, munus suum commendat, non expro
3 brat. Respiciendae sunt cuique facultates suae vires
que, ne aut plus praestemus, quam possumus, au
minus. Aestimanda est eius persona, cui damus
quaedam enim minora sunt, quam ut exire a magni
viris debeant, quaedam accipiente maiora sunt
Utriusque itaque personam confer et ipsum inte
illas, quod donabis, examina, numquid aut danti grave
sit aut parum, numquid rursus, qui accepturus est,
aut fastidiat aut non capiat.

1   16. Urbem cuidam Alexander donabat, vesanus
et qui nihil animo nisi grande conciperet. Cum ille,
cui donabatur, se ipse mensus tanti muneris invidiam
refugisset dicens non convenire fortunae suae : " Non
quaero," inquit, " quid te accipere deceat, sed quid
me dare." Animosa vox videtur et regia, cum sit
stultissima. Nihil enim per se quemquam decet ;
refert, qui det, cui, quando, quare, ubi, et cetera, sine

---

[1] dedit *commonly added*.

not to the extent of bringing ruin upon myself, unless by so doing I shall purchase the safety of a great man or a great cause. I shall never give a benefit which I should be ashamed to ask for. I shall neither magnify the value of a small service, nor allow a great service to pass as a small one ; for, just as he who takes credit for what he gives destroys all feeling of gratitude, so he who makes clear the value of what he gives recommends his gift, does not make it a reproach. Each one of us should consider his own means and resources in order that we may not bestow either a larger or a smaller amount than we are able to give. We should take into account, too, the character of the person to whom we are giving ; for some gifts are too small to come fittingly from the hands of a great man, and some are too large for the other to take. Do you therefore compare the characters of the two concerned, and over against these weigh the gift itself in order to determine whether, in the case of the giver, it will be either too onerous or too small, and whether, on the other hand, the one who is going to receive it will either disdain it or find it too large.

Alexander—madman that he was, and incapable of conceiving any plan that was not grandiose—once presented somebody with a whole city. When the man to whom he was presenting it had taken his own measure, and shrank from incurring the jealousy that so great a gift would arouse, Alexander's reply was : " I am concerned, not in what is becoming for you to receive, but in what is becoming for me to give." This seems a spirited and regal speech, but in reality it is most stupid. For nothing, in itself, makes a becoming gift for any man ; it all depends upon who gives it and who receives it—the when, wherefore,

2 quibus facti ratio non constabit. Tumidissimum
animal! Si illum accipere hoc non decet, nec te dare;
habetur personarum ac dignitatium portio et, cum sit
ubique virtus modus, aeque peccat, quod excedit,
quam quod deficit. Liceat istud sane tibi et te in
tantum fortuna sustulerit, ut congiaria tua urbes sint
(quas quanto maioris animi fuit non capere quam
spargere!): est tamen aliquis minor, quam in sinu
eius condenda sit civitas!

1   17. Ab Antigono Cynicus petit talentum; respondit plus esse, quam quod Cynicus petere deberet.
Repulsus petit denarium; respondit minus esse,
quam quod regem deceret dare. "Turpissima eiusmodi cavillatio est; invenit, quomodo neutrum daret.
In denario regem, in talento Cynicum respexit, cum
posset et denarium tamquam Cynico dare et talentum tamquam rex. Ut sit aliquid maius, quam quod
Cynicus accipiat, nihil tam exiguum est, quod non
2 honeste regis humanitas tribuat." Si me interrogas,
probo; est enim intolerabilis res poscere nummos et
contemnere. Indixisti pecuniae odium; hoc professus es, hanc personam induisti: agenda est. Ini-
quissimum est te pecuniam sub gloria egestatis ad-

ᵃ A fundamental doctrine of Stoic ethics. Thus courage
is a mean between timidity and foolhardiness, candour a
mean between false modesty and boastfulness.

and where of the gift, and all the other items without which there can be no true reckoning of the value of the deed. You puffed-up creature! If it is not becoming for the man to accept the gift, neither is it becoming for you to give it ; the relation of the two in point of character and rank is taken into account, and, since virtue is everywhere a mean,*a* excess and defect are equally an error. Granted that you have such power, and that Fortune has lifted you to such a height that you can fling whole cities as largesses (but how much more magnanimous it would have been not to take, than to squander, them !), yet it is possible that there is someone who is too small to put a whole city in his pocket !

A certain Cynic once asked Antigonus for a talent ; his reply was that this was more than a Cynic had a right to ask for. After this rebuff the Cynic asked for a denarius ; here the reply was that this was less than a king could becomingly give. " Such sophistry," it may be said, " is most unseemly ; the king found a way of not giving either. In the matter of the denarius he thought only of the king, in the matter of the talent only of the Cynic, although he might well have given the denarius on the score that the man was a Cynic, or the talent on the score that he himself was a king. Grant that there may be some gift that is too large for a Cynic to receive, none is too small for a king to bestow with honour if it is given out of kindness." If you ask my opinion, I think the king was right ; for the situation is intolerable that a man should ask for money when he despises it. Your Cynic has a declared hatred of money ; he has published this sentiment, he has chosen this rôle—now he must play it. It is most unfair for him to obtain money while he

quirere. Adspicienda ergo non minus sua cuique persona est quam eius, de quo iuvando quis cogitat.

3 Volo Chrysippi nostri uti similitudine de pilae lusu, quam cadere non est dubium aut mittentis vitio aut excipientis ; tum cursum suum servat, ubi inter manus utriusque apte ab utroque et iactata et excepta versatur. Necesse est autem lusor bonus aliter illam conlusori longo, aliter brevi mittat. Eadem beneficii ratio est. Nisi utrique personae, dantis et accipientis, aptatur, nec ab hoc exibit nec ad illum perveniet, ut
4 debet. Si cum exercitato et docto negotium est, audacius pilam mittemus ; utcumque enim venerit, manus illam expedita et agilis repercutiet ; si cum tirone et indocto, non tam rigide nec tam excusse sed languidius et in ipsam eius derigentes manum remisse occurremus. Idem faciendum est in beneficiis ; quosdam doceamus et satis iudicemus, si conantur, si
5 audent, si volunt. Facimus autem plerumque ingratos et, ut sint, favemus, tamquam ita demum magna sint beneficia nostra, si gratia illis referri non potuit ; ut malignis lusoribus propositum est conlusorem traducere, cum damno scilicet ipsius lusus, qui non potest,

boasts of poverty. It is, then, every man's duty to consider not less his own character than the character of the man to whom he is planning to give assistance.

I wish to make use of an illustration that our Chrysippus once drew from the playing of ball. If the ball falls to the ground, it is undoubtedly the fault either of the thrower or the catcher ; it maintains its course only so long as it does not escape from the hands of the two players by reason of their skill in catching and throwing it. The good player, however, must of necessity use one method of hurling the ball to a partner who is a long way off, and another to one who is near at hand. The same condition applies to a benefit. Unless this is suited to the character of both, the one who gives and the one who receives, it will neither leave the hands of the one, nor reach the hands of the other in the proper manner. If we are playing with a practised and skilled partner, we shall be bolder in throwing the ball, for no matter how it comes his ready and quick hand will promptly drive it back ; if with an unskilled novice, we shall not throw it with so much tension and so much violence, but play more gently, and run slowly forward guiding the ball into his very hand. The same course must be followed in the case of benefits ; some men need to be taught, and we should show that we are satisfied if they try, if they dare, if they are willing. But we ourselves are most often the cause of ingratitude in others, and we encourage them to be ungrateful, just as if our benefits could be great only when it was impossible to return gratitude for them ! It is as if some spiteful player should purposely try to discomfit his fellow-player, to the detriment of the game, of course, which can be carried on only in a

6 nisi consentitur, extendi. Multi sunt tam pravae naturae, ut malint perdere, quae praestiterunt, quam videri recepisse, superbi et imputatores. Quanto melius quantoque humanius id agere, ut illis quoque partes suae constent, et favere, ut gratia sibi referri possit, benigne omnia interpretari, gratias agentem non aliter, quam si referat, audire, praebere se facilem 7 ad hoc, ut, quem obligavit, etiam exsolvi velit ! Male audire solet fenerator, si acerbe exigit, aeque, si in recipiendo tardus ac difficilis moras quaerit. Beneficium tam recipiendum est quam non exigendum. Optimus ille, qui facile dedit, numquam exegit, reddi gavisus est, bona fide, quid praestitisset, oblitus, qui accipientis animo recepit.

1 18. Quidam non tantum dant beneficia superbe, sed etiam accipiunt, quod non est committendum. Iam enim transeamus ad alteram partem tractaturi, quomodo se gerere homines in accipiendis beneficiis debeant.

Quodcumque ex duobus constat officium, tantundem ab utroque exigit. Qualis pater esse debeat, cum inspexeris, scies non minus operis illic superesse, ut dispicias, qualem esse oporteat filium ; sunt aliquae 2 partes mariti, sed non minores uxoris. In vicem ista,

spirit of co-operation. There are many, too, who are naturally so perverse that they would rather lose what they have bestowed than appear to have had any return—arrogant, purse-proud men. But how much better, how much more kindly would it be to aim at having the recipients also do regularly their part, to encourage a belief in the possibility of repaying with gratitude, to put a kindly interpretation upon all that they do, to listen to words of thanks as if they were an actual return, to show oneself complaisant to the extent of wishing that the one upon whom the obligation was laid should also be freed from it. A money-lender usually gets a bad name if he is harsh in his demands, likewise, too, if he is reluctant to accept payment, and obstinately seeks to defer it. But in the case of a benefit it is as right to accept a return as it is wrong to demand it. The best man is he who gives readily, never demands any return, rejoices if a return is made, who in all sincerity forgets what he has bestowed, and accepts a return in the spirit of one accepting a benefit.

Some men are arrogant, not only in giving, but even in receiving, benefits, a mistake which is never excusable. For let me now pass to the other side of the subject in order to consider how men ought to conduct themselves in accepting a benefit.

Every obligation that involves two people makes an equal demand upon both. When you have considered the sort of person a father ought to be, you will find that there remains the not less great task of discovering the sort that a son should be ; it is true that a husband has certain duties, yet those of the wife are not less great. In the exchange of

quantum exigunt, praestant et parem desiderant
regulam, quae, ut ait Hecaton, difficilis est; omne
enim honestum in arduo est, etiam quod vicinum
honesto est; non enim tantum fieri debet, sed ratione
fieri. Hac duce per totam vitam eundum est, minima
maximaque ex huius consilio gerenda; quomodo
haec suaserit, dandum.

Haec autem hoc primum censebit non ab omnibus
3 accipiendum. A quibus ergo accipiemus? Ut breviter tibi respondeam: ab his, quibus dedissemus.
Videamus, num etiam maiore dilectu quaerendus est,
cui debeamus, quam cui praestemus. Nam ut non
sequantur ulla incommoda (secuntur autem plurima),
grave tamen tormentum est debere, cui nolis; contra
iucundissimum ab eo accepisse beneficium, quem
amare etiam post iniuriam possis, ubi amicitiam
alioqui iucundam causa fecit et iustam. Illud vero
homini verecundo et probo miserrimum est, si eum
4 amare oportet, quem non iuvat. Totiens admoneam
necesse est non loqui me de sapientibus, quos, quidquid oportet, et iuvat, qui animum in potestate habent
et legem sibi, quam volunt, dicunt, quam dixerunt,
servant, sed de imperfectis hominibus honestam viam
sequi volentibus, quorum adfectus saepe contumaciter

obligations each in turn renders to the other the service that he requires, and they desire that the same rule of action should apply to both, but this rule, as Hecaton says, is a difficult matter; for it is always hard to attain to Virtue, even to approach Virtue; for there must be, not merely achievement, but achievement through reason. Along the whole path of life Reason must be our guide, all our acts, from the smallest to the greatest, must follow her counsel; as she prompts, so also must we give.

Now her first precept will be that it is not necessary for us to receive from everybody. From whom, then, shall we receive? To answer you briefly, from those to whom we could have given. Let us see, in fact, whether it does not require even greater discernment to find a man to whom we ought to owe, than one on whom we ought to bestow, a benefit. For, even though there should be no unfortunate consequences (and there are very many of them), yet it is grievous torture to be under obligation to someone whom you object to; on the other hand, it is a very great pleasure to have received a benefit from one whom you could love even after an injury, when his action has shown a friendship that was in any case agreeable to be also justified. Surely, an unassuming and honest man will be in a most unhappy plight if it becomes his duty to love someone when it gives him no pleasure. But I must remind you, again and again, that I am not speaking of the ideal wise man to whom every duty is also a pleasure, who rules over his own spirit, and imposes upon himself any law that he pleases, and always observes any that he has imposed, but of the man who with all his imperfections desires to follow the perfect path, yet has passions

87

5 parent. Itaque eligendum est, a quo beneficium ac
cipiam; et quidem diligentius quaerendus benefici
quam pecuniae creditor. Huic enim reddendum est
quantum accepi, et, si reddidi, solutus sum ac liber
at illi et plus solvendum est, et nihilo minus etiam
relata gratia cohaeremus; debeo enim, cum reddidi
rursus incipere, manetque amicitia; et ut in amicitiam[1] non reciperem indignum, sic ne in beneficiorum quidem sacratissimum ius, ex quo amicitia oritur.

6 "Non semper," inquit, "mihi licet dicere: 'nolo';
aliquando beneficium accipiendum est et invito. Dat
tyrannus crudelis et iracundus, qui munus suum fastidire te iniuriam iudicaturus est: non accipiam?
Eodem loco latronem pone, piratam, regem animum
latronis ac piratae habentem. Quid faciam? Parum

7 dignus est, cui debeam?" Cum eligendum dico, cui
debeas, vim maiorem et metum excipio, quibus ad-
hibitis electio perit. Si liberum est tibi, si arbitrii tui
est, utrum velis an non, id apud te ipse perpendes;
si necessitas tollit arbitrium, scies te non accipere, sed
parere. Nemo id accipiendo obligatur, quod illi re-

---

[1] et ut in amicitiam *added by Haase.*

[a] *i.e.*, the lasting quality of friendship protracts the payment of gratitude.

that often are reluctant to obey. And so it is necessary for me to choose the person from whom I wish to receive a benefit ; and, in truth, I must be far more careful in selecting my creditor for a benefit than a creditor for a loan. For to the latter I shall have to return the same amount that I have received, and, when I have returned it, I have paid all my debt and am free ; but to the other I must make an additional payment, and, even after I have paid my debt of gratitude, the bond between us still holds ; for, just when I have finished paying it, I am obliged to begin again, and friendship endures [a] ; and, as I would not admit an unworthy man to my friendship, so neither would I admit one who is unworthy to the most sacred privilege of benefits, from which friendship springs. " But," you reply, " I am not always permitted to say, ' I refuse ' ; sometimes I must accept a benefit even against my wish. If the giver is a cruel and hot-tempered tyrant, who will deem the spurning of his gift an affront, shall I not accept it ? Imagine in a like situation a brigand or a pirate or a king with the temper of a brigand or a pirate. What shall I do ? Is such a man altogether unworthy of my being indebted to him ? " When I say that you must choose the person to whom you would become indebted, I except the contingency of superior force or of fear, for, when these are applied, all choice is destroyed. But, if you are free, if it is for you to decide whether you are willing or not, you will weigh the matter thoroughly in your mind ; if necessity removes any possibility of choice, you will realize that it is for you, not to accept, but to obey. No man contracts an obligation by accepting something that he had no power to reject ; if you wish to

pudiare non licuit ; si vis scire, an velim, effice, ut
8 possim nolle. " Vitam tamen tibi dedit ! " Non
refert, quid sit, quod datur, nisi a volente, nisi volenti
datur ; si servasti me, non ideo servator es. Venenum
aliquando pro remedio fuit ; non ideo numeratur inter
salubria. Quaedam prosunt nec obligant. Tuber
quidam tyranni gladio divisit, qui ad occidendum
eum venerat ; non ideo illi tyrannus gratias egit,
quod rem, quam medicorum manus reformidaverant,
nocendo sanavit.

1 **19.** Vides non esse magnum in ipsa re momen-
tum, quoniam non videtur dedisse beneficium, qui a
malo animo profuit ; casus enim beneficium est,
hominis iniuria. Leonem in amphitheatro specta-
vimus, qui unum e bestiariis agnitum, cum quondam
eius fuisset magister, protexit ab impetu bestiarum.
Num ergo beneficium est ferae auxilium ? Minime,
2 quia nec voluit facere nec faciendi animo fecit. Quo
loco feram posui, tyrannum pone ; et hic vitam dedit
et illa, nec hic nec illa beneficium. Quia non est
beneficium accipere cogi, non est beneficium debere,
cui nolis. Ante des oportet mihi arbitrium mei,
deinde beneficium.

discover whether I am willing, make it possible for me to be unwilling. " Yet suppose it was life that he gave you ! " It makes no difference what the gift is if it is not given willingly to one who accepts willingly; though you have saved my life, you are not for that reason my saviour. Poison at times serves as a remedy, but it is not for that reason counted as a wholesome medicine. Some things are beneficial, and yet impose no obligation. A man, who had approached a tyrant for the purpose of killing him, lanced a tumour for him by the blow of his sword ; he did not, however, for that reason receive the thanks of the tyrant, though by doing him injury he cured him of the disorder to which the surgeons had not had the courage to apply the knife.

You see that the act itself is of no great consequence, since it appears that the man who from evil intent actually renders a service has not given a benefit ; for chance designs the benefit, the man designs injury. We have seen in the amphitheatre a lion, who, having recognized one of the beast-fighters as the man who had formerly been his keeper, protected him from the attack of the other beasts. Is, then, the assistance of the wild beast to be counted a benefit ? By no means, for it neither willed to do one, nor actually did one with the purpose of doing it. In the same category, in which I have placed the wild beast, do you place your tyrant—the one as well as the other has given life, neither the one or the other a benefit. For, since that which I am forced to receive is not a benefit, that also which puts me under obligation to someone against my will is not a benefit. You ought to give me first the right to choose for myself, then the benefit.

1 20. Disputari de M. Bruto solet, an debuerit accipere ab divo Iulio vitam, cum occidendum eum
2 iudicaret. Quam rationem in occidendo secutus sit, alias tractabimus ; mihi enim, cum vir magnus in aliis fuerit, in hac re videtur vehementer errasse nec ex institutione Stoica se egisse. Qui aut regis nomen extimuit, cum optimus civitatis status sub rege iusto sit, aut ibi speravit libertatem futuram, ubi tam magnum praemium erat et imperandi et serviendi, aut existimavit civitatem in priorem formam posse revocari amissis pristinis moribus futuramque ibi aequalitatem civilis iuris et staturas suo loco leges, ubi viderat tot milia hominum pugnantia, non an servirent, sed utri ! Quanta vero illum aut rerum naturae aut urbis suae tenuit oblivio, qui uno interempto defuturum credidit alium, qui idem vellet, cum Tarquinius esset inventus post tot reges ferro ac
3 fulminibus occisos ! Sed vitam accipere debuit, ob hoc tamen non habere illum parentis loco, quia in ius dandi beneficii iniuria venerat ; non enim servavit is, qui non interfecit, nec beneficium dedit, sed missionem.

1 21. Illud magis venire in aliquam disputationem potest, quid faciendum sit captivo, cui redemptionis pretium homo prostituti corporis et infamis ore pro-

It is an oft-debated question whether Marcus Brutus ought to have received his life from the hands of the deified Julius when in his opinion it was his duty to kill him. The reason that led him to kill Caesar I shall discuss elsewhere, for, although in other respects he was a great man, in this particular he seems to me to have acted very wrongly, and to have failed to conduct himself in accordance with Stoic teaching. Either he was frightened by the name of king, though a state reaches its best condition under the rule of a just king, or he still hoped that liberty could exist where the rewards both of supreme power and of servitude were so great, or that the earlier constitution of the state could be restored after the ancient manners had all been lost, that equality of civil rights might still exist and laws maintain their rightful place there where he had seen so many thousands of men fighting to decide, not whether, but to which of the two masters, they would be slaves ! How forgetful, in truth, he was, either of the law of nature or of the history of his own city, in supposing that, after one man had been murdered, no other would be found who would have the same aims—although a Tarquin had been discovered after so many of the kings had been slain by the sword or lightning ! But Brutus ought to have received his life, yet without regarding Caesar in the light of a father, for the good reason that Caesar had gained the right to give a benefit by doing violence to right ; for he who has not killed has not given life, and has given, not a benefit, but quarter.

A question that offers more opportunity for debate is what should be the course of a captive if the price of his ransom is offered to him by a man who prostitutes his body and dishonours his mouth. Shall I permit a

mittit. Patiar me ab impuro servari ? Servatus deinde quam illi gratiam referam ? Vivam cum obsceno ? Non vivam cum redemptore ? Quid ergo

2 placeat, dicam. Etiam a tali accipiam pecuniam, quam pro capite dependam, accipiam autem tamquam creditum, non tamquam beneficium ; solvam illi pecuniam et, si occasio fuerit servandi periclitantem, servabo ; in amicitiam, quae similes iungit, non descendam, nec servatoris illum loco numerabo sed feneratoris, cui sciam reddendum, quod accepi.

3 Est aliquis dignus, a quo beneficium accipiam, sed danti nociturum est ; ideo non accipiam, quia ille paratus est mihi cum incommodo aut etiam periculo suo prodesse. Defensurus est me reum, sed illo patrocinio regem sibi facturus inimicum ; inimicus sum, si, cum ille pro me periclitari velit, ego, quod facilius est, non facio, ut sine illo pericliter.

4 Ineptum et frivolum hoc Hecaton ponit exemplum Arcesilai, quem ait a filio familiae adlatam pecuniam non accepisse, ne ille patrem sordidum offenderet. Quid fecit laude dignum, quod furtum non recepit, quod maluit non accipere quam reddere ? Quae est enim alienam rem non accipere moderatio ?

5 Si exemplo magni animi opus est, utamur Graecini

---

^a All members of the Roman family were subject to the authority of the father ; a son, even if he were of age, had no independent legal rights.

filthy wretch to save me ? Then, if I have been saved, how shall I return my gratitude ? Shall I live with a lewd fellow ? Shall I not live with my deliverer ? I shall tell you what in that case would be my course. Even from such a man I shall receive the money that will buy my freedom. I shall, however, receive it, not as a benefit, but as a loan ; then I shall repay the money to him, and, if I ever have an opportunity to save him from a perilous situation, I shall save him ; as for friendship, which is a bond between equals, I shall not condescend to that, and I shall regard him, not as a preserver, but as a banker, to whom I am well aware that I must return the amount that I have received.

It is possible that, while a man may be a worthy person for me to receive a benefit from, it will injure him to give it ; this I shall not accept for the very reason that he is ready to do me a service with inconvenience, or even with risk, to himself. Suppose that he is willing to defend me in a trial, but by his defence of me will make an enemy of the king ; I am his enemy if, since he is willing to run a risk for my sake, I do not do the easier thing—run my risk without him.

A foolish and silly example of this is a case that Hecaton cites. Arcesilaus, he says, refused to accept a sum of money that was offered to him by a man who was not yet his own master [a] for fear that the giver might offend his miserly father. But what was praiseworthy in his act of refusing to come into possession of stolen property, of preferring not to receive it than to restore it ? For what self-restraint is there in refusing to accept the gift of another man's property ?

If there is need of an example of a noble spirit, let

95

Iulii, viri egregii, quem C. Caesar occidit ob hoc unum, quod melior vir erat, quam esse quemquam tyranno expedit. Is cum ab amicis conferentibus ad impensam ludorum pecunias acciperet, magnam pecuniam a Fabio Persico missam non accepit et obiurgantibus iis, qui non aestimant mittentes, sed missa, quod repudiasset : " Ego," inquit, " ab eo beneficium accipiam, a quo propinationem accepturus non sum ? "

6 Cum illi Rebilus consularis, homo eiusdem infamiae, maiorem summam misisset instaretque, ut accipi iuberet : " Rogo," inquit, " ignoscas ; et a Persico non accepi." Utrum hoc munera accipere est an senatum legere ?

22. Cum accipiendum iudicaverimus, hilares accipiamus profitentes gaudium, et id danti manifestum sit, ut fructum praesentem capiat ; iusta enim causa laetitiae est laetum amicum videre, iustior fecisse. Quam grate ad nos pervenisse indicemus effusis adfectibus, quos non ipso tantum audiente sed ubique testemur. Qui grate beneficium accipit, primam eius pensionem solvit.

1 23. Sunt quidam, qui nolint nisi secreto accipere ; testem beneficii et conscium vitant ; quos scias licet male cogitare. Quomodo danti in tantum producenda notitia est muneris sui, in quantum de-

us take the case of Julius Graecinus, a rare soul, whom Gaius Caesar killed simply because he was a better man than a tyrant found it profitable for anyone to be. This man, when he was receiving contributions from his friends to meet the expense of the public games, refused to accept a large sum of money that Fabius Persicus had sent; and, when those who were thinking, not of the senders, but of what was sent, reproached him because he had rejected the contribution, he replied : " Am I to accept a benefit from a man from whom I would not accept a toast to my health ? " And, when a consular named Rebilus, a man of an equally bad reputation, had sent an even larger sum and insisted that he should order it to be accepted, he replied : " I beg your pardon ; but I have already refused to accept money from Persicus." Is this accepting a present or is it picking a senate ?

When we have decided that we ought to accept, let us accept cheerfully, professing our pleasure and letting the giver have proof of it in order that he may reap instant reward ; for, as it is a legitimate source of happiness to see a friend happy, it is a more legitimate one to have made him so. Let us show how grateful we are for the blessing that has come to us by pouring forth our feelings, and let us bear witness to them, not merely in the hearing of the giver, but everywhere. He who receives a benefit with gratitude repays the first instalment on his debt.

There are some who are not willing to receive a benefit unless it is privately bestowed ; they dislike having a witness to the fact or anyone aware of it. But these, you may be sure, take a wrong view. As the giver should add to his gift only that measure of publicity which will please the one to whom he gives

lectatura est, cui datur, ita accipienti adhibenda contio
2 est ; quod pudet debere, ne acceperis. Quidam fur-
tive gratias agunt et in angulo et ad aurem ; non est
ista verecundia, sed infitiandi genus ; ingratus est, qui
remotis arbitris agit gratias. Quidam nolunt nomina
secum fieri nec interponi pararios nec signatores ad-
vocari, chirographum[1] dare. Idem faciunt, qui dant
operam, ut beneficium in ipsos conlatum quam ignotis-
3 simum sit. Verentur palam ferre, ut sua potius virtute
quam alieno adiutorio consecuti dicantur ; rariores in
eorum officiis sunt, quibus vitam aut dignitatem debent, et, dum opinionem clientium timent, graviorem
subeunt ingratorum.
1   24. Alii pessime locuntur de optime meritis.
Tutius est quosdam offendere quam demeruisse ; argumentum enim nihil debentium odio quaerunt. Atqui
nihil magis praestandum est, quam ut memoria nobis
meritorum haereat, quae subinde reficienda est, quia
nec referre potest gratiam, nisi qui meminit, et, qui
meminit,[2] eam refert.
2   Nec delicate accipiendum est nec summisse et humi-
liter ; nam qui neclegens est in accipiendo, cum omne
beneficium recens pateat, quid faciat, cum prima eius

---

[1] chirographum *N, Préchac*: vix chirographum *Hosius
after Havet.*
[2] et qui meminit *commonly added.*

---

a Influential Romans received their clients, friends, and
admirers at the morning *salutatio.*

it, so the recipient should invite the whole city to witness it ; a debt that you are ashamed to acknowledge you should not accept. Some return their thanks stealthily, in a corner, in one's ear ; this is not discretion, but, in a manner, repudiation ; the man who returns his thanks only when witnesses have been removed shows himself ungrateful. Some men object to having any record made of their indebtedness, to the employment of factors, to the summoning of witnesses to seal the contract, to giving their bond. These are in the same class with those who take pains to keep as secret as possible the fact that they have had a benefit bestowed upon them. They shrink from taking it openly for fear that they may be said to owe their success to the assistance of another rather than to their own merit ; they are only rarely found paying their respects to those *a* to whom they owe their living or their position, and, while they fear the reputation of being a dependent, they incur the more painful one of being an ingrate.

Others speak worst of those who have treated them best. It is safer to offend some men than to have done them a service ; for, in order to prove that they owe nothing, they have recourse to hatred. And yet nothing ought to be made more manifest than that services rendered to us linger in our memory, but the memory must constantly be renewed ; for only the man who remembers is able to repay gratitude, and he who remembers does thereby repay it.

In receiving a benefit we should appear neither fastidious nor yet submissive and humble ; for, if anyone shows indifference in the act of receiving it, when the whole benefit is freshly revealed, what will he do when the first pleasure in it has cooled ? One

SENECA

voluptas refrixit ? Alius accipit fastidiose, tamquam
3 qui dicat : " Non quidem mihi opus est, sed quia tam
valde vis, faciam tibi mei potestatem " ; alius supine,
ut dubium praestanti relinquat, an senserit ; alius vix
labra diduxit et ingratior, quam si tacuisset, fuit.

4   Loquendum est pro magnitudine rei impensius et
illa adicienda : " Plures, quam putas, obligasti " (nemo
enim non gaudet beneficium suum latius patere) ;
" nescis, quid mihi praestiteris, sed scire te oportet,
quanto plus sit, quam existimas " (statim gratus est,
qui se onerat) ; " numquam tibi referre gratiam
potero ; illud certe non desinam ubique confiteri me
referre non posse."

1   25. Nullo magis Caesarem Augustum demeruit
et ad alia impetranda facilem sibi reddidit Furnius,
quam quod, cum patri Antonianas partes secuto
veniam impetrasset, dixit : " Hanc unam, Caesar,
habeo iniuriam tuam : effecisti, ut et viverem et
morerer ingratus." Quid est tam grati animi, quam
nullo modo sibi satis facere, quam ne ad spem quidem
exaequandi umquam beneficii accedere ?

2   His atque eiusmodi vocibus id agamus, ut voluntas
nostra non lateat, sed aperiatur et luceat. Verba
cessent licet : si, quemadmodum debemus, adfecti

100

man receives it disdainfully, as if to say : " I really do not need it, but since you so much wish it, I will surrender my will to yours " ; another accepts listlessly, so that he leaves the bestower doubtful about his being conscious of the benefit ; still another barely opens his lips, and shows himself more ungrateful than if he had kept silent.

The greater the favour, the more earnestly must we express ourselves, resorting to such compliments as : " You have laid more people under obligation than you think " (for every one rejoices to know that a benefit of his extends farther than he thought) ; " you do not know what it is that you have bestowed upon me, but you have a right to know how much more it is than you think " (he who is overwhelmed shows gratitude forthwith) ; " I shall never be able to repay to you my gratitude, but, at any rate, I shall not cease from declaring everywhere that I am unable to repay it."

No single fact more earned the goodwill of Augustus Caesar, and made it easy for Furnius to obtain from him other favours than his saying, when Augustus at his request had granted pardon to his father, who had supported the side of Antony : " The only injury, Caesar, that I have ever received from you is this—you have forced me both to live and to die without expressing my gratitude ! " For what so much proves a grateful heart as the impossibility of ever satisfying oneself, or of even attaining the hope of ever being able to make adequate return for a benefit ?

By these and similar utterances, instead of concealing, let us try to reveal clearly our wishes. Though words should fail, yet, if we have the feelings

3 sumus, conscientia eminebit in vultu. Qui gratus
futurus est, statim, dum accipit, de reddendo cogitet.
Chrysippus quidem ait illum velut in certamen cursus
compositum et carceribus inclusum opperiri debere
tempus suum, ad quod velut dato signo prosiliat ; et
quidem magna illi contentione opus est, magna celeri-
tate, ut consequatur antecedentem.

1 26. Videndum est nunc, quid maxime faciat
ingratos. Facit aut nimius sui suspectus et insitum
mortalitati vitium se suaque mirandi aut aviditas aut
invidia.

2 Incipiamus a primo. Nemo non benignus est sui
iudex. Inde est, ut omnia meruisse se existimet et
in solutum accipiat nec satis suo pretio se aestimatum putet. " Hoc mihi dedit, sed quam sero, sed post
quot labores ! Quanto consequi plura potuissem, si
illum aut illum aut me[1] colere maluissem ! Non hoc
speraveram ; in turbam coniectus sum. Tam exiguo
dignum me iudicavit ? Honestius praeteriri fuit."

1 27. Cn. Lentulus augur, divitiarum maximum
exemplum, antequam illum libertini pauperem
facerent, hic, qui quater milies sestertium suum
vidit (proprie dixi ; nihil enim amplius quam vidit),
ingenii fuit sterilis, tam pusilli quam animi. Cum

---

[1] aut me, *O, Préchac* : ita me *Hosius after Feldmann.*

---

[a] Consul 14 B.C. Driven to suicide by Tiberius, he was
forced to make the emperor his sole heir (Suetonius, *Tib.* 49).
102

we ought to have, the consciousness of them will show in our face. The man who intends to be grateful, immediately, while he is receiving, should turn his thought to repaying. Such a man, declares Chrysippus, like a racer, who is all set for the struggle and remains shut up within the barriers, must await the proper moment to leap forth when, as it were, the signal has been given; and, truly, he will need to show great energy, great swiftness, if he is to overtake the other who has the start of him.

And now we must consider what are the principal causes of ingratitude. The cause will be either a too high opinion of oneself and the weakness implanted in mortals of admiring oneself and one's deeds, or greed, or jealousy.

Let us begin with the first. Every man is a generous judge of himself. The result is that he thinks he has deserved all that he gets, and receives it as given in payment, yet considers that he has not been appraised at nearly his own value. " He has given me this," he says, " but how late, and after how much trouble ! How much more I might have accomplished if I had chosen to court So-and-so or So-and-so—or myself ! I had not expected this—I have been classed with the herd. Was I worth so little in his eyes ? It would have been more complimentary if he had passed me by ! "

Gnaeus Lentulus,[a] the augur, who, before his freedmen reduced him to poverty, was the most conspicuous example of wealth—this man, who saw his four hundred millions (I have spoken with strict accuracy, for he did no more than " see " them !), was destitute of intelligence, as contemptible in intellect as he was

2 esset avarissimus, nummos citius emittebat quam
verba : tanta illi inopia erat sermonis. Hic cum
omnia incrementa sua divo Augusto deberet, ad
quem attulerat paupertatem sub onere nobilitatis
laborantem, princeps iam civitatis et pecunia et gratia
subinde de[1] Augusto solebat queri dicens a studiis se
abductum ; nihil tantum in se congestum esse, quantum perdidisset relicta eloquentia. At illi inter alia
hoc quoque divus Augustus praestiterat, quod illum
derisu et labore irrito liberaverat !

3   Non patitur aviditas quemquam esse gratum ; numquam enim improbae spei, quod datur, satis est, et
maiora cupimus, quo maiora venerunt, multoque con-
citatior est avaritia in magnarum opum congestu collocata, ut flammae infinito acrior vis est, quo ex maiore
incendio emicuit.

4   Aeque ambitio non patitur quemquam in ea mensura honorum conquiescere, quae quondam eius fuit
impudens votum. Nemo agit de tribunatu gratias,
sed queritur, quod non est ad praeturam usque perductus ; nec haec grata est, si deest consulatus ; ne
hic quidem satiat, si unus est. Ultra se cupiditas
porrigit et felicitatem suam non intellegit, quia non,
unde venerit, respicit, sed quo tendat.

1   28. Omnibus his vehementius et importunius
malum est invidia, quae nos inquietat, dum comparat :

[1] de *commonly added.*

in heart. Though he was the greatest miser, it was easier for him to disgorge coins than words—so great was his poverty when it came to talking. Though he owed all his advancement to the deified Augustus, to whom he had come with nothing but the poverty that was struggling under the burden of a noble name, yet, when he had now become the chief citizen of the state, both in wealth and influence, he used to make constant complaint, saying that Augustus had enticed him away from his studies ; that he had not heaped upon him nearly so much as he had lost by surrendering the practice of eloquence. Yet the deified Augustus, besides loading him with other benefits, had also rescued him from ridicule and vain endeavour !

Nor does greed suffer any man to be grateful ; for incontinent hope is never satisfied with what is given and, the more we get, the more we covet ; and just as the greater the conflagration from which the flame springs, the fiercer and more unbounded is its fury, so greed becomes much more active when it is employed in accumulating great riches.

And just as little does ambition suffer any man to rest content with the measure of public honours that was once his shameless prayer. No one renders thanks for a tribuneship, but grumbles because he has not yet been advanced to the praetorship ; nor is he grateful for this if he is still short of the consulship ; and even this does not satisfy him if it is a single one. His greed ever reaches to what is beyond, and he does not perceive his own happiness because he regards, not whence he came, but what he would reach.

But more powerful and insistent than all these is the evil of jealousy, which disquiets us by making comparisons. It argues : " He bestowed this on me,

" Hoc mihi praestitit, sed illi plus, sed illi maturius " ;
et deinde nullius causam agit, contra omnes sibi favet.
Quanto est simplicius, quanto prudentius beneficium
acceptum augere, scire neminem tanti ab alio, quanti
2 a se ipso aestimari ! " Plus accipere debui, sed illi
facile non fuit plus dare ; in multos dividenda liberalitas erat ; hoc initium est, boni consulamus et animum
eius grate excipiendo evocemus ; parum fecit, sed
saepius faciet ; illum mihi praetulit, et me multis ; ille
non est mihi par virtutibus nec officiis, sed habuit suam
Venerem ; querendo non efficiam, ut maioribus dignus
sim, sed ut datis indignus. Plura illis hominibus tur-
pissimis data sunt ; quid ad rem ? Quam raro fortuna
3 iudicat ! Cotidie querimur malos esse felices ; saepe,
quae agellos pessimi cuiusque transierat, optimorum
virorum segetem grando percussit ; fert sortem suam
4 quisque ut in ceteris rebus ita in amicitiis." Nullum est tam plenum beneficium, quod non vellicare
malignitas possit, nullum tam angustum, quod non
bonus interpres extendat. Numquam deerunt causae
querendi, si beneficia a deteriore parte spectaveris.

1   29. Vide, quam iniqui sint divinorum munerum
aestimatores et quidem professi sapientiam. Queruntur, quod non magnitudine corporum aequemus ele-
phantos, velocitate cervos, levitate aves, impetu
tauros ; quod solida sit cutis beluis, decentior dam-

---

[a] The complaint against Nature was a stock theme of the
Epicureans. *Cf.* Lucretius, v. 195-234.

but more on So-and-so, and an earlier gift upon
So-and-so " ; and, too, it pleads no man's case, it is
for itself against everybody. But how much simpler,
how much more sensible it is to magnify the benefit
received, to be convinced that no one is as highly
esteemed by another as he is by himself ! "I ought
to have received more, but it was not easy for him
to give more ; he had to portion out his liberality
amongst many others ; this is simply the beginning,
let us take it in good part and attract his notice by
accepting it gratefully ; he has done too little, but he
will do something oftener ; he preferred So-and-so to
me, and me to many others ; So-and-so is not my
equal either in virtue or in services, but he has a
charm of his own ; by complaining I shall show, not
that I am deserving of greater favours, but that I am
undeserving of those that have been given. More
favours have been given to the basest of men, but what
does it matter ? How rarely is Fortune judicious !
Every day we complain that the wicked are prosperous ; often the hail-storm that has passed over the
fields of the greatest sinners smites the corn of the
most upright men ; each one must endure his lot, in
friendship as well as in everything else." No benefit
is so ample that it will not be possible for malice to
belittle it, none is so scanty that it cannot be enlarged
by kindly interpretation. Reasons for complaint will
never be lacking if you view benefits on their un-
favourable side.

See how unjust men are in appraising the gifts of
the gods, even those who profess to be philosophers.[a]
They grumble because we are inferior to elephants in
size of body, to stags in swiftness, to birds in lightness,
to bulls in energy ; because the skin of beasts is tough,

107

mis, densior ursis, mollior fibris ; quod sagacitate nos
narium canes vincant, quod acie luminum aquilae,
spatio aetatis corvi, multa animalia nandi facilitate.
2 Et cum quaedam ne coire quidem in idem natura
patiatur, ut velocitatem corporum et vires, ex diversis
ac dissidentibus bonis hominem non esse compositum
iniuriam vocant et neclegentes nostri deos, quod non
bona valetudo etiam vitiis inexpugnabilis data sit,
quod non futuri scientia. Vix sibi temperant, quin eo
usque impudentiae provehantur, ut naturam oderint,
quod infra deos sumus, quod non in aequo illis stetimus.
3 Quanto satius est ad contemplationem tot tantorum-
que beneficiorum reverti et agere gratias, quod nos in
hoc pulcherrimo domicilio voluerunt secundas sortiri,
quod terrenis praefecerunt! Aliquis ea animalia comparat nobis, quorum potestas penes nos est ? Quidquid nobis negatum est, dari non potuit.
4 Proinde, quisquis es iniquus aestimator sortis
humanae, cogita, quanta nobis tribuerit parens noster,
quanto valentiora animalia sub iugum miserimus,
quanto velociora consequamur, quam nihil sit mortale
5 non sub ictu nostro positum. Tot virtutes accepimus,
tot artes, animum denique, cui nihil non eodem, quo

that of deer more comely, of bears thicker, of beavers softer than ours ; because dogs surpass us in keenness of scent, eagles in sharpness of vision, crows in length of life, and many creatures in the ability to swim. And, though Nature does not suffer certain qualities, as for instance speed of body and strength, even to meet in the same creature, yet they call it an injustice that man has not been compounded of various good qualities that are incompatible, and say that the gods are neglectful of us because we have not been given the good health that can withstand even the assaults of vice, because we have not been gifted with a knowledge of the future. Scarcely can they restrain themselves from mounting to such a pitch of impertinence as actually to hate Nature because we mortals are inferior to the gods, because we are not placed on an equality with them. But how much better would it be to turn to the contemplation of our many great blessings, and to render thanks to the gods because they were pleased to allot to us a position second only to their own in this most beautiful dwelling-place, because they have appointed us to be the lords of earth ! Will anyone compare us with the creatures over whom we have absolute power ? Nothing has been denied to us that could possibly have been granted to us.

Accordingly, whoever thou art, thou unfair critic of the lot of mankind, consider what great blessings our Father has bestowed upon us, how much more powerful than ourselves are the creatures we have forced to wear the yoke, how much swifter those that we are able to catch, how nothing that dies has been placed beyond the reach of our weapons. So many virtues have we received, so many arts, in fine, the

intendit, momento pervium est, sideribus velociorem,
quorum post multa saecula futuros cursus antecedit ;
tantum deinde frugum, tantum opum, tantum rerum
aliarum super alias acervatarum. Circumeas licet
cuncta et, quia nihil totum invenies, quod esse te
malles, ex omnibus singula excerpas, quae tibi dari
velles ; bene aestimata naturae indulgentia confitearis
6 necesse est in deliciis te illi fuisse. Ita est : carissimos
nos habuerunt di immortales habentque, et, qui maximus tribui honos potuit, ab ipsis proximos collocave-
runt. Magna accepimus, maiora non cepimus.

1 30. Haec, mi Liberalis, necessaria credidi, et
quia loquendum aliquid de maximis beneficiis erat,
cum de minutis loqueremur, et quia inde manat etiam
in cetera huius detestabilis vitii audacia. Cui enim
respondebit grate, quod munus existimabit aut magnum aut reddendum, qui summa beneficia spernit ?
Cui salutem, cui spiritum debebit, qui vitam accepisse
2 se a dis negat, quam cotidie ab illis petit ? Quicumque
ergo gratos esse docet, et hominum causam agit et
deorum, quibus nullius rei indigentibus, positis extra

human mind, to which nothing is inaccessible the moment it makes the effort, which is swifter than the stars whose future courses through many ages it anticipates ; then, too, all the products of the field, all the store of wealth, and all the other blessings that are piled one upon the other. Though you should range through all creation, and, because you will fail to find there a thing which as a whole you would rather have been, should select from all creatures the particular qualities that you could wish had been given to you, yet any right estimate of the kindliness of Nature will force you to acknowledge that you have been her darling. The fact is, the immortal gods have held—still hold—us most dear, and in giving us a place next to themselves have bestowed upon us the greatest honour that was possible. Great things have we received, for greater we had no room.

These considerations, my dear Liberalis, I have thought necessary because, on the one hand, when speaking of insignificant benefits, I was forced to speak also of those that are supreme, and because, on the other, the abominable presumptuousness of the vice under consideration extends from these to all benefits. For, if a man scorns the highest benefits, to whom will he respond with gratitude, what gift will he deem either great or worthy of being returned ? If a man denies that he has received from the gods the gift of life that he begs from them every day, to whom will he be indebted for his preservation, to whom for the breath that he draws ? Whoever, therefore, teaches men to be grateful, pleads the cause both of men and of the gods, to whom, although there is no thing that they have need of since they have been placed beyond

desiderium, referre nihilo minus gratiam possumus.
Non est, quod quisquam excusationem mentis ingratae
ab infirmitate atque inopia petat et dicat : " Quid
enim faciam et quomodo ? Quando superioribus
dominisque rerum omnium gratiam referam ? " Referre facile est, si avarus es, sine impendio, si iners,
sine[1] opera. Eodem quidem momento, quo obligatus
es, si vis, cum quolibet paria fecisti, quoniam, qui
libenter beneficium accipit, reddidit.

1   31. Hoc ex paradoxis Stoicae sectae minime
mirabile, ut mea fert opinio, aut incredibile est eum,
qui libenter accipit, beneficium reddidisse. Nam cum
omnia ad animum referamus, fecit quisque, quantum
voluit ; et cum pietas, fides, iustitia, omnis denique
virtus intra se perfecta sit, etiam si illi manum exserere
non licuit, gratus quoque homo esse potest voluntate.
2 Quotiens, quod proposuit, quisque consequitur, capit
operis sui fructum. Qui beneficium dat, quid pro-
ponit ? Prodesse ei, cui dat, et voluptati esse. Si,
quod voluit, effecit pervenitque ad me animus eius ac
mutuo gaudio adfecit, tulit, quod petit. Non enim in
vicem aliquid sibi reddi voluit ; aut non fuit bene-
3 ficium, sed negotiatio. Bene navigavit, qui quem
destinavit portum tenuit ; teli iactus certae manus
peregit officium, si petita percussit ; beneficium qui

---

[1] sine *added by Muretus.*

all desire, we can nevertheless offer our gratitude. No one is justified in making his weakness and his poverty an excuse for ingratitude, in saying : " What am I to do, and how begin ? When can I ever repay to my superiors, who are the lords of creation, the gratitude that is due ? " It is easy to repay it—without expenditure if you are miserly, without labour if you are lazy. In fact, the very moment you have been placed under obligation, you can match favour for favour with any man if you wish to do so ; for he who receives a benefit gladly has already returned it.

This, in my opinion, is the least surprising or least incredible of the paradoxes of the Stoic school : that he who receives a benefit gladly has already returned it. For, since we Stoics refer every action to the mind, a man acts only as he wills ; and, since devotion, good faith, justice, since, in short, every virtue is complete within itself even if it has not been permitted to put out a hand, a man can also have gratitude by the mere act of will. Again, whenever anyone attains what he aimed at, he receives the reward of his effort. When a man bestows a benefit, what does he aim at ? To be of service and to give pleasure to the one to whom he gives. If he accomplishes what he wished, if his intention is conveyed to me and stirs in me a joyful response, he gets what he sought. For he had no wish that I should give him anything in exchange. Otherwise, it would have been, not a benefaction, but a bargaining. A man has had a successful voyage if he reaches the port for which he set out ; a dart hurled by a sure hand performs its duty if it strikes the mark ; he who gives a benefit wishes it to be gratefully accepted ; if it is cheerfully

113

dat, vult excipi grate ; habet, quod voluit, si bene
acceptum est. Sed speravit emolumenti aliquid. Non
fuit hoc beneficium, cuius proprium est nihil de reditu
4 cogitare. Quod accipiebam, eo animo accepi, quo
dabatur : reddidi. Alioqui pessima optimae rei condicio est : ut gratus sim, ad fortunam mittor ! Si illa
invita respondere non possum, sufficit animus animo.
5 "Quid ergo ? non, quidquid potuero, et faciam, ut
reddam, et temporum rerumque occasionem sequar et
implere eius sinum cupiam, a quo aliquid accepi ? "
Sed malo loco beneficium est, nisi et excussis manibus
esse grato licet !

1 32. "Qui accepit," inquit, "beneficium, licet
animo benignissimo acceperit, nondum consummavit
officium suum ; restat enim pars reddendi ; sicut in
lusu est aliquid pilam scite ac diligenter excipere, sed
non dicitur bonus lusor, nisi qui apte et expedite
2 remisit, quam acceperat." Exemplum hoc dissimile
est ; quare ? Quia huius rei laus in corporis motu est
et in agilitate, non in animo ; explicari itaque totum
debet, de quo oculis iudicatur. Nec tamen ideo non
bonum lusorem dicam, qui pilam, ut oportebat, excepit, si per ipsum mora, quominus remitteret, non
3 fuit. "Sed quamvis," inquit, "arti ludentis nihil

received he gets what he wanted. " But," you say, " he wished to gain something besides!" Then it was not a benefit, for the chief mark of one is that it carries no thought of a return. That which I have received I received in the same spirit in which it was given— thus I have made return. Otherwise, this best of things is subjected to the worst possible condition— in order to show gratitude, I must turn to Fortune! If I can make no other response because she is ad- verse, the answer from heart to heart is enough. " What, then," you say, " shall I make no effort to return whatever I can, shall I not hunt for the right time and opportunity, and be eager to fill the pocket of the one from whom I have received ? " Yes, but truly benefaction is in a sorry state if a man may not have gratitude even if his hands are empty !

" He who has received a benefit," you say, " although he may have received it in the most generous spirit, has not yet fulfilled his whole duty, for the part of returning it still remains ; just as in playing ball there is some merit in catching the ball with adroitness and accuracy, yet a man is not said to be a really good player unless he is clever and prompt in sending back the ball that he has received." But your example is not well taken ; and why ? Because success in the game depends, not upon the mind of the player, but upon the motion and the agility of his body, and so an exhibition of which the eye is to be the judge must be shown in its entirety. Yet, for all that, I am not willing to say that a man who caught the ball as he ought was not a good player if, through no fault of his own, he was prevented from sending it back. " But," you say, " although

115

desit, quia partem quidem fecit, sed partem, quam non fecit, potest facere, lusus ipse imperfectus est, qui 4 consummatur vicibus mittendi ac remittendi." Nolo diutius hoc refellere ; existimemus ita esse, desit aliquid lusui, non lusori ; sic et in hoc, de quo disputamus, deest aliquid rei datae, cui par alia debetur, non animo, qui animum parem sibi nanctus est et, quantum in illo est, quod voluit, effecit.

1   33. Beneficium mihi dedit ; accepi non aliter, quam ipse accipi voluit : iam habet, quod petit, et quod unum petit, ergo gratus sum. Post hoc usus mei restat et aliquod ex homine grato commodum ; hoc non imperfecti officii reliqua pars est, sed perfecti ac- 2 cessio. Facit Phidias statuam ; alius est fructus artis, alius artificii : artis est fecisse, quod voluit, artificii fecisse cum fructu ; perfecit opus suum Phidias, etiam si non vendidit. Triplex illi fructus est operis sui : unus conscientiae ; hunc absoluto opere percipit ; alter famae ; tertius utilitatis, quem allatura est aut 3 gratia aut venditio aut aliqua commoditas. Sic bene-

the player may not be lacking in skill since, while he did only half of his duty, the half that he did not do he is able to do, yet the playing itself remains imperfect, for its perfection lies in the interchange of throwing backwards and forwards." I do not wish to refute the point further ; let us agree to this, that, not the player, but the playing, lacks something ; so also in this matter which we are now discussing, the object given lacks something, for another corresponding to it is still due, but the spirit of the gift lacks nothing, for it has discovered on the other side a corresponding spirit, and, so far as the purpose of the giver is concerned, it has accomplished all that it wished.

A benefit has been bestowed upon me ; I have received it in precisely the spirit in which the giver wished it to be received : he consequently has the reward he seeks, and the only reward he seeks ; therefore I show myself grateful. There remain after this his use of me and some advantage from having a person grateful ; but this comes, not as the remainder of a duty only partially fulfilled, but as an addition consequent to its fulfilment. Phidias makes a statue ; the fruit of his art is one thing, that of the pursuit of his art another ; that of his art lies in his having made what he wished to make, that of the pursuit of his art in his having made it to some profit ; the work of Phidias was completed even if it was not sold. The fruit of his work he finds is threefold : the first is the consciousness of it ; this he experiences after the completion of his work ; another is the glory of it ; a third is the benefit which he will gain either from recognition or from the sale of it or from some other advantage. In the same way the

ficii fructus primus ille est conscientiae ; hunc percipit, qui, quo voluit, munus suum pertulit ; secundus
et tertius[1] est et famae et eorum, quae praestari in
vicem possunt. Itaque cum benigne acceptum est
beneficium, qui dedit, gratiam quidem iam recepit,
mercedem nondum ; debeo itaque, quod extra beneficium est, ipsum quidem bene accipiendo persolvi.

1   34. " Quid ergo ? ", inquit, " rettulit gratiam, qui
nihil fecit ? " Primum fecit : bono animo bonum
obtulit et, quod est amicitiae, ex aequo. Post deinde
aliter beneficium, aliter creditum solvitur ; non est,
quod expectes, ut solutionem tibi ostendam ; res inter
animos geritur.

2   Quod dico, non videbitur durum, quamvis primo
contra opinionem tuam pugnet, si te commodaveris
mihi et cogitaveris plures esse res quam verba. Ingens
copia est rerum sine nomine, quas non propriis appella-
tionibus notamus, sed alienis commodatisque. Pedem
et nostrum dicimus et lecti et veli et carminis, canem
et venaticum et marinum et sidus ; quia non suffici-
mus, ut singulis singula adsignemus, quotiens opus
3 est, mutuamur. Fortitudo est virtus pericula iusta
contemnens aut scientia periculorum repellendorum,

---

[1] et tertius *added by Haase.*

first fruit of a benefaction is the consciousness of it ;
a man experiences this from carrying out his gift as
he wished ; the second and the third are, respectively,
the glory of it and the things which may be bestowed
in exchange. And so, when a benefit has been
graciously received, the giver has forthwith received
gratitude in return, but not yet his full reward ; my
indebtedness, therefore, is for something apart from
the benefit, for the benefit itself I have repaid in full
by cheerfully accepting it.

"What, then ?" you say, "does a man repay
gratitude by doing nothing ?" But he has done
the chief thing—by showing a good spirit he has conferred a good, and—what is the mark of friendship—in
equal measure. Then, in the second place, a benefit
is paid in one way, a loan in another ; there is no
reason why you should expect me to flourish the
payment before your eyes—the transaction is performed in our minds !

You will come to see that what I am saying is not
too bold, although at first it may not accord with your
own ideas, if only you will give me your attention, and
reflect that there are many things for which there are
no words. There is a vast number of things that have
no name, and the terms by which we designate them,
instead of being their own, belong to other things
from which they are borrowed. We say that we ourselves, a couch, a sail, and a poem, have a "foot," and
we apply the word "dog" to a hound, to a creature
of the sea, and to a constellation ; since there are
not enough words to make it possible for us to assign
a separate one to each separate thing, we borrow
whenever it becomes necessary. Bravery is the virtue
that scorns legitimate dangers, or knowing how to

excipiendorum, provocandorum ; dicimus tamen et
gladiatorem fortem virum et servum nequam, quem
4 in contemptum mortis temeritas impulit. Parsimonia
est scientia vitandi sumptus supervacuos aut ars re
familiari moderate utendi ; parcissimum tamen hominem vocamus pusilli animi et contracti, cum infinitum
intersit inter modum et angustias. Haec alia sunt
natura, sed efficit inopia sermonis, ut et hunc et illum
parcum vocemus, ut et ille fortis dicatur cum ratione
fortuita despiciens et hic sine ratione in pericula
5 excurrens. Sic beneficium est et actio, ut diximus,
benefica et ipsum, quod datur per illam actionem, ut
pecunia, ut domus, ut praetexta ; unum utrique
nomen est, vis quidem ac potestas longe alia.

1 35. Itaque attende, iam intellegis nihil me, quod
opinio tua refugiat, dicere. Illi beneficio, quod actio
perficit, relata gratia est, si illud benevole excipi-
mus ; illud alterum, quod re continetur, nondum
reddidimus, sed volemus reddere. Voluntati voluntate
satis fecimus ; rei rem debemus. Itaque, quamvis
rettulisse illum gratiam dicamus, qui beneficium libenter accipit, iubemus tamen et simile aliquid ei, quod
accepit, reddere.

2 A consuetudine quaedam, quae dicimus, abhorrent,
deinde alia via ad consuetudinem redeunt. Negamus

ward off, to meet, and to court dangers ; yet we call both a gladiator and the worthless slave whose rashness has forced him into scorn of death a " brave " man. Frugality is knowing how to avoid unnecessary expenditure, or the art of applying moderation to the use of private means ; yet we call a petty-minded and close-fisted man a very " frugal " person although there is an infinite difference between moderation and meanness. These are essentially different things, yet our poverty of language leads us to call each of the two types a " frugal " person, and likewise to say that both the man who by the exercise of reason scorns the blows of Fortune and the one who rushes into dangers unreasoningly are " brave." So a " benefit," as we have said, is both a beneficent act and likewise the object itself which is given by means of the aforesaid act, as money, a house, the robe of office ; the two things bear the same name, but they are very different in their import and operation.

Attend, therefore, and you will soon understand that I am advancing nothing that your own conviction will reject. For the benefit that is accomplished by an act has been repaid by our gratitude if we give it friendly welcome ; the other, which consists of some object, we have not yet returned, but we shall have the desire to return it. Goodwill we have repaid with goodwill ; for the object we still owe an object. And so, although we say that he who receives a benefit gladly has repaid it, we, nevertheless, also bid him return some gift similar to the one he received.

Some of the utterances that we Stoics make avoid the ordinary meaning of the terms, and then by a different line of thought are restored to their ordinary

iniuriam accipere sapientem, tamen, qui illum pugno percusserit, iniuriarum damnabitur ; negamus stulti quidquam esse, et tamen eum, qui rem aliquam stulto surripuit, furti condemnabimus ; insanire omnes dicimus, nec omnes curamus elleboro ; his ipsis, quos vocamus insanos, et suffragium et iuris dictionem 3 committimus. Sic dicimus eum, qui beneficium bono animo accipit, gratiam rettulisse, nihilo minus illum in aere alieno relinquimus gratiam relaturum, etiam cum rettulit. Exhortatio est illa, non infitiatio beneficii, ne[1] beneficia timeamus, ne ut intolerabili sarcina pressi deficiamus animo. " Bona mihi donata sunt et fama defensa, detractae sordes, spiritus servatus[2] et libertas spiritu potior. Et quomodo referre gratiam potero ? Quando ille veniet dies, quo illi animum 4 meum ostendam ? " Hic ipse est, quo ille suum ostendit ! Excipe beneficium, amplexare, gaude, non quod accipias, sed quod reddas debiturusque sis ; non adibis tam magnae rei periculum, ut casus ingratum facere te possit. Nullas tibi proponam difficultates, ne despondeas animum, ne laborum ac longae servitutis expectatione deficias ; non differo te, de praesenti- 5 bus fiat. Numquam eris gratus, nisi statim es. Quid ergo facies ? Non arma sumenda sunt : at fortasse

---

[1] beneficii ne *added by Gertz.*
[2] servatus *added by Haase.*

meaning. We deny that the wise man can receive injury, yet the man who strikes him with his fist will be sentenced on the charge of doing him an injury ; we deny that a fool possesses anything, and yet a man who steals some object from a fool will be punished for theft ; we declare that all men are mad, and yet we do not dose all men with hellebore ; and to the very men whom we call mad we entrust the right of suffrage and the jurisdiction of a judge. So we declare that he who receives a benefit in a kindly spirit has repaid it by gratitude, yet, nevertheless, we leave him in debt—still bound to repay gratitude even after he has repaid it. The aim of this is, not to forbid beneficence, but to encourage us not to be fearful of benefits, not to faint under them as if we were weighed down by an intolerable burden. "Good things," you exclaim, "have been given to me, my reputation has been protected, my ignominy has been removed, my life has been preserved, and my liberty that is dearer than life. And how shall I ever be able to repay my gratitude ? When will there come the day on which I can show to my benefactor my heart ? " This is the very day—the day on which he is showing his own heart ! Accept the benefit, embrace it, rejoice, not because you are receiving it, but because you are returning it and yet will still be in debt ; you will then avoid the risk of the great mishap that some chance may cause you to be ungrateful. No difficult terms will I set before you for fear that you may be discouraged, that you may faint at the prospect of long labour and servitude. I do not put you off—you may pay with what you have ! Never will you be grateful if you are not so at this moment. What, then, shall you do ? There is no need for you to take up

erunt. Non maria emetienda : fortasse etiam ventis minantibus solves. Vis reddere beneficium? Benigne accipe ; rettulisti gratiam, non ut solvisse te putes, sed ut securior debeas.

arms—perhaps some day there will be. There is no need for you to traverse the seas—perhaps some day you will set sail even when storm-winds are threatening. Do you wish to return a benefit ? Accept it with pleasure ; you have repaid it by gratitude—not so fully that you may feel that you have freed yourself from debt, yet so that you may be less concerned about what you still owe !

LIBER III

1 1. Non referre beneficiis gratiam et est turpe et apud omnes habetur, Aebuti Liberalis ; ideo de ingratis etiam ingrati queruntur, cum interim hoc omnibus haeret, quod omnibus displicet, adeoque in contrarium itur, ut quosdam habeamus infestissimos **2** non post beneficia tantum sed propter beneficia. Hoc pravitate naturae accidere quibusdam non negaverim, pluribus, quia memoriam tempus interpositum subducit ; nam quae recentia apud illos viguerunt, ea interiecto spatio obsolescunt. De quibus fuisse mihi tecum disputationem scio, cum tu illos non ingratos vocares sed oblitos, tamquam ea res ingratum excuset, quae facit, aut, quia hoc accidit alicui, non sit ingratus, cum hoc non accidat nisi ingrato.

3 Multa sunt genera ingratorum, ut furum, ut homicidarum, quorum una culpa est, ceterum in partibus varietas magna. Ingratus est, qui beneficium accepisse se negat, quod accepit ; ingratus est, qui dis-

BOOK III

NOT to return gratitude for benefits is a disgrace, and the whole world counts it as such, Aebutius Liberalis. Therefore even the ungrateful complain of ingratitude, while the vice that all find so distasteful nevertheless continues its hold upon all, and we go so far to the opposite extreme that sometimes, not merely after having received benefits, but because we have received them, we consider the givers our worst enemies. I cannot deny that, while some fall into the vice from a natural perversity, more show it because remembrance disappears with the passing of time ; for benefits that at first lived fresh in their memory wither as the days go by. On the subject of such persons you and I, I am well aware, have already had a discussion, in which you said that they were, not ungrateful, but forgetful ; just as if that which caused a man to be ungrateful could be any excuse for his being so, or as if the fact that a man had this misfortune kept him from being grateful, whereas it is only the ungrateful man who has this misfortune.

There are many sorts of ungrateful men, just as there are many sorts of thieves and of murderers— they all show the same sin, but their types the greatest diversity. The man is ungrateful who denies that he has received a benefit, which he has in fact received ; he is ungrateful who pretends that he has

simulat; ingratus, qui non reddit, ingratissimus
4 omnium, qui oblitus est. Illi enim si non solvunt,
tamen debent, et extat apud illos vestigium certe
meritorum intra malam conscientiam inclusorum;
aliquando ad referendam gratiam converti ex aliqua
causa possunt, si illos pudor admonuerit, si subita
honestae rei cupiditas, qualis solet ad tempus etiam
in malis pectoribus exsurgere, si invitaverit facilis occasio; hic numquam fieri gratus potest, cui beneficium
totum elapsum est. Et utrum tu peiorem vocas, apud
quem gratia beneficii intercidit, an apud quem etiam
5 memoria? Vitiosi oculi sunt, qui lucem reformidant,
caeci, qui non vident; et parentes suos non amare impietas est, non adgnoscere insania!

1   2. Quis tam ingratus est, quam qui, quod in prima
parte animi positum esse debuit et semper occurrere,
ita seposuit et abiecit, ut in ignorantiam verteret?
Apparet illum non saepe de reddendo cogitasse, cui
2 obrepsit oblivio. Denique ad reddendam gratiam et
virtute opus est et tempore et facultate et adspirante
fortuna; qui meminit, sat sine[1] impendio gratus est.
Hoc, quod non operam exigit, non opes, non felicitatem, qui non praestat, nullum habet, quo lateat,
patrocinium; numquam enim voluit gratus esse, qui

---

[1] sat sine *Préchac*: sine *after erasures N*, sine *Hosius*:
et sine *Gertz*.

not received one ; he, too, is ungrateful who fails to
return one ; but the most ungrateful of all is the man
who has forgotten a benefit. For the others, even
if they do not pay, continue in debt, and reveal at
least some trace of the services that they have locked
in the depths of their evil hearts. These, it may be,
for one reason or another, may some day turn to
the expression of gratitude, whether urged to it by
shame, or by the sudden impulse toward honourable
action that is wont to spring up for a moment even
in the hearts of bad men, or perhaps by the call of a
favourable opportunity. But there is no possibility
of a man's ever becoming grateful, if he has lost all
memory of his benefit. And which of the two would
you call the worse—the man whose heart is dead to
gratitude for a benefit, or the one whose heart is
dead even to the memory of a benefit ? Eyes
that shrink from the light are weak, those that
cannot see are blind ; and not to love one's parents
is to be unfilial, not to recognize them is to be
mad !

Who is so ungrateful as the man who has so completely excluded and cast from his mind the benefit
that ought to have been kept uppermost in his
thought and always before him, as to have lost all
knowledge of it ? It is evident that he has not
thought very often about returning it if it has faded
into oblivion. In short, the repaying of gratitude
requires right desire and opportunity and means and
the favour of Fortune ; but he who remembers shows
sufficient gratitude without any outlay. Since this
duty demands neither effort nor wealth nor good
fortune, he who fails to render it has no excuse in
which he may find shelter ; for he who has thrust a

beneficium tam longe proiecit, ut extra conspectum
3 suum poneret. Quemadmodum, quae in usu sunt et
manum cotidie tactumque patiuntur, numquam periculum situs adeunt, illa, quae ad oculos non revocantur,
sed extra conversationem ut supervacua iacuerunt,
sordes ipsa colligunt vetustate, ita, quidquid frequens
cogitatio exercet ac renovat, memoriae numquam sub-
ducitur, quae nihil perdit, nisi ad quod non saepe
respexit.

1 3. Praeter hanc causam aliae quoque sunt, quae
nobis merita non numquam maxima evellant. Prima
omnium ac potentissima, quod novis semper cupiditatibus occupati non, quid habeamus, sed quid petamus,
spectamus[1]; in id, quod adpetitur, intentis, quidquid
2 est domi, vile est. Sequitur autem, ut, ubi quod acceperis leve novorum cupiditas fecit, auctor quoque eorum
non sit in pretio. Amavimus aliquem et suspeximus et
fundatum ab illo statum nostrum professi sumus, quamdiu nobis placebant ea, quae consecuti sumus ; deinde
irrumpit animum aliorum admiratio, et ad ea impetus
factus est, uti mortalibus mos est ex magnis maiora
cupiendi. Protinus excidit, quidquid ante apud nos
beneficium vocabatur, nec ea intuemur, quae nos aliis
praeposuere, sed ea sola, quae fortuna praecedentium
3 ostentat. Non potest autem quisquam et invidere et

---

[1] spectamus *added by Madvig.*

benefit so far from him that he has actually lost sight of it never could have wished to be grateful for it. Just as tools that are in use and are every day subjected to the contact of our hands never run any risk of becoming rusty, while those that are not brought before the eyes, and, not being required, have remained apart from constant use, gather rust from the mere passing of time, so anything that our thought repeatedly busies itself with and keeps fresh does not slip from the memory, which loses only that which it has over and over again failed to regard.

Besides this, there are still other causes that tend to uproot from our minds services that sometimes have been very great. The first and most powerful of all is the fact that, busied as we are with ever new desires, we turn our eyes, not to what we possess, but to what we seek to possess. To those who are intent upon something they wish to gain all that they have already gained seems worthless. It follows, too, that, when the desire of new benefits has diminished the value of one that has already been received, the author of them also is less esteemed. We love someone, and look up to him, and avow that he laid the foundation of our present position so long as we are satisfied with what we have attained ; then the desirability of other things assails our mind, and we rush toward those, as is the way of mortals, who, having great things, always desire greater. And everything that we were formerly inclined to call a benefit straightway slips from our memory, and we turn our eyes, not to the things that have set us above others, but to the things that the good fortune of those who outstrip us displays. But it is possible for no man to show envy and gratitude at

131

gratias agere, quia invidere querentis et maesti est,
gratias agere gaudentis.

4 Deinde quia nemo nostrum novit nisi id tempus,
quod cum maxime transit, ad praeterita rari animum
retorquent ; sic fit, ut praeceptores eorumque beneficia intercidant, quia totam pueritiam reliquimus ;
sic fit, ut in adulescentiam nostram collata pereant,
quia ipsa numquam retractatur. Nemo, quod fuit,
tamquam in praeterito sed tamquam in perdito ponit,
ideoque caduca memoria est futuro imminentium.

1 4. Hoc loco reddendum est Epicuro testimonium,
qui adsidue queritur, quod adversus praeterita simus
ingrati, quod, quaecumque percipimus bona, non re-
ducamus nec inter voluptates numeremus, cum certior
nulla sit voluptas, quam quae iam eripi non potest.

2 Praesentia bona nondum tota in solido sunt, potest
illa casus aliquis incidere ; futura pendent et incerta
sunt ; quod praeteriit, inter tuta sepositum est. Quomodo gratus esse quisquam adversus beneficia potest,
qui omnem vitam suam transilit praesentium totus ac
futurorum ? Memoria gratum facit ; memoriae minimum tribuit, quisquis spei plurimum.

1 5. Quemadmodum, mi Liberalis, quaedam res
semel perceptae haerent, quaedam, ut scias, non est
satis didicisse (intercidit enim eorum scientia, nisi con-

the same time, for envy goes with complaint and unhappiness, gratitude with rejoicing.

In the second place, because each one of us is actually aware of only the particular moment of time that is passing, only now and then do men turn their thought back to the past ; so it happens that the memory of our teachers and of their benefits to us vanishes because we have left boyhood wholly behind ; so, too, it happens that the benefits conferred upon us in youth are lost because youth itself is never relived. No one regards what has been as something that has passed, but as something that has perished, and so the memory of those who are intent upon a future benefit is weak.

At this point I must bear testimony to Epicurus, who constantly complains because we are ungrateful for past blessings, because we do not recall those that we have enjoyed, nor count them in the list of pleasures, while no pleasure exists more certainly than one that can no longer be snatched away. Present blessings are not yet wholly established upon a firm basis, it is still possible that some mischance may interrupt them ; future blessings are still in the air and are uncertain ; but what is past has been stored away in safety. How can a man who is wholly absorbed in the present and the future, who skips over all his past life, ever be grateful for benefits ? It is memory that makes him grateful ; the more time one gives to hope, the less one has for memory.

There are some subjects, my dear Liberalis, that remain fixed in our memory when we have once grasped them, and others that, if they are to be known, require more than a first acquaintance provides (for knowledge of them is lost unless it is con-

tinuetur), geometriam dico et sublimium cursum et si
qua alia propter suptilitatem lubrica sunt, ita beneficia
quaedam magnitudo non patitur excidere, quaedam
minora sed numero plurima et temporibus diversa
effluunt, quia, ut dixi, non subinde illa tractamus nec
2 libenter, quid cuique debeamus, recognoscimus. Audi
voces petentium. Nemo non victuram semper in animo
suo memoriam dixit, nemo non deditum se et devotum
professus est, et si quod aliud humilius verbum, quo
se oppigneraret, invenit. Post exiguum tempus idem
illi verba priora quasi sordida et parum libera evitant ;
perveniunt deinde eo, quo, ut ego existimo, pessimus
quisque atque ingratissimus pervenit, ut obliviscantur.
Adeo enim ingratus est, qui oblitus est, ut ingratus
sit, cui beneficium in mentem venit.

1   6. Hoc tam invisum vitium an impunitum esse
debeat, quaeritur, et an haec lex, quae in scholis exercetur, etiam in civitate ponenda sit, qua ingrati datur
actio ; quae videtur aequa omnibus. " Quidni ? cum
urbes quoque urbibus, quae praestitere, exprobrent et
2 in¹ maiores collata a posteris exigant." Nostri maiores,
maximi scilicet viri, ab hostibus tantum res repe-

---

¹ in *added by Gruter.*

ᵃ The schools of rhetoric were largely concerned in debat-
ing legal questions and imaginary cases in court, and in these,
apparently, actions for ingratitude were a common theme.
134

tinued)—I am thinking of the knowledge of geometry and of the motions of the heavenly bodies and of other similar subjects that, on account of their nicety, have a slippery hold. Just so, in the matter of benefits, there are some whose very magnitude will not allow them to slip from our mind, while others that are smaller, yet countless in number and bestowed at various times, escape from our memory because, as I have said, we do not repeatedly revert to them, and are not glad to recognize what we owe to each. Listen to the words of petitioners. No one of them fails to say that the memory of the benefit will live for ever in his heart; no one of them fails to declare himself your submissive and devoted slave, and, if he can find any more abject language in which to express his obligation, he uses it. But after a very little time these same men avoid their earlier utterances, counting them degrading and unworthy of a free man; and then they reach the state, to which, in my opinion, all the worst and the most ungrateful men come—they grow forgetful. For so surely is he ungrateful who has forgotten that a man is ungrateful when a benefit only "comes into his mind."

Some raise the question whether a vice so odious as this ought to go unpunished, or whether this law, by which, as it operates in the schools,[a] the ungrateful man becomes liable to prosecution, ought to be applied also in the state; for it seems to everybody to be a just one. "Why not?" they say, "since even cities bring charges against cities for services rendered, and force later generations to pay for what had been bestowed upon their forefathers." But our forefathers, who were undoubtedly very great men, demanded restitution only from their enemies;

tierunt, beneficia magno animo dabant, magno
perdebant; excepta Macedonum gente non est in
ulla data adversus ingratum actio. Magnumque hoc
argumentum est dandam non fuisse, quia adversus
maleficium omne consensimus, et homicidii, veneficii,
parricidii, violatarum religionum aliubi atque aliubi
diversa poena est, sed ubique aliqua, hoc frequentis-
simum crimen nusquam punitur, ubique improbatur.
Neque absolvimus illud, sed cum difficilis esset incertae
rei aestimatio, tantum odio damnavimus et inter ea
reliquimus, quae ad iudices deos mittimus.

1   7. Rationes autem multae mihi occurrunt, propter quas crimen hoc in legem cadere non debeat.
Primum omnium pars optima beneficii periit, si actio
sicut certae pecuniae aut ex conducto et locato datur.
Hoc enim in illo speciosissimum est, quod dedimus vel
perdituri, quod totum permisimus accipientium arbitrio; si appello, si ad iudicem voco, incipit non beneficium esse, sed creditum.

2   Deinde cum res honestissima sit referre gratiam,
desinit esse honesta, si necessaria est; non magis
enim laudabit quisquam gratum hominem, quam eum,
qui depositum reddidit aut, quod debebat, citra
3 iudicem solvit. Ita duas res, quibus in vita humana
nihil pulchrius est, corrumpimus, gratum hominem et
beneficium; quid enim aut in hoc magnificum est, si

ᵃ See Seneca's story of Philip in iv. 37. According to
Valerius Maximus (ii. 6. 6) ingratitude had its penalty at
Athens too : " age, quid illud institutum Athenarum, quam
memorabile, quod convictus a patrono libertus ingratus iure
libertatis exuitur."

benefactions they would bestow magnanimously, and lose them magnanimously. With the exception of the people of Macedonia,[a] in no state has the ungrateful man become liable to prosecution. And ample proof that there ought not to have been any such liability is shown by the fact that we are in full accord in opposing all crime ; the penalty for homicide, for poisoning, for parricide, and for the desecration of religion is different in different places, but they have some penalty everywhere, whereas this crime that is the commonest of all is nowhere punished, but is everywhere denounced. And yet we have not wholly acquitted it, but, because it is difficult to form an opinion of a thing so uncertain, we have only condemned it to hatred, and have left it among the sins that are referred to the gods for judgement.

But many reasons occur to me why this crime should not come under the law. First of all, the best part of a benefit is lost if it can become actionable, as is possible in the case of a fixed loan or of something rented or leased. For the most beautiful part of a benefit is that we gave it even when we were likely to lose it, that we left it wholly to the discretion of the one who received it. If I arrest him, if I summon him before a judge, it gets to be, not a benefit, but a loan.

In the second place, although to repay gratitude is a most praiseworthy act, it ceases to be praiseworthy if it is made obligatory ; for in that case no one will any more praise a man for being grateful than he will praise one who has returned a deposit of money, or paid a debt without being summoned before a judge. So we spoil the two most beautiful things in human life—a man's gratitude and a man's benefit. For what nobility does either one show—the one if, instead of

beneficium non dat, sed commodat, aut in illo, qui
reddit, non quia vult, sed quia necesse est? Non est
gloriosa res gratum esse, nisi tutum est ingratum
fuisse.

4   Adice nunc, quod huic uni legi omnia fora vix sufficient. Quis erit, qui non agat? Quis, cum quo non
agatur? Omnes sua extollunt, omnes etiam minima,
quae in alios contulere, dilatant.

5   Praeterea, quaecumque in cognitionem cadunt, com-
prendi possunt et non dare infinitam licentiam iudici;
ideo melior videtur condicio causae bonae, si ad
iudicem quam si ad arbitrum mittitur, quia illum
formula includit et certos, quos non excedat, terminos
ponit, huius libera et nullis adstricta vinculis religio et
detrahere aliquid potest et adicere et sententiam
suam, non prout lex aut iustitia suadet, sed prout
humanitas aut misericordia impulit, regere. Ingrati
6 actio non erat iudicem adligatura sed regno liber-
rimo positura. Quid sit enim beneficium, non constat, deinde, quantum sit; refert, quam benigne illud
interpretetur iudex. Quid sit ingratus, nulla lex
monstrat; saepe et qui reddidit, quod accepit, in-
7 gratus est, et qui non reddidit, gratus. De quibusdam
et imperitus iudex demittere tabellam potest, ubi
fecisse aut non fecisse pronuntiandum est, ubi prolatis

ᵃ In the *formula* prepared by the praetor, which summed
up the points of the accusation and the defence, and prescribed
the basis of judgement.

giving, he lends a benefit, the other if he makes return, not because he wishes, but because he is forced ? There is no glory in being grateful unless it would have been safe to be ungrateful.

Add, too, the fact that for the application of this one law all the law-courts in the world would scarcely be enough ! Where is the man who will not bring action ? Where is the man against whom action will not be brought ? For all exalt their own merits, all magnify the smallest services they have rendered to others.

Again, in all matters that become the basis of legal action it is possible to define [a] the procedure and to prohibit the judge from unlimited liberty ; it is clear, accordingly, that a just case is in a better position if it is brought before a judge than if it is brought before an " arbiter," because the judge is restricted by the formula of instructions, which sets definite bounds that he cannot exceed, whereas the other has entire liberty of conscience and is hampered by no bonds ; he can lessen the value of some fact or augment it, and can regulate his opinion, not according to the dictates of law or justice, but according to the promptings of humanity or pity. But an action for ingratitude would not place any restriction on the judge, but would set him in a position of absolutely untrammelled authority. For it is not clearly determined what a benefit is, nor, too, how great it is ; that depends upon how generously the judge may interpret it. No law shows what an ungrateful person is ; often one who has returned what he received is ungrateful, and one who has not returned it is grateful. On certain matters even an inexperienced judge is able to give a verdict ; for instance, when an opinion must be

cautionibus controversia tollitur, ubi inter disputantes ratio ius dicit. Ubi vero animi coniectura capienda est, ubi id, de quo sola sapientia decernit, in controversiam incidit, non potest sumi ad haec iudex ex turba selectorum, quem census in album et equestris hereditas misit.

1 8. Itaque non haec parum idonea res visa est, quae deduceretur ad iudicem, sed nemo huic rei satis idoneus iudex inventus est ; quod non admiraberis, si excusseris, quid habiturus fuerit difficultatis, quisquis 2 in eiusmodi reum exisset. Donavit aliquis magnam pecuniam, sed dives, sed non sensurus impendium ; donavit alius, sed toto patrimonio cessurus. Summa eadem est, beneficium idem non est. Etiamnunc adice : hic pecuniam pro addicto dependit, sed cum illam domo protulisset ; ille dedit eandem, sed mutuam sumpsit aut rogavit et se obligari ingenti merito passus est. Eodem existimas loco esse illum, qui beneficium ex facili largitus est, et hunc, qui ac- 3 cepit, ut daret ? Tempore quaedam magna fiunt, non summa. Beneficium est donata possessio, cuius fertilitas laxare possit annonam, beneficium est unus

---

^a The jurors appointed to try criminal cases were required to have a certain fortune, and were drawn chiefly from the senators and knights.

delivered on whether something has, or has not, been done, when the dispute is terminated by the giving of bonds, when common sense pronounces judgement between the litigants. When, however, a conjecture of motive has to be made, when a point concerning which wisdom alone can decide happens to be in dispute, it cannot be that for such purposes a judge is to be taken from the general crowd of jurors [a]—a man whom income and the inheritance of equestrian fortune have placed upon the roll.

Therefore the truth is, not that this offence has appeared quite unfitted to be brought before a judge, but that no one has been found who was quite fitted to be its judge ; and this will cause you no surprise if you will thresh out all the difficulties that anyone would have if he should appear against a man arraigned on a charge of this sort. A gift has been made by someone of a large sum of money, but the giver was rich, he was not likely to feel the sacrifice ; the same gift was made by another, but the giver was likely to lose the whole of his patrimony. The sum given is the same, but the benefit is not the same. Take another case. Suppose a man paid out money for one who had been adjudged to his creditor, but in doing so drew from his own private means ; another gave the same amount, but borrowed it or begged it, and in doing a great service was willing to burden himself with an obligation. Do you think that the one, for whom it was easy to bestow a benefit, and the other, who received in order that he might give a benefit, are both in the same class ? The timeliness, not the size, of a gift makes some benefits great. It is a benefit to bestow the gift of an estate that by reason of its fertility may lower the price of grain, it

in fame panis ; beneficium est donare regiones, per quas magna flumina et navigabilia decurrant, beneficium est arentibus siti et vix spiritum per siccas fauces ducentibus monstrare fontem. Quis inter se ista comparabit ? Quis expendet ? Difficilis est sententia, quae non rem, sed vim rei quaerit ; eadem licet 4 sint, aliter data non idem pendent. Dedit hic mihi beneficium, sed non libenter, sed dedisse se questus est, sed superbius me, quam solebat, adspexit, sed tam tarde dedit, ut plus praestaturus fuerit, si cito negasset. Horum quomodo iudex inibit aestimationem, cum sermo et dubitatio et vultus meriti gratiam destruant ?

1 9. Quid, quod quaedam beneficia vocantur, quia nimis concupiscuntur, quaedam non sunt ex hac vulgari nota sed maiora, etiam si minus apparent ?
2 Beneficium vocas dedisse potentis populi civitatem, in quattuordecim deduxisse et defendisse capitis reum. Quid utilia suasisse ? Quid retinuisse, ne in scelus rueret ? Quid gladium excussisse morituro ? Quid efficacibus remediis lugentem et, quos desiderabat,

---

a The first fourteen rows in the theatre were reserved for the knights.

142

is a benefit to bestow one loaf of bread in time of famine; it is a benefit to bestow lands that have large and navigable rivers flowing through them; it is a benefit to point out a spring of water to a man when he is parched with thirst and can scarce'y draw breath through his dry throat. Who will match these one against another? Who will weigh them in the balance? The decision is difficult when it is concerned, not with the thing, but with the significance of the thing. Though the gifts are the same, if they are differently given, their weight is not the same. A man may have bestowed on me a benefit, but suppose he did not do it willingly, suppose he complained about having bestowed it, suppose he regarded me more haughtily than was his wont, suppose he was so slow to give that he would have conferred a greater service if he had been quick to refuse. How will a judge set about appraising these benefits when the giver's words, his hesitation, and expression may destroy all gratitude for his favour?

And what shall we say of some gifts that are called benefits because they are excessively coveted, while others, though they lack this common ear-mark, are really greater benefits even if they do not appear so? It is called a " benefit " if you have given someone the citizenship of a powerful people, if you have escorted him to the fourteen rows [a] of the knights, if you have defended him when he was on trial for his life. But what of having given him useful advice? What of having kept him from plunging into crime? What of having struck the sword from his hands when he planned to die? What of having brought him effective consolation in sorrow, and of having restored

volentem sequi ad vitae consilium reduxisse? Quid adsedisse aegro et, cum valetudo eius ac salus momentis constaret, excepisse idonea cibo tempora et cadentes venas vino refecisse et medicum adduxisse morienti?

3 Haec quis aestimabit? Quis dissimilibus beneficiis iubebit beneficia pensari? "Donavi tibi domum." Sed ego tuam supra te ruere praedixi. "Dedi tibi patrimonium." Sed ego naufrago tabulam. "Pugnavi pro te et vulnera excepi." At ego vitam tibi silentio dedi. Cum aliter beneficium detur, aliter reddatur, paria facere difficile est.

1 10. Dies praeterea beneficio reddendo non dicitur, sicut pecuniae creditae; itaque potest, qui nondum reddidit, reddere. Dic enim, intra quod tempus 2 deprendatur ingratus. Maxima beneficia probationem non habent, saepe intra tacitam duorum conscientiam latent; an hoc inducimus, ut non demus beneficia sine teste?

3 Quam deinde poenam ingratis constituimus? Unam omnibus, cum disparia sint? Inaequalem et pro cuiusque beneficio maiorem, aut minorem? Age, intra pecuniam versabitur taxatio. Quid, quod quaedam vitae beneficia sunt et maiora vita? His quae pro-

in him a resolve to live when he was wishing to follow those for whom he grieved ? What of having sat at his side when he was sick, and, when his health and recovery were a matter of moments, of having seized the right times to administer food, of having revived his failing pulse with wine, and brought in a physician when he was dying ? Who will estimate the value of such services ? Who will decree that benefits of one sort counterbalance benefits of another ? " I gave you a house," you say. Yes, but I warned you that yours was tumbling down upon your head ! " I gave you a fortune," you say. Yes, but I gave you a plank when you were shipwrecked ! " I fought for you and received wounds for your sake," you say. Yes, but I by my silence gave you your life ! Since benefits may be given in one form and repaid in another, it is difficult to establish their equality.

Besides, for the repayment of a benefit no date is set, as there is for a loan of money ; and so it is possible that one who has not yet repaid may still repay. Pray tell me, at the expiration of what time is a man to be arrested for ingratitude ? Of the greatest benefits there is no visible evidence ; they often lie hidden in a silent consciousness that only two share. Or shall we introduce the rule of not giving a benefit without a witness ?

And then what punishment shall we fix upon for the ungrateful ? Shall there be the same one for all though their benefits are unequal ? Or shall it be variable, a larger or smaller one according to the benefit each one has received ? Very well, then, the standard of evaluation shall be money. But what of some benefits that have the value of life or are even greater than life ? What punishment will be pro-

nuntiabitur poena ? Minor beneficio ? Iniqua est.
Par et capitalis ? Quid inhumanius quam cruentos
esse beneficiorum exitus ?

1 11. " Quaedam," inquit, " privilegia parentibus
data sunt ; quomodo horum extra ordinem habita
ratio est, sic aliorum quoque beneficorum haberi
debet." Parentium condicionem sacravimus, quia expediebat liberos tolli ; sollicitandi ad hunc laborem
erant incertam adituri fortunam. Non poterat illis
dici, quod beneficia dantibus dicitur : " Cui des,
elige ; ipse tecum, si deceptus es, querere ; dignum
adiuva." In liberis tollendis nihil iudicio tollentium
licet, tota res voti est. Itaque, ut aequiore animo
adirent aleam, danda aliqua illis potestas fuit.

2 Deinde alia condicio parentium est, qui beneficia,
quibus dederunt, dant nihilo minus daturique sunt,
nec est periculum, ne dedisse ipsos mentiantur. In
ceteris quaeri debet, non tantum an receperint, sed an
dederint, horum in confesso merita sunt, et, quia utile
est iuventuti regi, imposuimus illi quasi domesticos
magistratus, sub[1] quorum custodia contineretur.[2]

---

[1] sub *GMP, Hosius* : sed *NR* : scilicet *Préchac.*
[2] et quia . . . contineretur *placed by Gertz after* potestas
fuit § 1 : *bracketed by Préchac.*

nounced upon ingratitude for these ? One smaller than the benefit ? That would be unjust ! One that is its equal—death ? But what could be more inhuman than that benefits should end in bloodshed !

"Certain prerogatives," it is argued, " have been accorded to parents ; and, in the same way in which the case of these has been considered to be exceptional, the case of other benefactors must also be considered to be so." But we have given sanctity to the position of parents because it was expedient that they should rear children ; it was necessary to encourage them to the task because they were going to face an uncertain hazard. You could not say to them what you say to those who give benefits : " Choose the one to whom you will give ; you have only yourself to blame if you have been deceived ; help the deserving man." In the rearing of children nothing is left to the choice of those who rear them—it is wholly a matter of hope. And so, in order that parents might be more content to run the risk, it was necessary to give to them a certain authority.

Then, too, the situation of parents is very different ; for to those to whom they have already given they none the less give, and will continue to give, benefits, nor is there any danger of their making false claims about having given them. In the case of other benefactors there must be the question not only of whether they have received a return, but also of whether they have actually given, while in the case of parents their services are unquestionable, and, because it is expedient that the young should be controlled, we have placed over them household magistrates, as it were, under whose custody they may be held in check.

147

3   Deinde omnium parentium unum erat beneficium,
itaque aestimari semel potuit ; alia diversa sunt, dissimilia, infinitis inter se intervallis distantia ; itaque
sub nullam regulam cadere potuerunt, cum aequius
esset omnia relinqui quam omnia aequari.

1   12. Quaedam magno dantibus constant, quaedam
accipientibus magna sunt, sed gratuita tribuentibus.
Quaedam amicis data sunt, quaedam ignotis ; plus est,
quamvis idem detur, si ei datur, quem nosse a beneficio tuo incipis.   Hic auxilia tribuit, ille ornamenta,
2 ille solacia.   Invenies, qui nihil putet esse iucundius,
nihil maius quam habere, in quo calamitas adquiescat ;
invenies rursus, qui dignitati suae, quam securitati
consuli malit ; est, qui plus ei debere se iudicet, per
quem tutior est, quam ei, per quem honestior. Proinde
ista maiora aut minora erunt, prout fuerit iudex aut
huc aut illo inclinatus animo.

3   Praeterea creditorem mihi ipse eligo, beneficium
saepe ab eo accipio, a quo nolo, et aliquando ignorans
obligor.   Quid facies ?   Ingratum vocabis eum, cui
beneficium inscio et, si scisset, non accepturo impositum est ?   Non vocabis eum, qui utcumque ac-

Again, the benefit from a parent was the same for all, and so it could be evaluated once for all. Benefits from others are diverse in character, are unrelated and separated from each by incalculable distances ; and so they could not be brought under any fixed norm, since it was more equitable to leave all unclassified than to place them all in the same category.

Certain benefits cost the givers a great price, others have great value in the eyes of the recipients, but cost the bestowers of them nothing. Some are given to friends, some to strangers ; although the same amount is given, it counts for more if it is given to one with whom the beginning of an acquaintance dates from the gift of your benefit. This one bestowed help, that other distinctions, another consolations. You will find the person who thinks that there is no greater pleasure, no greater boon than to have some breast on which he may find rest in misfortune ; again, you will find another who would prefer to have concern shown for his prestige rather than for his security ; there is the man, too, who will feel more indebted to one who adds to his safety than to his honour. Consequently, these benefits will assume greater or less value according as the temper of the judge leans in the one direction or the other.

Moreover, while I myself choose my creditor, yet I often receive a benefit from one from whom I do not wish it, and sometimes even unwittingly I contract an obligation. What in this case will you do ? Will you call a man ungrateful when, without his knowing it, a benefit has been forced upon him which, had he known it, he would not have accepted ? Will you not call him ungrateful if he does not repay it, no matter how he may have received it ? Suppose that

149

4 ceptum non reddidit ? Aliquis dedit mihi beneficium,
sed idem postea fecit iniuriam. Utrum uno munere ad
patientiam iniuriarum omnium adstringor, an proinde
erit, ac si gratiam rettulerim, quia beneficium suum
ipse insequenti iniuria rescidit ? Quomodo deinde
aestimabis, utrum plus sit, quod accepit, an quo laesus
est ? Dies me deficiet omnes difficultates persequi
temptantem.

1 13. "Tardiores," inquit, "ad beneficia danda
facimus non vindicando data nec infitiatores eorum
adficiendo poena." Sed illud quoque tibi e contrario
occurrat multo tardiores futuros ad accipienda beneficia, si periculum causae dicundae adituri erunt et
2 innocentiam sollicitiore habituri loco. Deinde erimus
per hoc ipsi quoque ad danda tardiores ; nemo enim
libenter dat invitis, sed quicumque ad bene faciendum
bonitate invitatus est et ipsa pulchritudine rei, etiam
libentius dabit nihil debituris nisi quod volent. Minui-
tur enim gloria eius officii, cui diligenter cautum est.

1 14. Deinde pauciora erunt beneficia, sed veriora ;
quid autem mali est inhiberi beneficiorum temeritatem ? Hoc enim ipsum secuti sunt, qui nullam
legem huic constituerunt, ut circumspectius dona-
remus, circumspectius eligeremus eos, in quos merita
2 conferuntur. Etiam atque etiam, cui des, considera :

someone has bestowed upon me a benefit, and that the same man later has done me an injury. Am I bound to endure every sort of injury because of his one gift, or will it be the same as if I had repaid his favour because he himself cancelled the benefit by his later injury? And then how will you tell whether the benefit that he received or the injury was the greater? Time will fail me if I attempt to enumerate all the difficulties.

"By not coming to the defence of benefits that have been given, and, by not inflicting punishment on those who deny them, we only make men more reluctant," you say, "to bestow others." But, on the other hand, remember, too, that men will be much more reluctant to accept benefits if they are going to run the risk of being forced to defend their case in court, and of having their integrity placed in a very dubious position. Then, too, we ourselves, because of this possibility, will be more reluctant to give; for no one gives willingly to the unwilling recipient, but every one, whose own goodness and the very beauty of his action has urged him to perform a generous deed, will give even more willingly to those who will incur no indebtedness except what they wish to feel. For a good deed that looks carefully to its own interests loses some of its glory.

Then, again, while benefits will become fewer, they will be more genuine; but what harm is there in checking the reckless giving of benefits? For the very aim of those who have designed no law for this matter has been that we should be more cautious in making gifts, more cautious in picking those upon whom we bestow our favours. Consider again and again to whom you are giving: you will have no

nulla actio erit, nulla repetitio. Erras, si existimas succursurum tibi iudicem ; nulla lex te in integrum restituet, solam accipientis fidem specta. Hoc modo beneficia auctoritatem suam tenent et magnifica sunt;
3 pollues illa, si materiam litium feceris. Aequissima vox est et ius gentium prae se ferens : " Redde, quod debes " ; haec turpissima est in beneficio. " Redde ! " Quid ? Reddet vitam, quam debet ? Dignitatem ?
4 Securitatem ? Sanitatem ? Reddi maxima quaeque non possunt. " At pro iis," inquit, " aliquid, quod tanti sit." Hoc est, quod dicebam, interituram tantae rei dignitatem, si beneficium mercem facimus. Non est irritandus animus ad avaritiam, ad querellas, ad discordiam ; sua sponte in ista fertur. Quantum possumus, resistamus et quaerenti occasiones amputemus.

1 15. Utinam quidem persuadere possemus, ut pecunias creditas tantum a volentibus acciperent ! Utinam nulla stipulatio emptorem venditori obligaret nec pacta conventaque impressis signis custodirentur, fides potius illa servaret et aecum colens animus !
2 Sed necessaria optimis praetulerunt et cogere fidem quam expectare malunt. Adhibentur ab utraque parte testes. Ille per tabulas plurium nomina interpositis parariis facit ; ille non est interrogatione con-

recourse to law, no claim to restitution. You are mistaken if you think that some judge will come to your aid ; no law will restore you to your original estate—look only to the good faith of the recipient. In this way benefits maintain their prestige and are lordly ; you disgrace them if you make them the ground of litigation. "Pay what you owe" is a proverb most just and one that is stamped with the approval of all nations ; but in the case of a benefit it becomes most shameful. "Pay!" But what ? Shall a man pay the life that he owes ? The position ? The security ? The sound health ? All the greatest benefits are incapable of being repaid. "Yet make some return for them," you say, "that is of equal value." But this is just what I was saying, that, if we make merchandise of benefits, all the merit of so fine an action will perish. The mind does not need to be incited to greed, to accusations, and to discord ; it tends to these by a natural impulse. But, as far as we can, let us oppose it, and cut it off from the opportunities that it seeks.

Would that I could persuade the lenders of money to accept payment only from those who are willing to pay ! Would that no compact marked the obligation of buyer to seller, and that no covenants and agreements were safeguarded by the impress of seals, but that, instead, the keeping of them were left to good faith and a conscience that cherishes justice ! But men have preferred what is necessary to what is best, and would rather compel good faith than expect it. Witnesses are summoned on both sides. One creditor, by having recourse to factors, causes the record to be made in the books of several people ; another is not content with oral promises, but must

3 tentus, nisi reum manu sua tenuit. O turpem humani
generis fraudis ac nequitiae publicae confessionem!
Anulis nostris plus quam animis creditur. In quid isti
ornati viri adhibiti sunt? In quid imprimunt signa?
Nempe ne ille neget accepisse se, quod accepit! Hos
incorruptos viros et vindices veritatis existimas? At
his ipsis non aliter statim pecuniae committentur. Ita
non honestius erat a quibusdam fidem falli, quam ab
4 omnibus perfidiam timeri? Hoc unum deest avaritiae,
ut beneficia sine sponsore non demus! Generosi
animi est et magnifici iuvare, prodesse; qui dat beneficia, deos imitatur, qui repetit, feneratores. Quid
illos, dum vindicamus, in turbam sordidissimam
redigimus?

1   16. "Plures," inquit, "ingrati erunt, si nulla adversus ingratum datur actio." Immo pauciores, quia
maiore dilectu dabuntur beneficia. Deinde non
expedit notum omnibus fieri, quam multi ingrati sint;
pudorem enim rei tollet multitudo peccantium, et
2 desinet esse probri loco commune maledictum. Numquid iam ulla repudio erubescit, postquam illustres
quaedam ac nobiles feminae non consulum numero
sed maritorum annos suos computant et exeunt
matrimonii causa, nubunt repudii? Tamdiu istuc
timebatur, quamdiu rarum erat; quia nulla sine

also bind his victim by a written signature. O, what a shameful admission of the open frauds and wickedness of the human race ! More trust is placed in our seal-rings than in our consciences. To what end have these notable men been summoned ? To what end do they leave the impress of their signets ? In order, for-sooth, that the debtor may not deny that what he has received has been received ! Think you that these men are incorruptible and champions of truth ? Yet to these very men money will not be entrusted at this hour on any other terms. So would it not have been more desirable to allow some men to break their word than to cause all men to fear treachery ? The only thing that avarice lacks now is that we should not even give benefits without a bondsman ! To help, to be of service, is the part of a noble and chivalrous soul ; he who gives benefits imitates the gods, he who seeks a return, money-lenders. Why, in wishing to protect benefactors, do we reduce them to the level of the most disreputable class ?

"More men," you say, "will become ungrateful if no action can be brought against ingratitude." No, fewer men, because benefits will be given with a greater discrimination. Then, too, it is not advisable that all men should know how many are ungrateful ; for the multitude of the offenders will remove the shame of the thing, and what is a general reproach will cease to be a disgrace. Is there any woman that blushes at divorce now that certain illustrious and noble ladies reckon their years, not by the number of consuls, but by the number of their husbands, and leave home in order to marry, and marry in order to be divorced ? They shrank from this scandal as long as it was rare ; now, since every gazette has a

divortio acta sunt, quod saepe audiebant, facere
3 didicerunt. Numquid iam ullus adulterii pudor est,
postquam eo ventum est, ut nulla virum habeat, nisi
ut adulterum irritet? Argumentum est deformitatis
pudicitia. Quam invenies tam miseram, tam sordidam,
ut illi satis sit unum adulterorum par, nisi singulis
divisit horas? Et non sufficit dies omnibus, nisi apud
alium gestata est, apud alium mansit. Infrunita et
antiqua est, quae nesciat matrimonium vocari unum
4 adulterium. Quemadmodum horum delictorum iam
evanuit pudor, postquam res latius evagata est, ita
ingratos plures efficies et auctiores,[1] si numerare se
coeperint.

1 17. "Quid ergo? impunitus erit ingratus?" Quid
ergo, impunitus erit impius? Quid malignus? Quid
avarus? Quid impotens? Quid crudelis? Impunita
tu credis esse, quae invisa sunt, aut ullum supplicium
2 gravius existimas publico odio? Poena est, quod non
audet ab ullo beneficium accipere, quod non audet
ulli dare, quod omnium designatur oculis aut designari
se iudicat, quod intellectum rei optimae ac dulcissimae
amisit. An tu infelicem vocas, qui caruit acie, cuius
aures morbus obstruxit, non vocas miserum eum, qui
3 sensum beneficiorum amisit? Testes ingratorum

---

[1] auctiores *O, Préchac*: auctores *N.*

divorce case, they have learned to do what they used to hear so much about. Is there any shame at all for adultery now that matters have come to such a pass that no woman has any use for a husband except to inflame her paramour? Chastity is simply a proof of ugliness. Where will you find any woman so wretched, so unattractive, as to be content with a couple of paramours—without having each hour assigned to a different one? And the day is not long enough for them all, but she must be carried in her litter to the house of one, and spend the night with another. She is simple and behind the times who is not aware that living with one paramour is called "marriage"! As the shame of these offences has disappeared now that their practice has spread more broadly, so you will make ingrates more numerous and increase their importance if once they begin to count their number.

"What, then," you say, "shall the ingrate go unpunished?" What, then, shall the undutiful man go unpunished? And the spiteful? And the greedy? And the overbearing? And the cruel? Do you imagine that qualities that are loathed do go unpunished, or that there is any greater punishment than public hate? The penalty of the ingrate is that he does not dare to accept a benefit from any man, that he does not dare to give one to any man, that he is a mark, or at least thinks that he is a mark, for all eyes, that he has lost all perception of a most desirable and pleasant experience. Or do you call that man unhappy who has lost his sight, whose ears have been closed by some malady, and yet do not call him wretched who has lost all sense of benefits? He dwells in fear of the gods, who are the witnesses of all

omnium deos metuit, urit illum et angit intercepti beneficii conscientia. Denique satis haec ipsa poena magna est, quod rei, ut dicebam, iucundissimae fructum non percipit.

At quem iuvat accepisse, aequali perpetuaque voluptate fruitur et animum eius, a quo accepit, non rem intuens gaudet. Gratum hominem semper bene-
4 ficium delectat, ingratum semel. Comparari autem potest utriusque vita, cum alter tristis sit et sollicitus, qualis esse infitiator ac fraudulentus solet, apud quem non parentium, qui debet, honor est, non educatoris, non praeceptorum, alter laetus, hilaris, occasionem referendae gratiae expectans et ex hoc ipso adfectu gaudium grande percipiens nec quaerens, quomodo decoquat, sed quemadmodum plenius uberiusque respondeat non solum parentibus et amicis, sed humilioribus quoque personis ? Nam etiam si a servo suo beneficium accepit, aestimat, non a quo, sed quid acceperit.

1 18. Quamquam quaeritur a quibusdam, sicut ab Hecatone, an beneficium dare servus domino possit. Sunt enim, qui ita distinguant, quaedam beneficia esse, quaedam officia, quaedam ministeria ; beneficium esse, quod alienus det (alienus est, qui potuit sine reprehensione cessare) ; officium esse filii, uxoris, earum personarum, quas necessitudo suscitat et ferre opem iubet ; ministerium esse servi, quem condicio

ingratitude, he is tortured and distressed by the consciousness of having thwarted a benefit. In short, this in itself is punishment great enough, the fact that he does not reap enjoyment from an experience that, as I just said, is the most delightful.

But he who is happy in having received a benefit tastes a constant and unfailing pleasure, and rejoices in viewing, not the gift, but the intention of him from whom he received it. The grateful man delights in a benefit over and over, the ungrateful man but once. But is it possible to compare the lives of these two? For the one, as a disclaimer of debts and a cheat are apt to be, is downcast and worried, he denies to his parents, to his protector, to his teachers, the consideration that is their due, while the other is joyous, cheerful, and, watching for an opportunity to repay his gratitude, derives great joy from this very sentiment, and seeks, not how he may default in his obligations, but how he may make very full and rich return, not only to his parents and friends, but also to persons of lower station. For, even if he has received a benefit from his slave, he considers, not from whom it came, but what he received.

And yet some raise the question, for example Hecaton, whether it is possible for a slave to give a benefit to his master. For there are those who distinguish some acts as benefits, some as duties, some as services, saying that a benefit is something that is given by a stranger (a stranger is one who, without incurring censure, might have done nothing); that a duty is performed by a son, or a wife, or by persons that are stirred by the ties of kinship, which impels them to bear aid; that a service is contributed by a slave, whose condition has placed him in such a

sua eo loco posuit, ut nihil eorum, quae praestat,
imputet superiori.[1]

2   Praeterea servum qui negat dare aliquando domino
beneficium, ignarus est iuris humani ; refert enim,
cuius animi sit, qui praestat, non cuius status. Nulli
praeclusa virtus est ; omnibus patet, omnes admittit,
omnes invitat, et ingenuos et libertinos et servos et
reges et exules ; non eligit domum nec censum, nudo
homine contenta est. Quid enim erat tuti adversus
repentina, quid animus magnum promitteret sibi, si
3 certam virtutem fortuna amitteret ? Si non dat beneficium servus domino, nec regi quisquam suo nec duci
suo miles ; quid enim interest, quali quis teneatur
imperio, si summo tenetur ? Nam si servo, quominus
in nomen meriti perveniat, necessitas obstat et
patiendi ultima timor, idem istuc obstabit et ei, qui
regem habet, et ei, qui ducem, quoniam sub dispari
titulo paria in illos licent. Atqui dant regibus suis,
4 dant imperatoribus beneficia ; ergo et dominis. Potest
servus iustus esse, potest fortis, potest magni animi ;
ergo et beneficium dare potest, nam et hoc virtutis est.
Adeo quidem dominis servi beneficia possunt dare, ut
ipsos saepe beneficii sui fecerint.[a]

1   19. Non est dubium, quin servus beneficium dare

---

[1] *Hosius after Lipsius marks a lacuna here.*

[a] *i.e.*, they have saved their masters' lives.

position that nothing that he can bestow gives him a claim upon his superior.

Moreover, he who denies that a slave can sometimes give a benefit to his master is ignorant of the rights of man ; for, not the status, but the intention, of the one who bestows is what counts. Virtue closes the door to no man ; it is open to all, admits all, invites all, the freeborn and the freedman, the slave and the king, and the exile ; neither family nor fortune determines its choice—it is satisfied with the naked human being. For what protection would it find against sudden events, what great assurance would the human mind be able to hold out to itself if Fortune could rob it of unchangeable Virtue ? If a slave cannot give a benefit to his master, no subject can give one to his king, no soldier to his general ; for, if a man is restrained by supreme authority, what difference does it make what the nature of the authority is that restrains him ? For, if the necessity of his lot and his fear of having to endure untold punishment prevent a slave from attaining the right to do a thankworthy act, the same condition will also prevent the man who is under a king, and the man who is under a general ; for these, under a different title, exercise equal authority. But a man can give a benefit to his king, a man can give a benefit to his general ; therefore a slave also can give one to a master. It is possible for a slave to be just, it is possible for him to be brave, it is possible for him to be magnanimous ; therefore it is possible also for him to give a benefit, for this also is one part of virtue. So true is it that slaves are able to give benefits to their masters that they have often caused their benefit to be their masters themselves.[a]

There is no doubt that a slave is able to give a

possit cuilibet ; quare ergo non et domino suo possit ?
" Quia non potest," inquit, " creditor domini sui fieri,
si pecuniam illi dederit. Alioqui cotidie dominum
suum obligat ; peregrinantem sequitur, aegro mini-
strat, rus eius labore summo colit ; omnia tamen ista,
quae alio praestante beneficia dicerentur, praestante
servo ministeria sunt. Beneficium enim id est, quod
quis dedit, cum illi liceret et non dare. Servus autem
non habet negandi potestatem ; ita non praestat, sed
paret, nec id se fecisse iactat, quod non facere non
potuit."

2 Iam sub ista ipsa lege vincam et eo perducam
servum, ut in multa liber sit. Interim dic mihi, si tibi
ostendero aliquem pro salute domini sui sine respectu
sui dimicantem et confossum vulneribus reliquias
tamen sanguinis ab ipsis vitalibus fundentem et, ut
ille effugiendi tempus habeat, moram sua morte
quaerentem, hunc tu negabis beneficium dedisse, quia
3 servus est ? Si tibi ostendero aliquem, ut secreta
domini prodat, nulla tyranni pollicitatione corruptum,
nullis territum minis, nullis cruciatibus victum aver-
tisse, quantum potuerit, suspiciones quaerentis et
impendisse spiritum fidei, hunc tu negabis beneficium
4 domino dedisse, quia servus est ? Vide, ne eo maius
162

benefit to anyone he pleases ; why not, therefore, also to his master ? " Because," you say, " it is not possible for him to become his master's ' creditor ' if he has given him money. Otherwise, he makes his master in debt to him every day ; he attends him when he travels, he nurses him when he is sick, he expends the greatest labour in cultivating his farm ; nevertheless all these boons, which when supplied by another are called benefits, are merely ' services ' when they are supplied by a slave. For a benefit is something that some person has given when it was also within his power not to give it. But a slave does not have the right to refuse ; thus he does not confer, but merely obeys, and he takes no credit for what he has done because it was not possible for him to fail to do it."

Even under these conditions I shall still win the day and promote a slave to such a position that he will, in many respects, be a free man. Meanwhile, tell me this—if I show to you one who fights for the safety of his master without any regard for his own, and, pierced with wounds, pours forth the last drops of his life-blood drawn from his very vitals, who, in order to provide time for his master to escape, seeks to give him a respite at the cost of his own life, will you deny that this man has bestowed a benefit simply because he is a slave ? If I show to you one who, refusing to betray to a tyrant the secrets of his master, was bribed by no promises, terrified by no threats, overcome by no tortures, and, as far as he was able, confounded the suspicions of his questioner, and paid the penalty of good faith with his life, will you deny that this man bestowed a benefit on his master simply because he was his slave ? Consider, rather, whether

sit, quo rarius est exemplum virtutis in servis, eoque gratius, quod, cum fere invisa imperia sint et omnis necessitas gravis, commune servitutis odium in aliquo domini caritas vicit. Ita non ideo beneficium non est, quia a servo profectum est, sed ideo maius, quia deterrere ab illo ne servitus quidem potuit.

1 20. Errat, si quis existimat servitutem in totum hominem descendere. Pars melior eius excepta est. Corpora obnoxia sunt et adscripta dominis; mens quidem sui iuris, quae adeo libera et vaga est, ut ne ab hoc quidem carcere, cui inclusa est, teneri queat, quominus impetu suo utatur et ingentia agat et in 2 infinitum comes caelestibus exeat. Corpus itaque est, quod domino fortuna tradidit; hoc emit, hoc vendit; interior illa pars mancipio dari non potest. Ab hac quidquid venit, liberum est; nec enim aut nos omnia iubere possumus aut in omnia servi parere coguntur; contra rem publicam imperata non facient, nulli sceleri manus commodabunt.

1 21. Quaedam sunt, quae leges nec iubent nec vetant facere; in iis servus materiam beneficii habet. Quam diu praestatur, quod a servo exigi solet, ministerium est; ubi plus, quam quod servo necesse est, beneficium est; ubi in adfectum amici transit, desinit 2 vocari ministerium. Est aliquid, quod dominus prae-

in the case of slaves, a manifestation of virtue is not the more praiseworthy the rarer it is, and, too, whether it is not all the more gratifying that, despite their general aversion to domination and the irksomeness of constraint, some slave by his affection for his master has overcome the common hatred of being a slave. So, therefore, a benefit does not cease to be a benefit because it proceeded from a slave, but is all the greater on that account, because he could not be deterred from it even by being a slave.

It is a mistake for anyone to believe that the condition of slavery penetrates into the whole being of a man. The better part of him is exempt. Only the body is at the mercy and disposition of a master ; but the mind is its own master, and is so free and unshackled that not even this prison of the body, in which it is confined, can restrain it from using its own powers, following mighty aims, and escaping into the infinite to keep company with the stars. It is, therefore, the body that Fortune hands over to a master ; it is this that he buys, it is this that he sells ; that inner part cannot be delivered into bondage. All that issues from this is free ; nor, indeed, are we able to command all things from slaves, nor are they compelled to obey us in all things ; they will not carry out orders that are hostile to the state, and they will not lend their hands to any crime.

There are certain acts that the law neither enjoins nor forbids ; it is in these that a slave finds opportunity to perform a benefit. So long as what he supplies is only that which is ordinarily required of a slave, it is a " service " ; when he supplies more than a slave need do, it is a " benefit " ; it ceases to be called a service when it passes over into the domain of friendly

stare servo debeat, ut cibaria, ut vestiarium ; nemo
hoc dixit beneficium. At indulsit, liberalius educavit,
artes, quibus erudiuntur ingenui, tradidit : beneficium
est. Idem e contrario fit in persona servi. Quidquid
est, quod servilis officii formulam excedit, quod non ex
imperio, sed ex voluntate praestatur, beneficium est,
si modo tantum est, ut hoc vocari potuerit quolibet
alio praestante.

1   22. Servus, ut placet Chrysippo, perpetuus mer-
cennarius est. Quemadmodum ille beneficium dat,
ubi plus praestat, quam in[1] quod operas locavit, sic
servus : ubi benevolentia erga dominum fortunae suae
modum transit et altius aliquid ausus, quod etiam
felicius natis decori esset, spem domini antecessit,
2 beneficium est intra domum inventum. An aecum
videtur tibi, quibus, si minus debito faciant, irascimur,
non haberi gratiam, si plus debito solitoque fecerint ?
Vis scire, quando non sit beneficium ? Ubi dici
potest : " Quid, si nollet ? " Ubi vero id praestitit,
quod nolle licuit, voluisse laudandum est.

3   Inter se contraria sunt beneficium et iniuria ; potest
dare beneficium domino, si a domino iniuriam accipere. Atqui de iniuriis dominorum in servos qui

---

[1] in *commonly added*

affection. There are certain things, as for instance food and clothing, which the master must supply to the slave ; no one calls these benefits. But suppose the master is indulgent, gives him the education of a gentleman, has him taught the branches in which the freeborn are schooled—all this will be a benefit. Conversely, the same is true in the case of the slave. All that he does in excess of what is prescribed as the duty of a slave, what he supplies, not from obedience to authority, but from his own desire, will be a benefit, provided that its importance, if another person were supplying it, would entitle it to that name.

A slave, according to the definition of Chrysippus, is " a hireling for life." And, just as a hireling gives a benefit if he supplies more than he contracted to do, so a slave—when he exceeds the bounds of his station in goodwill toward his master, and surpasses the expectation of his master by daring some lofty deed that would be an honour even to those more happily born, a benefit is found to exist inside the household. Or do you think it fair that those with whom we become angry if they do less than they ought should not draw our gratitude if they do more than they ought or are wont ? Do you want to know when what a slave does is not a benefit ? When one might say of it : " What if he had refused ? " But when he has bestowed something that he had a right to refuse to bestow, the fact that he was willing deserves to be praised.

Benefit and injury are the opposites of each other ; it is possible for a slave to give a benefit to his master if it is possible for him to receive an injury from his master. But cognizance of the injuries inflicted by masters upon their slaves has been committed to an

167

audiat positus est, qui et saevitiam et libidinem et in
praebendis ad victum necessariis avaritiam compescat.
Quid ergo ? Beneficium dominus a servo accipit ?
4 Immo homo ab homine. Denique, quod in illius
potestate fuit, fecit : beneficium domino dedit ; ne a
servo acceperis, in tua potestate est. Quis autem
tantus est, quem non fortuna indigere etiam infimis
cogat ?

1 23. Multa iam beneficiorum exempla referam
et dissimilia et quaedam inter se contraria. Dedit
aliquis domino suo vitam, dedit mortem, servavit
periturum et, hoc si parum est, pereundo servavit ;
alius mortem domini adiuvit, alius decepit.

2 Claudius Quadrigarius in duodevicensimo annalium
tradit, cum obsideretur Grumentum et iam ad summam desperationem ventum esset, duos servos ad
hostem transfugisse et operae pretium fecisse. Deinde
urbe capta passim discurrente victore illos per nota
itinera ad domum, in qua servierant, praecucurrisse
et dominam suam ante egisse ; quaerentibus, quae-
nam esset, dominam et quidem crudelissimam ad supplicium ab ipsis duci professos esse. Eductam deinde
extra muros summa cura celasse, donec hostilis ira
consideret ; deinde, ut satiatus miles cito ad Romanos
mores rediit, illos quoque ad suos redisse et dominam

official who restrains their cruelty and lust and their stinginess in supplying them with the necessities of life. What, then, is the case? Does a master receive a benefit from a slave? No, but a human being from a human being. After all, whatever was in his power, he did—he gave a benefit to his master; that you should not receive one from a slave is in your power. But who is so exalted that Fortune may not force him to have need of even the most lowly?

I shall proceed now to cite a number of instances of benefits that differ from each other and are in some cases contradictory. One gave to his master life, one gave death, one saved him when he was about to perish, and, if this is not enough, one saved him by perishing himself; another helped his master to die, another baffled his desire.

Claudius Quadrigarius relates, in the eighteenth book of his *Annals*, that, during the siege of Grumentum, just when the city had reached its most desperate plight, two slaves deserted to the enemy and there did good service. Later, after the city had been captured, while the victors were rushing hither and thither, that the two ran ahead along the well-known streets to the house in which they had been slaves, and drove forth their mistress in front of them; that, if anyone asked who she was, they stated that she had been their mistress, and, indeed, a most cruel one, and that they were taking her off to punishment. But that afterwards, when they had brought her outside the walls, they concealed her with the utmost care until the fury of the enemy subsided, and later, when the soldiers, quickly glutted, returned to the normal conduct of Romans, that they, too, returned to theirs, and of their own accord gave themselves into the

3 sibi ipsos dedisse. Manu misit utrumque e vestigio
illa nec indignata est ab his se vitam accepisse, in
quos vitae necisque potestatem habuisset. Potuit
sibi hoc vel magis gratulari; aliter enim servata
munus notae et vulgaris clementiae habuisset, sic servata nobilis fabula et exemplum duarum urbium fuit.
4 In tanta confusione captae civitatis cum sibi quisque
consuleret, omnes ab illa praeter transfugas fugerunt;
at hi, ut ostenderent, quo animo facta esset prior illa
transitio, a victoribus ad captivam transfugerunt personam parricidarum ferentes; quod in illo beneficio
maximum fuit, tanti iudicaverunt, ne domina occide-
retur, videri dominam occidisse. Non est, mihi crede,
non dico[1] servilis, sed vilis[2] animi egregium factum
fama sceleris emisse.

5   Vettius, praetor Marsorum, ducebatur ad Romanum
imperatorem; servus eius gladium militi illi ipsi, a
quo trahebatur, eduxit et primum dominum occidit,
deinde: "Tempus est," inquit, "me et mihi con-
sulere! iam dominum manu misi," atque ita traiecit
se uno ictu. Da mihi quemquam, qui magnificentius
dominum servaverit.

   24. Corfinium Caesar obsidebat, tenebatur in-
clusus Domitius; imperavit medico eidemque servo
suo, ut sibi venenum daret. Cum tergiversantem

---

[1] non dico *O, Préchac* : condicio *Hosius.*
[2] sed vilis *added by Préchac.*

power of their mistress. She manumitted both on the spot, and did not think it beneath her to have received her life at the hands of those over whom she had once had the power of life and death. Instead, she might even have congratulated herself upon this fact ; for, if she had been saved by other hands, she would have had the mere gift of well-known and common mercy, but, as it was, she became famous in story, and an example to two cities. In the great confusion of the city, at a time when every one was thinking of his own interest, she was deserted by all except these deserters ; but they, playing the rôle of being her murderers, deserted from the victors to the captive lady in order to reveal the purpose that had led them to make their first desertion ; and the crowning touch to their benefit was that, in order to save the life of their mistress, they thought it was worth the price of seeming to have put her to death. Believe me, it is not the act—I will not say of a " slavish," but—of a commonplace soul to purchase a noble deed at the cost of being thought a criminal !

When Vettius, the praetor of the Marsians, was being conducted to the Roman general, his slave snatched a sword from the very soldier who was dragging him along, and first slew his master. Then he said : " Now that I have given my master his freedom, the time has come for me to think also of myself," and so with one blow he stabbed himself. Name to me anyone who has saved his master more gloriously.

When Caesar was besieging Corfinium, Domitius, who was confined in the city by the blockade, ordered one of his slaves, who was likewise his physician, to give him poison. Observing his reluctance, he said :

videret : " Quid cunctaris," inquit, " tamquam in tua
potestate totum istud sit ?   Mortem rogo armatus."
Tum ille promisit et medicamentum innoxium biben-
dum illi dedit ; quo cum sopitus esset, accessit ad
filium eius et : " Iube," inquit, " me adservari, dum
ex eventu intellegis, an venenum patri tuo dederim."
Vixit Domitius et servatus a Caesare est ; prior tamen
illum servus servaverat.

25. Bello civili proscriptum dominum servus abscondit et, cum anulos eius sibi aptasset ac vestem
induisset, speculatoribus occurrit nihilque se deprecari,
quo minus imperata peragerent, dixit et deinde cer-
vicem porrexit.   Quanti viri est pro domino eo tempore
mori velle, quo rara erat fides dominum mori nolle !
in publica crudelitate mitem inveniri, in publica per-
fidia fidelem ! cum praemia proditionis ingentia osten-
dantur, praemium fidei mortem concupiscere !

1 26. Nostri saeculi exempla non praeteribo. Sub
Tib. Caesare fuit accusandi frequens et paene publica
rabies, quae omni civili bello gravius togatam civitatem
confecit ;   excipiebatur ebriorum sermo, simplicitas
iocantium ; nihil erat tutum ; omnis saeviendi place-
bat occasio, nec iam reorum expectabantur eventus,
cum esset unus.

Cenabat Paulus praetorius in convivio quodam

" Why do you hesitate, as though this matter were wholly in your own power ; I am asking for death, but I have my sword." Whereupon the slave assented, and gave him a concoction to drink that was harmless. When Domitius had fallen asleep because of it, the slave went to his master's son, and said : " Have me put under guard until you discover from the outcome whether I have given your father poison." Domitius did not die, and Caesar saved his life ; but his life had first been saved by a slave.

During the Civil War, a slave hid away his master, who had been proscribed, and, having put on his rings and dressed himself in his clothes, presented himself to those searching for his master, and, saying that he asked for nothing better than that they should carry out their orders, forthwith offered his neck for their swords. What a hero !—to wish to die in place of a master in times when not to wish a master to die was a rare show of loyalty ; to be found kind when the state was cruel, faithful when it was treacherous ; to covet death as a reward for loyalty in face of the huge rewards that are offered for disloyalty !

And I will not omit some examples from our own age. Under Tiberius Caesar there was such a common and almost universal frenzy for bringing charges of treason, that it took a heavier toll of the lives of Roman citizens than any Civil War ; it seized upon the talk of drunkards, the frank words of jesters ; nothing was safe—anything served as an excuse to shed blood, and there was no need to wait to find out the fate of the accused since there was but one outcome.

Paulus, a praetorian, while dining on a certain

imaginem Tib. Caesaris habens ectypa et eminente
2 gemma. Rem ineptissimam fecero, si nunc verba
quaesiero, quemadmodum dicam illum matellam
sumpsisse ; quod factum simul et Maro ex notis illius
temporis vestigatoribus notavit et servus eius, quoi
nectebantur insidiae, ei ebrio anulum extraxit. Et
cum Maro convivas testaretur admotam esse imaginem obscenis et iam subscriptionem componeret,
ostendit in manu sua servus anulum. Si quis hunc
servum vocat, et illum convivam vocabit.

1   27. Sub divo Augusto nondum hominibus verba
sua periculosa erant, iam molesta. Rufus, vir
ordinis senatorii, inter cenam optaverat, ne Caesar
salvus rediret ex ea peregrinatione, quam parabat;
et adiecerat idem omnes et tauros et vitulos optare.
Fuerunt, qui illa diligenter audirent. Ut primum
diluxit, servus, qui cenanti ad pedes steterat, narrat,
quae inter cenam ebrius dixisset, et hortatur, ut
2 Caesarem occupet atque ipse se deferat. Usus consilio descendenti Caesari occurrit et, cum malam
mentem habuisse se pridie iurasset, id ut in se et in
filios suos recideret, optavit et Caesarem, ut igno-
3 sceret sibi rediretque in gratiam secum, rogavit. Cum
dixisset se Caesar facere : " Nemo," inquit, " credet

---

festive occasion, was wearing a ring with a conspicuous stone on which the portrait of Tiberius Caesar was engraved in relief. I should be acting in very silly fashion if I tried, at this point, to find a polite way of saying that he took in his hands a chamber-pot—an action that was noticed simultaneously by Maro, one of the notorious informers of that time, and by a slave of the victim for whom the trap was being set, who drew off the ring from the finger of his drunken master. And, when Maro called the company to witness that the emperor's protrait had been brought in contact with something foul, and was drawing up the indictment, the slave showed that the ring was on his own hand. Whoever calls such a man a slave, will also call Maro a boon companion !

Under the deified Augustus, it was not yet true that a man's utterances endangered his life, but they did cause him trouble. Rufus, a man of senatorial rank, once at a dinner expressed the hope that Caesar would not return safe from the journey that he was planning ; and he added that all the bulls and the calves[a] wished the same thing. Some of those who were present carefully noted these words. At the break of day, the slave who had stood at his feet when he was dining told him what he had said at dinner while he was drunk, and urged him to be the first to get Caesar's ear and volunteer charges against himself. Following this advice, Rufus met Caesar as he was going down to the forum, and, having sworn that he had been out of his mind the night before, expressed the hope that his words might recoil upon his own head and the head of his children, and begged Caesar to pardon him and restore him to favour. When Caesar had consented to do so, he said : " No one

te mecum in gratiam redisse, nisi aliquid mihi dona-
veris," petitque non fastidiendam etiam a propitio
summam et impetravit. Caesar ait: " Mea causa
4 dabo operam, ne umquam tibi irascar!" Honeste
fecit Caesar, quod ignovit, quod liberalitatem clementiae adiecit. Quicumque hoc audierit exemplum,
necesse est Caesarem laudet, sed cum servum ante
laudaverit. Non expectas, ut tibi narrem manu missum, qui hoc fecerat. Nec tamen gratis: pecuniam
pro libertate eius Caesar numeraverat.

1   28. Post tot exempla num dubium est, quin
beneficium aliquando a servo dominus accipiat?
Quare potius persona rem minuat, quam personam res
ipsa cohonestet? Eadem omnibus principia eadem-
que origo; nemo altero nobilior, nisi cui rectius in-
2 genium et artibus bonis aptius. Qui imagines in atrio
exponunt et nomina familiae suae longo ordine ac
multis stemmatum inligata flexuris in parte prima
aedium collocant, non noti magis quam nobiles sunt?
Unus omnium parens mundus est, sive per splendidos
sive per sordidos gradus ad hunc prima cuiusque origo
perducitur. Non est, quod te isti decipiant, qui, cum
maiores suos recensent, ubicumque nomen inlustre
3 defecit, illo deum infulciunt. Neminem despexeris,
etiam si circa illum obsoleta sunt nomina et parum
indulgente adiuta fortuna. Sive libertini ante vos

will believe that you have restored me to favour unless you bestow upon me a gift," and he asked for a sum that no favourite need have scorned, and actually obtained it. " For my own sake," said Caesar, " I shall take pains never to be angry with you ! " Caesar acted nobly in pardoning him and in adding to his forgiveness liberality. Every one who hears of this incident must necessarily praise Caesar, but the first to be praised will be the slave. You need not wait for me to tell you that the slave who had done this was set free. Yet it was not a gratuitous act— Caesar had paid the price of his liberty !

After so many instances, can there be any doubt that a master may sometimes receive a benefit from a slave ? Why should a man's condition lessen the value of a service, and the very value of the service not exalt the man's condition ? We all spring from the same source, have the same origin ; no man is more noble than another except in so far as the nature of one man is more upright and more capable of good actions. Those who display ancestral busts in their halls, and place in the entrance of their houses the names of their family, arranged in a long row and entwined in the multiple ramifications of a genealogical tree—are these not notable rather than noble ? Heaven is the one parent of us all, whether from his earliest origin each one arrives at his present degree by an illustrious or obscure line of ancestors. You must not be duped by those who, in making a review of their ancestors, wherever they find an illustrious name lacking, foist in the name of a god. Do not despise any man, even if he belongs with those whose names are forgotten, and have had too little favour from Fortune. Whether your line before

177

habentur sive servi sive exterarum gentium homines,
erigite audacter animos et, quidquid in medio sordidi
iacet, transilite ; expectat vos in summo magna nobili-
4 tas. Quid superbia in tantam vanitatem attollimur,
ut beneficia a servis indignemur accipere et sortem
eorum spectemus obliti meritorum ? Servum tu
quemquam vocas, libidinis et gulae servus et adulterae,
5 immo adulterarum commune mancipium ? Servum
vocas quemquam tu ? Quo tandem ab istis gerulis
raperis cubile istud tuum circumferentibus ? Quo te
penulati in militum quidem non vulgarem cultum
subornati, quo, inquam, te isti efferunt ? Ad ostium
alicuius ostiarii, ad hortos alicuius, ne ordinarium
quidem habentis officium ; et deinde negas tibi a
servo tuo beneficium dari posse, cui osculum alieni
6 servi beneficium est ? Quae est tanta animi discordia ?
Eodem tempore servos despicis et colis, imperiosus
intra limen atque impotens, humilis foris et tam con-
temptus quam contemnens. Neque enim ulli magis
abiciunt animos, quam qui improbe tollunt, nullique
ad calcandos alios paratiores, quam qui contumelias
facere accipiendo didicerunt.

1 29. Dicenda haec fuerunt ad contundendam
insolentiam hominum ex fortuna pendentium vindi-
candumque ius beneficii dandi servis, ut filiis quoque
vindicaretur. Quaeritur enim, an aliquando, liberi

---

a The idea recurs in Seneca's *Epistles* (xliv. 1) : " omnes,
si ad originem primam revocantur, *a dis* sunt."

you holds freedmen or slaves or persons of foreign extraction, boldly lift up your head, and leap over the obscure names in your pedigree ; great nobility awaits you at its source.[a] Why are we raised by our pride to such a pitch of vanity that we scorn to receive benefits from slaves, and, forgetting their services, look only upon their lot ? You who are a slave of lust, of gluttony, of a harlot—nay, who are the common property of harlots—do you call any other man a slave ? *You* call any other man a slave ? Whither, pray, are you being rushed by those bearers who carry around your cushioned litter ? Whither are those fellows in cloaks, tricked out in remarkable livery to look like soldiers—whither, I say, are these conveying you ? To some door-keeper's door, to the gardens of some slave whose duties are not even fixed ; and then you deny that your own slave is capable of giving you a benefit, when in your eyes it is a benefit to have from another man's slave a kiss ? What great inconsistency is this ? At the same time you both despise slaves and court them—inside your threshold you are imperious and violent, outside abject, and scorned as greatly as ever you scorn. For none are more prone to abase themselves than those who are presumptuously puffed up, and none are more ready to trample upon others than those who from receiving insults have learned how to give them.

These things needed to be said in order to crush the arrogance of men who are themselves dependent upon Fortune, and to claim for slaves the right of bestowing benefits to the end that it may be claimed also for our sons. For the question is raised whether children can sometimes bestow on their

maiora beneficia dare parentibus suis possint, quam
acceperint.

2 Illud conceditur multos filios maiores potentiores-
que extitisse quam parentes suos ; aeque et illud
meliores fuisse. Quod si constat, potest fieri, ut
meliora tribuerint, cum et fortuna illis maior esset et
3 melior voluntas. " Quidquid," inquit, " est, quod det
patri filius, utique minus est, quia hanc ipsam dandi
facultatem patri debet. Ita numquam beneficio vincitur, cuius beneficium est ipsum, quod vincitur."

Primum quaedam initium ab aliis trahunt et tamen
initiis suis maiora sunt ; nec ideo aliquid non est maius
eo, quo coepit, quia non potuisset in tantum procedere,
4 nisi coepisset. Nulla non res principia sua magno
gradu transit. Semina omnium rerum causae sunt et
tamen minimae partes sunt eorum, quae gignunt.
Adspice Rhenum, adspice Euphraten, omnes denique
inclutos amnes. Quid sunt, si illos illic, unde effluunt,
aestimes ? Quidquid est, quo timentur, quo nominan-
5 tur, in processu paraverunt. Adspice trabes, sive
proceritatem aestimes, altissimas, sive crassitudinem
spatiumque ramorum, latissime fusas. Quantulum est
his comparatum illud, quod radix tenui fibra complectitur ! Tolle radicem : nemora non surgent, nec tanti

parents greater benefits than they have received from them.

It is granted me that there have been many examples of sons who were greater and more powerful than their parents, and just as freely, too, that they were better men. If this is true, it is quite possible that they bestowed on them better gifts, since they were endowed both with greater good fortune and with better intentions. "However that may be," you reply, " what a son gives to a father is, in any case, less, because he owes to his father this very power of giving. So a father is never surpassed in the matter of a benefit, for the very benefit in which he is surpassed is really his own."

But, in the first place, there are some things that derive their origin from others, and yet are greater than their origins ; nor is it true that a thing cannot be greater than that from which it begins on the ground that it could not have advanced to its great size unless it had had a beginning. All things exceed by a great degree their origins. Seeds are the causes of all growing things, and yet are the tiniest parts of what they produce. Look at the Rhine, look at the Euphrates, in fact, at all the famous rivers. What are they if you judge of them from what they are at their source ? Whatever makes them feared, whatever makes them renowned, has been acquired in their progress. Look at the trunks of trees—the tallest if you are considering their height, the broadest if you are considering their thickness and the reach of their branches ; compared with all this, how small a compass the slender thread of the root embraces ! Yet take away the root, and there will be no springing up of forests, and the mighty moun-

montes vestientur. Innituntur fundamentis suis
templa excelsa urbis ; tamen, quae in firmamentum
6 totius operis iacta sunt, latent. Idem in ceteris evenit ;
principia sua semper sequens magnitudo obruet. Non
potuissem quicquam consequi, nisi parentum beneficium antecessisset ; sed non ideo, quidquid consecutus sum, minus est eo, sine quo consecutus non
7 essem. Nisi me nutrix aluisset infantem, nihil eorum,
quae consilio ac manu gero, facere potuissem nec in
hanc emergere nominis claritatem, quam civili ac
militari industria merui ; numquid tamen ideo maximis operibus praeferes nutricis officium ? Atqui quid
interest, cum aeque sine patris beneficio quam sine
nutricis non potuerim ad ulteriora procedere ? Quod
8 si initio meo, quidquid iam possum, debeo, cogita non
esse initium mei patrem, ne avum quidem ; semper
enim erit ulterius aliquid, ex quo originis proximae
origo descendat. Atqui nemo dicet me plus debere
ignotis et ultra memoriam positis maioribus quam
patri ; plus autem debeo, si hoc ipsum, quod genuit
me pater meus, maioribus debet.

1   30. " Quidquid praestiti patri, etiam si magnum

tains will lack their vesture. The lofty temples of the city rise upon their foundations; yet all that was thrown down to support their whole structure lies out of sight. The same is true in the case of all other things; always their subsequent greatness will conceal their first beginnings. It would not have been possible for me to attain anything unless there had been the preceding benefit from my parents; but it does not follow that whatever I have attained is inferior to that without which I could not have attained it. Unless my nurse had suckled me when I was an infant, I should not have been able to do any of the things that I now perform by brain and hand, nor should I have risen to the present distinction and fame that my civil and military labours have earned for me; yet, for all that, surely you will not set more value on the service of my nurse than on my very weighty achievements? But what difference is there, since it is just as true that I should not have been able to advance to my later accomplishments without the benefit from my nurse as without that from my father? But if I am indebted for all that I can now do to the source of my being, reflect that the source of my being is not my father, nor my grandfather, either; for there will always be something farther removed, from which the source of a succeeding source is derived. Yet no one will say that I am more indebted to ancestors that are unknown and have passed from memory than to my father; I *am*, however, more indebted, if the very fact that my father has begotten me is a debt that he owes to his ancestors.

" Whatever I have bestowed on my father," you say, " even if it is great, falls short of the value of my

est, infra aestimationem paterni muneris est, quia non esset, si non genuisset." Isto modo etiam, si quis patrem meum aegrum ac moriturum sanaverit, nihil praestare ei potero, quod non beneficio eius minus sit; non enim genuisset me pater, nisi sanatus esset. Sed vide, ne illud verius sit aestimari, an id, quod potui, et id, quod feci, meum sit, mearum virium, meae 2 voluntatis. Illud, quod natus sum, per se intuere, quale sit : animadvertis exiguum et incertum et boni malique communem materiam, sine dubio primum ad omnia gradum, sed non ideo maiorem omnibus, quia primus est.

3 Servavi patrem meum et ad summam provexi digni-tatem et principem urbis suae feci nec tantum rebus a me gestis nobilitavi, sed ipsi quoque gerendarum in-gentem ac facilem nec tutam minus quam gloriosam dedi materiam ; honores, opes, quidquid humanos ad se animos rapit, congessi, et cum supra omnes starem, 4 infra illum steti. Dic nunc : " Hoc ipsum, quod ista potuisti, patris munus est " ; respondebo tibi : " Est prorsus, si ad ista facienda nasci satis est ; sed si ad bene vivendum minima portio est vivere et id tribuisti, quod cum feris mihi et animalibus quibusdam minimis, quibusdam etiam foedissimis commune est, noli tibi

father's gift to me, for, if he had not begotten me, there would be no gift." Then, too, by this manner of reasoning, if anyone healed my father when he was sick and about to die, I shall not be able to bestow on him any benefit that will not be less than his to me ; for my father would not have begotten me if he had not been healed. But take thought whether it would not be nearer the truth to count both what I have been able to do, and what I have done, as something of my own—the product of my own powers and of my own will. Consider what the fact of my birth is in itself—a small matter of uncertain character, with a like potentiality of good and evil, without doubt the first step to everything else, but not greater than everything else simply because it comes first.

I have saved the life of my father, and raised him to the highest position ; I have made him the chief citizen of his city, and have not only made him famous by my own achievements, but also have provided him with a vast and easy opportunity, not less safe than it is glorious, of achieving something himself; I have loaded him with honours, with wealth, with everything that attracts the minds of men, and, although I had place above all others, I have taken a place below him. Let my father now say : " The very fact that you have been able to do these things is a gift from your father," and I shall reply : " Yes, undoubtedly, if, in order to do all these things, it is only necessary to be born ; but, if the factor that contributes least to successful living is being alive, and, if you have bestowed on me merely that which I have in common with wild beasts and some of the tiniest, even some of the foulest, creatures, then do not take

adserere, quod non ex tuis beneficiis, etiam si non sine tuis, oritur."

1 31. Puta me vitam pro vita reddidisse. Sic quoque munus tuum vici, cum ego dederim sentienti, cum sentiens me dare, cum vitam tibi non voluptatis meae causa aut certe per voluptatem dederim, cum tanto maius sit retinere spiritum quam accipere, 2 quanto levius mori ante mortis metum. Ego vitam dedi statim illa usuro, tu nescituro, an viveret ; ego vitam dedi mortem timenti, tu vitam dedisti, ut mori possem ; ego tibi vitam dedi consummatam, perfectam, tu me expertem rationis genuisti, onus 3 alienum. Vis scire, quam non sit magnum beneficium vitam sic dare ? Exposuisses ; nempe iniuria erat genuisse ! Quo quid colligo ? Minimum esse beneficium patris matrisque concubitum, nisi accesserunt alia, quae prosequerentur hoc initium muneris et aliis 4 officiis ratum facerent. Non est bonum vivere, sed bene vivere. At bene vivo. Sed potui et male ; ita hoc tantum est tuum, quod vivo. Si vitam imputas mihi per se, nudam, egentem consilii, et id ut magnum bonum iactas, cogita te mihi imputare muscarum ac 5 vermium bonum. Deinde, ut nihil aliud dicam, quam

credit to yourself for something that does not arise out of your benefits, even if it does not arise without them."

Suppose that I have given back life for life. Even in this case I have surpassed your gift, since I gave to one who was conscious of the gift, and I was conscious that I was giving it; since, when I gave you your life, it was not to indulge my own pleasure, or, at any rate, by means of my own pleasure; since, as it is a lighter thing to die before one learns to fear death, so it is a greater thing to retain the breath of life than to receive it. I gave life to one who would straightway enjoy it, you gave it to one who would not know whether he was alive; I gave life to one who was afraid of death, you gave life to me, and made me subject to death; I gave to you life that was complete and perfect, when you begot me, I was a creature without reason and a burden to others. Do you wish to know how small a benefit it is to give life in this way? You should have exposed me to death as a child; of course by begetting me you did me a wrong! What, then, is my conclusion? That the fact of their coition constitutes a very small benefit on the part of a father and a mother unless they add others which will follow up this initial gift, and confirm it by still other services. It is not a blessing to live, but to live well. But you say I do live well. Yes, but I might also have lived ill; so the only thing that I have from you is that I am alive. If you claim credit for giving me mere life, life stripped bare and bereft of purpose, and boast of it as a great blessing, reflect that you are claiming credit for giving me a blessing that flies and worms possess. Finally, though I should mention no more than that I have

187

bonis artibus me studuisse et cursum ad rectum iter
vitae direxisse, in ipso beneficio tuo maius, quam quod
dederas, recepisti ; tu enim me mihi rudem, imperitum
dedisti, ego tibi filium, qualem genuisse gauderes.

1   32. Aluit me pater. Si idem praesto, plus
reddo, quia non tantum ali se, sed a filio ali gaudet et
maiorem ex animo meo quam ex ipsa re percipit
voluptatem, illius alimenta ad corpus tantum meum
2 pervenerunt. Quid ? si quis in tantum processit, ut
aut eloquentia per gentes notesceret aut iustitia aut
bellicis rebus et patri quoque ingentem circumfunderet
famam tenebrasque natalium suorum clara luce discu-
teret, non inaestimabile in parentes suos beneficium
3 contulit ? An quisquam Aristonem et Gryllum nisi
propter Xenophontem ac Platonem filios nosset ?
Sophroniscum Socrates expirare non patitur. Ceteros
enumerare longum est, qui durant ob nullam aliam
causam, quam quod illos liberorum eximia virtus
4 tradidit posteris. Utrum maius beneficium dedit M.
Agrippae pater ne post Agrippam quidem notus, an
patri dedit Agrippa navali corona insignis, unicum
adeptus inter dona militaria decus, qui tot in urbe
maxima opera excitavit, quae et priorem magnifi-

---

a Of obscure origin, he attained fame as a commander and
statesman in the reign of Augustus, and married Julia, the
emperor's daughter.

applied myself to liberal studies, and have directed the course of my life along the path of rectitude, in the case of the very benefit I had from you, you have received in return a greater one than you gave ; for you gave to me a self that was ignorant and inexperienced, and I have given to you a son such as you might be happy to have begotten.

True, my father has supported me. But, if I bestow the same on him, I return more than I got, for he has joy, not only from being supported, but from being supported by a son, and he derives greater pleasure from the spirit of my act than from the act itself, but the food he gave me reached only the needs of the body. Tell me, if a man has attained so much eminence as to be renowned throughout the world by reason either of his eloquence or of his justice or his military prowess, if he has been able to encompass his father also in the greatness of fame, and by the glory of his name to dispel the obscurity of his birth, has he not conferred upon his parents a benefit that is beyond all estimate ? Or would anyone ever have heard of Aristo and Gryllus except for the fact that Xenophon and Plato were their sons ? It is Socrates that does not allow the name of Sophroniscus to die. It would take too long to recount all the others whose names endure only because they have been handed down to posterity owing to the exceptional worth of their children. Which was the greater benefit—what Marcus Agrippa [a] received from his father, who was unknown even after having had a son like Agrippa, or what the father received from Agrippa, who, by the glory of a naval crown, gained a distinction that was unique among the honours of war, who reared in the city so many mighty works that not only surpassed

189

5 centiam vincerent et nulla postea vincerentur?
Utrum Octavius maius beneficium dedit filio an patri
divus Augustus, quamvis illum umbra adoptivi patris
abscondit? Quantam cepisset voluptatem, si illum
post debellata arma civilia vidisset securae paci prae-
sidentem, non adgnoscens bonum suum nec satis
credens, quotiens ad se respexisset, potuisse illum
virum in domo sua nasci! Quid nunc ceteros pro-
sequar, quos iam consumpsisset oblivio, nisi illos
filiorum gloria e tenebris eruisset et adhuc in luce
retineret?

6 Deinde, cum quaeramus, non quis filius patri maiora
beneficia reddiderit, quam a patre acceperat, sed an
aliquis possit maiora reddere, etiam si, quae rettuli,
exempla nondum satis faciunt nec beneficia parentium
suorum superiaciunt, capit tamen hoc natura, quod
nondum ulla aetas tulit. Si singula paternorum
meritorum magnitudinem exsuperare non possunt,
plura in unum congesta superabunt.

1 33. Servavit in proelio patrem Scipio et prae-
textatus in hostes ecum concitavit. Parum est, quod,
ut perveniret ad patrem, tot pericula maximos duces
cum maxime prementia contempsit, tot oppositas difficultates, quod ad primam pugnam exiturus tiro per

---

    a *i.e.*, Julius Caesar.
    b Upon the bank of the Ticinus in 218 B.C., where Hannibal
gained his first victory over the Romans.

all former grandeur, but later could be surpassed by none ? Which was the greater benefit—what Octavius bestowed on his son, or what the deified Augustus bestowed on his father, obscured as he was by the shadow of an adoptive father ? [a] What joy would Octavius have experienced if he had seen his son, after he had brought the Civil War to an end, watching over well - established peace : he would not have recognized the good that he had himself bestowed, and would scarcely have believed, whenever he turned his gaze backward to himself, that so great a hero could have been born in his house. Why continue now to mention all the others who would long have been buried in oblivion, had not the glory of their sons rescued them from darkness, and kept them in the light even to this day ?

Moreover, since the question is, not what son bestowed greater benefits on his father than he received from his father, but whether it is possible for any son to bestow greater benefits, even if the instances that I have cited are not convincing, and the benefits of parents are not overtopped by those of their sons, nevertheless that which no age has as yet produced still lies within the bounds of nature. If single acts may not be able to surpass the magnitude of a father's services, yet several of them combined together will exceed it.

Scipio saved the life of his father in battle,[b] and, lad as he was, spurred his horse into the midst of the enemy. Is it, then, too small a thing, if, in order to reach his father, he despised all the dangers, by which at that very time the greatest leaders were being hard pressed, despised all the difficulties that blocked his path, if, in order to make his way into the

veteranorum corpora cucurrit, quod annos suos tran-
2 siluit ? Adice, ut idem patrem reum defendat et con-
spirationi inimicorum potentium eripiat, ut alterum
illi consulatum ac tertium aliosque honores etiam consularibus concupiscendos congerat, ut pauperi raptas
belli iure opes tradat et, quod est militaribus viris
speciosissimum, divitem illum spoliis etiam hostilibus
3 faciat. Si adhuc parum est, adice, ut provincias et
extraordinaria imperia continuet, adice, ut dirutis
maximis urbibus Romani imperii sine aemulo ad ortus
occasusque venturi defensor et conditor maiorem nobi-
litatem nobili viro adiciat, dici Scipionis patrem !
Dubium est, quin generandi vulgare beneficium vicerit
eximia pietas et virtus ipsi urbi nescio utrum maius
4 praesidium adferens an decus ? Deinde, si hoc parum
est, finge aliquem tormenta patris discussisse, finge in
se transtulisse. Licet tibi, in quantum velis, extendere
beneficia filii, cum paternum munus et simplex sit et
facile et danti voluptarium, quod necesse est ille
multis dederit, etiam quibus dedisse se nescit, in quo
consortem habet, in quo spectavit legem, patriam,
praemia patrum, domus ac familiae perpetuitatem,
5 omnia potius quam eum, cui dabat. Quid ? si quis

front of the fight, he, tiro that he was, galloped through the ranks of veterans, if in one bound he outstripped his years ? Then add to this, that he also defended his father in court, and rescued him from a conspiracy of powerful enemies, that he heaped upon him a second and a third consulship and other honours that even consulars might covet and that, when his father was poor, he handed over to him the wealth that he had seized by right of war, and made him rich even with the spoils taken from the enemy, which to a military hero is his greatest glory. If this is still too little, add that he prolonged his father's extraordinary powers in his government of the provinces, add that, after having destroyed the mightiest cities, he, the defender and founder of the Roman Empire that was destined to reach without a rival from the rising to the setting sun, added to a hero already renowned the greater renown of being called the father of Scipio ! Is there any doubt that the commonplace benefit of his birth was surpassed by his rare filial devotion and his valour, which brought to the city itself, I might almost say, greater glory than protection ? Then, if this is still too little, imagine some son that rescued his father from tortures, imagine that he transferred them to himself. You may extend the benefits of a son to any length you please, whereas the gift of a father is of one sort only, easily given, and fraught with pleasure to the giver—one that he must necessarily have given to many others, even to some to whom he does not know that he gave it, one in which he has a partner, in which he has had regard for the law, his country, the rewards that accrue to fathers, the continuance of his house and family, for everything, in fact, but the recipient of his gift. Tell me,

sapientiam consecutus hanc patri tradiderit, etiamnunc disputabimus, an maius aliquid iam dederit,
quam acceperat, cum vitam beatam patri reddiderit,
acceperit tantum vitam ?

34. "Sed patris," inquit, "beneficium est, quidquid facis, quidquid praestare illi potes." Et praeceptoris mei, quod institutis liberalibus profeci;
ipsos tamen, qui tradiderunt illa, transcendimus,
utique eos, qui prima elementa docuerunt, et quamvis
sine illis nemo quicquam adsequi posset, non tamen,
quantumcumque quis adsecutus est, infra illos est.
Multum inter prima ac maxima interest, nec ideo
prima maximorum instar sunt, quia sine primis maxima
esse non possunt.

1 **35.** Iam tempus est quaedam ex nostra, ut ita
dicam, moneta proferre. Qui id beneficium dedit, quo
est aliquid melius, potest vinci. Pater dedit filio
vitam, est autem aliquid vita melius; ita pater vinci
potest, quia dedit beneficium, quo est aliquid melius.
2 Etiamnunc, qui dedit alicui vitam, si et semel et
iterum liberatus est mortis periculo, maius accepit
beneficium quam dedit. Pater autem vitam dedit
potest ergo, si saepius periculo mortis liberatus a filio

ᵃ The phrase is technical, and means the ideal life that is
attained only through philosophy. See Seneca's essay *De
Vita Beata* in Volume II.

ᵇ *i.e.*, the syllogisms, which were characteristic of the Stoic
school.

if a son has attained the wisdom of philosophy and has transmitted it to his father, shall we still be able to argue as to whether he gave something greater than he received, though the gift he returned to his father was the Happy Life,[a] and that which he received was merely life ?

" But," you say, " whatever you do, whatever you are able to bestow on your father, is a part of his benefit to you." Yes, and the progress I have made in liberal studies is a benefit from my teacher ; nevertheless we leave behind the very teachers who have transmitted their knowledge, particularly those who have taught us the alphabet, and, although no one could have accomplished anything without them, it is, nevertheless, not true that, no matter how much anyone has accomplished, he is still their inferior. There is a great deal of difference between what is first in time and what is first in importance, and it does not follow that what is first in time is the equivalent of what is first in importance on the ground that without the first in time there could be no first in importance.

It is now time to produce something coined, so to speak, in the Stoic mint.[b] He who has given a benefit that falls short of being the best faces the possibility of being outdone. A father has given life to his son, but there is something better than life ; so the father can be outdone because he has given a benefit that falls short of being the best. Again, if a man who has given life to another has been freed, time and again, from the peril of death, he has received a greater benefit than he gave. Now, a father has given life ; if, therefore, he should be repeatedly freed from the peril of death by his son, it is possible

3 fuerit, maius beneficium accipere quam dedit. Qui
beneficium accipit, maius accipit, quo magis eo indiget.
Magis autem indiget vita, qui vivit, quam qui natus
non est, ut qui ne indigere quidem omnino possit ;
maius ergo beneficium accipit pater, si vitam a filio
4 accipit, quam filius a patre, quod natus est. " Patris
beneficia vinci a filii beneficiis non possunt. Quare ?
Quia vitam accepit a patre, quam nisi accepisset, nulla
dare beneficia potuisset." Hoc commune est patri
cum omnibus, qui vitam alicui dederunt ; non potuis-
sent enim referre gratiam, nisi vitam accepissent.
Ergo nec medico gratia in maius referri potest (solet
enim et medicus vitam dare), nec nautae, si naufragum
sustulit. Atqui et horum et aliorum, qui aliquo modo
nobis vitam dederunt, beneficia vinci possunt ; ergo
5 et patrum possunt. Si quis mihi beneficium dedit,
quod multorum beneficiis adiuvandum esset, ego
autem illi beneficium dedi id, quod nullius egeret
adiutorio, maius dedi quam accepi. Pater filio vitam
dedit perituram, nisi multa accessissent, quae illam
tuerentur ; filius patri si dedit vitam, dedit eam, quae
nullius desideraret auxilium in hoc, ut permaneret ;
ergo maius beneficium accepit a filio pater, qui vitam
accepit, quam ipse illi dedit.

1   36. Haec non destruunt parentium venerationem

for him to receive a greater benefit than he gave. The more need a man has of a benefit, the greater is the benefit he receives. Now, one who is alive has more need of life than one who has not been born, since such a one can feel no need at all ; consequently, if a father has received life from his son, he has received a greater benefit from the son than the son received from his father by being born. " Benefits from a father," you say, " cannot be surpassed by benefits from a son. And why ? Because the son received life from his father, and, unless he had received it, he could not have given any benefits at all." But a father has this in common with all men who have at any time given life to others ; for these would not have been able to return gratitude unless they had received the gift of their lives. Consequently, you cannot return too much gratitude to a physician (for physicians also habitually give life), nor to a sailor if he has rescued you from shipwreck. Yet the benefits of these and of others, who have in some fashion given us life, are capable of being surpassed ; therefore those of a father also are capable of it. If anyone has given to me the sort of benefit that needs to be supplemented by benefits from many others, while I have given to him the benefit that needs a supplement from no man, then I have given a greater one than I have received. Now a father gave to his son a life which, unless it had had many accessories that preserved it, would have perished ; whereas a son, if he has given life to his father, gave that which needed the help of no man to make it endure ; therefore a father who received his life from a son received a greater benefit than he himself gave.

These considerations do not destroy respect for

nec deteriores illis liberos faciunt, immo etiam
meliores ; natura enim gloriosa virtus est et anteire
priores cupit. Alacrior erit pietas, si ad reddenda
beneficia cum vincendi spe venerit. Ipsis patribus id
volentibus laetisque contigerit, quoniam pleraque
2 sunt, in quibus nostro bono vincimur. Unde certamen
tam optabile ? Unde tantam felicitatem parentibus,
ut fateantur ipsos liberorum beneficiis impares ? Nisi
hoc ita iudicamus, excusationem damus liberis et illos
segniores ad referendam gratiam facimus, quibus
stimulos adicere debemus et dicere :

"Hoc agite, optimi iuvenes ! Proposita est inter
parentes ac liberos honesta contentio, dederint maiora
3 an receperint. Non ideo vicerunt, quia occupaverunt.
Sumite modo animum, qualem decet, et deficere
nolite : vincetis optantes. Nec desunt tam pulchro
certamini duces, qui ad similia vos cohortentur ac per
vestigia sua ire ad victoriam saepe iam partam ex
parentibus iubeant.

1 37. "Vicit Aeneas patrem, ipse eius in[1] infantia leve tutumque gestamen, gravem senio per
media hostium agmina et per cadentis circa se urbis
ruinas ferens, cum complexus sacra ac penates deos

---

[1] in added by Pincianus.

parents, nor render children worse than their parents, but even better ; for by its very nature Virtue loves to shine, and is eager to push ahead of any in front. Filial devotion will be all the more ardent if it approaches the repayment of benefits with the hope of surpassing them. And the fathers themselves will be willing and glad to have it happen since, in the case of a great many things, it is to our advantage to be surpassed. How else comes a rivalry so desirable ? How else comes to parents a happiness so great that, in the matter of benefits, they acknowledge themselves to be no match for their children ? Unless we adopt this view of the matter, we supply children with an excuse, and make them less ready to return gratitude, whereas we ought to spur them on and say to them :

" To your task, young heroes ! A glorious contest is set before you—the contest between parents and children to decide whether they have given, or received, the greater benefits. Your fathers have not won the victory for the mere reason that they were first on the field. Only show the spirit that befits you, and do not lose courage—they desire to have you win. Nor, in this glorious struggle, will there be any lack of leaders to encourage you to do as they did, and bid you follow their footsteps to the victory that often ere now has been won from parents.

" Aeneas won the victory from his father ; for, though he himself, in his infancy, had been but a light and safe burden to his father's arms, he bore his father, heavy with years, through the midst of the lines of the enemy, through the destruction of the city that was crashing around him, while the pious old man, clasping in his arms his sacred relics and household gods,

religiosus senex non simplici vadentem sarcina
premeret ; tulit illum per ignes et (quid non pietas
potest ?) pertulit colendumque inter conditores Romani imperii posuit.

2 " Vicere Siculi iuvenes : cum Aetna maiore vi
peragitata in urbes, in agros, in magnam insulae partem effudisset incendium, vexerunt parentes suos ;
discessisse creditum est ignes et utrimque flamma
recedente limitem adapertum, per quem transcur-
rerent iuvenes dignissimi, qui magna tuto auderent.

3 " Vicit Antigonus, qui, cum ingenti proelio supe-
rasset hostem, praemium belli ad patrem transtulit et
imperium illi Cypri tradidit. Hoc est regnum nolle
regnare, cum possis.

4 " Vicit patrem imperiosum quidem Manlius, qui,
cum ante ad tempus relegatus esset a patre ob adulescentiam brutam et hebetem, ad tribunum plebis, qui
patri suo diem dixerat, venit ; petito tempore, quod
ille dederat sperans fore proditorem parentis invisi,
(et bene meruisse se de iuvene credebat, cuius exilium
pro gravissimo crimine inter alia Manlio obiciebat),
nanctus adulescens secretum stringit occultatum sinu
ferrum et : ' Nisi iuras,' inquit, ' te diem patri remis-
surum, hoc te gladio transfodiam. In tua potestate

---

^a In Virgil's story he shared Aeneas's wanderings as far
as Drepanum in Sicily.
^b An allusion to the story of Amphinomus and Anapius
of Catana.

burdened his son's progress with more than his simple weight; he bore him through flames, and (what cannot filial love accomplish!) bore him out of danger,[a] and placed him, for our worship, among the founders of the Roman Empire.

" Those young Sicilians[b] won the victory; for, when Aetna, aroused to unusual fury, poured forth its fire upon cities, upon fields, upon a great part of the island, they conveyed their parents to safety. The fires parted, so it was believed, and, as the flames retired on either side, a path was opened up for the passage of the youths, who greatly deserved to perform their heroic tasks in safety.

" Antigonus won the victory; for, having vanquished the enemy in a mighty battle, he transferred to his father the prize of the war, and handed over to him the sovereignty of Cyprus. This is true kingship, to refuse to be king when you might have been.

" Manlius won the victory from his father, tyrant though he was; for, although his father had previously banished him for a time because of his dullness and stupidity as a youth, he went to the tribune of the people, who had appointed a day for his father's trial; having asked for an interview, which the tribune granted, expecting to find him a traitor to his detested father—he believed, too, that he had earned the gratitude of the young man, for, among other charges that he was bringing against Manlius, the gravest was his son's exile—the youth, when he had obtained his private audience, drew forth a sword, that he had had concealed beneath his robe, and cried : ' Unless you swear that you will remit the charges against my father, I shall run you through

est, utro modo pater meus accusatorem non habeat.'
Iuravit tribunus nec fefellit et causam actionis omissae
contioni reddidit.   Nulli alii licuit impune tribunum
in ordinem redigere.

1   38. " Alia ex aliis exempla sunt eorum, qui
parentes suos periculis eripuerint, qui ex infimo ad
summum protulerint et e plebe acervoque ignobili
2 numquam tacendos saeculis dederint.   Nulla vi verborum, nulla ingenii facultate exprimi potest, quantum opus sit, quam laudabile quamque numquam
memoria hominum exiturum, posse hoc dicere :
' Parentibus meis parui, cessi imperio eorum, sive
aecum sive inicum ac durum fuit, obsequentem sub-
missumque me praebui ; ad hoc unum contumax fui,
3 ne beneficiis vincerer.'   Certate, obsecro vos, et fessi
quoque restituite aciem.   Felices, qui vincent, felices,
qui vincentur !   Quid eo adulescente praeclarius, qui
sibi ipsi dicere poterit (neque enim est fas alteri
dicere) : ' Patrem meum beneficiis vici ' ?   Quid eo
fortunatius sene, qui omnibus ubique praedicabit a
filio se suo beneficiis victum ?   Quid autem est felicius
quam ibi cedere ? "

with this sword. It lies with you to decide which way my father shall have of escaping his accuser.' The tribune took the oath and did not break it, and he reported to the assembly his reason for abandoning the action. No other man was ever permitted to put a tribune in his place without being punished.

" There are countless instances of others who have snatched their parents from dangers, who have advanced them from the lowest to the highest station, and, taking them from the nameless mass of commoners, have given them a name that will sound throughout the ages. No power of words, no wealth of genius can express how great, how laudable, how sure of living in the memory of men will be the achievement of being able to say : ' I obeyed my parents, I gave way to their authority, whether it was just or unjust and harsh, I showed myself humble and submissive ; in only one thing was I stubborn—the resolve not to be outdone by them in benefits.' Struggle on, I beg of you, and, even though wearied, renew the fight. Happy they who shall conquer, happy they who shall be conquered. What can be more glorious than the youth who can say to himself (for to say it to another would be an impiety) : ' I have surpassed my father in benefits ' ? What can be more fortunate than the old man who, to all ears and in all places, will declare that in benefits he has been surpassed by his son ? But what can be happier than to lose that victory ? "

BOOK IV

1 1. Ex omnibus, quae tractavimus, Aebuti Liberalis, potest videri nihil tam necessarium aut magis, ut ait Sallustius, cum cura dicendum, quam quod in manibus est : an beneficium dare et in vicem gratiam referre per se res expetendae sint.

2 Inveniuntur, qui honesta in mercedem colant quibusque non placeat virtus gratuita ; quae nihil habet in se magnificum, si quicquam venale. Quid enim est turpius, quam aliquem computare, quanti vir bonus sit, cum virtus nec lucro invitet nec absterreat damno adeoque neminem spe ac pollicitatione corrumpat, ut contra impendere in se iubeat et saepius in ultro tributis sit ? Calcatis ad illam utilitatibus eundum est ; quocumque vocavit, quocumque misit, sine respectu rei familiaris, interdum etiam sine ulla sanguinis sui parsimonia vadendum nec umquam
3 imperium eius detractandum. "Quid consequar," inquit, "si hoc fortiter, si hoc grate fecero ?" Quod feceris ; nihil tibi extra promittitur. Si quid commodi forte obvenerit, inter accessiones numerabis.

204

BOOK IV

Of all the questions that we have discussed, Aebutius
Liberalis, none can seem so essential, or to need, as
Sallust puts it, such careful treatment, as the one
that is now before us : whether to bestow a benefit
and to return gratitude for it are in themselves
desirable ends.

Some are to be found who cultivate honourable
practices for the recompense, and care nothing for
virtue that is unrewarded ; whereas it has nothing
glorious in it if it shows any element of profit. For
what is more shameful than for anyone to calculate
the value to a man of being good, since Virtue neither
invites by the prospect of gain, nor deters by the
prospect of loss, and, so far is she from bribing any
man with hopes and promises, that, on the contrary,
she bids him spend upon her, and is more often
found in voluntary contributions. We must go to
her, trampling under foot all self-interest ; whithersoever she calls, whithersoever she sends us we must
go, without any regard for our fortunes, sometimes
even without sparing our own blood, and we must
never refuse her demands. " And what shall I gain,"
you ask, " if I do this bravely, if I do it gladly ? "
Only the gain of having done it—she promises you
nothing besides. If you should chance to encounter
some profit, count it as something additional. The

Rerum honestarum pretium in ipsis est. Si honestum
per se expetendum est, beneficium autem honestum
est, non potest alia eius condicio esse, cum eadem
natura sit. Per se autem expetendum esse honestum
saepe et abunde probatum est.

1 2. In hac parte nobis pugna est cum Epicureis, de-
licata et umbratica turba in convivio suo philosophan-
tium, apud quos virtus voluptatum ministra est, illis
paret, illis deservit, illas supra se videt. " Non est,"
2 inquis, " voluptas sine virtute." Sed quare ante
virtutem est ? De ordine putas disputationem esse ?
De re tota et de potestate eius ambigitur. Non est
virtus, si sequi potest ; primae partes eius sunt, ducere
debet, imperare, summo loco stare ; tu illam iubes
3 signum petere ! " Quid," inquit, " tua refert ? Et
ego sine virtute nego beatam vitam posse constare.
Ipsam voluptatem, quam sequor, cui me emancipavi,
remota illa improbo et damno. De hoc uno dis-
putatur, utrum virtus summi boni causa sit an ipsa
summum bonum." Ut hoc unum quaeratur, ordinis
tantum existimas mutationem ? Ista vero confusio
est et manifesta caecitas primis postrema praeferre.
4 Non indignor, quod post voluptatem ponitur virtus,
sed quod omnino cum voluptate, contemptrix eius et

ᵃ Literally, " shade-loving," *i.e.*, shrinking from the
hardships of active life. Epicurus's doctrine of ἀταραξία
fostered aloofness from practical affairs.

reward of virtuous acts lies in the acts themselves. If a virtuous act is in itself a desirable end, if, further, a benefit is a virtuous act, it follows that, since they bear the same nature, they cannot be subject to a different condition. But that the virtuous course is in itself a desirable end has been often and abundantly proved.

On this point we Stoics are in arms against the Epicureans, an effeminate, sheltered [a] set, who philosophize over their cups, and hold that Virtue is but the handmaid of Pleasures, that she obeys them, that she is their slave, and sees them enthroned above herself. " There can be no pleasure," you say, " without virtue." But why does it come before virtue ? Do you suppose that the question is one of mere precedence ? The whole principle and power of virtue are thrown into doubt. Virtue does not exist if it is possible for her to follow ; hers is the first place, she must lead, must command, must have the supreme position ; you bid her ask for the watchword ! " What difference," you say, " does it make ? Even I affirm that there can be no happy life without virtue. The very pleasure at which I aim, to which I am enslaved, I disapprove of and condemn if she is banished. The only point in question is whether virtue is the cause of the highest good, or is itself the highest good." Do you suppose that the answer to this question turns upon merely making a shift in the order ? It does indeed show confusion and obvious blindness to give preference to last things over first things. But what I protest against is, not that virtue is placed second to pleasure, but that virtue is associated with pleasure at all, for virtue despises pleasure, is its enemy, and recoils from it as far as it

hostis et longissime ab illa resiliens, labori ac dolori familiarior, virilibus incommodis, quam isti effeminato bono.

1   3. Inserenda haec, mi Liberalis, fuerunt, quia beneficium, de quo nunc agitur, dare virtutis est et turpissimum id causa ullius alterius rei dare, quam ut datum sit. Nam si recipiendi spe tribueremus, locupletissimo cuique, non dignissimo daremus ; nunc vero diviti importuno pauperem praeferimus. Non 2 est beneficium, quod ad fortunam spectat. Praeterea, si, ut prodessemus, sola nos invitaret utilitas, minime beneficia distribuere deberent, qui facillime possent, locupletes et potentes et reges aliena ope non indigentes ; di vero tot munera, quae sine intermissione diebus ac noctibus fundunt, non darent ; in omnia enim illis natura sua sufficit plenosque et tutos et inviolabiles praestat ; nulli ergo beneficium dabunt, si una dandi causa est se intueri ac suum commodum. 3 Istud non beneficium, sed fenus est circumspicere, non ubi optime ponas, sed ubi quaestuosissime habeas, unde facillime tollas. Quod cum longe a dis remotum sit, sequitur, ut inliberales sint ; nam si una beneficii dandi causa sit dantis utilitas, nulla autem ex nobis utilitas deo speranda est, nulla deo dandi beneficii causa est.

can, being more acquainted with labour and sorrow, which are manly ills, than with this womanish good of yours.

It has been needful, my Liberalis, to introduce these considerations here, because the bestowal of the kind of benefit that is now under discussion is a mark of virtue, and to bestow it for any reason other than the mere bestowing of it is a most shameful act. For, if we made contributions with the expectation of receiving a return, we should give, not to the most worthy, but to the richest, men; as it is, we prefer a poor man to an importunate rich man. That is not a benefit which has regard for the fortune of the recipient. Moreover, if it were only self-interest that moved us to help others, those who could most easily dispense benefits, such as the rich and powerful and kings, who need no help from others, would not be under the least obligation to bestow them; nor, indeed, would the gods bestow the countless gifts that, day and night, they unceasingly pour forth, for their own nature is sufficient to them for all their needs, and renders them fully provided and safe and inviolable; they will, therefore, give to no man a benefit if their only motive in bestowing it is a regard for themselves and their own advantage. To take thought, not where you can best place your benefit, but where you can derive the most gain, and from whom you can most readily collect, is to be, not a benefactor, but a money-lender. And, since the gods are far removed from such concern, it follows that they will not be liberal; for, if the only reason for giving a benefit is the advantage of the giver, and if God can hope for no advantage from us, then no motive is found for God's giving a benefit.

1   4. Scio, quid hoc loco respondeatur : " Itaque non
dat deus beneficia, sed securus et neclegens nostri,
aversus a mundo aliud agit aut, quae maxima Epicuro
felicitas videtur, nihil agit, nec magis illum beneficia
2 quam iniuriae tangunt." Hoc qui dicit, non exaudit
precantium voces et undique sublatis in caelum manibus vota facientium privata ac publica ; quod profecto
non fieret, nec in hunc furorem omnes profecto mor-
tales consensissent adloquendi surda numina et in-
efficaces deos, nisi nossemus illorum beneficia nunc
oblata ultro, nunc orantibus data, magna, tempestiva,
3 ingentes minas interventu suo solventia. Quis est
autem tam miser, tam neclectus, quis tam duro fato
et in poenam genitus, ut non tantam deorum munificentiam senserit ? Ipsos illos complorantes sortem
suam et querulos circumspice : invenies non ex toto
beneficiorum caelestium expertes, neminem esse, ad
quem non aliquid ex illo benignissimo fonte manaverit.
Parum est autem id, quod nascentibus ex aequo dis-
tribuitur ? Ut quae secuntur inaequali dispensata
mensura transeamus, parum dedit natura, cum se
dedit?

1   5. " Non dat deus beneficia." Unde ergo ista,
quae possides, quae das, quae negas, quae servas,
quae rapis ? Unde haec innumerabilia oculos, aures,

I know the answer that can be made to this : " Yes,
and therefore God does not give benefits, but, free
from all care and unconcerned about us, he turns
his back on the world, and either does something
else, or—that which Epicurus counts supreme happiness—does nothing at all, and benefits no more
concern him than injuries." But he who says this
does not hearken to the voices of those who pray and
of those who all around him, lifting their hands to
heaven, offer vows for blessings public and private.
Assuredly this would not be the case, assuredly all
mortals would not have agreed upon this madness of
addressing divinities that were deaf and gods that
were ineffectual, unless we were conscious of their
benefits that sometimes are presented unasked, sometimes are granted in answer to prayer—great and
timely gifts, which by their coming remove grave
menaces. And who is so wretched, so uncared for,
who has been born to so cruel a destiny and punishment as never to have experienced the great bounty
of the gods ? Look at those who bemoan and
deplore their lot—you will find that even these are
not wholly excluded from heavenly benefits, that
there is not one to whom some benefit has not trickled
from that most bountiful spring. And the gift that at
birth is dispensed equally to all—is this too small a
thing ? Though the fortunes to which we pass in
later life are dispensed in unequal measure, was it too
small a thing that Nature gave when she gave to us
herself ?

" God gives no benefits," you say. Whence, then,
comes all that you possess, all that you give, all that
you withhold, all that you hoard, all that you steal ?
Whence come the countless things that delight your

animum mulcentia ? Unde illa luxuriam quoque
instruens copia (neque enim necessitatibus tantum-
modo nostris provisum est ; usque in delicias ama-
2 mur) ? Tot arbusta non uno modo frugifera, tot
herbae salutares, tot varietates ciborum per totum
annum digestae, ut inerti quoque fortuita terrae
alimenta praeberent ? Iam animalia omnis generis,
alia in sicco solidoque, alia in umido nascentia, alia
per sublime demissa, ut omnis rerum naturae pars
3 tributum aliquod nobis conferret ? Flumina haec
amoenissimis flexibus campos cingentia, illa praebitura
commercio viam vasto et navigabili cursu vadentia,
ex quibus quaedam aestatis diebus mirabile incre-
mentum trahunt, ut arida et ferventi subiecta caelo
loca subita vis aestivi torrentis irriget ? Quid medi-
catorum torrentium venae ? Quid in ipsis litoribus
aquarum calentium exundatio ?

> Te, Lari maxime, teque,
> fluctibus et fremitu adsurgens, Benace, marino ?

1 6. Si pauca quis tibi donasset iugera, accepisse te
diceres beneficium ; immensa terrarum late patentium
spatia negas esse beneficium ? Si pecuniam tibi aliquis donaverit et arcam tuam, quoniam tibi id ma
gnum videtur, impleverit, beneficium vocabis ; tot
metalla deus[1] defodit, tot flumina emisit terra, super
quae decurrunt sola, aurum vehentia ; argenti, aeris,

---

[1] deus *added by Hosius.*

eyes, your ears, your mind ? Whence the profusion that supplies even our luxury ? For it is not merely our necessities that are provided—we are loved to the point of being spoiled ! Whence all the trees yielding their varied fruits, all the healing plants, all the different sorts of foods distributed throughout the whole year, so that even the slothful find sustenance from the chance produce of the earth ? Whence, too, the living creatures of every kind, some born upon dry and solid ground, others in the waves, others that descend through the air, in order that every part of Nature's domain might pay to us some tribute ? Whence the rivers—these that encircle the fields in loveliest curves, those that, as they flow on in their vast and navigable courses, provide a channel for commerce, some of which in the days of summer undergo a wonderful increase in size in order that, by the sudden overflow of the summer torrent, they may water the parched lands that lie outstretched beneath a burning sky ? And what of the springs of healing waters ? What of the warm waters that bubble forth upon the very coast of the sea ?

> And thee, O lordly Larius, and, Benacus, thee,
> Rising with a roar of billows like the sea ? [a]

If anyone had made you a gift of but a few acres, you would say that you had received a benefit ; and do you say that the illimitable stretches that the earth opens to you are not a benefit ? If anyone has presented you with money, and, since this is a great thing in your eyes, has filled your coffer, you will call it a benefit. God has planted in the earth countless mines, has drawn forth from its depths countless rivers that over the lands where they flow carry down

ferri immane pondus omnibus locis obrutum, cuius
investigandi tibi facultatem dedit, ac latentium divitiarum in summa terra signa disposuit : negas te
2 accepisse beneficium ?   Si domus tibi donetur, in qua
marmoris aliquid resplendeat et tectum nitidius auro
aut coloribus sparsum, non mediocre munus vocabis.
Ingens tibi domicilium sine ullo incendii aut ruinae
metu struxit, in quo vides non tenues crustas et ipsa,
qua secantur, lamna graciliores, sed integras lapidis
pretiosissimi moles, sed totas variae distinctaeque
materiae, cuius tu parvula frusta miraris, tectum vero
aliter nocte, aliter interdiu fulgens : negas te ullum
3 munus accepisse ?   Et cum ista, quae habes, magno
aestimes, quod est ingrati hominis, nulli debere te
iudicas ?   Unde tibi istum, quem trahis, spiritum ?
Unde istam, per quam actus vitae tuae disponis atque
ordinas, lucem ?   Unde sanguinem, cuius cursu vitalis
continetur calor ?   Unde ista palatum tuum saporibus
exquisitis ultra satietatem lacessentia ?   Unde haec
irritamenta iam lassae voluptatis ?   Unde ista quies,
4 in qua putrescis ac marces ?   Nonne, si gratus es,
dices :

gold ; silver and copper and iron in huge store have been buried in all places, and he has given to you the means of discovering them by placing upon the surface of the earth the signs of its hidden treasures—yet do you say that you have received no benefit ? If you should receive the gift of a house that was resplendent with marble and a ceiling gleaming with gold or decked out with colours, you would call it no commonplace gift. God has built for you a huge mansion that need not fear conflagration or ruin, a house in which you see, not flimsy veneers ^a thinner than the very blade by which they are sawn, but virgin masses of most precious stone, whole masses of a substance with such a variety of markings that the tiniest fragments of it fill you with wonder, and a ceiling gleaming in one fashion by night, and in another by day—yet do you say that you have received no gift ? And, though you prize greatly these blessings that you possess, do you act the part of an ungrateful man, and consider that you are indebted to no one for them ? Whence do you have that breath which you draw ? Whence that light by which you distribute and order the acts of your life ? Whence the blood that by its circulation maintains the heat of life ? Whence those dainties that by rare flavours excite your palate when it is already sated ? Whence those provocatives of pleasure when it palls ? Whence this repose in which you wither and rot ? Will you not, if you are grateful, say :

<hr>

^a *i.e.*, of marble.

SENECA

Deus nobis haec otia fecit.
namque erit ille mihi semper deus, illius aram
saepe tener nostris ab ovilibus inbuet agnus.
ille meas errare boves, ut cernis, et ipsum
ludere, quae vellem, calamo permisit agresti.

5 Ille deus est, non qui paucas boves, sed qui per
totum orbem armenta dimisit, qui gregibus ubique
passim vagantibus pabulum praestat, qui pascua
hibernis aestiva substituit, qui non calamo tantum
cantare et agreste atque inconditum carmen ad aliquam tamen observationem modulari docuit, sed tot
artes, tot vocum varietates, tot sonos alios spiritu
nostro, alios externo cantus edituros commentus est.
6 Neque enim nostra ista, quae invenimus, dixeris, non
magis, quam quod crescimus, quam quod ad constitutum temporum sua corpori officia respondent : nunc
puerilium dentium lapsus, nunc ad surgentem iam
aetatem et in robustiorem gradum transeuntem
pubertas et ultimus ille dens surgenti iuventae
terminum ponens. Insita sunt nobis omnium aetatium, omnium artium semina, magisterque ex occulto
deus producit ingenia.
1 7. " Natura," inquit, " haec mihi praestat." Non
intellegis te, cum hoc dicis, mutare nomen deo ?
Quid enim aliud est natura quam deus et divina ratio
toti mundo partibusque eius inserta ? Quotiens voles,
tibi licet aliter hunc auctorem rerum nostrarum

---

a Virgil, *Eclogues*, i. 6 *sqq.*, where the poet refers to his
own indebtedness to the bounty of Octavian.

b A reference, apparently, to the wind produced by
bellows as in the water-organ, with which the emperors and
opulent Romans entertained the populace.

A god for us this ease hath wrought.   For he
Shall ever be a god indeed to me,
And many a firstling lamb his altar stain
From out our flock.   You see what boons I gain :
My oxen by his bounty roam at will,
While I fond airs upon my pipe can trill ? [a]

But God is he who has set free, not a few oxen, but
herds throughout the whole earth, who everywhere
supplies food to the flocks as they range far and wide,
who after pastures of summer has provided pastures
of winter, who has not merely taught how to play
upon the pipe and to fashion a tune that, rustic and
artless as it is, yet shows some regard for form, but
has invented countless arts, the countless variations
of the voice, the countless tones that will produce
melodies, some by the breath of our body, others by
the breath of an instrument.[b]   For you must not say
that whatever we have invented is our own any more
than the fact of our growth, or the fact that the
behaviour of our body corresponds with the fixed
periods of life ; now comes the loss of childhood's
teeth, now, as age gradually advances and passes into
the hardier stage, puberty and the last tooth that
marks the end of the progress of youth.   In us are
implanted the seeds of all ages, the seeds of all the
arts, and it is God, our master, who draws forth from
the secret depths of our being our various talents.

" It is Nature," you say, " who supplies me with
these things."   But do you not understand that,
when you say this, you merely give another name to
God ?   For what else is Nature but God and the
Divine Reason that pervades the whole universe and
all its parts ?   You may, as often as you like, address
this being who is the author of this world of ours by

compellare ; et Iovem illum Optimum ac Maximum
rite dices et Tonantem et Statorem, qui non, ut histo-
rici tradiderunt, ex eo, quod post votum susceptum
acies Romanorum fugientium stetit, sed quod stant
beneficio eius omnia, stator stabilitorque est.   Hunc
2 eundem et Fatum si dixeris, non mentieris ; nam cum
fatum nihil aliud sit, quam series implexa causarum,
ille est prima omnium causa, ex qua ceterae pendent.
Quaecumque voles, illi nomina proprie aptabis vim
aliquam effectumque caelestium rerum continentia :
tot appellationes eius possunt esse, quot munera.
1   8. Hunc et Liberum patrem et Herculem ac Mercurium nostri putant : Liberum patrem, quia omnium
parens sit, cui primum inventa seminum vis est vitae[1]
consultura per voluptatem ; Herculem, quia vis eius
invicta sit quandoque lassata fuerit operibus editis,
in ignem recessura ; Mercurium, quia ratio penes
2 illum est numerusque et ordo et scientia.   Quocumque te flexeris, ibi illum videbis occurrentem tibi ;
nihil ab illo vacat, opus suum ipse implet.   Ergo nihil
agis, ingratissime mortalium, qui te negas deo debere,
sed naturae, quia nec natura sine deo est nec deus sine
3 natura, sed idem est utrumque, distat officio.   Si,
quod a Seneca accepisses, Annaeo te debere diceres
vel Lucio, non creditorem mutares, sed nomen,
quoniam, sive praenomen eius sive nomen dixisses

---

[1] vitae *added by Basore*: vitae perpetuitati *added by
Préchac after* voluptatem.

---

[a] *i.e.*, of Romulus in a battle with the Sabines.
[b] An allusion to the Stoic idea that God is Creative Fire,
into which all other elements are periodically resolved. So
Hercules, after completing his labours, passed away in fire.
[c] The speaker's full name was Lucius Annaeus Seneca.

different names ; it will be right for you to call him Jupiter Best and Greatest, and the Thunderer and the Stayer, a title derived, not from the fact that, as the historians have related, the Roman battle-line stayed its flight in answer to prayer,[a] but from the fact that all things are stayed by his benefits, that he is their Stayer and Stabilizer. If likewise you should call him Fate, it would be no falsehood ; for, since Fate is nothing but a connected chain of causes, he is the first of all the causes on which the others depend. Any name that you choose will be properly applied to him if it connotes some force that operates in the domain of heaven—his titles may be as countless as are his benefits.

Our school regard him both as Father Liber and as Hercules and as Mercury—Father Liber, because he is the father of all things, he who first discovered the seminal power that is able to subserve life through pleasure ; Hercules, because his power is invincible, and, whenever it shall have grown weary with fulfilling its works, shall return into primal fire [b] ; Mercury, because to him belong reason and number and order and knowledge. In whatever direction you turn, you will see God coming to meet you ; nothing is void of him, he himself fills all his work. For this reason, O most ungrateful of mortals, it is futile for you to say that you are indebted, not to God, but to Nature, for there is no Nature without God, nor God without Nature, but both are the same thing, they differ only in their function. If, having received a gift from Seneca, you were to say that you were indebted to Annaeus or to Lucius,[c] you would be changing, not your creditor, but his name, for, whether you designated him by his first, his second,

sive cognomen, idem tamen ille esset. Sic nunc
naturam voca, fatum, fortunam; omnia eiusdem
dei nomina sunt varie utentis sua potestate. Et
iustitia, probitas, prudentia, fortitudo, frugalitas unius
animi bona sunt; quidquid horum tibi placuit, animus
placet.

1 9. Sed ne aliam disputationem ex obliquo habeam,
plurima beneficia ac maxima in nos deus defert sine
spe recipiendi, quoniam nec ille conlato eget nec nos
ei quidquam conferre possumus; ergo beneficium per
se expetenda res est. Una spectatur in eo accipientis
utilitas; ad hanc accedamus sepositis commodis
nostris.

2 " Dicitis," inquit, " diligenter eligendos, quibus
beneficia demus, quia ne agricolae quidem semina
harenis committant; quod si verum est, nostram
utilitatem in beneficiis dandis sequimur, quemadmodum in arando serendoque; neque enim serere
per se res expetenda est. Praeterea quaeritis, ubi
et quomodo detis[1] beneficium, quod non esset faciendum, si per se beneficium dare expetenda res esset,
quoniam, quocumque loco et quocumque modo da-
3 retur, beneficium erat." Honestum propter nullam
aliam causam quam propter ipsum sequimur; tamen,
etiam si nihil aliud sequendum est, quaerimus, quid[2]
faciamus et quando et quemadmodum; per haec enim
constat. Itaque, cum eligo, cui dem beneficium, id

----

[1] ubi et quomodo detis *added by Gertz.*
[2] quid *O* : cui *Hosius after Gertz.*

----

[a] The others in the list represent the four cardinal virtues
of Stoic teaching.

or his third name, he would nevertheless be the same person. So, if you like, speak of Nature, Fate, Fortune, but all these are names of the same God, who uses his power in various ways. And justice, honesty,[a] prudence, courage, temperance are the good qualities of only one mind ; if you take pleasure in any of these, you take pleasure in that mind.

But, not to be drawn aside into further controversy, God bestows upon us very many and very great benefits, with no thought of any return, since he has no need of having anything bestowed, nor are we capable of bestowing anything on him ; consequently, a benefit is something that is desirable in itself. It has in view only the advantage of the recipient ; so, putting aside all interests of our own, let us aim solely at this.

" Yet you say," someone retorts, " that we ought to take care to select those to whom we would give benefits, since even the farmer does not commit his seeds to sand ; but if this is true, then in giving benefits we are seeking our own advantage, just as surely as in ploughing and sowing ; for sowing is not something that is desirable in itself. Moreover, you inquire where and how you should bestow a benefit, which there would be no need of doing if giving a benefit is something that is desirable in itself, since, in whatever place and in whatever fashion it was bestowed, it would still be a benefit." But we pursue honour solely for its own sake ; yet, even if we should have no other reason for pursuing it, we do inquire what we should do, and when and how we should do it ; for it is just through these considerations that honour has its being. And so, when I select the person to whom I would give a benefit, I am thinking

221

ago, ut quandoque beneficium sit, quia, si turpi datur, nec honestum esse potest nec beneficium.

1   10. Depositum reddere per se res expetenda est; non tamen semper reddam nec quolibet loco nec quolibet tempore. Aliquando nihil interest, utrum infitier an palam reddam. Intuebor utilitatem eius, cui redditurus sum, et nociturum illi depositum 2 negabo. Idem in beneficio faciam. Videbo, quando dem, cui dem, quemadmodum, quare. Nihil enim sine ratione faciendum est; non est autem beneficium, nisi quod ratione datur, quoniam ratio omnis 3 honesti comes est. Quam saepe hominum donationem suam inconsultam obiurgantium hanc exaudimus vocem: " Mallem perdidisse quam illi dedisse "! Turpissimum genus damni est inconsulta donatio multoque gravius male dedisse beneficium quam non recepisse; aliena enim culpa est, quod non recipimus; quod, cui daremus, non elegimus, nostra. 4 In electione nihil minus quam hoc, quod tu existimas, spectabo, a quo recepturus sim; eligo enim eum, qui gratus, non qui redditurus sit, saepe autem et non 5 redditurus gratus est et ingratus,[1] qui reddidit. Ad animum tendit aestimatio mea; ideo locupletem sed

---

[1] est et ingratus *commonly added.*

of this—how and when a gift is a benefit; for if it is given to one who is base, it can be neither an honourable act nor a benefit.

To restore a deposit is something that is desirable in itself ; yet I shall not always restore it, nor at every time or in every place. Sometimes it is a matter of indifference whether I deny a deposit or restore it openly. I shall always regard the interest of the one to whom I am intending to restore a deposit, and shall refuse to do so if it will do him harm. I shall proceed in the same way in the matter of a benefit. I shall consider when to give it, to whom to give it, and how and why. For reason should be applied to everything we do ; and no gift can be a benefit unless it is given with reason, since every virtuous act is accompanied by reason. How often, when men are reproaching themselves for some thoughtless benefaction, do we hear the words : " I would rather have lost it than have given it to him " ! Thoughtless benefaction is the most shameful sort of loss, and it is a much greater offence to have ill bestowed a benefit than to have received no return ; for it is the fault of another if we have received no return, while, if we did not select the one to whom we were giving, the fault is our own. In making my choice no considerations will influence me so little as the one you suppose—who will be likely to make me some return ; for I choose a person who will be grateful, not one who is likely to make a return, and it often happens that the grateful man is one who is not likely to make a return, while the ungrateful man is one who has made a return. It is to the heart that my estimate is directed ; consequently I shall pass by the man who, though rich, is unworthy, and shall

indignum praeteribo, pauperi viro bono dabo ; erit
enim in summa inopia gratus et, cum omnia illi
deerunt, supererit animus.

1   11. Non lucrum ex beneficio capto, non voluptatem,
non gloriam ; uni placere contentus in hoc dabo, ut
quod oportet faciam.   Quod oportet autem non est
sine electione.   Quae qualis futura sit, interrogas ?
Eligam   virum   integrum,   simplicem,   memorem,
gratum, alieni abstinentem, sui non avare tenacem,
benevolum ;   hunc ego cum elegero, licet nihil illi
fortuna tribuat, ex quo referre gratiam possit, ex
2 sententia gesta res erit.   Si utilitas me et sordida
computatio liberalem facit, si nulli prosum, nisi ut in
vicem ille mihi prosit, non dabo beneficium profici-
scenti   in diversas longinquasque regiones, afuturo
semper ;   non dabo sic adfecto, ut spes ei nulla sit
convalescendi ;   non dabo ipse deficiens, non enim
3 habeo recipiendi tempus.   Atqui ut scias rem per se
expetendam esse bene facere, advenis modo in nostrum delatis portum, statim abituris, succurrimus ;
ignoto naufrago navem, qua revehatur, et damus et
struimus.   Discedit ille vix satis noto salutis auctore
et numquam amplius in conspectum nostrum rever-
surus debitores nobis deos delegat precaturque, illi
pro se gratiam referant ;   interim nos iuvat sterilis

give to one who, though poor, is good ; for he will be grateful in the midst of extreme poverty, and, when he lacks all else, this heart he will still have.

It is not gain that I try to get from a benefit, nor pleasure, nor glory ; content with giving pleasure to one human being, I shall give with the single purpose of doing what I ought. But I am not without choice in doing what I ought. Do you ask what the nature of this choice will be ? I shall choose a man who is upright, sincere, mindful, grateful, who keeps his hands from another man's property, who is not greedily attached to his own, who is kind to others ; although Fortune may bestow upon him nothing with which he may repay my favour, I shall have accomplished my purpose when I have made choice of such a man. If I am made liberal by self-interest and mean calculation, if my only purpose in doing a service to a man is to have him in turn do a service to me, I shall not give a benefit to one who is setting out for distant and foreign countries, never to return ; I shall not give to one who is so ill that he has no hope of recovery ; I shall not give when my own health is failing, for I shall have no time to receive a return. And yet, that you may know that generous action is something desirable in itself, the foreigner who has just put into our harbour, and will straightway depart, receives our assistance ; to a shipwrecked stranger, in order that he may sail back home, we both give a ship and equip it. He leaves us scarcely knowing who was the author of his salvation, and, expecting never more to see our faces again, he deputes the gods to be our debtors, and prays that they may repay the favour in his stead ; meanwhile we rejoice in the consciousness of having given a

4 beneficii conscientia. Quid ? cum in ipso vitae fine
constitimus, cum testamentum ordinamus, non beneficia nihil nobis profutura dividimus ? Quantum
temporis consumitur, quam diu secreto agitur, quantum et quibus demus ! Quid enim interest, quibus
5 demus a nullo recepturi ? Atqui numquam diligentius damus, numquam magis iudicia nostra torque-
mus, quam ubi remotis utilitatibus solum ante oculos
honestum stetit, tam diu officiorum mali iudices,
quam diu illa depravat spes ac metus et inertissimum
vitium, voluptas. Ubi mors interclusit omnia et ad
ferendam sententiam incorruptum iudicem misit,
quaerimus dignissimos, quibus nostra tradamus, nec
quicquam cura sanctiore componimus, quam quod ad
6 nos non pertinet. At mehercules tunc magna voluptas subit cogitantem : " Hunc ego locupletiorem
faciam, et huius dignitati adiectis opibus aliquid
splendoris adfundam." Si non damus beneficia nisi
recepturi, intestatis moriendum sit !

1 12. " Dicitis," inquit, " beneficium creditum insolubile esse ; creditum autem non est res per se expetenda." Cum creditum dicimus, imagine et trans-
latione utimur ; sic enim et legem dicimus iusti
iniustique regulam esse, et regula non est res per se
expetenda. Ad haec verba demonstrandae rei causa
descendimus ; cum dico creditum, intellegitur tamquam creditum. Vis scire ? Adicio insolubile, cum

benefit that will yield no fruit. And tell me, when we have reached the very end of life, and are drawing up our will, do we not dispense benefits that will yield us nothing ? How much time is spent, how long do we debate with ourselves to whom and how much we shall give ! For what difference does it make to whom we give since no one will make us any return ? Yet never are we more careful in our giving, never do we wrestle more in making decisions than when, with all self-interest banished, only the ideal of good remains before our eyes ; we are bad judges of our duties only so long as they are distorted by hope and fear and that most slothful of vices, pleasure. But when death has shut off all these, and has brought us to pronounce sentence as incorrupt judges, we search for those who are most worthy to inherit our possessions, and there is nothing that we arrange with more scrupulous care than this which is of no concern to ourselves. Yet, heavens ! the great joy that comes to us as we think : " Through me this man will become richer, and I, by increasing his wealth, shall add new lustre to his high position." If we give only when we may expect some return, we ought to die intestate !

" You say," someone retorts, " a benefit is a loan that cannot be repaid ; but a loan is not something that is desirable in itself." When I use the term " loan," I resort to a figure, a metaphor ; for in the same way I can also say that a law is the measure of justice and injustice, and a measure is not something desirable in itself. We resort to such terms for the purpose of making something clear ; when I say a " loan," a quasi-loan is understood. Do you wish to know the difference ? I add the words " that

creditum nullum non solvi aut possit aut debeat.
2 Adeo beneficium utilitatis causa dandum non est, ut
saepe, quemadmodum dixi, cum damno ac periculo
dandum sit. Sic latronibus circumventum defendo,
ut tuto transire permittatur ; reum gratia laborantem
tueor et hominum potentium factionem in me con-
verto, quas illi detraxero sordes, sub accusatoribus
isdem fortasse sumpturus, cum abire in partem
alteram possim et securus spectare aliena certamina ;
spondeo pro iudicato et suspensis amici bonis libellum
deicio creditoribus eius me obligaturus ; ut possim
servare proscriptum, ipse proscriptionis periculum
adeo.
3   Nemo Tusculanum aut Tiburtinum paraturus salu-
britatis causa et aestivi secessus, quoto anno empturus
4 sit, disputat ; cum erit,[1] tuendum est. Eadem in
beneficio ratio est ; nam cum interrogaveris, quid
reddat, respondebo : bonam conscientiam. Quid
reddat beneficium ? Dic tu mihi, quid reddat iustitia,
quid innocentia, quid magnitudo animi, quid pudicitia, quid temperantia ; si quicquam praeter ipsas,

   [1] cum erit *O* : cui e re sit *Hosius* : *alii alia.*

---

   [a] The conventional garb of the defendant, as shown
notably by Plutarch, *Cicero*, 30. 4 κινδυνεύων οὖν καὶ
διωκόμενος ἐσθῆτα μετήλλαξε καὶ κόμης ἀνάπλεως περιϊὼν ἱκέτευε
τὸν δῆμον.

   [b] *Quoto anno*, as the English " purchase," is technical ;
it means how many years it will take for the total return from
the estate to equal the price paid for it. The point seems
to be that the man who is buying an estate primarily for
the purpose of health and pleasure will be prone to disregard
the question of financial return.

   [c] The Latin is vague and the text uncertain ; with *erit*

cannot be repaid," whereas every true loan either can or ought to be repaid. So far from its being right for us to give a benefit from a motive of self-interest, often, as I have said, the giving of it must involve one's own loss and risk. For instance, I come to the rescue of a man who has been surrounded by robbers although I am at liberty to pass by in safety. By defending an accused man, who is battling with privilege, I turn against myself a clique of powerful men, and shall be forced perhaps by the same accusers to put on the mourning^a that I have removed from him, although I might take the other side, and look on in safety at struggles that do not concern me ; I go bail for a man who has been condemned, and, when a friend's goods are put up for sale, I quash the indictment, and shall probably make myself responsible for what he owes to his creditors ; in order to save a proscribed person, I myself run the risk of proscription.

No one, when he wishes to acquire an estate at Tusculum or at Tibur because of their healthfulness and the retreat they afford in summer, stops to consider at how many years' purchase^b he is going to buy ; when once he has bought^c it, he must look after it. In the case of a benefit the same principle applies ; for, when you ask me what the return will be, I answer, " the reward of a good conscience." What return does one have from a benefit ? Do you, pray, tell me what return one has from justice, from innocence, from greatness of soul, from chastity, from temperance ; if you seek for anything besides the

of the MSS. perhaps *emptum* is to be supplied with *praedium* as a subject. The sense will be that the owner will, naturally, try to make the estate pay.

5 ipsas[1] non petis. In quid mundus vices suas solvit ?
In quid sol diem extendit et contrahit ? Omnia ista
beneficia sunt, fiunt enim nobis profutura. Quomodo
mundi officium est circumagere rerum ordinem, quomodo solis loca mutare, ex quibus oriatur, in quae
cadat, et haec salutaria nobis facere sine praemio,
ita viri officium est inter alia et beneficium dare.
Quare ergo dat ? Ne non det, ne occasionem bene
faciendi perdat.

1   13. Vobis voluptas est inertis otii facere corpu-
sculum et securitatem sopitis simillimam appetere et
sub densa umbra latitare tenerrimisque cogitationi-
bus, quas tranquillitatem vocatis, animi marcentis
oblectare torporem et cibis potionibusque intra hor-
torum latebram corpora ignavia pallentia saginare ;
2 nobis voluptas est dare beneficia vel laboriosa, dum
aliorum labores levent, vel periculosa, dum alios
periculis extrahant, vel rationes nostras adgravatura,
3 dum aliorum necessitates et angustias laxent. Quid
mea interest, an recipiam beneficia ? Etiam cum re-
cepero, danda sunt. Beneficium eius commodum
spectat, cui praestatur, non nostrum ; alioquin nobis
illud damus. Itaque multa, quae summam utilitatem
aliis adferunt, pretio gratiam perdunt. Mercator

---

[1] ipsas *added by Modius.*

virtues themselves, it is not the virtues themselves that you seek. To what end does heaven perform its revolutions? To what end does the sun lengthen and shorten the day? These are all benefits, for they take place in order to work good to us. Just as it is the office of heaven to perform its revolutions in the fixed order of Nature, and that of the sun to shift the points at which it rises and sets, and to do these things that are serviceable to us without any reward, so it is the duty of man, amongst other things, to give also benefits. Why, then, does he give? For fear that he should fail to give, for fear that he should lose an opportunity of doing good.

You count it pleasure to surrender your miserable body to sluggish ease, to court a repose that differs not much from sleep, to lurk in a covert of thick shade and beguile the lethargy of a languid mind with the most delicate thoughts, which you call tranquillity, and in the secret retreats of your gardens to stuff with food and drink your bodies that are pallid from inaction; we count it pleasure to give benefits, even at the price of labour, if only they will lighten the labours of others, even at the price of danger, if only they will extricate others from dangers, even at the expense of burdening our budgets, if only they will relieve the needs and distresses of others. What difference does it make whether my benefits are returned? Even after they have been returned, they must be given again. A benefit views the interest, not of ourselves, but of the one upon whom it is bestowed; otherwise, it is to ourselves that we give it. And so, many services that confer the utmost advantage on others lose claim to gratitude because they are paid for. The trader renders service to

urbibus prodest, medicus aegris, mango venalibus ;
sed omnes isti, quia ad alienum commodum pro suo
veniunt, non obligant eos, quibus prosunt. Non est
beneficium, quod in quaestum mittitur. " Hoc dabo
et hoc recipiam " auctio est.

1   14. Non dicam pudicam, quae amatorem ut in-
cenderet reppulit, quae aut legem aut virum timuit ;
ut ait Ovidius :

> Quae, quia non licuit, non dedit, illa dedit.

Non immerito in numerum peccantium refertur, quae
pudicitiam timori praestitit, non sibi. Eodem modo,
2 qui beneficium ut reciperet dedit, non dedit. Ergo
et nos beneficium damus animalibus, quae aut usui
aut alimento futura nutrimus ! Beneficium damus
arbustis, quae colimus, ne siccitate aut immoti et
3 neclecti soli duritia laborent ! Nemo ad agrum
colendum ex aequo et bono venit nec ad ullam rem,
cuius extra ipsam fructus est ; ad beneficium dandum
non adducit cogitatio avara nec sordida, sed humana,
liberalis, cupiens dare, etiam cum dederit, et augere
novis ac recentibus vetera, unum habens propositum,
quanto ei, cui praestat, bono futura sit ; alioqui
humile est, sine laude, sine gloria, prodesse, quia
4 expedit. Quid magnifici est se amare, sibi parcere,
sibi adquirere ? Ab omnibus istis vera beneficii

---

cities, the physician to the sick, the slave-monger to those he sells ; but all these, because they arrive at the good of others through seeking their own, do not leave those whom they serve under any obligation. That which has gain as its object cannot be a benefit. " I shall give so much and get so much in return " is pure barter.

I should not call that woman chaste who repulses a lover in order to inflame him, who is afraid either of the law or of her husband. As Ovid [a] puts it :

> She who sinned not because she could not—sinned.

A woman who owes her chastity, not to herself, but to fear, is very rightly put in the class of sinners. In the same way, he who has given a benefit in order that he may get something back has really not given it. At this rate, we also give a benefit to the animals that we rear in order that they may provide us either with service or with food ! We give a benefit to the orchards that we tend in order that they may not suffer from drought or the hardness of untilled and neglected ground. But it is not justice nor goodness that moves anyone to cultivate a field, or to perform any act that involves some reward apart from the act itself. The motive that leads to the giving of a benefit is not greedy nor mean, but is humane and generous, a desire to give even when one has already given, and to add new and fresh gifts to old ones, having as its sole aim the working of as much good as it can for him upon whom it bestows ; whereas it is a contemptible act, without praise and without glory, to do anyone a service because it is to our own interest. What nobleness is there in loving oneself, in sparing oneself, in getting gain for oneself ? The true desire

dandi cupido avocat, ad detrimentum iniecta manu trahit et utilitates relinquit ipso bene faciendi opere laetissima.

1 15. Numquid dubium est, quin contraria sit beneficio iniuria ? Quomodo iniuriam facere per se vitanda ac fugienda res est, sic beneficium dare per se expetenda. Illic turpitudo contra omnia praemia in scelus hortantia valet ; ad hoc invitat honesti per se 2 efficax species. Non mentiar, si dixero neminem non amare beneficia sua, neminem non ita compositum animo, ut libentius eum videat, in quem multa congessit, cui non causa sit iterum dandi beneficii semel dedisse. Quod non accideret, nisi ipsa nos delectarent 3 beneficia. Quam saepe dicentem audias : " Non sustineo illum deserere, cui dedi vitam, quem e periculo eripui. Rogat me, ut causam suam contra homines gratiosos agam ; nolo, sed quid faciam ? Iam illi semel, iterum adfui." Non vides inesse isti rei propriam quandam vim, quae nos dare beneficia cogit, primum quia oportet, deinde quia dedimus ? 4 Cui initio ratio non fuisset praestandi aliquid, ei praestamus ob hoc, quia praestitimus ; adeoque ad beneficia nos non impellit utilitas, ut inutilia tueri ac

of giving a benefit summons us away from all these motives, and, laying hand upon us, forces us to put up with loss, and, forgoing self-interest, finds its greatest joy in the mere act of doing good.

Can there be any doubt that the opposite of a benefit is an injury ? Just as doing an injury is something that in itself must be avoided and shunned, so giving a benefit is something that is desirable in itself. In one case, the baseness of the action outweighs all the rewards that urge us to the crime, in the other, we are incited to the action by the idea of virtue, which is in itself a powerful incentive. I shall not be guilty of misstatement if I say that everyone takes delight in the benefits he does, that everyone is so disposed that he is made more happy by seeing the one upon whom he has heaped benefits, that everyone finds in the fact of having given one benefit a reason for giving a second one. And this would not happen if the benefits themselves were not the source of his pleasure. How often will you hear a man say : " I cannot bear to desert him, for I have given him his life, I have rescued him from peril. He now begs me to plead his cause against men of influence ; I do not want to, but what can I do ? I have already helped him once, no, twice." Do you not see that there is, inherent in the thing itself, some peculiar power that compels us to give benefits, first, because we ought, then, because we have already given them ? Though in the beginning we may have had no reason for bestowing anything upon a man, we continue to bestow because we have already bestowed ; and so untrue is it that we are moved to give benefits from a motive of profit, that we persist in maintaining and cherishing those that are unprofitable, solely from an

fovere perseveremus sola beneficii caritate, cui etiam
infeliciter dato indulgere tam naturale est quam
liberis pravis.

1 16. Idem isti gratiam referre ipsos fatentur, non
quia honestum est, sed quia utile. Quod non esse
ita minore opera probandum est, quia, quibus argumentis collegimus beneficium dare per se rem ex-
2 petendam esse, isdem etiam hoc colligimus. Fixum
illud est, a quo in cetera probationes nostrae exeunt,
honestum ob nullam aliam causam, quam quia
honestum sit, coli. Quis ergo controversiam facere
audebit, an gratum esse honestum sit ? Quis non
ingratum detestetur, hominem sibi ipsum inutilem ?
Quid autem cum tibi narratur, " Adversus summa
beneficia amici sui ingratus est," quomodo adficeris ?
Utrum tamquam rem turpem fecerit, an tamquam
rem utilem sibi et profuturam omiserit ? Puto,
nequam hominem existimas, cui poena, non cui cura-
tore opus sit ; quod non accideret, nisi gratum esse
3 per se expetendum honestumque esset. Alia fortasse minus dignitatem suam praeferunt et, an sint
honesta, interprete egent. Hoc expositum est pul-
chriusque, quam ut splendor eius dubie ac parum
luceat. Quid tam laudabile, quid tam aequaliter in
omnium animos receptum quam referre bene meritis
gratiam ?

1 17. Ad hoc, dic mihi, quae causa nos perducit ?
Lucrum ? Quod qui non contemnit, ingratus est.

---

^a *i.e.*, the Epicureans.

affection for the benefit, to which, even though it has been unfortunately placed, we show indulgence as naturally as we might to children who misbehave.

These same opponents[a] admit that they themselves return gratitude, yet not because it is right, but because it is expedient. But to prove that this is false is an easier task, because the same arguments by which we have established that to give a benefit is something that is desirable in itself establish this also. The one fixed principle from which we proceed to the proof of other points is that the honourable is cherished for no other reason than because it is honourable. Who, therefore, will dare to raise the question whether it is honourable to be grateful? Who does not loathe the ungrateful man, a person who is unprofitable even to himself? And tell me, when you hear it said of someone : " He is ungrateful for very great benefits," what are your feelings? Is it as though he had done something base, or as though he had omitted to do something that was expedient and likely to be profitable to himself? I imagine you count him a worthless fellow, who should have, not a guardian, but punishment ; but this would not be the case unless to be grateful were something that is desirable in itself and honourable. Other qualities, perhaps, manifest their worth less clearly, and, in order to decide whether they are honourable, we need an interpreter. This one is open to the view, and is too beautiful to have its glory dimmed or obscured. What is so praiseworthy, upon what are all our minds so uniformly agreed, as the repayment of good services with gratitude?

Tell me, what is the motive that leads to this? Gain? But he who does not scorn gain is ungrateful.

237

Ambitio ? Et quae iactatio est solvisse, quod debeas ? Metus ? Nullus ingrato ; huic enim uni rei
non posuimus legem, tamquam satis natura cavisset.
2 Quomodo nulla lex amare parentes, indulgere liberis
iubet (supervacuum est enim, in quod imus, impelli),
quemadmodum nemo in amorem sui cohortandus est,
quem adeo, dum nascitur, trahit, ita ne ad hoc quidem,
ut honesta per se petat ; placent suapte natura,
adeoque gratiosa virtus est, ut insitum sit etiam malis
probare meliora. Quis est, qui non beneficus videri
velit, qui non inter scelera et iniurias opinionem boni-
tatis adfectet, qui non ipsis, quae impotentissime
fecit, speciem aliquam induat recti velitque etiam
3 his videri beneficium dedisse, quos laesit ? Gratias
itaque agi sibi ab iis, quos adflixere, patiuntur bonos-
que se ac liberales fingunt, quia praestare non possunt.
Quod non facerent, nisi illos honesti et per se ex-
petendi amor cogeret moribus suis opinionem con-
trariam quaerere et nequitiam abdere, cuius fructus
concupiscitur, ipsa vero odio pudorique est ; nec quisquam tantum a naturae lege descivit et hominem
4 exuit, ut animi causa malus sit. Dic enim cuilibet
ex istis, qui rapto vivunt, an ad illa, quae latrociniis
et furtis consecuntur, malint ratione bona pervenire :
optabit ille, cui grassari et transeuntes percutere

---

^a So Ovid (*Met.* vii. 20 *sq.*) makes Medea exclaim :
"" video meliora proboque,
deteriora sequor.""

Vainglory ? And what is there to boast about in
having paid what you owe ? Fear ? The ungrateful
man has none ; for this is the only crime for which
we have provided no law, on the theory that Nature
has taken sufficient precautions against it. Just as
there is no law that bids us love our parents or indulge
our children, for it is useless to push us in the direction
in which we are already going, just as no one needs
to be urged to self-love, which he imbibes even while
he is being born, so, too, there is none for this, no
law that bids us seek the honourable in and for itself ;
it pleases us by its very nature, and so attractive is
virtue that even the wicked instinctively approve of
the better course.[a] Who is there who does not wish
to seem beneficent ? who, even in the midst of his
crimes and injuries, does not aspire to a reputation for
goodness ? who does not clothe even his most violent
acts with some semblance of righteousness, and wish
to have the appearance of having given a benefit even
to those whom he has injured ? And so men suffer
those whom they have ruined to render them thanks,
and they make a pretence of being good and generous
because they are not able to prove themselves so.
But they would not do this unless the love of what is
right and desirable in itself forced them to seek a
reputation at variance with their characters, and
conceal the wickedness, which they regard with
hatred and shame, while they covet its fruits ; no one
has ever so far revolted from Nature's law and put
aside humanity as to be evil for the pleasure of it.
For ask any of the men who live by robbery whether
they would not prefer to attain by honourable means
the things that they get by brigandage and theft.
The man who gets his living by highway robbery and

quaestus est, potius illa invenire quam eripere;
neminem reperies, qui non nequitiae praemiis sine
nequitia frui malit.   Maximum hoc habemus naturae
meritum, quod virtus lumen suum in omnium animos
permittit; etiam, qui non secuntur illam, vident.

1   18. Ut scias per se expetendam esse grati animi
adfectionem, per se fugienda res est ingratum esse,
quoniam nihil aeque concordiam humani generis dis-
sociat ac distrahit quam hoc vitium.   Nam quo alio
tuti sumus, quam quod mutuis iuvamur officiis ?   Hoc
uno instructior vita contraque incursiones subitas
2 munitior est, beneficiorum commercio.   Fac nos
singulos, quid sumus ?   Praeda animalium et vic-
timae ac bellissimus et facillimus sanguis.   Quoniam
ceteris animalibus in tutelam sui satis virium est,
quaecumque vaga nascebantur et actura vitam
segregem, armata sunt, hominem imbecilla cutis[1]
cingit; non unguium vis, non dentium terribilem
ceteris fecit, nudum et infirmum societas munit.

Duas deus[2] res dedit, quae illum obnoxium validis-
simum facerent, rationem et societatem; itaque, qui
par esse nulli posset, si seduceretur, rerum potitur.
3 Societas illi dominium omnium animalium dedit;
societas terris genitum in alienae naturae transmisit
imperium et dominari etiam in mari iussit; hoc[3]

---

[1] cutis *added by Madvig.*   [2] deus *added by Haase.*
[3] hoc *O*: haec *M, Hosius.*

by murdering travellers will desire rather to find his booty than to snatch it ; you will discover no one who would not prefer to enjoy the rewards of wickedness without the wickedness. Of all the benefits that we have from Nature this is the greatest, the fact that Virtue causes her light to penetrate into the minds of all ; even those who do not follow her see her.

To prove to you that the sentiment of gratitude is something to be desired in itself, ingratitude is something to be avoided in itself because there is nothing that so effectually disrupts and destroys the harmony of the human race as this vice. For how else do we live in security if it is not that we help each other by an exchange of good offices ? It is only through the interchange of benefits that life becomes in some measure equipped and fortified against sudden disasters. Take us singly, and what are we ? The prey of all creatures, their victims, whose blood is most delectable and most easily secured. For, while other creatures possess a strength that is adequate for their self-protection, and those that are born to be wanderers and to lead an isolated life have been given weapons, the covering of man is a frail skin ; no might of claws or of teeth makes him a terror to others, naked and weak as he is, his safety lies in fellowship.

God has given to him two things, reason and fellowship, which, from being a creature at the mercy of others, make him the most powerful of all ; and so he who, if he were isolated, could be a match for none is the master of the world. Fellowship has given to him dominion over all creatures ; fellowship, though he was begotten upon the land, has extended his sovereignty to an element not his own, and has bidden him be lord even upon the sea ; it is this that has

morborum impetus arcuit, senectuti adminicula pro-
spexit, solacia contra dolores dedit ; hoc[1] fortes nos
4 facit, quod licet contra fortunam advocare. Hanc
societatem tolle, et unitatem generis humani, qua
vita sustinetur, scindes ; tolletur autem, si efficis, ut
ingratus animus non per se vitandus sit, sed quia
aliquid illi timendum est ; quam multi enim sunt,
quibus ingratis esse tuto licet ! Denique ingratum
voco, quisquis metu gratus est.

1   19. Deos nemo sanus timet ; furor est enim
metuere salutaria, nec quisquam amat, quos timet.
Tu denique, Epicure, deum inermem facis, omnia illi
tela, omnem detraxisti potentiam et, ne cuiquam
metuendus esset, proiecisti illum extra metum.
2 Hunc igitur insaeptum ingenti quidem et inexplicabili
muro divisumque a contactu et a conspectu mortalium
non habes quare verearis ; nulla illi nec tribuendi
nec nocendi materia est ; in medio intervallo huius
et alterius caeli desertus sine animali, sine homine,
sine re ruinas mundorum supra se circaque se caden-
tium evitat non exaudiens vota nec nostri curiosus.
3 Atqui hunc vis videri colere non aliter quam parentem
grato, ut opinor, animo ; aut, si non vis gratus videri,
quia nullum habes illius beneficium, sed te atomi
et istae micae tuae forte ac temere conglobaverunt,
4 cur colis ? " Propter maiestatem," inquis, " eius

---

[1] hoc *O* : haec *M, Hosius.*

---

[a] According to the Epicureans, the gods dwelt in the
intermundia—the spaces between the countless worlds of
infinity.
[b] The atomic theory of matter, upon which the Epicurean
system was founded, was a common source of ridicule.

checked the assaults of disease, has made ready supports for old age, has provided solace for sorrow ; it is this that makes us brave, this that we may invoke as a help against Fortune. Take away this fellowship, and you will sever the unity of the human race on which its very existence depends ; yet you will take it away if you succeed in proving that ingratitude is to be avoided, not because of itself, but because it has something to fear ; for how many there are who might safely be ungrateful ! In fine, any man who is made grateful by fear I call ungrateful.

No sane man fears the gods ; for it is madness to fear what is beneficial, and no one loves those whom he fears. You, Epicurus, in the end leave God unarmed, you have stripped him of all his weapons, of all his power, and, in order that no one may have need to fear him, you have thrust him beyond the range of fear. Surrounded, therefore, as he is, by a vast and impassable wall, and removed beyond the reach and sight of mortals, you have no reason to stand in awe of him ; he has no means of bestowing either blessing or injury ; in the space that separates our own from some other heaven [a] he dwells alone, without a living creature, without a human being, without a possession, and avoids the destruction of the worlds that crash around and above him, having no ear for our prayers and no concern for us. And yet you wish to seem to worship this being, from a feeling of gratitude, I suppose, as if he were a father ; or, if you do not wish to seem grateful, because you have from him not a single benefit, but are yourself merely a combination of atoms [b] and of those mites of yours that have met blindly and by chance, why do you worship him? "Because of his glorious majesty,"

eximiam ac singularem naturam." Ut concedam tibi, nempe hoc facis nullo pretio inductus, nulla spe; est ergo aliquid per se expetendum, cuius te ipsa dignitas ducit, id est honestum. Quid est autem honestius, quam gratum esse? Huius virtutis materia tam late patet quam vita.

1 20. "Sed inest," inquit, "huic bono etiam utilitas aliqua." Cui enim virtuti non inest? Sed id propter se expeti dicitur, quod, quamvis habeat aliqua extra commoda, sepositis quoque illis ac remotis placet. Prodest gratum esse; ero tamen gratus, etiam si 2 nocet. Gratus quid sequitur? Ut haec res illi alios amicos, alia beneficia conciliet? Quid ergo? Si quis sibi offensas concitaturus est, si quis intellegit adeo per hoc se nihil consecuturum, ut multa etiam ex reposito adquisitoque perdenda sint, non libens 3 in detrimenta descendit? Ingratus est, qui in referenda gratia secundum datum videt, qui sperat, cum reddit. Ingratum voco, qui aegro adsidit, quia testamentum facturus est, cui de hereditate aut de legato vacat cogitare. Faciat licet omnia, quae facere bonus amicus et memor officii debet: si animo eius obversatur spes lucri, captator est et hamum iacit. Ut aves, quae laceratione corporum aluntur, lassa morbo pecora et casura ex proximo speculantur, ita hic imminet morti et circa cadaver volat.

you say, " and his exceptional nature." Granting
that you do this, you clearly do it without the inducement of any reward, of any expectation ; there is,
therefore, something that is desirable in itself, whose
very worth induces you, that is, the honourable.
But what is more honourable than gratitude ? The
opportunity for this virtue is limited only by life.

" But this good," you say, " has in it also some
element of profit." What virtue, indeed, has not ?
But that is said to be desired because of itself
which, although it possesses some outside advantages, still pleases even when these have been
stripped off and removed. There is advantage in
being grateful ; yet I shall be grateful even if it
harms me. And what is the aim of one who is
grateful ? Is it that his gratitude may win for him
more friends, more benefits ? What, then, if a man is
likely to arouse disfavour by it, if a man knows that,
so far from being likely to gain anything by it, he
must lose much from the store that he has already
acquired, does he not gladly submit to his losses ?
He is ungrateful who in the act of repaying gratitude
has an eye on a second gift—who hopes while he
repays. I call him ungrateful who sits at the bedside
of a sick man because he is going to make his will,
who finds room for any thought of an inheritance or
a legacy. Though he should do everything that a
good and thoughtful friend ought to do, if his mind
is haunted by the hope of gain, he is only a fisher for
legacies and is just dropping his hook. As birds of
prey that feed upon carcasses keep watch near by
the flocks that are spent with disease and are ready
to drop, so such a man gloats over a death-bed and
hovers about the corpse.

1   21. Gratus animus ipsa virtute propositi sui capitur.
Vis scire hoc ita esse nec illum utilitate corrumpi?
Duo genera sunt grati hominis. Dicitur gratus, qui
aliquid pro eo, quod acceperat, reddidit; hic fortasse
ostentare se potest, habet, quod iactet, quod proferat.
Dicitur gratus, qui bono animo accepit beneficium,
2 bono debet; hic intra conscientiam clusus est. Quae
illi contingere potest utilitas ex adfectu latenti?
Atqui hic, etiam si ultra facere nil potest, gratus est.
Amat, debet, referre gratiam cupit; quidquid ultra
3 desideras, non ipse deest.[a] Artifex est etiam, cui ad
exercendam artem instrumenta non suppetunt, nec
minus canendi peritus, cuius vocem exaudiri fremitus
obstrepentium non sinit. Volo referre gratiam: post
hoc aliquid superest mihi, non ut gratus, sed ut solutus
sim; saepe enim et qui gratiam rettulit, ingratus
est, et qui non rettulit, gratus. Nam ut omnium
aliarum virtutum, ita huius ad animum tota aestimatio redit; hic si in officio est, quidquid defuit,
4 fortuna peccat. Quomodo est disertus etiam qui
tacet, fortis etiam qui compressis manibus vel etiam
adligatis, quomodo gubernator etiam, qui in sicco est,
quia consummatae scientiae nihil deest, etiam si quid
obstat, quominus se utatur, ita gratus est etiam, qui
vult tantum nec habet huius voluntatis suae ullum

---

        [a] *i.e.*, a man shows himself grateful by the mere desire to
repay; he then frees himself from all obligation by actual
repayment.

But the grateful heart is attracted by the very excellence of its purpose. Do you wish proof that this is so, and that it is not corrupted by the idea of profit ? There are two classes of grateful men. One man is said to be grateful because he has made return for something that he received ; he, perhaps, is able to make himself conspicuous, has something to boast about, something to publish. He, too, is said to be grateful who has accepted a benefit in good spirit, who owes in good spirit ; this man keeps his gratitude shut up in his heart. What profit can he gain from this hidden feeling ? Yet such a man, even if he is able to do no more than this, is grateful. He loves, is conscious of his debt, desires to repay the favour ; whatever else you may find wanting, nothing is wanting in the man himself. A man may be an artist even if he does not have at hand the tools for practising his craft, nor is one less a trained singer if the noise of those who are crying him down does not permit his voice to be heard. I wish to repay a favour : after this something is left for me to do, not in order to become grateful, but in order to become free [a] ; for it often happens that he who has repaid a favour is ungrateful, and he who has not repaid it is grateful. For, as in the case of all the others, the true estimate of this virtue is concerned wholly with the heart ; if this does its duty, whatever else is lacking is the fault of Fortune. Just as a man can be fluent in speech even if he is silent, brave even if his hands are folded, or even tied, just as a man can be a pilot even when he is on dry land, since there is no deficiency in the completeness of his knowledge even though something prevents him from using it, so also a man is grateful who only wishes to be so, and has

5 alium quam se testem. Immo amplius adiciam : est
aliquando gratus etiam qui ingratus videtur, quem
mala interpres opinio contrarium tradidit. Hic quid
aliud sequitur quam ipsam conscientiam ? Quae
etiam obruta delectat, quae contioni ac famae re-
clamat et in se omnia reponit et, cum ingentem ex
altera parte turbam contra sentientium adspexit, non
6 numerat suffragia, sed una sententia vincit. Si vero
bonam fidem perfidiae suppliciis adfici videt, non
descendit e fastigio et supra poenam suam consistit.
" Habeo," inquit, " quod volui, quod petii ; nec
paenitet nec paenitebit nec ulla iniquitate me eo
fortuna perducet, ut hanc vocem audiat : ' Quid mihi
volui ? Quid nunc mihi prodest bona voluntas ? ' "
Prodest et in eculeo, prodest et in igne ; qui si
singulis membris admoveatur et paulatim vivum
corpus circumeat, licet ipsum cor plenum bona conscientia stillet : placebit illi ignis, per quem bona
fides conlucebit.

1 22. Nunc illud quoque argumentum quamvis dictum iam reducatur : quid est, quare grati velimus
esse, cum morimur, quare singulorum perpendamus
officia, quare id agamus in omnem vitam nostram
memoria decernente, ne cuius officii videamur obliti ?
Nihil iam superest, quo spes porrigatur ; in illo tamen

none besides himself to bear witness to this desire. And I will go even further than this—sometimes a man is grateful even when he appears to be ungrateful, when rumour with its evil tongue has given the opposite report of him. What guide has this man but his own conscience ? Crushed though it be, this gives him cheer, this cries out against the mob and hearsay, and relies wholly upon itself, and, when it sees the vast crowd of those on the other side who think differently, it does not take trouble to count votes, but wins the victory by its single vote. If it sees its own loyalty subjected to the chastisements reserved for treachery, it does not descend from its pinnacle, but abides there superior to its punishment. " I have," it says, " what I wished, what I strove for ; I do not regret it, nor shall I ever regret it, and no injustice of Fortune shall ever bring me to such a pass that she will hear me say : ' What was it I wished ? What profit have I now from my good intention ? ' " I have profit even on the rack, I have profit even in the fire ; though fire should devour my limbs one by one, and gradually encircle my living body, though my very heart, brimming with conscious virtue, should drip with blood, it will delight in the flame through which its loyalty will shine forth.

The following argument also, although it has already been used, may be reapplied here : why is it that we wish to be grateful at the hour of death, that we carefully weigh the services of each one, that, with memory as judge of the whole of our life, we try to avoid the appearance of having forgotten the service of any ? Nothing then is left for us to hope for ; nevertheless, as we pause upon the threshold, we

cardine positi abire e rebus humanis quam gratissimi
2 volumus. Est videlicet magna in ipso opere merces
rei et ad adliciendas mentes hominum ingens honesti
potentia, cuius pulchritudo animos circumfundit et
delenitos admiratione luminis ac fulgoris sui rapit.
3 At multa hoc commoda oriuntur, et tutior est vita
melioribus amorque et secundum bonorum iudicium
aetasque securior, quam innocentia, quam grata mens
prosequitur. Fuisset enim iniquissima rerum natura,
si hoc tantum bonum miserum et anceps et sterile
fecisset. Sed illud intuere, an ad istam virtutem,
quae saepe tuta ac facili aditur via, etiam per saxa
et rupes et feris ac serpentibus obsessum iter fueris
4 iturus. Non ideo per se non est expetendum, cui
aliquid extra quoque emolumenti adhaeret ; fere enim
pulcherrima quaeque multis et adventiciis comitata
sunt dotibus, sed illas trahunt, ipsa praecedunt.
1 23. Num dubium est, quin hoc humani generis
domicilium circumitus solis ac lunae vicibus suis tem-
peret ? Quin alterius calore alantur corpora, terrae
relaxentur, immodici umores comprimantur, adli-
gantis omnia hiemis tristitia frangatur, alterius tepore
efficaci et penetrabili regatur maturitas frugum ?
Quin ad huius cursum fecunditas humana respondeat?

wish to appear as grateful as possible at the time of our departure from human affairs. It is evident that the great reward for an action lies in the deed itself, and that virtue has great power in influencing the minds of men, for souls are flooded with its beauty, and, marvelling at the brilliance and splendour of it, are transported with enchantment. " But there are many advantages," you say, " that spring from it; good men live in greater security, and have the love and respect of good men, and existence is less troubled when accompanied by innocence and gratitude." Nature would, indeed, have been most unjust if she had made so great a good an unhappy and uncertain and unfruitful thing. But the point to consider is whether you would turn your steps toward this virtue, which often is reached by a safe and easy way, even though the path lay over rocks and precipices, and was beset with wild beasts and serpents. It is not true, therefore, that that which has also some extraneous profit closely attached to it is not something to be desired in itself; for in most cases the things that are most beautiful are accompanied by many accessory advantages, but they follow in the train of beauty while she leads the way.

Does anyone doubt that the sun and the moon in their periodic revolutions exercise an influence upon this abiding-place of the human race ? That the heat of the one gives life to our bodies, loosens the hard earth, reduces excessive moisture, and breaks off the bonds of gloomy winter that enchains all things, while the warmth of the other with its efficacious and pervasive power determines the ripening of the crops ? That there is some relation between human fecundity and the course of the moon ? That the one by its

251

Quin ille annum observabilem fecerit circumactu suo,
2 haec mensem minoribus se spatiis flectens? Ut
tamen detrahas ista, non erat ipse sol idoneum oculis
spectaculum dignusque adorari, si tantum praeteriret?
Non erat digna suspectu luna, etiam si otiosum sidus
transcurreret? Ipse mundus, quotiens per noctem
ignes suos fudit et tantum stellarum innumerabilium
refulsit, quem non intentum in se tenet? Quis sibi
3 illa tunc, cum miratur, prodesse cogitat? Adspice
ista tanto superne coetu labentia, quemadmodum
velocitatem suam sub specie stantis atque immoti
operis abscondant. Quantum ista nocte, quam tu in
numerum ac discrimen dierum observas, agitur!
Quanta rerum turba sub hoc silentio evolvitur!
4 Quantam fatorum seriem certus limes educit! Ista,
quae tu non aliter, quam in decorem sparsa consideras,
singula in opere sunt. Nec enim est, quod existimes
septem sola discurrere, cetera haerere; paucorum
motus comprehendimus, innumerabiles vero longius-
que a conspectu seducti di eunt redeuntque, et ex
his, qui oculos nostros patiuntur, plerique obscuro
gradu pergunt et per occultum aguntur.
1   24. Quid ergo? Non caperis tantae molis adspectu, etiam si te non tegat, non custodiat, non
foveat generetque ac spiritu suo riget? Quemadmodum haec cum primum usum habeant et neces-

---

^a The Stoics counted the heavenly bodies divine.

circuit marks out the year, and the other, moving in
a smaller orbit, the month ? Yet, although these
advantages should be removed, would not the sun
itself form a fitting spectacle for our eyes, and be
worthy of our adoration if it merely passed across the
sky ? Would not the moon be a sight worthy of our
eyes even if it traversed heaven as idly as a star ?
And the firmament itself—who is not held spellbound
by it whenever it pours forth its fires by night and
glitters with its horde of countless stars ? Who, when
he marvels at them, stops to think of their utility to
himself ? Behold the mighty company as it glides
by overhead, how, under the appearance of an
organism that is immovable and at rest, its members
conceal from us their speed. How much takes place
in that night of which we take note only for the
purpose of numbering and distinguishing the days !
What a multitude of events is being unrolled beneath
this silence ! What a chain of destiny is being traced
by their unerring path ! These bodies, which you
imagine have been strewn about for no other purpose
than for ornament, are one and all at work. For there
is no reason why you should suppose that there are
only seven wandering stars, and that all the others are
fixed ; there are a few whose movements we appre-
hend, but, farther removed from our sight, are countless divinities *a* that go their rounds, and very many
of those that our eyes can reach proceed at an im-
perceptible pace and veil their movements.

Tell me, would you not be captivated by the sight
of such a mighty structure even if it did not cover
you, guard you, cherish you and give you birth, and
permeate you with its spirit ? As the heavenly
bodies have primarily their use, and are necessary

saria vitaliaque sint, maiestas tamen eorum totam
mentem occupat, ita omnis illa virtus et in primis
grati animi multum quidem praestat, sed non vult
ob hoc diligi ; amplius quiddam in se habet nec satis
ab eo intellegitur a quo inter utilia numeratur.

2 Gratus est, quia expedit ? Ergo et quantum expedit ?
Non recipit sordidum virtus amatorem ; soluto ad
illam sinu veniendum est. Ingratus hoc cogitat :
" Volebam gratiam referre, sed timeo impensam,
timeo periculum, vereor offensam ; faciam potius,
quod expedit." Non potest eadem ratio et gratum
facere et ingratum ; ut diversa illorum opera, ita
diversa inter se proposita sunt. Ille ingratus est,
quamvis non oporteat, quia expedit ; hic gratus est,
quamvis non expediat, quia oportet.

1 25. Propositum est nobis secundum rerum naturam
vivere et deorum exemplum sequi. Di autem, quodcumque faciunt, in eo quid praeter ipsam faciendi
rationem secuntur ? Nisi forte illos existimas fructum operum suorum ex fumo extorum et turis odore

2 percipere ! Vide, quanta cotidie moliantur, quanta
distribuant ; quantis terras fructibus impleant, quam
opportunis et in omnes oras ferentibus ventis maria
permoveant, quantis imbribus repente deiectis solum
molliant venasque fontium arentes redintegrent et
infuso per occulta nutrimento novent. Omnia ista

---

a *i.e.*, the Stoic God, the active principle in the universe,
must by the very necessity of his being be given to action.

254

and vital to us, while it is their majesty that wholly occupies our minds, so virtue in general, and particularly that of gratitude, while it does indeed bestow much upon us, does not wish to be cherished because of this ; it has in it something more, and he who counts it merely among the useful things has not properly comprehended it. Is a man grateful because it is to his advantage ? Accordingly, also to the extent that it is to his advantage ? But Virtue does not open her door to a niggardly lover ; he must come to her with an open purse. It is the ungrateful man who thinks : " I should have liked to return gratitude, but I fear the expense, I fear the danger, I shrink from giving offence ; I would rather consult my own interest." It is not possible to render men grateful and ungrateful by the same line of reasoning ; as their actions are different, their intentions are different. The one is ungrateful, although he ought not to be, because it is to his interest ; the other is grateful, although it is not to his interest, because he ought to be.

It is our aim to live according to Nature, and to follow the example of the gods. Yet, in all their acts, what inducement have the gods other than the very principle of action [a] ? Unless perchance you suppose that they obtain a reward for their deeds from the smoke of burnt offerings and the odour of incense ! See the gigantic efforts they make every day, the great largesses they dispense ; with what wealth of crops they fill the land, with what favourable winds that bear us to all shores they ruffle the seas, with what mighty rains, suddenly hurled down, they soften the soil, renew the dried sources of springs, and, flooding them with secret nourishment, give them new life.

sine mercede, sine ullo ad ipsos perveniente commodo
3 faciunt.   Hoc nostra quoque ratio, si ab exemplari
suo non aberrat, servet, ne ad res honestas conducta
veniat.   Pudeat ullum venale esse beneficium : gra-
tuitos habemus deos !

1   26. " Si deos," inquit, " imitaris, da et ingratis
beneficia ; nam et sceleratis sol oritur et piratis patent
maria."   Hoc loco interrogant, an vir bonus daturus
sit beneficium ingrato sciens ingratum esse.   Per-
mitte mihi aliquid interloqui, ne interrogatione insi-
2 diosa capiamur.   Duos ex constitutione Stoica accipe
ingratos.   Alter est ingratus, quia stultus est ; stultus
etiam malus est ; quia malus est, nullo vitio caret :
ergo et ingratus est.   Sic omnes malos intemperantes
dicimus, avaros, luxuriosos, malignos, non quia omnia
ista singulis magna et nota vitia sunt, sed quia esse
possunt ; et sunt, etiam si latent.   Alter est ingratus, qui volgo dicitur, in hoc vitium natura pro-
3 pensus.   Illi ingrato, qui sic hac culpa non caret,
quomodo nulla caret, dabit beneficium vir bonus ;
nulli enim dare poterit, si tales homines submoverit.
Huic ingrato, qui beneficiorum fraudator est et in

---

a According to a Stoic commonplace, the *sapiens* has all
the virtues, and so the *stultus* all the vices.
256

They do all these things without any reward, without attaining any advantage for themselves. Our rule also, if it would not depart from its model, should observe this principle of never proceeding to virtuous acts for pay. We should be ashamed to set a price on any benefit whatsoever—the gods are ours for nothing !

"If you are imitating the gods," you say, "then bestow benefits also upon the ungrateful ; for the sun rises also upon the wicked, and the sea lies open also to pirates." This point raises the question whether a good man would bestow a benefit upon one who was ungrateful, knowing that he was ungrateful. Permit me here to put in a brief remark for fear that we may be trapped by the tricky question. Understand that, according to the system of the Stoics, there are two classes of ungrateful persons. One man is ungrateful because he is a fool ; a fool is also a bad man [a] ; because he is a bad man, he possesses every vice : therefore he is also ungrateful. Thus we say that all bad men are intemperate, greedy, voluptuous, and spiteful, not because every individual has all these vices in a great or marked degree, but because he is capable of having them ; and he does have them even if they are not visible. Another man is ungrateful, and this is the common meaning of the term, because he has a natural tendency to this vice. To an ingrate of the first type, the man who possesses this fault for the reason that there is no fault that he does not possess, a good man will give his benefit ; for, if he were to eliminate all such men, there would be no one to whom he could give. To the ingrate of the second type, the man who in the matter of benefits shows himself a cheat, and has a natural bent

hanc partem procubuit animo, non magis dabit beneficium, quam decoctori pecuniam credet aut depositum committet ei, qui iam pluribus abnegavit.

1 27. Timidus dicitur aliquis, quia stultus est: et
hoc malos sequitur, quos indiscreta et universa vitia
circumstant; dicitur timidus proprie natura etiam
ad inanes sonos pavidus. Stultus omnia vitia habet,
sed non in omnia natura pronus est; alius in avaritiam, alius in luxuriam, alius in petulantiam inclinatur.

2 Itaque errant illi, qui interrogant Stoicos : "Quid
ergo ? Achilles timidus est ? Quid ergo ? Aristides,
cui iustitia nomen dedit, iniustus est ? Quid ergo ?
Et Fabius, qui 'cunctando restituit rem,' temerarius
est ? Quid ergo ? Decius mortem timet ? Mucius
proditor est ? Camillus desertor ?" Non hoc dicimus sic omnia vitia esse in omnibus, quomodo in
quibusdam singula eminent, sed malum ac stultum
nullo vitio vacare ; ne audacem quidem timoris absol-

3 vimus, ne prodigum quidem avaritia liberamus. Quomodo homo omnes sensus habet nec ideo tamen
omnes homines aciem habent Lynceo similem, sic,
qui stultus est, non tam acria et concitata habet
omnia, quam quidam quaedam. Omnia in omnibus
vitia sunt, sed non omnia in singulis extant. Hunc
natura ad avaritiam impellit ; hic vino, hic libidini
deditus est aut, si nondum deditus, ita formatus, ut
in hoc illum mores sui ferant.

---

[a] An oft-quoted characterization drawn from the *Annales*
of Ennius.

[b] In legend he could see through the earth and discern
objects at the distance of many miles.

in this direction, he will no more give a benefit than he will lend money to a spendthrift, or entrust a deposit to a man whom many have already found false.

There is the man who is called timid because he is a fool; and because of this he is classed with the bad men who are beset by all vices without distinction and without exception. But, strictly speaking, a timid man is one who because of a natural weakness grows alarmed even at unmeaning noises. The fool possesses all vices, but he is not inclined by nature to all; one man inclines to greed, another to luxury, another to insolence. Therefore it is a mistake for persons to put such questions as these to the Stoics: "Tell me, is Achilles timid? Tell me, is Aristides, whose name stood for justice, unjust? Tell me, is even Fabius, 'who retrieved the situation by his delays,'[a] rash? Tell me, is Decius afraid of death? Mucius a traitor? Camillus a deserter?" We do not say that all men possess all vices in the same way in which certain men display particular vices, but that the bad and foolish man is not exempt from any vice; we do not acquit even the bold man of fear, nor absolve even the spendthrift from avarice. Just as a man has all the five senses, and yet all men do not for that reason have as keen sight as Lynceus,[b] so, if a man is a fool, he does not possess all the vices in the same active and vigorous form in which some persons possess some of them. All the vices exist in all men, yet not all are equally prominent in each individual. This man's nature impels him to greed; this one is a victim of wine, this one of lust, or, if he is not yet a victim, he is so constituted that his natural impulses lead him in this direction.

4 Itaque, ut ad propositum revertar, nemo non ingratus est, qui malus : habet enim omnia nequitiae
semina ; tamen proprie ingratus appellatur, qui ad
hoc vitium vergit. Huic ergo beneficium non dabo.
5 Quomodo male filiae suae consulet, qui illam con-
tumelioso et saepe repudiato collocavit, malus pater
familiae habebitur, qui negotiorum gestorum damnato
patrimonii sui curam mandaverit, quomodo demen-
tissime testabitur, qui tutorem filio reliquerit pupil-
lorum spoliatorem, sic pessime beneficia dare dicetur,
quicumque ingratos eligit, in quos peritura conferat.
1 28. " Di quoque," inquit, " multa ingratis tri-
buunt." Sed illa bonis paraverunt ; contingunt
autem etiam malis, quia separari non possunt. Satius
est autem prodesse etiam malis propter bonos, quam
bonis deesse propter malos. Ita, quae refers, diem,
solem, hiemis aestatisque cursus et media veris
autumnique temperamenta, imbres et fontium
haustus, ventorum statos flatus pro universis in-
2 venerunt ; excerpere singulos non potuerunt. Rex
honores dignis dat, congiarium et indignis ; frumentum publicum tam fur quam periurus et adulter
accipiunt et sine dilectu morum, quisquis incisus est ;

And so, to return to my original proposition, everyone who is bad is ungrateful, for he has in him all the seeds of wrongdoing ; yet, strictly speaking, the man who is termed ungrateful is one who has a bent toward this vice. To such a man, consequently, I shall not give a benefit. As a father who betroths his daughter to an overbearing man who has been often divorced will disregard her best interests, as he who entrusts the care of his patrimony to one who has been condemned for the bad management of his affairs will be considered a poor head of a household, as it will be the veriest madness for a man to make a will naming as the guardian of his son one who is known to be a robber of wards, so he will be counted the worst of benefactors who chooses ungrateful persons in order to bestow upon them gifts that are doomed to perish.

"Even the gods," you say, "confer many blessings upon the ungrateful." But they designed them for the good ; yet the bad also share in them because they cannot be separated from the others. It is better, too, to benefit also the bad for the sake of the good than to fail the good for the sake of the bad. So the blessings you cite—the day, the sun, the succession of summer and winter and the intermediate seasons of spring and autumn with their milder temperature, rains and springs to drink from, and winds that blow in fixed season—these the gods have devised for the good of all ; they could not make an exception of individuals. A king gives honours to the worthy, but largesses even to the unworthy ; the thief no less than the perjurer and the adulterer and everyone, without distinction of character, whose name appears on the register receives grain from the state ; whatever else

quidquid aliud est, quod tamquam civi, non tamquam
3 bono datur, ex aequo boni ac mali ferunt. Deus
quoque quaedam munera universo humano generi
dedit, a quibus excluditur nemo. Nec enim poterat
fieri, ut ventus bonis viris secundus esset, contrarius
malis, communi autem bono erat patere commercium
maris et regnum humani generis relaxari ; nec poterat
lex casuris imbribus dici, ne in malorum improborum-
4 que rura defluerent. Quaedam in medio ponuntur.
Tam bonis quam malis conduntur urbes ; monumenta
ingeniorum et ad indignos perventura publicavit
editio ; medicina etiam sceleratis opem monstrat ;
compositiones remediorum salutarium nemo sup-
5 pressit, ne sanarentur indigni. In iis exige censuram
et personarum aestimationem, quae separatim tamquam digno dantur, non in his, quae promiscue turbam admittunt. Multum enim refert, utrum aliquem
non excludas an eligas. Ius et furi dicitur ; pace et
homicidae fruuntur ; sua repetunt etiam, qui aliena
rapuerunt ; percussores et domi ferrum exercentes
murus ab hoste defendit ; legum praesidio, qui pluri-
6 mum in illas peccaverunt, proteguntur. Quaedam non
poterant ceteris contingere, nisi universis darentur ;
non est itaque, quod de istis disputes, ad quae publice

a man may be, he gets his dole, not because he is
good, but because he is a citizen, and the good and the
bad share alike.   God also has given certain gifts to
the whole human race, and from these no man is shut
out.   For, while it was to the common good that traffic
on the sea should be open to all, and that the kingdom
of mankind should be enlarged, it was impossible to
cause the same wind to be favourable for the good and
adverse for the bad ; nor was it possible to appoint a
law for the fall of the rains in order that they might
not descend upon the fields of wicked and dishonest
men.   Certain blessings are offered to all.   Cities are
founded as much for the bad as for the good ; works
of genius, even if they will fall into the hands of the
unworthy, are published for everybody ; medicine
points out its healing power even to criminals ; no
one has banned the compounding of wholesome
remedies for fear that they may heal the unworthy.
In the case of the gifts that are specifically bestowed
because the recipient is worthy, apply the rule of
censorship and of rating the person, but not so in the
case of those that are open to the mob.   There is a
great difference between not excluding a man and
choosing him.   Justice is vouchsafed even to the
thief ; even murderers taste the blessings of peace ;
those who have stolen the property of others even
recover their own ; assassins and those who ply their
swords on the city streets are protected from the
public enemy by the city wall ; the laws shield with
their protection those who have sinned most against
them.   There are certain blessings that could not
have fallen to a few unless they were given to all ;
there is no need, therefore, for you to argue about
the benefits to which we have received a public

invitati sumus. Illud, quod iudicio meo ad aliquem pervenire debebit, ei, quem esse ingratum sciam, non dabo.

1 29. "Ergo," inquit, "nec consilium deliberanti dabis ingrato nec aquam haurire permittes nec viam monstrabis erranti ? An haec quidem facies, sed nihil donabis ? " Distinguam istud, certe temptabo 2 distinguere. Beneficium est opera utilis, sed non omnis opera utilis beneficium est ; quaedam enim tam exigua sunt, ut beneficii nomen non occupent. Duae res coire debent, quae beneficium efficiant. Primum rei magnitudo ; quaedam enim sunt infra huius nominis mensuram. Quis beneficium dixit quadram panis aut stipem aeris abiecti aut ignis accendendi factam potestatem ? Et interdum ista plus prosunt, quam maxima ; sed tamen vilitas sua illis, etiam ubi temporis necessitate facta sunt neces-3 saria, detrahit pretium. Deinde hoc, quod potentissimum est, oportet accedat, ut eius causa faciam, ad quem volam pervenire beneficium, dignumque eum iudicem et libens id tribuam percipiensque ex munere meo gaudium, quorum nihil est in istis, de quibus loquebamur ; non enim tamquam dignis illa tribuimus, sed neclegenter tamquam parva, et non homini damus, sed humanitati.

1 30. Aliquando daturum me etiam indignis quaedam non negaverim in honorem aliorum, sicut in

invitation. But that which must go to a beneficiary of my own choosing will not be given to a man whom I know to be ungrateful.

"Will you, then," you ask, "neither give counsel to an ungrateful man when he is perplexed, nor permit him to have a drink of water, nor point out the path to him if he has lost his way? Or will you do all these services, and yet not be making a gift?" Here I shall draw a distinction, or at least endeavour to do so. A benefit is a useful service, but not every useful service is a benefit; for some services are too small to have the right to be called benefits. In order to produce a benefit, there must be a combination of two conditions. The first is the importance of the service; for there are some that fall short of the dignity of the claim. Who ever called a morsel of bread a benefit, or tossing anyone a copper, or enabling him to get a light? And sometimes these are more helpful than very large gifts; yet, for all that, their cheapness detracts from their value even when the necessity of the moment has made them necessities. A second condition, which is most important, that must supplement the other, is that the motive of my action must be the interest of the one for whom the benefit is destined, that I should deem him worthy of it, should bestow it willingly and derive pleasure from my gift; but none of those services of which we were just speaking bears any of these marks, for we bestow them, not with the thought that the recipients are worthy, but carelessly and as mere trifles, and our gift is made, not so much to a man, as to humanity.

I shall not deny that sometimes I shall give even to the unworthy in order to do honour to others; as,

265

petendis honoribus quosdam turpissimos nobilitas
industriis sed novis praetulit non sine ratione. Sacra
est magnarum virtutum memoria, et esse plures bonos
2 iuvat, si gratia bonorum non cum ipsis cadit. Cicero-
nem filium quae res consulem fecit nisi pater ?
Cinnam nuper quae res ad consulatum recepit ex
hostium castris, quae Sex. Pompeium aliosque Pom-
peios, nisi unius viri magnitudo tanta quondam, ut
satis alte omnes suos etiam ruina eius attolleret ?
Quid nuper Fabium Persicum, cuius osculum etiam
impudici denotabant, sacerdotem non in uno collegio
fecit nisi Verrucosi et Allobrogici et illi trecenti, qui
hostium incursioni pro re publica unam domum
3 obiecerant ? Hoc debemus virtutibus, ut non prae-
sentes solum illas, sed etiam ablatas e conspectu
colamus ; quomodo illae id egerunt, ut non in unam
aetatem prodessent, sed beneficia sua etiam post ipsas
relinquerent, ita nos non una aetate grati simus. Hic
magnos viros genuit : dignus est beneficiis, qualis-
4 cumque est ; dignos dedit. Hic egregiis maioribus
ortus est : qualiscumque est, sub umbra suorum
lateat. Ut loca sordida repercussu solis illustrantur,
ita inertes maiorum suorum luce resplendeant.

---

[a] Gnaeus Cinna, grandson of Pompey the Great.
[b] Paullus Fabius Persicus, consul A.D. 34, a scion of the
old and distinguished family of the Fabii, to which specific
reference is made below. Verrucosus, "the Warty," better
known as *Cunctator*, "the Delayer," was the famous
opponent of Hannibal after the disaster at Lake Trasumenus
(217 B.C.) ; Allobrogicus, consul 121 B.C., by his victory over
the Allobroges decided the mastery of southern Gaul.
[c] Livy (ii. 50) tells the story of the brave action of the
whole clan, three hundred and six in number, against the
Veientes in 477 B.C.

for instance, in the competition for public office some of the most disreputable men are preferred to others who are industrious, but of no family, by reason of their noble birth, and not without reason. For sacred is the memory of great virtues, and more people find pleasure in being good, if the influence of good men does not end with their lives. To what did Cicero's son owe the consulship if not to his father ? What recently took Cinna [a] from the camp of the enemy, and raised him to the consulship, what Sextus Pompeius and the other Pompeii, unless it was the greatness of one man, who once reached such a height that even his downfall sufficed to exalt all his descendants ? What recently made Fabius Persicus [b] a priest in more than one college, a man whose kiss even the shameless counted an insult ? What but a Verrucosus and an Allobrogicus and the famous three hundred,[c] who, to save their country, blocked the invasion of the enemy with their single family ? This is the duty we owe to the virtuous—to honour them, not only when they are present with us, but even when they have been taken from our sight ; as they have made it their aim, not to confine their services to one age alone, but to leave behind their benefits even after they themselves have passed away, so let us not confine our gratitude to one age alone. So-and-so was the father of great men : whatever he may be, he is worthy of our benefits ; he has given us worthy sons. So-and-so is descended from glorious ancestors : whatever he may be, let him find refuge under the shadow of his ancestry. As filthy places become bright from the radiance of the sun, so let the degenerate shine in the light of their forefathers.

1   31. Excusare hoc loco tibi, mi Liberalis, deos volo.
Interdum enim solemus dicere : " Quid sibi voluit
providentia, quae Arrhidaeum regno imposuit ? "
2 Illi putas hoc datum ? Patri eius datum est et fratri.
" Quare C.¹ Caesarem orbi terrarum praefecit, hominem sanguinis humani avidissimum, quem non
aliter fluere in conspectu suo iubebat, quam si ore
excepturus esset ? " Quid ergo ? Tu hoc illi datum
existimas ? Patri eius Germanico datum, avo pro-
avoque et ante hos aliis non minus claris viris, etiam
3 si privati paresque aliis vitam exegerunt. Quid ?
Tu, cum Mamercum Scaurum consulem faceres,
ignorabas ancillarum illum suarum menstruum ore
hiante exceptare ? Numquid enim ipse dissimulabat?
Numquid purus videri volebat ? Referam tibi dictum
eius in se, quod circumferri memini et ipso praesente
4 laudari. Pollioni Annio iacenti obsceno verbo usus
dixerat se facturum id, quod pati malebat ; et cum
Pollionis adtractiorem vidisset frontem : " Quidquid," inquit, " mali dixi, mihi et capiti meo ! " Hoc
5 dictum suum ipse narrabat. Hominem tam palam ob-
scenum ad fasces et ad tribunal admisisti ? Nempe
dum veterem illum Scaurum senatus principem cogitas
et indigne fers subolem eius iacere.

¹ C. *added by Muretus.*

ᵃ The imbecile half-brother of Alexander the Great.
ᵇ A dissolute orator and poet under the emperor Tiberius.
ᶜ Marcus Aemilius Scaurus, consul 115 B.C., raised his
family from obscurity to the highest distinction.

At this point, Liberalis, I wish to offer a defence of the gods. For sometimes we are moved to say : " What could Providence mean by putting on the throne an Arrhidaeus *a* ? " Was it to him, think you, that the honour was accorded ? It was accorded to his father and to his brother. " Why did it make Gaius Caesar the ruler of the world ?—a man so greedy of human blood that he ordered it to be shed in his presence as freely as if he intended to catch the stream in his mouth ! " But tell me, do you think that it was to him this was accorded ? It was accorded to his father Germanicus, to his grandfather and to his great-grandfather, and to others before them, men who were no less glorious, even if they passed their lives as private citizens on a footing of equality with others. Why, when you yourself were supporting Mamercus Scaurus *b* for the consulship, were you not aware that he would try to catch in his open mouth the menstrual discharge of his own maidservants ? Did he himself make any mystery of it ? Did he wish to appear to be decent ? I will repeat to you a story that he told on himself—it went the rounds, I recall, and was recounted in his presence. To Annius Pollio who was lying down he had proposed, using an obscene word, an act that he was more ready to submit to, and when he saw Pollio frown, he added : " If there is anything bad in what I have said, may it fall upon me and my head ! " This story he used to tell against himself. Is it this man, so openly obscene, that you have admitted to the fasces and the tribunal ? Of course it was while you were thinking of the great old Scaurus,*c* who was president of the senate, and chafing to see his offspring obscure !

1 32. Idem facere[1] deos veri simile est, ut alios indulgentius tractent propter parentes avosque, alios propter futuram nepotum pronepotumque ac longe sequentium posterorum indolem ; nota enim illis est operis sui series, omniumque illis rerum per manus suas iturarum scientia in aperto semper est ; nobis ex abdito subit, et, quae repentina putamus, illis provisa veniunt ac familiaria.

2 " Sint hi reges, quia maiores eorum non fuerunt, quia pro summo imperio habuerunt iustitiam, abstinentiam, quia non rem publicam sibi, sed se rei publicae dicaverunt. Regnent hi, quia vir bonus quidam ante proavus eorum fuit, qui animum supra fortunam gessit, qui in dissensione civili, quoniam ita expediebat rei publicae, vinci quam vincere maluit ; referri gratia illi tam longo spatio non potuit ; in illius respectum iste populo praesideat, non quia scit **3** aut potest, sed quia alius pro illo meruit. Hic corpore deformis est, adspectu foedus et ornamenta sua traducturus ; iam me homines accusabunt, caecum ac temerarium dicent, nescientem, quo loco, quae summis atque excelsissimis debentur, ponam ; at ego scio alii me istud dare, alii olim debitum solvere.

[1] idem facere *added by Madvig.*

---

[a] Seemingly, an allusion to the emperor Claudius, whose physical infirmities and absent-mindedness made him a frequent butt.

The gods, it is probable, act in the same manner—some are treated with more indulgence because of their parents and ancestors, others because of their grandchildren and great-grandchildren and the long line of their descendants, whose qualities are as yet unrevealed ; for the gods know well the complete evolution of their work, and the knowledge of all that will hereafter pass through their hands is always to them clearly revealed. The events that appear suddenly to us out of the unknown, and all that we count unexpected are to them familiar happenings, long foreseen.

God says : " Let these men be kings because their forefathers have not been, because they have regarded justice and unselfishness as their highest authority, because, instead of sacrificing the state to themselves, they have sacrificed themselves to the state. Let these others reign, because some one of their grandsires before them was a good man who displayed a soul superior to Fortune, who, in times of civil strife, preferred to be conquered than to conquer, because in this way he could serve the interest of the state. Despite the long lapse of time, it has not been possible to pay to him the debt of gratitude ; out of regard for him, now let this other rule over the people, not because he has the knowledge or the ability, but because another has served in his place. This one [a] is deformed in body, hideous in aspect, and will bring ridicule upon the insignia of his office ; then men will blame me, they will say that I am blind and rash, that I little know what disposition I am making of honours that are due to none but the greatest and loftiest of men ; yet I am well aware that I am making this gift to one man, and thereby paying an ancient

4 Unde isti norunt illum quondam gloriae sequentis
fugacissimum, eo voltu ad pericula euntem, quo alii
e periculo redeunt, numquam bonum suum a publico
distinguentem? 'Ubi,' inquis, 'iste aut quis est?'
Unde vos scitis? Apud me istae expensorum ac-
ceptorumque rationes dispunguntur, ego, quid cui
debeam, scio. Aliis post longam diem repono, aliis
in antecessum ac prout occasio et rei publicae meae
facultas tulit." Ingrato ergo aliquando quaedam,
sed non propter ipsum dabo.

1 33. "Quid? Si," inquit, "nescis, utrum ingratus
sit an gratus, expectabis, donec scias, an dandi beneficii tempus non amittes? Expectare longum est
(nam, ut ait Platon, difficilis humani animi coniectura
2 est), non expectare temerarium est." Huic respon-
debimus numquam expectare nos certissimam rerum
comprehensionem, quoniam in arduo est veri explo-
ratio, sed ea ire, qua ducit veri similitudo. Omne hac
via procedit officium. Sic serimus, sic navigamus,
sic militamus, sic uxores ducimus, sic liberos tollimus;
cum omnium horum incertus sit eventus, ad ea accedi-
mus, de quibus bene sperandum esse credidimus.
Quis enim pollicetur serenti proventum, naviganti
portum, militanti victoriam, marito pudicam uxorem,
patri pios liberos? Sequimur, qua ratio, non qua
3 veritas traxit. Expecta, ut nisi bene cessura non
facias et nisi comperta veritate nil noveris: relicto
omni actu vita consistit. Cum veri similia me in hoc

debt to another. How can these critics know that hero of old, who persistently fled from the glory that followed him, who, going into danger, had the air that others show when they return from danger, who never separated his own interest from that of the state? 'Where,' you ask, ' is this man, or who is he?' But how could you know these things? It is for me to balance the debits and credits of such accounts, I know what and to whom I owe. Some I repay after a long term, others in advance, and according as opportunity and the resources of my governance permit." Consequently, I, too, shall sometimes bestow certain gifts on an ungrateful man, but not because of the man himself.

"Tell me," you say, " if you do not know whether a man is grateful or ungrateful, will you wait until you do know, or will you refuse to lose the opportunity of giving a benefit? To wait is a long matter, —for, as Plato says, the human heart is hard to divine,—not to wait hazardous." Our answer to this will be that we never wait for absolute certainty, since the discovery of truth is difficult, but follow the path that probable truth shows. All the business of life proceeds in this way. It is thus that we sow, that we sail the sea, that we serve in the army, that we take wives, that we rear children ; since in all these actions the issue is uncertain, we follow the course that we believe offers the hope of success. For who will promise to the sower a harvest, to the sailor a port, to the soldier a victory, to a husband a chaste wife, to a father dutiful children ? We follow, not where truth, but where reason, directs us. If you wait to do only what is assured of success and to have only the knowledge that comes from ascertained truth, all activity is given up, and life comes to a halt. Since

aut in illud impellant, non vera, ei beneficium dabo,
quem veri simile erit gratum esse.

1   34. " Multa," inquit, " intervenient, propter quae
et malus pro bono surrepat et bonus pro malo dis-
pliceat ; fallaces enim sunt rerum species, quibus
credidimus." Quis negat ? Sed nihil aliud invenio,
per quod cogitationem regam. His veritas mihi
vestigiis sequenda est, certiora non habeo ; haec ut
quam diligentissime aestimem, operam dabo nec cito
2 illis adsentiar. Sic enim in proelio potest accidere,
ut telum meum in commilitonem manus dirigat aliquo
errore decepta et hosti tamquam meo parcam ; sed
hoc et raro accidet et non vitio meo, cuius propositum
est hostem ferire, civem defendere. Si sciam ingratum esse, non dabo beneficium. At obrepsit, at
imposuit : nulla hic culpa tribuentis est, quia tamquam grato dedi.

3   " Si promiseris," inquit, " te daturum beneficium
et postea ingratum esse scieris, dabis an non ? Si
facis sciens, peccas, das enim, cui non debes dare ; si
negas, et hoc modo peccas : non das ei, cui promisisti.
Conscientia vestra hoc loco titubat et illud superbum
promissum numquam sapientem facti sui paenitere
nec umquam emendare, quod fecerit, nec mutare
4 consilium." Non mutat sapiens consilium omnibus

274

it is, not truth, but the probable truth, that impels me in one direction or another, I shall give my benefit to the man who in all probability will be grateful.

" Many circumstances," you say, " will arise that will enable a bad man to steal into the place of a good one, and the good man will lose favour instead of the bad one ; for appearances are deceptive, and it is these we trust." Who denies it ? Yet I find nothing else from which to form an opinion. These are the footprints I must follow in my search for truth, I have nothing that is more trustworthy ; I shall take pains to consider these with all possible care, and shall not be hasty in granting my assent. For the same thing may happen in battle, and my hand, deceived by some mistake, may direct my weapon against a comrade, and spare an enemy as though he were a friend ; but this will happen but rarely, and from no fault of my own, for my intention is to smite the enemy, and to defend my countryman. If I know that a man is ungrateful, I shall not give him a benefit. Yet if he has tricked me, if he has imposed upon me, no blame attaches to the giver because I made the gift supposing that the man would be grateful.

" Suppose," you say, " that you have promised to give a benefit, and later have discovered that the man is ungrateful, will you or will you not bestow it ? If you do so knowingly, you do wrong, for you give to one to whom you ought not to give ; if you refuse, you likewise do wrong—you do not give to one to whom you promised to give. This case would upset your conscience and your proud assurance that the wise man never regrets his action, or amends what he has done, or changes his purpose." The wise man does not change his purpose if the situation remains as it

275

his manentibus, quae erant, cum sumeret ; ideo numquam illum paenitentia subit, quia nihil melius illo
tempore fieri potuit, quam quod factum est, nihil
melius constitui, quam constitutum est ; ceterum ad
omnia cum exceptione venit : " Si nihil inciderit,
quod impediat." Ideo omnia illi succedere dicimus
et nihil contra opinionem accidere, quia praesumit
animo posse aliquid intervenire, quod destinata pro-
5 hibeat. Imprudentium ista fiducia est fortunam sibi
spondere ; sapiens utramque partem eius cogitat ;
scit, quantum liceat errori, quam incerta sint humana,
quam multa consiliis obstent ; ancipitem rerum ac
lubricam sortem suspensus sequitur, consiliis certis
incertos eventus expendit. Exceptio autem, sine
qua nihil destinat, nihil ingreditur, et hic illum tuetur.

1 35. Promisi beneficium, nisi si quid incidisset, quare
non deberem dare. Quid enim, si, quod illi pollicitus
sum, patria sibi dare iusserit ? Si lex lata erit, ne id
quisquam faciat, quod ego me amico meo facturum
promiseram ? Promisi tibi in matrimonium filiam ;
postea peregrinus apparuisti ; non est mihi cum
externo conubium ; eadem res me defendit, quae
2 vetat. Tunc fidem fallam, tunc inconstantiae crimen
audiam, si, cum eadem omnia sint, quae erant pro-
mittente me, non praestitero promissum ; alioquin,
quidquid mutatur, libertatem facit de integro con-

was when he formed it ; he is never filled with regret because at the time nothing better could have been done than was done, no better decision could have been made than was made ; yet all that he undertakes is subject to the reservation : " If nothing happens to prevent." If we say that all his plans prosper, and that nothing happens contrary to his expectation, it is because he has presupposed that something might happen to thwart his designs. It is the imprudent man who is confident that Fortune is plighted to himself ; the wise man envisages her in both of her aspects ; he knows how great is the chance of mistake, how uncertain are human affairs, how many obstacles block the success of our plans ; he follows alert the doubtful and slippery course of chance, weighs uncertain outcome against his certainty of purpose. But the reservation without which he makes no plan, undertakes nothing, protects him here also.

I have promised a benefit in case nothing occurs to show that I ought not to give it. For what if my country should bid me give to her what I have promised to another ? What if a law should be passed, forbidding anyone to do what I had promised that I would do for my friend ? Suppose I have promised you my daughter in marriage, but find out later that you are not a citizen ; I have no right to contract a marriage with a foreigner ; the same circumstance that forbids it provides my defence. Only then shall I be breaking faith, only then shall I listen to a charge of inconstancy, if I fail to fulfil a promise though all the circumstances remain the same as they were when I made my promise ; otherwise, any change that takes place gives me the liberty of revising my decision, and frees me from my

sulendi et me fide liberat. Promisi advocationem :
postea apparuit per illam causam praeiudicium in
patrem meum quaeri ; promisi me peregre exiturum :
sed iter infestari latrociniis nuntiatur ; in rem praesentem venturus fui : sed aeger filius, sed puerpera
3 uxor tenet. Omnia esse debent eadem, quae fuerunt,
cum promitterem, ut promittentis fidem teneas ;
quae autem maior fieri mutatio potest, quam si te
malum virum et ingratum comperi ? Quod tamquam digno dabam, indigno negabo et irascendi quoque causam habebo deceptus.

1   36. Inspiciam tamen et, quantum sit, de quo agitur;
dabit mihi consilium promissae rei modus. Si exiguum est, dabo, non quia dignus es, sed quia promisi,
nec tamquam munus dabo, sed verba mea redimam
et aurem mihi pervellam. Damno castigabo promittentis temeritatem : " Ecce, ut doleat tibi, ut
postea consideratius loquaris ! " Quod dicere sole-
2 mus, linguarium dabo. Si maius erit, non committam,
quemadmodum Maecenas ait, ut sestertio centies
obiurgatus sim. Inter se enim utrumque comparabo.
Est aliquid in eo, quod promiseris, perseverare ; est
rursus multum in eo, ne indigno beneficium des ; hoc
tamen quantum est ? Si leve, coniveamus ; si vero
magno mihi aut detrimento aut rubori futurum, malo

---

[a] *i.e.*, remember not to be rash a second time.   The gesture
was an appeal to memory.
278

pledge. Suppose I have promised my legal assistance, but afterwards discover that a precedent was
being sought from that case to harm my father;
suppose I have promised that I will go abroad, but
word is brought that the way is beset with robbers;
suppose I was about to go to keep an appointment,
but am detained by the illness of my son or by my
wife's confinement. If you are to hold me to the
fulfilment of my promise, all the circumstances must
remain the same as they were when I promised; but
what greater change can there be than my discovery
that you are a bad and ungrateful man? I shall
refuse to an unworthy man what I was willing to give
to him supposing him to be worthy, and I shall even
have reason to be angry because I was deceived.

Nevertheless I shall also examine into the value of
the gift in question; for the amount of the sum
promised will help my decision. If it is a trifle, I
shall give it to you, not because you deserve it, but
because I have promised, and I shall not count it as a
gift, but shall keep my word, and give my ear a twitch.[a]
I shall punish my rashness in promising by suffering
loss: " You see how sorry you are for yourself; next
time take more care before you speak!" As the
saying is, I shall pay for my tongue. If the amount
is a larger one, " I shall not," as Maecenas puts it,
" let my punishment cost me ten million sesterces."
For I shall match the two sides of the question one
against the other. There is something in abiding by
what you have promised; on the other hand, there is
much in the principle of not bestowing a benefit on
one who is unworthy. Yet how great is this benefit?
If it is a slight one, let us wink at it; if, however, it
is likely to cause me either great loss or shame, I

semel excusare, quare negaverim, quam semper,
quare dederim. Totum, inquam, in eo est, quanti
3 promissi mei verba taxentur. Non tantum, quod
temere promisi, retinebo, sed, quod non recte dedi,
repetam ; demens est, qui fidem praestat errori.

1 37. Philippus Macedonum rex habebat militem
manu fortem, cuius in multis expeditionibus utilem
expertus operam subinde ex praeda aliquid illi virtutis causa donaverat et hominem venalis animae
crebris auctoramentis accendebat. Hic naufragus
in possessiones cuiusdam Macedonis expulsus est ;
quod ut nuntiatum est, accucurrit, spiritum eius recol-
legit, in villam illum suam transtulit, lectulo suo cessit,
adfectum semianimemque recreavit, diebus triginta
sua impensa curavit, refecit, viatico instruxit subinde
dicentem : " Gratiam tibi referam, videre tantum
2 mihi imperatorem meum contingat." Narravit Philippo naufragium suum, auxilium tacuit et protinus
petit, ut sibi cuiusdam praedia donaret. Ille quidam
erat hospes eius, is ipse, a quo receptus erat, a quo
sanatus. Multa interim reges in bello praesertim
opertis oculis donant. " Non sufficit homo iustus tot
armatis cupiditatibus, non potest quisquam eodem
tempore et bonum virum et bonum ducem agere.
Quomodo tot milia hominum insatiabilia satiabuntur ?
280

should rather excuse myself once for having refused it than ever afterward for having given it. It all depends, I say, upon how much value I attach to the letter of my promise. I shall not only keep back what I have rashly promised, but shall demand back what I have wrongly given. The man is mad who keeps a promise that was a mistake.

Philip, king of the Macedonians, had a soldier who was a valiant fighter, and, having found his services useful in many campaigns, he had from time to time presented him with some of the booty as a reward for his prowess, and, by his repeated bounties, was exciting the venal spirit of the man. Once after being shipwrecked he was cast ashore upon the estate of a certain Macedonian; this one, when he heard the news, rushed to his help, resuscitated his breath, brought him to his farmhouse, surrendered to him his bed, restored him from a weak and half-dead condition to new life, cared for him for thirty days at his own expense, put him upon his feet, provided him with money for his journey, and heard him say over and over : " I will show you my gratitude if only I have the good fortune to see my commander." To Philip he gave an account of his shipwreck, but said nothing of the help he had received, and promptly asked Philip to present him with a certain man's estate. The man was, in fact, his host, the very one who had rescued him, who had restored him to health. Kings sometimes, especially in time of war, make many gifts with their eyes closed. " One just man is no match for so many armed men fired with greed, it is not possible for any mortal to be a good man and a good general at the same time. How will he satiate so many thousands of insatiable men ? What will

3 Quid habebunt, si suum quisque habuerit ? " Haec
Philippus sibi dixit, cum illum induci in bona, quae
petebat, iussit. Expulsus bonis suis ille non ut rusticus iniuriam tacitus tulit contentus, quod non et ipse
donatus esset, sed Philippo epistulam strictam ac
liberam scripsit ; qua accepta ita exarsit, ut statim
Pausaniae mandaret, bona priori domino restitueret,
ceterum improbissimo militi, ingratissimo hospiti,
avidissimo naufrago stigmata inscriberet ingratum
4 hominem testantia. Dignus quidem fuit, cui non
inscriberentur illae litterae, sed insculperentur, qui
hospitem suum nudo et naufrago similem in id, in[1]
5 quo iacuerat ipse, litus expulerat. Sed videbimus,
quis modus poenae servandus fuerit ; auferendum
utique fuit, quod summo scelere invaserat. Quis
autem poena eius moveretur ? Id commiserat, propter quod nemo misereri misericors posset.

1 38. Dabit tibi Philippus, quia promisit, etiam si
non debet, etiam si iniuriam facturus est, etiam si
scelus facturus est, etiam si uno facto praeclusurus
est naufragis litora ? Non est levitas a cognito et
damnato errore discedere, et ingenue fatendum est :
" Aliud putavi, deceptus sum." Haec vero superbae
stultitiae perseverantia est : " Quod semel dixi,

---

[1] in *commonly added.*

---

[a] A member of Philip's body-guard and later his murderer.
[b] *i.e.*, no one would be willing to run the risk of losing
his property by succouring the shipwrecked.

they have if every man has only what is his own ? "
So Philip communed with himself as he gave order
that the soldier should be put in possession of the
property he asked for. The other, however, when he
was expelled from his property, did not, like a peasant,
endure his wrong in silence, thankful that he himself
had not been included in the present, but wrote a
concise and outspoken letter to Philip. Upon receiving this, Philip was so enraged that he immediately
ordered Pausanias [a] to restore the property to its
former owner, and, besides, to brand that most
dishonourable of soldiers, most ungrateful of guests,
most greedy of shipwrecked men with letters showing him to be an ungrateful person. He, indeed,
deserved, not merely to be branded with those letters,
but to have them carved in his flesh—a man who had
cast out his own host to lie like a naked and shipwrecked sailor upon that shore on which he himself
had lain. But we shall heed within what limits the
punishment ought to be kept; he had, in any case,
to be deprived of what he had seized with the
utmost villainy. Yet who would be moved by his
punishment ? He had committed a crime which
could stir no pitiful heart to pity him.

Will a Philip give to you because he promised, even
at the price of sacrificing duty, even at the price of
committing an injustice, even at the price of committing a crime, even at the price of closing all shores [b]
to the shipwrecked by this one act ? There is no
fickleness in leaving a wrong course when it has been
recognized as such and condemned, and we must
confess frankly : " I thought it was different, I have
been deceived." It is but the stubbornness of foolish
pride to declare : " What I have once said, be it what

2 qualecumque est, fixum ratumque sit." Non est
turpe cum re mutare consilium. Age, si Philippus
possessorem illum eorum litorum reliquisset, quae
naufragio ceperat, non omnibus miseris aqua et igni
interdixerat ? " Potius," inquit, " intra fines regni
mei tu litteras istas oculis inscribendas durissima
fronte circumfer. I, ostende, quam sacra res sit
mensa hospitalis ; praebe in facie tua legendum istuc
decretum, quo cavetur, ne miseros tecto iuvare
capital sit. Magis ista constitutio sic rata erit, quam
si illam in aes incidissem."

1 39. " Quare ergo," inquit, " Zeno vester, cum
quingentos denarios cuidam mutuos promisisset et
ipse illum parum idoneum comperisset, amicis sua-
dentibus, ne daret, perseveravit credere, quia pro-
2 miserat ? " Primum alia condicio est in credito, alia
in beneficio. Pecuniae etiam male creditae exactio
est ; et appellare debitorem ad diem possum et, si
foro cesserit, portionem feram ; beneficium et totum
perit et statim. Praeterea hoc mali viri est, illud
mali patris familiae. Deinde ne Zeno quidem, si
maior fuisset summa, credere perseverasset. Quin-
genti denarii sunt : illud quod dici solet, " in morbo
consumat " ; fuit tanti non revocare promissum
3 suum. Ad cenam, quia promisi, ibo, etiam si frigus
erit ; non quidem, si nives cadent. Surgam ad

---

a *i.e.*, made it a crime to afford them hospitality.

it may, shall remain fixed and unaltered." There is nothing wrong in changing a plan when the situation is changed. Tell me, if Philip had left the soldier in possession of the shores that he had obtained by shipwreck, is it not true that he would thereby have cut off all unfortunates from fire and water[a]? "Rather do you," he said, "within the bounds of my kingdom carry everywhere upon your most brazen brow these letters that ought to be stamped upon all men's eyes. Go, show how sacred a thing is the table of hospitality; display upon your countenance that decree, for all to read, which keeps it from being a capital crime to shelter the unfortunate beneath one's roof! This ordinance will thus have more authority than if I had engraved it upon bronze."

"Why, then," you say, "did your master Zeno, when he had promised a loan of five hundred denarii to a man, and had himself discovered that he was an altogether unsuitable person, persist in making the loan because he had promised it, although his friends advised him not to give it?" In the first place, one set of terms applies to a loan, another to a benefit. It is possible to recall money even if it has been badly placed; I can summon a debtor to pay on a given date, and, if he has gone bankrupt, I shall get my share; but a benefit is lost wholly and immediately. Besides, the one is the act of a bad man, the other of a bad manager. Again, if the sum had been a larger one, not even Zeno would have persisted in lending it. It was only five hundred denarii,—an amount, as we say, "one can spend on an illness,"—and not to break his promise was worth that much. I will go out to dinner because I have promised, even if the weather is cold; but not so if there is a snowstorm.

sponsalia, quia promisi, quamvis non concoxerim ;
sed non, si febricitavero. Sponsum descendam, quia
promisi ; sed non, si spondere me in[1] incertum iube-
4 bis, si fisco obligabis. Subest, inquam, tacita exceptio : "Si potero, si debebo, si haec ita erunt."
Effice, ut idem status sit, cum exigis, qui fuit, cum
promitterem ; destituere levitas erit. Si aliquid intervenit novi, quid miraris, cum condicio promittentis
mutata sit, mutatum esse consilium ? Eadem mihi
omnia praesta, et idem sum. Vadimonium promittimus, tamen deserti non in omnes datur actio :
deserentem vis maior excusat.

1 40. Idem etiam in illa quaestione responsum existima, an omni modo referenda sit gratia, et an beneficium utique reddendum sit. Animum praestare
gratum debeo, ceterum aliquando me referre gratiam
non patitur mea infelicitas, aliquando felicitas eius, cui
2 debeo. Quid enim regi, quid pauper diviti reddam,
utique cum quidam recipere beneficium iniuriam
iudicent et beneficia subinde aliis beneficiis onerent ?
Quid amplius in horum persona possum quam velle ?
Nec enim ideo beneficium novum reicere debeo, quia
nondum prius reddidi. Accipiam tam libenter, quam
dabitur, et praebebo me amico meo exercendae boni-

---

[1] in *added by Erasmus.*

[a] The condition seems to involve the forfeiture of money to
the emperor's privy purse.

I will rise from my table because I have promised to attend a betrothal, although I have not digested my food ; but not so if I shall have a fever. I will go down to the forum in order to go bail for you because I have promised ; but not so if you ask me to go bail for an uncertain amount, if you place me under obligation to the treasury.[a] There is understood, I say, the unexpressed reservations : " If I can, if I ought, if things remain so-and-so." When you exact fulfilment, see to it that the situation is the same as it was when I promised ; then, if I fail, I shall be guilty of fickleness. If something new has happened, why are you surprised that my intention has changed, since conditions have changed since I promised ? Put everything back as it was, and I shall be as I was. We promise to appear in court, yet not all are liable to prosecution if they default—a major necessity excuses the defaulter.

To the further question of whether in every case we ought to show gratitude, and whether a benefit ought in all cases to be returned, consider that I make the same reply. It is my duty to show a grateful heart, but sometimes my own ill fortune, sometimes the good fortune of the one to whom I am indebted, will not permit me to show gratitude. For what return can I make to a king, what to a rich man if I am poor, particularly since some men regard it as an injustice to have their benefit returned, and are continually piling benefits upon benefits ? In the case of such persons, what more can I do than have the desire ? Nor, indeed, ought I to refuse a fresh benefit simply because I have not yet repaid an earlier one. I shall accept it as willingly as it is given, and I shall allow my friend to find in me an ample opportunity for

tatis suae capacem materiam. Qui nova accipere non
3 vult, acceptis offenditur. Non refero gratiam : quid ad
rem ? Non est per me mora, si aut occasio mihi deest
aut facultas. Ille praestitit mihi, nempe cum occasionem haberet, cum facultatem. Utrum bonus vir
est an malus ? Apud bonum virum bonam causam
4 habeo, apud malum non ago. Ne illud quidem
existimo faciendum, ut referre gratiam etiam invitis
his, quibus refertur, properemus et instemus rece-
dentibus. Non est referre gratiam, quod volens
acceperis, nolenti reddere. Quidam, cum aliquod
illis missum est munusculum, subinde aliud intempestive remittunt et nihil se debere testantur ; re-
iciendi genus est protinus aliud in vicem mittere et
5 munus munere expungere. Aliquando et non reddam
beneficium, cum possim. Quando ? Si plus mihi
detracturus ero quam illi conlaturus, si ille non erit
sensurus ullam accessionem recepto eo, quo reddito
mihi multum abscessurum erit. Qui festinat utique
reddere, non habet animum grati hominis, sed debitoris ; et, ut breviter, qui nimis cupit solvere, invitus
debet ; qui invitus debet, ingratus est.

exercising his goodness. He who is unwilling to accept new benefits must resent those already received. I may not testify my gratitude—but what does it matter? I am not responsible for the delay if I lack either the opportunity or the means. He, of course, had both the opportunity and the means when he bestowed his benefit upon me. Is he a good man or a bad man? Before a good judge I have a good case; before a bad one I do not plead my case. Nor do I think that we ought to do this either—to hasten to show gratitude even against the will of those to whom we show it, and to press it upon them although they draw back. It is not displaying gratitude to repay something that you have willingly accepted to someone who is unwilling to accept it. Some people, when a trifling gift has been sent to them, forthwith, quite unseasonably, send back another, and then declare that they are under no obligation; but to send something back at once, and to wipe out a gift with a gift is almost a repulse. Sometimes, too, I shall not return a benefit although I am able. When? When I myself shall lose more than the other will gain, when he will not be aware of any increase of his store in taking back that which will cause me great loss by being returned. He who hastens at all odds to make return shows the feeling, not of a person that is grateful, but of a debtor. And, to put it briefly, he who is too eager to pay his debt is unwilling to be indebted, and he who is unwilling to be indebted is ungrateful.

LIBER V

1 1. In prioribus libris videbar consummasse propositum, cum tractassem, quemadmodum dandum esset beneficium, quemadmodum accipiendum ; hi enim sunt huius officii fines. Quidquid ultra moror, non servio materiae, sed indulgeo, quae, quo ducit, sequenda est, non quo invitat ; subinde enim nascetur, quo lacessat aliqua dulcedine animum, magis **2** non supervacuum quam necessarium. Verum, quia ita vis, perseveremus peractis, quae rem continebant, scrutari etiam ea, quae, si vis verum, conexa sunt, non cohaerentia ; quae quisquis diligenter inspicit, nec facit operae pretium nec tamen perdit operam.

3 Tibi autem, homini natura optimo et ad beneficia propenso, Liberalis Aebuti, nulla eorum laudatio satis facit. Neminem umquam vidi tam benignum etiam levissimorum officiorum aestimatorem ; iam bonitas tua eo usque prolapsa est, ut tibi dari putes beneficium, quod ulli datur ; paratus es, ne quem **4** beneficii paeniteat, pro ingratis dependere. Ipse

BOOK V

I thought that I had finished my task in the preceding books, having discussed there how a benefit
ought to be given, and how it ought to be received ;
for these two points are the boundary marks of this
particular service. In any further inquiry, I shall be,
not serving, but indulging, my subject, the only demand of which is that I follow whither it leads, not
whither it allures ; for now and then a suggestion
will be born that challenges the mind by a certain
charm, yet remains, if not a useless, an unnecessary
addition. Since, however, such is your wish, having
finished with the matters that bound the subject, let
us continue to examine further those that, if I must
tell the truth, are associated with it, yet are not
actually connected ; whoever examines these carefully will neither be repaid for his pains nor yet
wholly waste his pains.

To you, however, Aebutius Liberalis, who are
naturally the best of men and prone to benefits, no
laudation of them seems to be adequate. Never
have I seen anyone who was so generous in his
estimate of even the most trivial services ; your
goodness has reached such a degree that, when any
man is given a benefit, you count it as given to yourself ; in order that no one may regret the bestowal
of a benefit, you are ready to pay the debts of the

usque eo abes ab omni iactatione, usque eo statim vis
exonerare, quos obligas, ut, quidquid in aliquem confers, velis videri non praestare, sed reddere, ideoque
plenius ad te sic data revertentur. Nam fere secuntur beneficia non reposcentem et, ut gloria
fugientes magis sequitur, ita fructus beneficiorum
gratius respondet, per quos esse etiam ingratis
5 licet. Per te vero non est mora, quominus beneficia,
qui acceperunt, ultro repetant, nec recusabis conferre alia et suppressis dissimulatisque plura ac maiora
adicere : propositum optimi viri et ingentis animi
tam diu ferre ingratum, donec feceris gratum. Nec
te ista ratio decipiet ; succumbunt vitia virtutibus,
si illa non cito odisse properaveris.

1 2. Illud utique unice tibi placet velut magnifice
dictum turpe esse beneficiis vinci. Quod an sit
verum, non immerito quaeri solet, longeque aliud est,
quam mente concipis. Numquam enim in rerum
honestarum certamine superari turpe est, dummodo
arma non proicias et victus quoque velis vincere.
2 Non omnes ad bonum propositum easdem adferunt
vires, easdem facultates, eandem fortunam, quae
optimorum quoque consiliorum dumtaxat exitus temperat ; voluntas ipsa rectum petens laudanda est,

ungrateful. So far removed are you yourself from all
boasting, so eager at once to free those whom you
place under obligation from the burden of it, that,
in making a gift to anyone, you wish to appear, not
to be bestowing, but to be returning, one ; and so all
that is given in this manner will be returned to you
in richer measure. For benefits usually pursue the
man who asks no return, and just as glory is more apt
to pursue those who flee from it, so those who are
willing to allow men to be ungrateful reap a more
grateful return for the benefits they have given them.
Truly, so far as you are concerned, there is nothing to
prevent those who have received benefits from boldly
repeating their request, nor will you refuse to confer
others, and to add more and greater benefits to those
that have been covert and concealed—excellent man
that you are and a truly great soul, your aim is to bear
with an ungrateful man so long that he will in the end
become grateful. Nor will your method deceive you ;
vices will yield to virtue if you do not hasten too
quickly to hate them.

In any case the precept that it is disgraceful to be
outdone in bestowing benefits gives you unique pleasure as being a glorious utterance. Whether this is
true or not is often rightly questioned, and the case is
quite different from what you imagine. For it is never
disgraceful to be worsted in a struggle for something
honourable, provided that you do not throw down
your arms, and that, even when conquered, you still
wish to conquer. Not all bring the same strength to
the accomplishment of a good purpose, nor the same
resources, nor the same favour of Fortune, which
modifies at all events the issues of even the best
plans ; praise should be awarded to the very desire

etiam si illam alius gradu velociori antecessit. Non
ut in certaminibus ad spectaculum editis meliorem
palma declarat, quamquam in illis quoque saepe
3 deteriorem praetulit casus. Ubi de officio agitur,
quod uterque a sua parte esse quam plenissimum
cupit, si alter plus potuit et ad manum habuit
materiam sufficientem animo suo, si illi, quantum
conatus est, fortuna permisit, alter autem voluntate
par est, etiam si minora, quam accepit, reddidit aut
omnia non reddidit, sed vult reddere et toto in hoc
intentus est animo, non magis victus est, quam qui
in armis moritur, quem occidere facilius hostis potuit
4 quam avertere. Quod turpe existimas, id accidere
viro bono non potest, ut vincatur. Numquam enim
succumbet, numquam renuntiabit ; ad ultimum usque
vitae diem stabit paratus et in hac statione morietur
magna se accepisse prae se ferens, paria voluisse.

1   3. Lacedaemonii vetant suos pancratio aut caestu
decernere, ubi inferiorem ostendit victi confessio.
Cursor cretam prior contigit ; velocitate illum, non
animo antecessit. Luctator ter abiectus perdidit
palmam, non tradidit. Cum invictos esse Lacedaemonii cives suos magno aestimarent, ab iis certaminibus removerunt, in quibus victorem facit non iudex

---

^a A contest in which boxing and wrestling were combined.
^b A boxing-glove weighted with metal knobs.

that strives in the right direction even though another
by his swifter pace outstrips it. It is not as in the contests provided as a public spectacle, where the palm
declares which is the better contestant, although even
in these chance often gives the preference to the
poorer man. When the object of the struggle is a
service which both on their part are eager to make as
great as possible, if one of the two has had greater
power, and has had at hand ample resources to accomplish his purpose, if Fortune permits him to attain
all that he has attempted, while the other matches
him only in desire—even if the latter has returned
smaller gifts than he received, or has not returned
all, but wishes to make return, and strives with his
whole soul to do so, he is no more conquered than is
the soldier who dies in arms, whom the enemy could
more easily kill than turn from his purpose. You are
counting it a disgrace to be conquered, but that cannot possibly happen to a good man. For he will never
surrender, he will never give up ; to the last day of
his life he will stand prepared, and in that posture
will die, proud of having received great gifts and of
having desired to repay them.

The Lacedaemonians forbid their young men to con-
tend in the pancratium[a] or with the caestus,[b] where
the weaker contestant is shown by his own admission
that he has been conquered. A runner wins by being
the first to reach the chalk-line ; he surpasses his opponent, not in pluck, but in speed. A wrestler who
has been thrown three times, though he does not surrender the palm, loses it. Since the Lacedaemonians
thought it highly important to have their citizens invincible, they kept them out of those contests in
which the victor is determined, not by a judge, or

nec per se ipse exitus, sed vox cedentis et tradere
2 iubentis. Hoc, quod illi in suis civibus custodiunt,
virtus ac bona voluntas omnibus praestat, ne umquam vincantur, quoniam quidem etiam inter supe-
rantia animus invictus est. Ideo nemo trecentos
Fabios victos dicit, sed occisos ; et Regulus captus
est a Poenis, non victus, et quisquis alius saevientis
fortunae vi ac pondere oppressus non submittit
3 animum. In beneficiis idem est. Plura aliquis
accepit, maiora, frequentiora ; non tamen victus est.
Beneficia fortasse beneficiis victa sunt, si inter se data
et accepta computes ; si dantem et accipientem
comparaveris, quorum animi et per se aestimandi
sunt, penes neutrum erit palma. Solet enim fieri, ut,
etiam cum alter multis vulneribus confossus est, alter
leviter quidem saucius pares exisse dicantur, quamvis
alter videatur inferior.

1 4. Ergo nemo vinci potest beneficiis, si scit debere,
si vult referre : si, quem rebus non potest, animo
aequat. Hic quam diu in hoc permanet, quam diu
tenet voluntatem gratum animum signis approbandi,
quid interest, ab utra parte munuscula plura nume-
rentur ? Tu multa dare potes, et ego tantum accipere
possum ; tecum stat fortuna, mecum bona voluntas ;

purely by the outcome itself, but by the cry of the vanquished proclaiming surrender. This quality of never being conquered, which the Lacedaemonians safeguard for their citizens, is bestowed on all men by virtue and virtuous desire, since the spirit is unconquered even in the midst of defeat. For this reason no one speaks of the three hundred Fabii as conquered, but slaughtered ; and Regulus was captured by the Carthaginians, not conquered, nor is any other man who, though overwhelmed by the strength and weight of angry Fortune, does not yield in spirit. The same is true of benefits. A man may have received more than he gave, greater ones, more frequent ones, yet, for all that, he has not been conquered. If you reckon those that you have given over against those that you have received, it is true, perhaps, that benefits are surpassed by benefits ; but, if you match the giver against the recipient, taking into consideration, as you must, their intentions in themselves, the palm will belong to neither. For, even when one combatant has been pierced by many wounds, while the other has been but slightly wounded, it is customary to say that they left the arena evenly matched, although it is evident that one of them is the weaker man.

No one, therefore, can be outdone in benefits if he knows how to owe a debt, if he desires to make return—if he matches his benefactor in spirit, even though he cannot match him in deeds. So long as he continues in this state of mind, so long as he holds the desire to give proof of a grateful heart, what difference does it make on which side the greater number of gifts is reckoned ? You are able to give much, and I am able only to receive ; on your side stands good fortune, on my side good desire ; yet I am as

tamen tam par tibi sum, quam multis armatissimis
2 nudi aut leviter armati. Nemo itaque beneficiis
vincitur, quia tam gratus est quisque, quam voluit.
Nam si turpe est beneficiis vinci, non oportet a prae-
potentibus viris accipere beneficium, quibus gratiam
referre non possis, a principibus dico, a regibus, quos
eo loco fortuna posuit, ex quo largiri multa possent
3 pauca admodum et imparia datis recepturi. Reges
et principes dixi, quibus tamen potest opera navari
et quorum illa excellens potentia per minorum con-
sensum ministeriumque constat. At sunt quidam
extra omnem subducti cupiditatem, qui vix ullis
humanis desideriis continguntur ; quibus nihil potest
praestare ipsa fortuna. Necesse est a Socrate beneficiis vincar, necesse est a Diogene, qui per medias
Macedonum gazas nudus incessit calcatis regis
4 opibus. O ! ne ille tunc merito et sibi et ceteris,
quibus ad dispiciendam veritatem non erat obfusa
caligo, supra eum eminere visus est, infra quem
omnia iacebant. Multo potentior, multo locupletior
fuit omnia tunc possidente Alexandro ; plus enim
erat, quod hic nollet accipere, quam quod ille posset
dare.

1 5. Non est turpe ab his vinci ; neque enim minus
fortis sum, si cum invulnerabili me hoste committis,
nec ideo minus ignis urere potest, si in materiam

---

a A celebrated Cynic philosopher of Sinope, whose scorn
of Alexander gave point to many a story.

much your peer as naked or lightly armed soldiers are the peers of the many who are fully armed. No one, therefore, is outdone in benefits because each man's gratitude is to be measured by his desire. For, if it is disgraceful to be outdone in benefits, it is not right to accept a benefit from most powerful men whose kindness you are unable to return—I mean princes and kings, who have been placed by Fortune in a position that enables them to bestow many gifts, and are likely to receive very few and very inadequate returns for what they have given. I have spoken of kings and princes, to whom, nevertheless, it is possible for us to render assistance, and whose pre-eminent power rests upon the consent and service of their inferiors. But there are some men who, withdrawn beyond the reach of every lust, are scarcely touched at all by any human desires ; upon whom Fortune herself has nothing that she can bestow. In benefits I must of necessity be outdone by Socrates, of necessity by Diogenes,[a] who marched naked through the midst of the treasures of the Macedonians, treading under foot the wealth of a king. O ! in very truth, how rightly did he seem then, both to himself and to all others who had not been rendered blind to the perception of truth, to tower above the man beneath whose feet lay the whole world ! Far more powerful, far richer was he than Alexander, who then was master of the whole world ; for what Diogenes refused to receive was even more than Alexander was able to give.

It is not disgraceful to be outdone by such as these ; for it is not proved that I am the less brave if you pit me against an enemy that is invulnerable, nor that fire is the less able to burn if it falls upon a substance

incidit inviolabilem flammis, nec ideo ferrum secandi
vim perdidit, si non recipiens ictum lapis solidusque
et invictae adversus dura naturae dividendus est.
Idem tibi de homine grato respondeo. Non turpiter
vincitur beneficiis, si ab his obligatus est, ad quos
aut fortunae magnitudo aut eximia virtus aditum
2 redituris ad se beneficiis clusit. A parentibus fere
vincimur. Nam tam diu illos habemus, quam diu
iudicamus graves et quam diu beneficia illorum non
intellegimus. Cum iam aetas aliquid prudentiae col-
legit et apparere coepit propter illa ipsa eos amari a
nobis debere, propter quae non amabantur, admoni-
tiones, severitatem et inconsultae adulescentiae dili-
gentem custodiam, rapiuntur nobis. Paucos usque ad
verum fructum a liberis percipiendum perduxit aetas ;
3 ceteri filios onere senserunt. Non est tamen turpe
vinci beneficiis a parente ; quidni non sit turpe,
cum a nullo sit ? Quibusdam enim et pares et impares sumus, pares animo, quem solum illi exigunt,
quem nos solum promittimus, impares fortuna, quae
si cui obstitit, quominus referret gratiam, non ideo
illi tamquam victo erubescendum est. Non est turpe
4 non consequi, dummodo sequaris. Saepe necesse
est ante alia beneficia petamus, quam priora reddidimus, nec ideo non petimus aut turpiter, quia non
reddituri debebimus, quia non per nos erit mora,
quominus gratissimi simus, sed interveniet aliquid

that flames cannot harm, nor that iron has lost its power of cutting if it attempts to cleave stone that is solid, impervious to a blow, and by its very nature invincible to hard instruments. In regard to the grateful man I would answer you in the same way. He is not disgracefully outdone in benefits if he has become indebted to those whose exalted station or exceeding merit blocks the approach to any benefits that might return to them. Our parents almost always outdo us. For, so long as we count them severe, so long as we fail to understand the benefits they give us, we have them with us. When at last with age we have acquired some wisdom, and it begins to be evident that we ought to love them for the very things that kept us from loving them—their admonitions, their strictness, and their careful watch over our heedless youth, —they are snatched from us. Few reach the age when they can reap some true reward from their children ; the rest are aware of their sons by their burden. Yet there is no disgrace in being outdone in benefits by a parent ; how should there be, seeing that there is no disgrace in being outdone by anyone ? For there are some men to whom we are both equal and unequal—equal in intention, which is all that they require, unequal in fortune, and, if it is this that prevents anyone from repaying a favour, he has no need to blush on the ground that he has been outdone. It is no disgrace to fail to attain provided you keep striving. Very often it is necessary to ask for new benefits before we have returned older ones, and yet we do not fail to ask for them or feel any disgrace because we shall be indebted for them with no prospect of returning them, for, if we are prevented from showing ourselves most grateful, it will be the

extrinsecus, quod prohibeat. Nos tamen nec vince-
mur animo nec turpiter his rebus superabimur, quae
non sunt in nostra potestate.

1   6. Alexander Macedonum rex gloriari solebat a
nullo se beneficiis victum. Non est, quod nimius
animi Macedonas et Graecos et Caras et Persas et
nationes discriptas in exercitum suspiciat, nec hoc
sibi praestitisse regnum a[1] Thraciae angulo porre-
ctum usque ad litus incogniti maris iudicet. Eadem
re gloriari Socrates potuit, eadem Diogenes, a quo
utique victus est. Quidni victus sit illo die, quo homo
super mensuram iam humanae superbiae tumens
vidit aliquem, cui nec dare quicquam posset nec
eripere ?

2   Archelaus rex Socratem rogavit, ut ad se veniret ;
dixisse Socrates traditur nolle se ad eum venire, a quo
acciperet beneficia, cum reddere illi paria non posset.
Primum in ipsius potestate erat non accipere ; deinde
ipse dare beneficium prior incipiebat, veniebat enim
rogatus et id dabat, quod utique ille non erat Socrati
redditurus. Etiamnunc Archelaus daturus erat aurum et argentum recepturus contemptum auri et
argenti : non poterat referre Archelao Socrates

---

[1] a *commonly added.*

302

fault, not of ourselves, but of something from without that intervenes and deters us. Yet in intention we shall not be outdone, nor shall we be disgraced if we are overpowered by things that are beyond our control.

Alexander, king of the Macedonians, used to boast that no one had outdone him in benefits. But there is no reason why, in the excess of his pride, he should look up to the Macedonians and the Greeks and the Carians and the Persians and the other nations who were enrolled in his army, nor suppose that it was their benefit that had bestowed upon him a kingdom that extended from a corner of Thrace to the shore of the unknown sea! Socrates could have had the same reason to boast, and Diogenes the same reason, by whom, in any case, he was outdone. Why was he not outdone on that day when, puffed up as he was beyond the limits of human pride, he saw someone to whom he could give nothing, from whom he could take nothing away?

King Archelaus once invited Socrates to come to him. But Socrates is said to have replied that he was not willing to go to him in order that he might receive benefits from him, since he would be unable to make adequate return for them. Yet, in the first place, he was at liberty to refuse to accept them; in the second place, he would have anticipated him in bestowing a benefit, for he would have come because he was invited, and would, at any rate, have given something for which Archelaus could have made no return to Socrates. Furthermore, if Archelaus was going to give to him gold and silver, and was going to receive in return only a scorn for gold and silver, could not Socrates have repaid Archelaus with his

303

3 gratias ? Et quid tantum erat accepturus, quantum
dabat, si ostendisset hominem vitae ac mortis peritum
utriusque fines tenentem ? Si regem in luce media
errantem ad rerum naturam admisisset usque eo eius
ignarum, ut, quo die solis defectio fuit, regiam cluderet
et filium, quod in luctu ac rebus adversis moris est,
4 tonderet ? Quantum fuisset beneficium, si timentem
e latebris suis extraxisset et bonum animum habere
iussisset dicens : " Non est ista solis defectio, sed
duorum siderum coitus, cum luna humiliore currens
via infra ipsum solem orbem suum posuit et illum
obiectu sui abscondit ; quae modo partes eius exiguas,
si in transcursu strinxit, obducit, modo plus tegit, si
maiorem partem sui obiecit, modo excludit totius
adspectum, si recto libramento inter solem terrasque
5 media successit. Sed iam ista sidera hoc et illo
diducet velocitas sua ; iam recipient diem terrae, et
hic ibit ordo per saecula dispositosque ac praedictos
dies habet, quibus sol intercursu lunae vetetur omnes
radios effundere. Paulum expecta ; iam emerget,
iam istam velut nubem relinquet, iam exsolutus im-

---

^a *i.e.*, to avert the evil omen of long hair, the symbol of
grief and disaster. Pliny (*Letters*, vii. 27. 14) explains the
superstition : " ex quo coniectari potest, quia reis moris est
summittere capillum, recisos meorum capillos depulsi quod
imminebat periculi signum fuisse."

thanks ? And what could he have received that would have had the value of what he gave if he had revealed to Archelaus a man who was skilled in the knowledge of life and of death, and comprehended the ends of both ? If he had admitted into the secrets of Nature one who even in broad daylight had lost his way—a king, so ignorant of her ways that one day, when there was an eclipse of the sun, he shut up his palace, and, as is customary in times of grief and disaster, sheared his son's hair *a* ? How great a benefit it would have been if Socrates had dragged the frightened king from his hiding-place, and bidden him be of good cheer, saying : " This does not mean the disappearance of the sun, but that two heavenly bodies are in conjunction by reason of the fact that the moon, which travels by a lower path, has placed her disk exactly beneath the sun itself, and has hidden it by interposing her own body. Sometimes, if she just grazes the sun in passing, she veils only a small portion of it ; sometimes, if she thrusts the greater part of her body in front of it, she conceals a larger portion ; sometimes, if, being between the earth and the sun, she reaches a point where the three bodies are in a straight line, she shuts off completely the sight of the sun. But soon their own speed will draw these heavenly bodies apart, one to this position, the other to that ; soon the earth will recover the light of day. And this order will continue throughout the ages, and has its appointed days, that are known beforehand, on which the sun is prevented from sending forth all his rays because of the intervention of the moon. Wait just a little while ; soon he will emerge, soon he will leave behind this seeming cloud, soon he

6 pedimentis lucem suam libere mittet." Socrates
parem gratiam Archelao referre non posset, si illum
regnare vetuisset? Parum scilicet magnum beneficium a Socrate accipiebat, si ullum dare Socrati
potuisset. Quare ergo hoc Socrates dixit? Vir
facetus et cuius per figuras sermo procederet, derisor
omnium, maxime potentium, maluit illi nasute negare
quam contumaciter aut superbe; dixit se nolle beneficia ab eo accipere, cui non posset paria reddere.
Timuit fortasse, ne cogeretur accipere, quae nollet,
timuit, ne quid indignum Socrate accipere. Dicet
7 aliquis: "Negasset, si vellet." Sed instigasset in
se regem insolentem et omnia sua magno aestimari
volentem. Nihil ad rem pertinet, utrum dare aliquid
regi nolis an accipere a rege; in aequo utramque
ponit repulsam, et superbo fastidiri acerbius est quam
non timeri. Vis scire, quid vere voluerit? Noluit
ire ad voluntariam servitutem is, cuius libertatem
civitas libera ferre non potuit!

1   7. Satis, ut existimo, hanc partem tractavimus, an
turpe esset beneficiis vinci. Quod qui quaerit, scit
non solere homines sibi ipsos dare beneficium; manifestum enim fuisset non esse turpe a se ipsum vinci.
2 Atqui apud quosdam Stoicos et de hoc ambigitur, an

---

a *i.e.*, if he had taught him the true values of life.

will be rid of all obstructions, and will freely send forth his light." Could not Socrates have made adequate return to Archelaus for his favour if he had forbidden him to be king ^{a}? Assuredly the benefit he received from Socrates would have been too small if it had been possible for him to bestow any benefit on Socrates! Why, then, did Socrates say this? Being a clever person, who was given to talking in parables, a mocker of all, especially of the great, he preferred to couch his refusal in irony rather than in stubbornness or pride; he said that he was not willing to receive benefits from one to whom he could not make adequate return. Perhaps he feared that he might be forced to accept gifts that he did not wish, that he might be forced to accept something unworthy of Socrates. Someone will say: " He could have refused it if he wished." But he would have made an enemy of the king, who was arrogant, and wished all his favours to be highly valued. Whether you are unwilling to give something to a king, or to accept something from a king is of no consequence; both alike are in his eyes a rebuff, and to be treated with scorn is more bitter to a proud spirit than not to be feared. Would you like to know what Socrates really meant? He meant that the man whose freedom of speech even a free state could not endure declined to enter into voluntary servitude!

But I think that we have sufficiently discussed this topic of whether it is disgraceful to be outdone in benefits. Whoever raises the question must know that men are not in the habit of bestowing benefits upon themselves; for it would have been evident that there is no disgrace in a man's being outdone by himself. Yet among certain Stoics it is even debated

possit aliquis sibi beneficium dare, an debeat referre
sibi gratiam. Quod ut videretur quaerendum, illa
fecerunt : solemus dicere ; " gratias mihi ago " et
" de nullo queri possum alio quam de me " et " ego
mihi irascor " et " ego a me poenas exigam " et " odi
me," multa praeterea eiusmodi, per quae unusquisque
3 de se tamquam de altero loquitur. " Si nocere,"
inquit, " mihi possum, quare non et beneficium mihi
dare possim ? Praeterea quae, si in alium contulis-
sem, beneficia vocarentur, quare, si in me contuli,
non sint ? Quod, si ab altero accepissem, deberem,
quare, si mihi ipse dedi, non debeam ? Quare sim
adversus me ingratus, quod non minus turpe est
quam in se sordidum esse et in se durum ac saevum
4 et sui neclegentem ? Tam alieni corporis leno male
audit quam sui. Nempe reprenditur adsentator et
aliena subsequens verba, paratus ad falsa laudator ;
non minus placens sibi et se suspiciens, ut ita dicam,
adsentator suus. Vitia non tantum, cum foris pec-
5 cant, invisa sunt, sed cum in se retorquentur. Quem
magis admiraberis, quam qui imperat sibi, quam qui
se habet in potestate ? Gentes facilius est barbaras
impatientesque arbitrii alieni regere, quam animum
suum continere et tradere sibi. Platon, inquit, agit

whether it is possible for a man to bestow a benefit on himself, whether it is his duty to return gratitude to himself. The reason why it seemed necessary to raise the question was our habitual use of such expressions as : " I am thankful to myself," " I can blame no one but myself," " I am angry with myself," " I shall exact punishment from myself," " I hate myself," and many others of the same sort in which one speaks of oneself as if another person. " If," they say, " I am able to injure myself, why should I not be able also to bestow a benefit on myself ? Moreover, why should not things that would be called benefits if I had bestowed them on another still be benefits if I have bestowed them on myself ? Why should not something that would have placed me in debt if I had received it from another still place me in debt if I have given it to myself ? Why should I be ungrateful to myself, which is just as disgraceful as to be niggardly to oneself and harsh and cruel to oneself and neglectful of oneself ? The reputation of a pimp is equally bad whether he prostitutes himself or another. The flatterer, the man who subscribes to the words of another, and is ready to applaud falsehoods, is of course open to censure ; and not less so is the man who is pleased with himself, who, so to speak, looks up to himself, and is his own flatterer. The vices are hateful, not only when they are outwardly expressed, but when they are turned in upon themselves. Whom will you more admire than the man who governs himself, who has himself under control ? It is easier to rule savage nations, impatient as they are of the authority of others, than to restrain one's own spirit and submit to self-control. Plato, say they, was grateful to Socrates be-

Socrati gratias, quod ab illo didicit ; quare Socrates
sibi non agat, quod ipse se docuit ? M. Cato ait :
' Quod tibi deerit, a te ipso mutuare.' Quare donare
6 mihi non possim, si commodare possum ? Innumerabilia sunt, in quibus consuetudo nos dividit ; dicere
solemus : ' Sine, loquar mecum ' et ' Ego mihi aurem
pervellam.' Quae si vera sunt, quemadmodum aliquis sibi irasci debet, sic et gratias agere ; quomodo
obiurgare se, sic et laudare se ; quomodo damno sibi
esse, sic et lucro potest. Iniuria et beneficium contraria sunt ; si de aliquo dicimus : ' Iniuriam sibi
fecit,' poterimus dicere et : ' Beneficium sibi dedit.' "

1   8. Natura prius est, ut quis debeat, deinde, ut gratiam referat ; debitor non est sine creditore, non
magis quam maritus sine uxore aut sine filio pater ;
aliquis dare debet, ut aliquis accipiat. Non est dare
nec accipere in dexteram manum ex sinistra trans-
2 ferre. Quomodo nemo se portat, quamvis corpus
suum moveat et transferat, quomodo nemo, quamvis
pro se dixerit, adfuisse sibi dicitur nec statuam sibi
tamquam patrono suo ponit, quomodo aeger, cum
cura sua convaluit, mercedem a se non exigit, sic in
omni negotio, etiam cum aliquid, quod prodesset
sibi, fecerit, non tamen debebit referre gratiam sibi,

---

^a *i.e.*, jog my memory.

cause he learned from him ; why should not Socrates
be grateful to himself because he taught himself ?
Marcus Cato says : ' Borrow from yourself whatever
you lack.' If I am able to lend to myself, why
should I not be able to give to myself ? The instances in which habit leads us to divide ourselves
into two persons are countless ; we are prone to say :
' Let me converse with myself,' and, ' I will give my
ear a twitch.' [a] If there is any truth in these expressions, just as a man ought to be angry with himself, so he ought to render thanks to himself ; as he
ought to reprove himself, so also he ought to praise
himself ; as he can cause himself loss, so also he can
bring himself gain. Injury and benefit are the converse of each other ; if we say of anyone : ' He has
done himself an injury,' we may also say : ' He has
bestowed upon himself a benefit.' "

Nature's rule is that a man should first become a
debtor, and then should return gratitude ; there
cannot be a debtor without a creditor any more than
there can be a husband without a wife, or a father
without a son ; someone must give in order that
someone may receive. To transfer something from
the left hand to the right hand is neither to give nor
to receive. Just as no one carries himself although
he moves and transports his body, as no one, although
he has spoken in his own defence, is said to have appeared as his own advocate, or erects a statue to himself as his own patron, as no sick man, when he has
regained health by treating himself, demands from
himself a fee, so in transactions of every sort—even
though he may have done something that has been
to his advantage, yet he will be under no obligation
to return gratitude to himself because he will not find

311

3 quia non habebit, cui referat. Ut concedam aliquem
dare sibi beneficium, dum dat, et recipit ; ut concedam aliquem a se accipere beneficium, dum accipit,
reddit. Domi, quod aiunt, versura fit et velut luso-
rium nomen statim transit ; neque enim alius dat
quam accipit, sed unus atque idem. Hoc verbum
" debere " non habet nisi inter duos locum ; quomodo
4 ergo in uno consistet, qui se obligando liberat ? Ut
in orbe ac pila nihil imum est, nihil summum, nihil
extremum, nihil primum, quia motu ordo mutatur
et quae sequebantur praecedunt et quae occidebant
oriuntur, omnia, quomodocumque ierunt, in idem
revertuntur, ita in homine existima fieri ; cum illum
in multa mutaveris, unus est. Cecidit se : iniuriarum
cum quo agat, non habet ; adligavit et clusit : de vi
non tenetur ; beneficium sibi dedit : danti protinus
reddidit.
5 Rerum natura nihil dicitur perdere, quia, quidquid
illi avellitur, ad illam redit, nec perire quicquam
potest, quod, quo excidat, non habet, sed eodem re-
volvitur, unde discedit. " Quid simile," inquis, " hoc
exemplum habet huic propositae quaestioni ? "
6 Dicam. Puta te ingratum esse : non perit bene-

---

a *i.e.*, in the book-keeping a debit straightway becomes a
credit—you take from yourself and give to yourself by one
and the same act.

any person to whom he can return it. Though I grant that a man may bestow a benefit on himself, yet at the same time that he gives it, he also receives a return ; though I grant that a man may receive a benefit from himself, yet at the same time that he receives it, he returns it. "You borrow," as they say, "from your own pocket," and, just as if it were a game, the item immediately shifts to the other side [a] ; for the giver and the receiver are not to be differentiated, but are one and the same person. The word "owe" has no place unless two persons are involved ; how, then, will it apply to one person, who, in the act of incurring a debt, frees himself from it ? In a disk or a sphere there is no bottom, no top, no end, no beginning, because, as the object is moved, the relations change, and the part that was behind now precedes, and the part that was going down now comes up, yet all, in whatever direction they may move, come back to the same position. Imagine that the same principle applies in the case of a man ; though you may transform him into many different characters, he remains a simple human being. He strikes himself—there is no one whom he may charge with doing him an injury. He binds himself and locks himself up— he is not held for damages. He bestows a benefit on himself—he has forthwith made return to the giver.

In the realm of Nature, it is said, there is never any loss, for whatever is taken out of it, returns to it, and nothing is able to perish, because there is no place into which it can escape, but everything returns to whence it came. "What is the bearing," you ask, "of this illustration on the question that is before us ?" I will tell you. Suppose that you are un-

ficium, habet illud, qui dedit. Puta te recipere nolle : apud te est, antequam redditur. Non potes quicquam amittere, quia, quod detrahitur, nihilo minus tibi adquiritur. Intra te ipsum orbis agitur ; accipiendo das, dando accipis.

1 9. " Beneficium," inquit, " sibi dare oportet ; ergo et referre gratiam oportet." Primum illud falsum est, ex quo pendent sequentia ; nemo enim sibi beneficium dat, sed naturae suae paret, a qua ad caritatem sui compositus est, unde summa illi cura est nocitura 2 vitandi, profutura appetendi. Itaque nec liberalis est, qui sibi donat, nec clemens, qui sibi ignoscit, nec misericors, qui malis suis tangitur. Quod aliis praestare liberalitas est, clementia, misericordia, sibi praestare natura est. Beneficium res voluntaria est, at prodesse sibi necessarium est. Quo quis plura beneficia dedit, beneficentior est ; quis umquam laudatus est, quod sibi ipse fuisset auxilio ? Quod se eripuisset latronibus ? Nemo sibi beneficium dat, non magis quam hospitium ; nemo sibi donat, non magis quam credit.

3 Si dat sibi quisque beneficium, semper dat, sine intermissione dat, inire beneficiorum suorum non potest numerum. Quando ergo gratiam referet, cum per hoc ipsum, quo gratiam refert, beneficium

grateful—the benefit is not lost, for the one who bestowed it still has it. Suppose that you are unwilling to receive a return—it is already in your possession before it is returned. You are not able to lose anything, because what is withdrawn from you is none the less acquired by you. The operation proceeds in a circle within yourself—in receiving you give, in giving you receive.

"One ought," you say, "to bestow benefit on oneself; therefore one ought also to return gratitude to oneself." But the first proposition, on which the conclusion depends, is false; for no one bestows benefit on himself, but a man simply obeys a natural instinct that disposes him to show affection for himself, and it is this that causes him to take the utmost pains to avoid what is hurtful, and to seek what is beneficial. Consequently, the man who gives to himself is not generous, nor is he who pardons himself merciful, nor he who is touched by his own misfortunes pitiful. For generosity, mercy, and pity contribute to others; natural instinct contributes to oneself. A benefit is a voluntary act, but self-interest is a law of nature. The more benefits a man bestows, the more beneficent he becomes; but who was ever praised for having been of service to himself? for having rescued himself from brigands? No one any more bestows a benefit upon himself than he does hospitality; no one any more gives to himself than he lends to himself.

If every man does bestow benefits on himself, if he is always bestowing them, and bestows them without cessation, it will be impossible for him to reckon the number of his benefits. When, then, will he be able to return gratitude, since, by the act of returning gratitude, he will be giving a benefit? For how will

det ? Quomodo enim discernere poteris, utrum det
sibi beneficium an reddat, cum intra eundem hominem
res geratur ? Liberavi me periculo : beneficium
mihi dedi. Iterum me periculo libero : utrum do
beneficium an reddo ?

4   Deinde, ut primum illud concedam dare nos nobis
beneficium, quod sequitur, non concedam ; nam
etiam si damus, non debemus. Quare ? Quia
statim recipimus. Accipere beneficium me oportet,
deinde debere, deinde referre ; debendi locus non
est, quia sine ulla mora recipimus. Dat nemo nisi
alteri, debet nemo nisi alteri, reddit nemo nisi alteri.
Id intra unum non potest fieri, quod totiens duos
exigit.

1   10. Beneficium est praestitisse aliquid utiliter ;
verbum autem " praestitisse " ad alios spectat.
Numquid non demens videbitur, qui aliquid sibi ven-
didisse se dicet ? Quia venditio alienatio est et rei
suae iurisque in ea sui ad alium translatio. Atqui,
quemadmodum vendere, sic dare aliquid a se dimittere est et id, quod tenueris, habendum alteri tradere.
Quod si est, beneficium nemo sibi dedit, quia nemo
dat sibi ; alioqui duo contraria in uno coeunt, ut sit
2 idem dare et accipere. Etiamnunc multum interest
inter dare et accipere ; quidni ? cum ex diverso ista

you be able to tell whether he is giving, or returning, a benefit to himself, since the transactions take
place within one and the same man ? I have freed
myself from peril—I have, then, bestowed a benefit
upon myself. I free myself from peril a second time
—am I, then, giving, or returning, a benefit to myself ?

Again, although I should grant the first proposition, that we do bestow benefit upon ourselves, I shall
not grant the conclusion that is drawn from it ; for
even if we give, we owe nothing. Why ? Because
we immediately receive a return. I ought, properly,
to receive a benefit, then be indebted, then repay ;
but there is no opportunity here to be indebted, for
we receive a return without any delay. No one
really gives except to another, no one owes except
to another, no one returns except to another. An
act that so often requires two persons cannot be performed within the limits of one.

A benefit is the contribution of something useful ;
but " contribution " implies the existence of others.
If a man says that he has sold something to himself,
will he not be thought mad ? For selling means
alienation, the transferring of one's property and
one's right in it to another. Yet, just as is the case
in selling, giving implies the relinquishment of something, the surrendering of something that you have
held to the possession of another. And if this is so,
no one has ever bestowed a benefit upon himself because no one can " give " to himself ; otherwise two
opposites are combined in one act, so that giving and
receiving are the same thing. Yet there is a great
difference between giving and receiving ; why should
there not be, since these words are applied to exactly

317

verba posita sint. Atqui si quis sibi beneficium dat,
nihil interest inter dare et accipere. Paulo ante
dicebam quaedam ad alios pertinere et sic esse for-
mata, ut tota significatio illorum discedat a nobis :
frater sum, alterius, nemo est enim suus frater ;
par sum, sed alicui, quis enim par est sibi ? Quod
comparatur, sine altero non intellegitur ; quod iun-
gitur, sine altero non est ; sic et, quod datur, sine
altero non est, et beneficium sine altero non est.

3 Idem ipso vocabulo apparet, in quo hoc continetur,
" bene fecisse " ; nemo autem sibi bene facit, non
magis quam sibi favet, quam suarum partium est.
Diutius hoc et pluribus exemplis licet prosequi.

4 Quidni ? cum inter ea sit habendum beneficium,
quae secundam personam desiderant. Quaedam,
cum sint honesta, pulcherrima, summae virtutis, nisi
in altero non habent locum. Laudatur et inter
maxima humani generis bona fides colitur ; num quis
ergo dicitur sibi fidem praestitisse ?

1   11. Venio nunc ad ultimam partem. Qui gratiam
refert, aliquid debet impendere, sicut, qui solvit,
pecuniam ; nihil autem impendit, qui gratiam sibi
refert, non magis quam consequitur, qui beneficium
a se accepit. Beneficium et gratiae relatio ultro
citro ire debent ; intra unum hominem non est vicis-
situdo. Qui gratiam refert, invicem prodest ei, a

opposite actions ? Yet, if anyone can give a benefit to himself, there is no difference between giving and receiving. I said a little while ago that certain words imply the existence of other persons, and are of such fashion that their whole meaning is directed away from ourselves. I am a brother, but of another, for no one can be his own brother ; I am an equal, but of someone else, for can any man be the equal of himself ? Unless there are two objects, comparison is unintelligible ; unless there are two objects, there can be no coupling ; so also, unless there are two persons, there can be no giving, and, unless there are two persons, there can be no benefaction. This is clear from the very expression, " to do good to," by which the act is defined ; but no one any more does good to himself than he befriends himself, or belongs to his own party. I might pursue this theme further, and multiply examples. Of course, since benefaction must be included among those acts that require a second person. Certain actions, though honourable, admirable, and highly virtuous, find a field only in the person of another. Fidelity is praised, and honoured as one of the greatest blessings of the human race, yet is it ever said that anyone for that reason has kept his promise to himself ?

I come now to the last part of the subject. He who returns gratitude ought to expend something, just as he who pays a debt expends money ; but he who returns gratitude to himself expends nothing, just as surely as he who has received a benefit from himself gains nothing. A benefit and the repayment of gratitude must pass from one to the other ; no interchange is possible if only one person is involved. He who returns gratitude does good in his turn to the one

quo consecutus est aliquid. Qui sibi gratiam refert,
cui prodest ? Sibi. Et quis non alio loco rela-
tionem gratiae, alio beneficium cogitat ? Qui gratiam
refert sibi, sibi[1] prodest. Et quis umquam ingratus
hoc noluit facere ? Immo quis non ingratus fuit, ut
2 hoc faceret ? " Si gratias," inquit, " nobis agere
debemus, et gratiam referre debemus ; dicimus
autem : ' Ago gratias mihi, quod illam uxorem nolui
ducere ' et ' quod cum illo non contraxi societatem.' "
Cum hoc dicimus, laudamus nos et, ut factum nostrum
comprobemus, gratias agentium verbis abutimur.
3 Beneficium est, quod potest, cum datum est, et non
reddi ; qui sibi beneficium dat, non potest non recipere, quod dedit ; ergo non est beneficium. Alio
4 tempore beneficium accipitur, alio redditur. In[2]
beneficio et hoc est probabile, hoc suspiciendum, quod
aliquis, ut alteri prodesset, utilitatis interim suae
oblitus est, quod alteri dedit ablaturus sibi. Hoc non
5 facit, qui beneficium sibi dat. Beneficium dare
socialis res est, aliquem conciliat, aliquem obligat ;
sibi dare non est socialis res, neminem conciliat,
neminem obligat, neminem in spem inducit, ut dicat :
" Hic homo colendus est ; illi beneficium dedit, dabit
6 et mihi." Beneficium est, quod quis non sua causa

---

[1] sibi *added by Haase.*
[2] *Hosius after Haupt posits a hiatus before* in.

---

[a] Some editors posit after this a loss in the text which
removed a statement to the effect that a man, when he
bestows a benefit upon himself, receives and returns it at the
same time.

from whom he obtained something. But he who returns gratitude to himself—to whom does he do good? Only to himself. And who does not think of the repayment of gratitude as one act, and the bestowal of a benefit as another? He who returns gratitude to himself does good to himself. And what ingrate was ever unwilling to do this? Nay, rather, who was ever an ingrate except that he might do this? " If," you say, " we ought to render thanks to ourselves, we ought also to return gratitude ; yet we say : ' I am thankful to myself that I refused to marry that woman,' and ' that I did not conclude a partnership with that man.' " But when we say this, we are lauding ourselves, and, in order to show approval of our act, we misapply the language of those who render thanks. A benefit is something which, when given, may, or may not, be returned. Now he who gives a benefit to himself cannot help having what he has given returned ; therefore this is not a benefit. A benefit is received at one time, is returned at another.[a] A benefit, too, possesses this commendable, this most praiseworthy, quality, that a man forgets for the time being his own interest in order that he may give help to another, that he is ready to deprive himself of what he gives to another. But he who gives a benefit to himself does not do this. The giving of a benefit is a social act, it wins the goodwill of someone, it lays someone under obligation ; giving to oneself is not a social act, it wins no one's goodwill, it lays no one under obligation, it raises no man's hopes, or leads him to say : " I must cultivate this man ; he has given a benefit to So-and-so, he will give one to me also." A benefit is something that a man gives, not for his own sake, but for the sake

dat, sed eius, cui dat ; is autem, qui sibi beneficium
dat, sua causa dat ; non est ergo beneficium.

1   12. Videor tibi iam illud, quod in principio dixeram,
mentitus.   Dicis me abesse ab eo, qui operae pretium
facit, immo totam operam bona fide perdere.   Expecta, et iam hoc verius dices, simul te ad has latebras
perduxero, ex quibus cum evaseris, nihil amplius eris
adsecutus, quam ut eas difficultates effugeris, in quas
2 licuit non descendere.   Quid enim boni est nodos
operose solvere, quos ipse, ut solveres, feceris ?   Sed
quemadmodum quaedam in oblectamentum ac iocum
sic inligantur, ut eorum solutio imperito difficilis sit,
quae illi, qui implicuit, sine ullo negotio paret, quia
commissuras eorum et moras novit, nihilo minus illa
habent aliquam voluptatem (temptant enim acumen
animorum et intentionem excitant), ita haec, quae
videntur callida et insidiosa, securitatem ac segnitiam
ingeniis auferunt, quibus modo campus, in quo vagen-
tur, sternendus est, modo creperi aliquid et confragosi
obiciendum, per quod erepant et sollicite vestigium
faciant.

3   Dicitur nemo ingratus esse ; id sic colligitur :
" Beneficium est, quod prodest ; prodesse autem
nemo homini malo potest, ut dicitis Stoici ; ergo beneficium non accipit malus, * ingratus est.

ᵃ Something has been lost from the text.

of the one to whom he is giving. But he who gives a benefit to himself gives for his own sake; this, then, is not a benefit.

I seem to you now to have been false to the claim that I made at the beginning. For you say that I am far from doing anything worth while—nay, that, in honest truth, I am wasting all my trouble. But wait, and you will soon say this with more truth after I have led you into such obscurities that, even when you have found your way out, you will have accomplished nothing more than escape from difficulties into which you need never have plunged. For what is the good of laboriously untying knots which you yourself have made in order that you might untie them? But, just as it provides amusement and sport when certain objects are knotted up in such a way that an unskilled person has difficulty in unloosing them, while they yield without any trouble to the one who tied the knots because he knows the loops and the snarls, and nevertheless the problem affords some pleasure, for it tests sharpness of wits and provokes mental effort,—so these matters, which seem cunning and tricky, banish indifference and sloth from our minds, which, at one time, should find a level field in which to wander, and, at another, should encounter a dark and uneven stretch, through which we must merely creep, and place every footstep with care.

Some argue that no man is ungrateful, and support the statement as follows : " A benefit is that which does good ; but, according to you Stoics, no one is able to do good to a bad man ; therefore a bad man does not receive a benefit,[therefore he] is [not]*a* ungrateful.

"Etiamnunc beneficium honesta et probabilis res est; apud malum nulli honestae rei aut probabili locus est, ergo nec beneficio; quod si accipere non potest, ne reddere quidem debet, et ideo non fit ingratus.

4 "Etiamnunc, ut dicitis, bonus vir omnia recte facit; si omnia recte facit, ingratus esse non potest. Malo viro beneficium nemo dare potest. Bonus beneficium reddit, malus non accipit; quod si est, nec bonus quisquam ingratus est nec malus. Ita ingratus in rerum natura est nemo, et hoc inane nomen."[1]

5 Unum est apud nos bonum, honestum. Id pervenire ad malum non potest; desinet enim malus esse, si ad illum virtus intraverit; quam diu autem malus est, nemo illi dare beneficium potest, quia mala bonaque dissentiunt nec in unum eunt. Ideo nemo illi prodest, quia, quidquid ad illum pervenit, id pravo 6 usu corrumpitur. Quemadmodum stomachus morbo vitiatus et colligens bilem, quoscumque accepit cibos, mutat et omne alimentum in causam doloris trahit, ita animus scaevus, quidquid illi commiseris, id onus suum et perniciem et occasionem miseriae facit. Felicissimis itaque opulentissimisque plurimum aestus subest minusque se inveniunt, quo in maiorem 7 materiam inciderunt, qua fluctuarentur. Ergo nihil potest ad malos pervenire, quod prosit, immo nihil, quod non noceat. Quaecumque enim illis con-

---

[1] nomen *added by Erasmus; omitted by Hosius.*

" Furthermore, you say, a benefit is an honourable and commendable act ; but no honourable and commendable act has place in a bad man, therefore neither has a benefit ; and, if he cannot receive one, neither ought he to return one, and, therefore, he does not become ungrateful.

" Furthermore, according to you, a good man always acts rightly ; but, if he always acts rightly, he cannot be ungrateful. No one is able to give a benefit to a bad man. A good man returns a benefit, a bad man does not receive one ; and, if this is so, neither is any good man, nor any bad man, ungrateful. So in the whole realm of Nature, there is no such thing as an ungrateful man, and the term is an empty one."

According to us Stoics there is only one sort of good, the honourable. A bad man cannot possibly attain this ; for he will cease to be bad if virtue has entered into him ; but, so long as he is bad, no one is able to give him a benefit, because evils and goods are opposites, and cannot unite. Therefore, no one can do good to him, for whatever good reaches him is vitiated by his wrong use of it. Just as the stomach, when it is impaired by disease, gathers bile, and, changing all the food that it receives, turns every sort of sustenance into a source of pain, so, in the case of the perverse mind, whatever you entrust to it becomes to it a burden and a source of disaster and wretchedness. And so those who are most prosperous and wealthy are beset with most trouble, and the more property they have to cause them unrest, the less they find themselves. Nothing, therefore, which would be to their good can possibly come to bad men —nay, nothing which would not do them harm. For whatever good falls to their lot they change into their

tigerunt, in naturam suam vertunt et extra speciosa
profuturaque, si meliori darentur, illis pestifera sunt.
Ideo nec beneficium dare possunt, quoniam nemo
potest, quod non habet, dare; hic bene faciendi
voluntate caret.

1 13. Sed quamvis haec ita sint, accipere etiam malus
tamen quaedam potest, quae beneficiis similia sint,
quibus non redditis ingratus erit. Sunt animi bona,
sunt corporis, sunt fortunae. Illa animi bona a stulto
ac malo submoventur; ad haec admittitur, quae et
accipere potest et debet reddere, et, si non reddit,
ingratus est. Nec hoc ex nostra tantum constitutione. Peripatetici quoque, qui felicitatis humanae
longe lateque terminos ponunt, aiunt minuta beneficia perventura ad malos; haec qui non reddit, in-
2 gratus est. Nobis itaque beneficia esse non placet,
quae non sunt animum factura meliorem; commoda
tamen illa esse et expetenda non negamus. Haec et
viro bono dare malus potest et accipere a bono, ut
pecuniam et vestem et honores et vitam; quae si non
reddit, in ingrati nomen incidet.

3 " At quomodo ingratum vocas eo non reddito, quod
negas esse beneficium? " Quaedam, etiam si vera
non sunt, propter similitudinem eodem vocabulo
comprehensa sunt. Sic pyxidem et argenteam et
auream dicimus; sic inlitteratum non ex toto rudem,

---

^a The *pyxis* was originally a small box made of boxwood.

own evil nature, and seemingly attractive gifts that would be beneficial if they were given to a better man become baneful to them. Nor, therefore, are they able to give a benefit, since no one is able to give what he does not have ; such a man lacks the desire to benefit.

But, though this is so, still even a bad man is able to receive certain things that resemble benefits, and he will be ungrateful if he does not return them. There are goods of the mind, goods of the body, and goods of fortune. The fool and the bad man are debarred from the goods of the mind ; but he is admitted to the others—these he can receive and ought to return, and, if he does not return them, he is ungrateful. And ours is not the only school that holds this doctrine. The Peripatetics also, who widely extend the bounds of human happiness, say that trifling benefits come even to the bad, and that he who does not return such is ungrateful. We, therefore, do not agree that things that will not make the mind better are benefits ; nevertheless we do not deny that those things are advantageous and desirable. These things a bad man is able both to give to a good man and to receive from him, such as money and clothing and public office and life ; and, if he does not return them, he will fall into the class of the ungrateful.

" But," you retort, " how can you call a man ungrateful if he fails to return something which you will not admit to be a benefit ? " Certain things, on account of their similarity, are designated by the same term even at the expense of some inaccuracy. Thus we speak of a silver and a golden " pyxis *a* " ; thus, too, we call a man " illiterate," though he may

sed ad litteras altiores non perductum; sic, qui male
vestitum et pannosum vidit, nudum vidisse se dicit.
Beneficia ista non sunt, habent tamen beneficii
4 speciem. "Quomodo ista sunt tamquam beneficia,
sic et ille tamquam ingratus est, non ingratus." Falsum est, quia illa beneficia et qui dat appellat et qui
accipit. Ita, qui veri beneficii speciem fefellit, tam
ingratus est quam veneficus, qui soporem, cum venenum esse crederet, miscuit.

1 14. Cleanthes vehementius agit. "Licet," inquit,
"beneficium non sit, quod accepit, ipse tamen ingratus est, quia non fuit redditurus, etiam si ac-
2 cepisset." Sic latro est etiam antequam manus in-
quinet, quia ad occidendum iam armatus est et habet
spoliandi atque interficiendi voluntatem; exercetur
et aperitur opere nequitia, non incipit. Sacrilegi
dant poenas, quamvis nemo usque ad deos manus
porrigat.

3 "Quomodo," inquit, "adversus malum[b] ingratus
est quisquam, cum a[1] malo dari beneficium non
possit?" Ea scilicet ratione, quia ipsum, quod
accepit, beneficium non erat, sed vocabatur; qui[2]
accipiet ab illo aliquid ex his, quae apud imperitos
sunt, quorum et malis copia est, ipse quoque in simili
materia gratus esse debebit et illa, qualiacumque
sunt, cum pro bonis acceperit, pro bonis reddere.

---

[1] a *added by Haupt.*
[2] qui *added by Gertz.*

---

[a] Zeno's successor as head of the Stoic school.
[b] *i.e.,* the evil, since only the wise are good.

be not utterly untutored but only not acquainted with the higher branches of learning ; thus, too, one who has seen a man wretchedly clad and in rags says that the man he saw was " naked." The things that we mean are not really benefits, but have the appearance of benefits. " Then," you retort, " just as these things are quasi-benefits, so also the man is, not an ingrate, but a quasi-ingrate." No, not so, because both the giver and the recipient of these things call them benefits. So, he who fails to return the semblance of a true benefit is just as much an ingrate as he is a poisoner who, when he thought that he was concocting poison, concocted a sleeping-draught !

The words of Cleanthes [a] are even stronger. " Granted," he says, " that what the man received was not a benefit, yet he himself is an ingrate because, even if he had received a benefit, he would not have returned it." So, a man becomes a brigand even before he stains his hands with blood, because he has armed himself to kill, and possesses the desire to murder and rob ; he practises and manifests wickedness in action, but it does not begin there. Men are punished for sacrilege, but no man's hands can actually reach the gods.

" How," it is asked, " can anyone be ungrateful to a bad man, since a bad man is unable to give a benefit ? " For the reason, of course, that, while the gift that was received was not a benefit, it was called one. If anyone receives from a bad man any of these things that the ignorant [b] possess, of which even the bad have a store, it will be his duty to be grateful with a like offering, and, no matter what may be the nature of the gifts, to return them as true goods since he received them as true goods. A man is

4 Aes alienum habere dicitur et qui aureos debet et qui
corium forma publica percussum, quale apud Lace-
daemonios fuit, quod usum numeratae pecuniae
praestat. Quo genere obligatus es, hoc fidem ex-
5 solve. Quid sint beneficia, an et in hanc sordidam
humilemque materiam deduci magnitudo nominis
clari debeat, ad vos non pertinet; in alios quaeritur
verum. Vos ad speciem veri componite animum et,
dum honestum discitis, quidquid est, in quo nomen
honesti iactatur, id colite.

1 15. "Quomodo," inquit, "nemo per vos ingratus
est, sic rursus omnes ingrati sunt." Nam, ut dicimus,
omnes stulti mali sunt; qui unum autem habet
vitium, omnia habet; omnes autem stulti et mali
2 sunt; omnes ergo ingrati sunt. Quid ergo? Non
sunt? Non undique humano generi convicium fit?
Non publica querella est perisse beneficia et paucis-
simos esse, qui de bene merentibus non invicem pessime mereantur? Nec est, quod hanc nostram tantum murmurationem putes pro pessimo pravoque
numerantium, quidquid citra recti formulam cecidit.
3 Ecce nescioqui non ex philosophorum domo clamat,
ex medio conventu populos gentesque damnatura vox
mittitur:

> Non hospes ab hospite tutus,
> non socer a genero; fratrum quoque gratia rara est;
> imminet exitio vir coniugis, illa mariti.

---

a Literally, "to have another's *copper*," since all Roman
money was originally copper.

said to be in debt [a] whether he owes pieces of gold or pieces of leather stamped with the seal of the state, such as the Lacedaemonians used, which serve the purpose of coined money. Discharge your indebtedness in that kind by which you incurred it. What benefits are, whether so great and noble a term should be degraded by being applied to such mean and vulgar matter, does not concern you; your search for truth is to the detriment of others. Do you adjust your minds to the semblance of truth, and, while you are learning true virtue, honour whatever vaunts the name of virtue.

"As, according to you," someone retorts, "no man is ungrateful, so, on the other hand, all men are ungrateful." Yes, for, as we say, all fools are bad; moreover, he who has one vice has them all; but all men are foolish and bad; all men, therefore, are ungrateful. What, then? Are they not? Is it not an indictment that is everywhere brought against the human race? Is it not a universal complaint that benefits are thrown away, that there are only a very few who do not requite those who have treated them kindly with the greatest unkindness? Nor need you suppose that I am merely voicing the grumbling of the Stoics, who count every act as most evil and wrong that falls short of the standard of righteousness. Hear the voice of one who cries out condemnation upon all nations and peoples, a voice that issues, not from the home of philosophy, but from the midst of the crowd!

> No guest from host is safe, nor daughter's sire
> From daughter's spouse; e'en brothers' love is rare.
> The husband doth his wife, she him, ensnare.[b]

[b] Ovid, *Met.* i. 144 *sqq.*, cited also in *De Ira*, ii. 9. 2.

4 Hoc iam amplius est : beneficia in scelus versa sunt,
et sanguini eorum non parcitur, pro quibus sanguis
fundendus est ; gladio ac venenis beneficia sequimur.
Ipsi patriae manus adferre et fascibus illam suis premere potentia ac dignitas est ; humili se ac depresso
loco putat stare, quisquis non supra rem publicam
stetit ; accepti ab illa exercitus in ipsam convertuntur,
5 et imperatoria contio est : " Pugnate contra coniuges,
pugnate contra liberos ! Aras, focos, penates armis
incessite ! " Qui ne triumphaturi quidem inire
urbem iniussu senatus deberetis quibusque victorem
exercitum reducentibus curia extra muros prae-
beretur, nunc civibus caesis perfusi cruore cognato
6 urbem subrectis intrate vexillis. Obmutescat inter
militaria signa libertas, et ille victor pacatorque
gentium populus remotis procul bellis, omni terrore
compresso, intra muros obsessus aquilas suas horreat.

1   16. Ingratus est Coriolanus, sero et post sceleris
paenitentiam pius ; posuit arma, sed in medio parri-
cidio posuit.

Ingratus Catilina ; parum est illi capere patriam,
nisi verterit, nisi Allobrogum in illam cohortes im-
miserit et trans Alpes accitus hostis vetera et ingenita

---

a " The Invader of his Country," a Roman legendary hero
of the early period, who, banished from Rome, led a victorious
Volscian army against the city.
332

This goes even further — here crime takes the place of benefits, and the blood of those for whom blood ought to be shed is not spared ; we requite benefits with the sword and poison. To lay hands upon the fatherland itself and crush it with its own fasces is to gain rank and power. Whoever does not stand above the commonweal thinks that he stands in a position that is low and degraded. The armies that she has given are turned against herself, and the general now harangues his men with : "Fight against your wives, fight against your children ! Assail with arms your altars, hearths, and household gods !" Yes, you who had no right to enter the city without the permission of the senate even in order to triumph, who, when bringing back a victorious army, should have been given an audience outside the walls, now, after slaughtering your own countrymen, and stained with the blood of kinsmen, enter into the city with flying flags. Amidst the ensigns of soldiers let Liberty be dumb, and, now that all war has been banished afar, all terror suppressed, let that people who conquered and pacified the nations of the earth be beleaguered within its own walls, and shudder at the sight of its own eagles.

Ungrateful is Coriolanus,[a] who became dutiful too late, and after penitence for crime ; he laid down his arms, but he laid them down in the midst of unholy war.

Ungrateful is Catiline ; he is not satisfied with seizing his fatherland—he must overturn it, he must let loose against it the cohorts of the Allobroges, he must summon an enemy from beyond the Alps to satiate its old and inborn hatred, and pay with the

odia satiaverit ac diu debitas inferias Gallicis bustis duces Romanos persolverit.

2 Ingratus C. Marius ad consulatus a caliga perductus, qui, nisi Cimbricis caedibus Romana funera aequaverit, nisi civilis exitii et trucidationis non tantum dederit signum, sed ipse signum fuerit, parum mutatam ac repositam in priorem locum fortunam suam sentiet.

3 Ingratus L. Sulla, qui patriam durioribus remediis, quam pericula erant, sanavit, qui, cum a Praenestina arce usque ad Collinam portam per sanguinem humanum incessisset, alia edidit in urbe proelia, alias caedes : legiones duas, quod crudele est, post victoriam, quod nefas, post fidem in angulo congestas contrucidavit et proscriptionem commentus est, di magni, ut, qui civem Romanum occidisset, impunitatem, pecuniam, tantum non civicam acciperet !

4 Ingratus Cn. Pompeius, qui pro tribus consulatibus, pro triumphis tribus, pro tot honoribus, quos ex maxima parte immaturus invaserat, hanc gratiam rei publicae reddidit, ut in possessionem eius alios quoque induceret quasi potentiae suae detracturus invidiam, si, quod nulli licere debebat, pluribus licuisset ; dum extraordinaria concupiscit imperia, dum provincias, ut eligat, distribuit, dum ita cum tertio rem publicam

---

^a According to a tradition, the bones of the Gauls, who invaded Rome in 387 B.C., were burned in the city after it had been retaken by Camillus.

^b An allusion to the members of the First Triumvirate formed in 60 B.C.

^c i.e., Crassus.

lives of Roman leaders the sacrifices long owed to Gallic tombs.[a]

Ungrateful is Gaius Marius, who, though raised from the rank of a common soldier to repeated consulships, will feel that the change in his fortune has been too slight, and that he would sink to his former position did he not match the slaughter of the Cimbrians with a sacrifice of Roman lives, did he not, not merely give, but himself become, the signal for the destruction and butchery of his countrymen.

Ungrateful is Lucius Sulla, who healed his fatherland by remedies that were harsher than her ills, who, having marched through human blood all the way from the citadel of Praeneste to the Colline Gate, staged other battles, other murders inside the city; two legions that had been crowded into a corner he butchered; O! the cruelty of it, after he had won the victory, O! the wickedness of it, after he had promised them quarter; and he devised proscription, great gods! in order that anyone who had killed a Roman citizen might claim impunity, money, all but a civic crown!

Ungrateful is Gnaeus Pompeius, who in return for three consulships, in return for three triumphs, in return for the many public offices into most of which he had thrust himself before the legal age, showed such gratitude to the commonwealth that he induced others[b] also to lay hands upon her—as if he could render his own power less odious by giving several others the right to do what no man ought to have had the right to do! While he coveted extraordinary commands, while he distributed the provinces to suit his own choice, while he divided the commonwealth in such a way, that though a third person[c] had a share,

335

dividit, ut tamen in sua domo duae partes essent, eo
redegit populum Romanum, ut salvus esse non posset
nisi beneficio servitutis.

5 Ingratus ipse Pompei hostis ac victor ; a Gallia
Germaniaque bellum in urbem circumegit, et ille
plebicola, ille popularis castra in circo Flaminio posuit
propius, quam Porsinae fuerant. Temperavit quidem
ius crudelitatemque victoriae ; quod dicere solebat,
praestitit : neminem occidit nisi armatum. Quid
ergo est ? Ceteri arma cruentius exercuerunt, satiata
tamen aliquando abiecerunt ; hic gladium cito condidit, numquam posuit.

6 Ingratus Antonius in dictatorem suum, quem iure
caesum pronuntiavit, interfectores eius in provincias
et imperia dimisit ; patriam vero proscriptionibus,
incursionibus, bellis laceratam post tot mala destinavit
ne Romanis quidem regibus, ut, quae Achaeis,
Rhodiis, plerisque urbibus claris ius integrum liber-
tatemque cum immunitate reddiderat, ipsa tributum
spadonibus penderet !

1 17. Deficiet dies enumerantem ingratos usque in
ultima patriae exitia. Aeque immensum erit, si per-
currere coepero, ipsa res publica quam ingrata in
optimos ac devotissimos sibi fuerit quamque non
minus saepe peccaverit, quam in ipsam peccatum est.

2 Camillum in exilium misit, Scipionem dimisit ;

---

^a An allusion to the fact that Pompey's wife was Julia,
the daughter of Caesar.

^b The name is omitted because " Caesar " had become an
imperial title.

^c The statement lacks other authority. Antony was
consul at the time of Caesar's murder, and so officially in
power.

two-thirds of it remained in his own family,[a] he reduced the Roman people to such a plight that only by
the acceptance of slavery were they able to survive.

The foe and conqueror [b] of Pompeius was himself
ungrateful. From Gaul and Germany he whirled
war to Rome, and that friend of the people, that
democrat, pitched his camp in the Circus Flaminius,
even nearer to the city than Porsina's had been. It
is true that he used the cruel privileges of victory
with moderation ; the promise that he was fond of
making he kept—he killed no man who was not in
arms. But what of it ? The others used their arms
more cruelly, yet, once glutted, flung them aside ; he
quickly sheathed his sword, but never laid it down.

Ungrateful was Antony to his dictator, who he declared was rightly slain,[c] and whose murderers he
allowed to depart to their commands in the provinces.
His country, torn as it had been by proscriptions, in-
vasions, and wars, after all her ills, he wished to make
subject to kings, who were not even Roman, in order
that a city that had restored sovereign rights,
autonomy, and immunity to the Achaeans, the
Rhodians, and many famous cities, might herself pay
tribute to eunuchs ! [d]

The day will fail me to enumerate those whose ingratitude resulted in the ruin of their country.
Equally endless will be the task if I attempt a survey
of how ungrateful the commonwealth herself has
been to its best and most devoted servants, and how
it has sinned not less often than it has been sinned
against.

Camillus it sent into exile, Scipio went with its con-

[d] An allusion to the Egyptian court and Antony's surrender
to the charms of Cleopatra.

337

exsulavit post Catilinam Cicero, diruti eius penates,
bona direpta, factum, quidquid victor Catilina fecisset;
Rutilius innocentiae pretium tulit in Asia latere;
Catoni populus Romanus praeturam negavit, consulatum pernegavit.

3 Ingrati publice sumus. Se quisque interroget:
nemo non aliquem queritur ingratum. Atqui non
potest fieri, ut omnes querantur, nisi querendum est
de omnibus: omnes ergo ingrati sunt. Ingrati sunt[1]
tantum? Et cupidi omnes et maligni omnes et
timidi omnes, illi in primis, qui videntur audaces.
Adice: et ambitiosi omnes sunt et impii omnes. Sed
non est, quod irascaris; ignosce illis, omnes in-
saniunt.

4 Nolo te ad incerta revocare, ut dicam: "Vide,
quam ingrata sit iuventus! Quis non patris sui
supremum diem, ut innocens sit, optat? Ut modera-
tus sit, expectat? Ut pius, cogitat? Quotus quisque uxoris optimae mortem timet, ut non et com-
putet? Cui, rogo, litigatori defenso tam magni
beneficii ultra res proximas memoria duravit?"

5 Illud in confesso est: quis sine querella moritur?
Quis extremo die dicere audet:

Vixi et quem dederat cursum fortuna peregi?

Quis non recusans, quis non gemens exit? Atqui
hoc ingrati est non esse contentum praeterito tem-

---

[1] Ingrati sunt *added by Gertz; omitted by Hosius.*

---

[a] Banished in 92 B.C. because of his sturdy opposition to
the extortions of the *publicani* in Asia.

[b] Virgil, *Aeneid*, iv. 653; cited also in *De Vita Beata*, 19. 1.

sent ; it exiled Cicero, even after the conspiracy of Catiline, destroyed his home, plundered his property, did everything that a victorious Catiline would have done ; Rutilius [a] found his blamelessness rewarded with a hiding-place in Asia ; to Cato the Roman people refused the praetorship, and persisted in refusing the consulship.

We are universally ungrateful. Let each one question himself—everyone will find someone to complain of for being ungrateful. But it is impossible that all men should complain, unless all men gave cause for complaint—all men, therefore, are ungrateful. Are they ungrateful only ? They are also covetous and spiteful and cowardly—especially those who appear to be bold. Besides, all are self-seeking, all are ungodly. But you have no need to be angry with them ; pardon them—they are all mad.

To refer you to uncertain instances is not my desire, so I say : " See how ungrateful is youth ! What young man does not long for his father's last day though his hands are clean ? Does not look forward to it though he curbs his desire ? Does not ponder it though he is dutiful ? How few there are who dread so much the death of their best of wives that they do not even calculate the probabilities ? What litigant, I ask you, after he has been defended, retains the memory of so great a benefit beyond the hour it happened ? "

And all agree in asking who dies without complaint ! Who on his last day ventures to say :

I've lived ; my destined course I now have run [b] ?

Who does not shrink from departure ? Who does not mourn it ? Yet not to be satisfied with the time

339

pore. Semper pauci dies erunt, si illos numeraveris.
6 Cogita non esse summum bonum in tempore ; quantumcumque est, boni consules. Ut prorogetur tibi
dies mortis, nihil proficitur ad felicitatem, quoniam
7 mora non fit beatior vita sed longior. Quanto satius
est gratum adversus perceptas voluptates non aliorum
annos computare, sed suos benigne aestimare et in
lucro ponere ! " Hoc me dignum iudicavit deus,
hoc satis est ; potuit plus, sed hoc quoque beneficium
est." Grati simus adversus deos, grati adversus
homines, grati adversus eos, qui aliquid nobis praestiterunt, grati etiam adversus eos, qui nostris praestiterunt.

1 18. " In infinitum ius," inquit, " me obligas, cum
dicis : ' et nostris ' ; itaque pone aliquem finem. Qui
filio beneficium dat, ut dicis, et patri eius dat : primum, de quo quaero. Deinde illud utique mihi de-
terminari volo : si et patri beneficium datur, numquid
et fratri ? Numquid et patruo ? Numquid et avo ?
Numquid et uxori et socero ? Dic mihi, ubi debeam
desinere, quousque personarum seriem sequar."

2 Si agrum tuum coluero, tibi beneficium dedero ;
si domum tuam ardentem restinxero aut, ne concidat,
excepero, tibi beneficium dabo ; si servum tuum
sanavero, tibi imputabo ; si filium tuum servavero,
non habebis beneficium meum ?

one has had is to be ungrateful. Your days will always seem few if you stop to count them. Reflect that your greatest blessing does not lie in mere length of time ; make the best of it however short it may be. Though the day of your death should be postponed, your happiness is in no whit enhanced, since life becomes, not more blissful, but merely longer, by the delay. How much better it is to be grateful for the pleasures that have been enjoyed, not to reckon up the years of others, but to set a generous value on one's own, and to score them down as gain ! " God deemed me worthy of this, this is enough ; he might have given more, but even this is a benefit." Let us be grateful to the gods, grateful to mankind, grateful to those who have bestowed anything upon ourselves, grateful also to those who have bestowed anything upon our dear ones.

" You render me liable," you retort, " to infinite obligation when you say ' also upon our dear ones ' ; so do set some limit. According to you, he who gives a benefit to a son, gives it also to his father. This is the first question I raise. Secondly, I should like particularly to have this point settled. If the benefit is given also to your friend's father, is it given also to his brother ? Also to his uncle ? Also to his grandfather ? Also to his wife ? Also to his father-in-law ? Tell me, where must I stop, how far am I to pursue the list of relatives ? "

If I cultivate your field, I shall give you a benefit ; if your house is on fire and I shall put it out, or if I keep it from tumbling down, I shall give you a benefit ; if I heal your slave, I shall charge the service to you ; if I save the life of your son, will you not have a benefit from me ?

1   19. " Dissimilia ponis exempla, quia, qui agrum meum colit, agro beneficium non dat sed mihi ; et qui domum meam, quo minus ruat, fulcit, praestat mihi, ipsa enim domus sine sensu est ; debitorem me habet, quia nullum habet ; et qui agrum meum colit, non illum, sed me demereri vult. Idem de servo dicam : mei mancipii res est, mihi servatur ; ideo ego pro illo debeo. Filius ipse beneficii capax est ; itaque ille accipit, ego beneficio laetor et contingor, non obligor."

2   Velim tamen, tu, qui debere te non putas, respondeas mihi. Filii bona valetudo, felicitas, patrimonium pertinet ad patrem ; felicior futurus est, si salvum filium habuerit, infelicior, si amiserit. Quid ergo ? Qui et felicior fit a me et infelicitatis maximae periculo liberatur, non accipit beneficium ?

3   " Non," inquit ; " quaedam enim in alios conferuntur, sed ad nos usque permanant ; ab eo autem exigi quidque debet, in quem confertur, sicut pecunia ab eo petitur, cui credita est, quamvis ad me illa aliquo modo venerit. Nullum beneficium est, cuius non commodum et proximos tangat, non num-
4 quam etiam longius positos ; non quaeritur, quo beneficium ab eo, cui datum est, transierit, sed ubi

" The instances you offer are of a different colour, for he who cultivates my field, gives a benefit, not to the field, but to me ; and he who props up my house to keep it from falling, bestows a benefit on me, for the house itself is without feeling ; because it has none, he makes me his debtor ; and he who cultivates my field, wishes to do a service, not to it, but to me. I should say the same of the slave ; he is a chattel of mine, it is to my advantage to have his life saved ; therefore the debt is mine instead of his. But my son is himself capable of receiving a benefit ; he, therefore, receives it, while I merely rejoice, and, though I am nearly concerned, I am not placed under obligation by it."

Nevertheless I should like you, who suppose that you are under no obligation, to answer me this. A father is concerned in the good health, the happiness, the inheritance of his son ; he is going to be made more happy if he keeps his son alive, more unhappy if he has lost him. What, then ? If any-one is made happier by me, if he is freed from the danger of the greatest unhappiness, does he not receive a benefit ?

" No," you answer, " for there are some things that, though they are conferred upon others, pass on to us ; but, in each case, the thing ought to be required of the one upon whom it was conferred, just as, in the case of a loan, money is sought from the one to whom it was lent, although it may by some means have come into my hands. There is no benefit whose advantage does not extend to those who are nearest to the recipient, sometimes even to those who are far removed ; the question is, not whither did the benefit pass from the one to whom it was given, but where

primo collocetur ; a reo tibi ipso et a capite repetitio
est."

Quid ergo ? Oro te, non dicis : " Filium mihi
donasti, et, si hic perisset, victurus non fui " ? Pro
eius vita beneficium non debes, cuius vitam tuae
praefers ? Etiamnunc, cum filium tuum servavi, ad
genua procumbis, dis vota solvis tamquam ipse ser-
5 vatus ; illae voces exeunt tibi : " Nihil mea interest,
an me servaveris ; duos servasti, immo me magis."
Quare ista dicis, si non accipis beneficium ?

" Quia et, si filius meus pecuniam mutuam sump-
serit, creditori numerabo, non tamen ideo ego
debuero ; quia et, si filius meus in adulterio deprensus
6 erit, erubescam, non ideo ego ero adulter. Dico me
tibi obligatum pro filio, non quia sum, sed quia volo
me offerre tibi debitorem voluntarium. At pervenit
ad me summa ex incolumitate eius voluptas, summa
utilitas, et orbitatis gravissimum vulnus effugi. Non
quaeritur nunc, an profueris mihi, sed an beneficium
dederis ; prodest enim et animal et lapis et herba, nec
tamen beneficium dant, quod numquam datur nisi a
7 volente. Tu autem non vis patri, sed filio dare, et
interim ne nosti quidem patrem. Itaque cum dixeris:
' Patri ergo beneficium non dedi filium eius ser-
vando ? ' contra oppone : ' Patri ergo beneficium

was it first placed. You must be repaid by the real debtor, the one who first received it."

What, then? I beg of you, do you not say to me: "You have given me the life of my son, and, if he had perished, I could not have survived him"? Do you not owe a benefit in return for the life of one whose safety you value above your own? Besides, when I have saved your son's life, you fall upon your knees, you pay vows to the gods just as if your own life had been saved; your lips utter these words: "Whether you have saved my own life is to me of no concern; you have saved both our lives—nay, rather, mine." Why do you say this if you do not receive a benefit?

"Because, also, if my son were to obtain a loan of money, I should pay his creditor, yet should not for that reason be indebted to him; because also, if my son should be caught in adultery, I should blush, yet should not for that reason become an adulterer. I say that I am indebted to you for my son's life, not because I really am, but because I wish to constitute myself your debtor of my own free will. But his safety has brought to me the greatest possible pleasure, the greatest possible advantage, and I have escaped the heaviest of all blows, the loss of a child. The question is now, not whether you have been of service to me, but whether you have given me a benefit; for a dumb animal, or a stone, or a plant, can be of service, and yet they cannot give a benefit, for a benefit is never given without an act of the will. But you wish to give, not to the father, but to the son, and sometimes you do not even know the father. Therefore, when you have said: 'Have I not, then, given a benefit to the father by saving the life of his son?' you must raise the counter-question: 'Have I, then,

dedi, quem non novi, quem non cogitavi ? ' Et quid
quod aliquando eveniet, ut patrem oderis, filium
serves ? Beneficium ei videberis dedisse, cui tunc
inimicissimus eras, cum dares ? "

8   Sed ut dialogorum altercatione seposita tamquam
iuris consultus respondeam, mens spectanda est
dantis ; beneficium ei dedit, cui datum voluit. Si
in patris honorem fecit, pater accepit beneficium ;
si filii in usum, pater beneficio in filium conlato non
obligatur, etiam si fruitur. Si tamen occasionem
habuerit, volet et ipse praestare aliquid, non tamquam
solvendi necessitatem habeat, sed tamquam inci-
piendi causam. Repeti a patre beneficium non debet ;
si quid pro hoc benigne facit, iustus, non gratus est.

9 Nam illud finiri non potest: si patri do beneficium,
et matri et avo et avunculo et liberis et adfinibus et
amicis et servis et patriae. Ubi ergo beneficium
incipit stare ? Sorites enim ille inexplicabilis subit,
cui difficile est modum imponere, quia paulatim sur-
repit et non desinit serpere.

1   20. Illud solet quaeri: "Fratres duo dissident; si alterum servo, an dem beneficium ei, qui fratrem invisum
non perisse moleste laturus est." Non est dubium,
quin beneficium sit etiam invito prodesse, sicut non

2 dedit beneficium, qui invitus profuit. " Beneficium,"

ᵃ A chain-argument, in which the conclusion of one syl-
logism becomes the premiss of the next.

given a benefit to the father, whom I do not know, of whom I had no thought ? ' And what if, as will sometimes happen, you hate the father, yet save the life of his son ? Will you be considered to have given a benefit to one to whom, at the very time that you gave it, you had the greatest hostility ? "

But, to lay aside the bickering of dialogue, and to reply, as it were, judicially, I should say that the purpose of the giver must be considered ; he gave the benefit to the one to whom he wished it to be given. If he did it as a compliment to the father, then the father received the benefit ; if, as a service to the son, the father is placed under no obligation by the benefit conferred upon the son, even if he is pleased by it. If, however, he gets the opportunity, he will himself wish to bestow something, not that he feels the necessity of repaying, but that he finds an excuse for offering, a service. Repayment of the benefit must not be sought from the father ; if he does a generous act because of it, he is, not grateful, but just. For there can be no end to it—if I am giving a benefit to my friend's father, I am giving it also to his mother, his grandfather, his uncle, his children, his relatives, his friends, his slaves, his country. Where, then, does a benefit begin to stop ? For there enters in the endless sorites,[a] to which it is difficult to set any limit, for it grows little by little, and never stops growing.

This, too, is a common question : " If two brothers are at variance, and I save the life of one, do I give a benefit to the other who will probably regret that the brother he hated did not die ? " There can be no doubt that to render a service to a man even against his will is a benefit, just as he who has rendered a service against his will has not given a benefit. " Do

347

inquit, " vocas, quo ille offenditur, quo torquetur ? "
Multa beneficia tristem frontem et asperam habent,
quemadmodum secare et urere, ut sanes, et vinclis
coercere. Non est spectandum, an doleat aliquis
beneficio accepto, sed an gaudere debeat ; non est
malus denarius, quem barbarus et ignarus formae
publicae reiecit. Beneficium et odit et accepit, si
modo id prodest, si is, qui dabat, ut prodesset, dedit.
Nihil refert, an bonam rem malo animo quis accipiat.
3 Agedum, hoc in contrarium verte. Odit fratrem
suum, quem illi habere expedit ; hunc ego occidi :
non est beneficium, quamvis ille dicat esse et gaudeat.
Insidiosissime nocet, cui gratiae aguntur pro iniuria !
4   " Video : prodest aliqua res et ideo beneficium
est ; nocet et ideo non est beneficium. Ecce, quod
nec prosit nec noceat, dabo, et tamen beneficium
erit. Patrem alicuius in solitudine exanimem inveni,
corpus eius sepelivi. Nec ipsi profui (quid enim illius
intererat, quo genere dilaberetur ?) nec filio (quid
enim illi per hoc commodi accessit ?)."
    Dicam, quid consecutus sit : officio sollemni et
5 necessario per me functus est ; praestiti patri eius,
quod ipse praestare voluisset nec non et debuisset.
Hoc tamen ita beneficium est, si non misericordiae et

you," you ask, " call that which vexes him, which torments him a benefit ? " Yes, many benefits are, on their face, stern and harsh, such as the cures wrought by surgery and cautery and confinement in chains. The point to consider is, not whether anyone is made unhappy, but whether he ought to be made happy, by receiving a benefit ; a coin is not necessarily a bad one because a barbarian who does not know the government stamp has rejected it. A man both hates, and yet accepts, a benefit provided that it does him good, provided that the giver gave it in order that it might do him good. It makes no difference whether anyone accepts a good thing with a bad spirit or not. Come, consider the converse case. A man hates his brother, but it is to his advantage to keep him ; if I have killed the brother, I do not do him a benefit, although he may say that it is, and be glad of it. It is a very artful enemy who gets thanked for the injury he has done !

" I understand ; a thing that does good is a benefit, a thing that does harm is not a benefit. But see here, I will give you an instance where neither good nor harm is done, and yet the act will be a benefit. Suppose I have found the corpse of someone's father in a lonely place, and bury it. I have done no good either to the man himself (for what difference would it make to him in what fashion he rotted ?), or to the son (for what advantage does he gain by the act ?)."

I will tell you what he has gained. Using me as his instrument, he has performed a customary and necessary duty ; I supplied to his father what he would have wished, what it would also have been his duty, to supply himself. Yet such an act becomes a benefit only if I performed it, not out of the sense

humanitati dedi, ut quodlibet cadaver absconderem,
sed si corpus adgnovi, si filio tunc hoc praestare me
cogitavi. At si terram ignoto mortuo inieci, nullum
in hoc habeo huius officii debitorem in publicum
humanus.

6   Dicet aliquis : " Quid tanto opere quaeris, cui dederis beneficium, tamquam repetiturus aliquando ?
Sunt, qui numquam iudicent esse repetendum, et has
causas adferunt. Indignus etiam repetenti non
reddet, dignus ipse per se referet. Praeterea, si bono
viro dedisti, expecta, ne iniuriam illi facias appellando,
tamquam sua sponte redditurus non fuisset. Si malo
viro dedisti, plectere ; beneficium vero ne corruperis
creditum faciendo. Praeterea lex, quod non iussit
repeti, vetuit."

7   Verba sunt ista. Quam diu me nihil urguet, quam
diu fortuna nihil cogit, perdam potius beneficium
quam repetam. Sed si de salute liberorum agitur,
si in periculum uxor deducitur, si patriae salus ac
libertas mittit me etiam, quo ire nollem, imperabo
pudori meo et testabor omnia me fecisse, ne opus
esset mihi auxilio hominis ingrati ; novissime recipiendi beneficii necessitas repetendi verecundiam
vincet. Deinde, cum bono viro beneficium do, sic
do tamquam numquam repetiturus, nisi fuerit necesse.

of pity and humanity that would lead me to hide away anybody's corpse, but because I recognized the body, and supposed that I was rendering a service to the son. But, if I have thrown earth over an unknown dead man, I have by the act made no one my debtor for this service—I am just generally humane.

But someone will say : " Why do you take so much trouble to discover to whom you should give a benefit as though you intended to ask repayment some day ? There are some who think that repayment ought never to be asked, and the reasons they adduce are these. An unworthy person will not make return even when he is asked to do so, and the worthy man will repay of his own accord. Moreover, if you have given to a good man, be patient ; do not do him an injustice by dunning him, as though he would not have made return of his own accord. If you have given to a bad man, you must blame yourself ; but do not spoil a benefit by making it a loan. Besides, the law, by not bidding you to ask repayment, forbids you."

These are mere words. So long as I have no pressing need, so long as I am not forced by fortune, I would rather lose a benefit than ask for repayment. If, however, the safety of my children is at stake, if my wife is threatened with danger, if the safety of my country and my liberty impel me to a course that I should prefer not to take, I shall conquer my scruples, and bear witness that I have done everything to avoid needing the help of an ungrateful person ; the necessity of receiving a return of my benefit will at last overcome my reluctance to ask a return. Again, when I give a benefit to a good man, I do so with the intention of never asking a return unless it should be necessary.

1 **21.** "Sed lex," inquit, "non permittendo exigere vetuit." Multa legem non habent nec actionem, ad quae consuetudo vitae humanae omni lege valentior dat aditum. Nulla lex iubet amicorum secreta non eloqui ; nulla lex iubet fidem etiam inimico praestare ; quae lex ad id praestandum nos, quod alicui promisimus, adligat ? Nulla. Querar tamen cum eo, qui arcanum sermonem non continuerit, et fidem datam nec servatam indignabor.

2 "Sed ex beneficio," inquit, "creditum facis." Minime ; non enim exigo, sed repeto, et ne repeto quidem, sed admoneo. Num ultima quoque me necessitas in hoc aget, ut ad eum veniam, cum quo mihi diu luctandum sit ? Si[1] quis tam ingratus est, ut illi non sit satis admoneri, eum transibo nec dignum

3 iudicabo, qui gratus esse cogatur. Quomodo fenerator quosdam debitores non appellat, quos scit decoxisse et in quorum pudorem nihil superest, nisi quod pereat, sic ego quosdam ingratos palam ac pertinaciter praeteribo nec ab ullo beneficium repetam, nisi a quo non ablaturus ero, sed recepturus.

1 **22.** Multi sunt, qui nec negare sciant, quod acceperunt, nec referre, qui nec tam boni sunt quam grati nec tam mali quam ingrati, segnes et tardi, lenta nomina, non mala. Hos ego non appellabo, sed commonefaciam et ad officium aliud agentes re-

---

[1] si *added by Gruter.*

" But," you say, " the law, by not authorizing, forbids the exaction." There are many things that do not come under the law or into court, and in these the conventions of human life, that are more binding than any law, show us the way. No law forbids us to divulge the secrets of friends ; no law bids us keep faith even with an enemy. What law binds us to keep a promise that we have made to anyone ? There is none. Yet I shall have a grievance against a person who has not kept the secret I told him, and I shall be indignant with one who, after giving a promise, has not kept it.

" But," you say, " you are turning a benefit into a loan." By no means ; for I do not demand, but request, and I do not even request, but simply remind. Shall even the most pressing necessity ever force me to go to one with whom there would be need for me to have a long struggle ? If anyone is so ungrateful that a simple reminder will not suffice, I shall pass him by, and judge him unworthy of being compelled to be grateful. As a money-lender makes no demand of certain debtors who he knows have become bankrupt, and, to their shame, have nothing left but what is already lost, so I shall pass over certain men who are openly and obstinately ungrateful, and I shall ask a benefit to be repaid by no one from whom I could not hope, not to extort, but to receive, a return.

There are many who do not know how either to disavow or to repay what they have received, who are neither good enough to be grateful, nor bad enough to be ungrateful—slow and dilatory people, backward debtors, but not defaulters. Of these I shall make no demand, but shall admonish them and turn them back from other interests to their duty. They will promptly

ducam. Qui statim mihi sic respondebunt: "Ignosce; non mehercules scivi hoc te desiderare, alioqui
ultro obtulissem; rogo, ne me ingratum existimes;
memini, quid mihi praestiteris." Hos ego quare
2 dubitem et sibi meliores et mihi facere? Quemcumque potuero, peccare prohibebo; multo magis
amicum, et ne peccet et ne in me potissimum peccet.
Alterum illi beneficium do, si illum ingratum esse non
patior; nec dure illi exprobrabo, quod praestiti, sed
quam potuero mollissime. Ut potestatem referendae
gratiae faciam, renovabo memoriam eius et petam
3 beneficium; ipse me intelleget repetere. Aliquando
utar verbis durioribus, si emendari illum posse spera-
vero; nam deploratum propter hoc quoque non
4 exagitabo, ne ex ingrato inimicum faciam. Quod
si admonitionis quoque sugillationem ingratis re-
mittimus, segniores ad reddenda beneficia faciemus;
quosdam vero sanabiles et qui fieri boni possint, si
quid illos momorderit, perire patiemur admonitione
sublata, qua et pater filium aliquando correxit et
uxor maritum aberrantem ad se reduxit et amicus
languentem amici fidem erexit.

1   23. Quidam, ut expergiscantur, non feriendi, sed
commovendi sunt; eodem modo quorundam ad referendam gratiam fides non cessat, sed languet.
Hanc pervellamus. "Noli munus tuum in iniuriam
vertere; iniuria est enim, si in hoc non repetis, ut
ingratus sim. Quid, si ignoro, quid desideres? Quid,

reply to me : " Pardon me ; upon my word, I did not know that you missed the money, or I would have offered it of my own accord ; I beg you not to think me ungrateful ; I am mindful of your favour to me." Why should I hesitate to make such as these better men both in their own eyes and in mine ? If I can keep anyone from doing wrong, I shall ; much more a friend —both from doing wrong and, most of all, from doing wrong to me. I bestow a second benefit upon him by not permitting him to be ungrateful ; nor will I reproach him harshly with what I had bestowed, but as gently as I can. In order to give him an opportunity to show his gratitude, I shall refresh his memory, and ask for a benefit ; he will himself understand that I am asking repayment. Sometimes, if I have hope of being able to correct his fault, I shall use harsher words ; yet, if he is beyond hope, I shall not exasperate him as well, for fear that I may turn an ingrate into an enemy. But if we spare ungrateful men even the affront of an admonition, we shall make them more dilatory in re- turning benefits. Some, indeed, who are curable, if conscience pricks them, and might become good men will be left to go to ruin if we withhold the admonition by which a father at times reclaims his son, by which a wife brings back to her arms an erring husband, and a friend stimulates the flagging loyalty of a friend.

In order to awaken some men, it is necessary only to shake, not to strike, them ; in the same way, in the case of some men, their sense of honour about return- ing gratitude is, not extinct, but only asleep. Let us arouse it. " Do not," they might say, " turn your gift into an injury ; for injury it will be if you fail to ask repayment for the express purpose of leaving me ungrateful. What if I do not know what you desire ?

si occupationibus districtus et in alia vocatus occasionem non observavi ? Ostende mihi, quid possim,
2 quid velis. Quare desperes, antequam temptes ? Quare properas et beneficium et amicum perdere ? Unde scis, nolim an ignorem, animus an facultas desit mihi ? Experire." Admonebo ergo non amare, non palam, sine convicio, sic, ut se redisse in memoriam, non reduci putet.

1   24. Causam dicebat apud divum Iulium ex veteranis quidam paulo violentior adversus vicinos suos et causa premebatur. "Meministi," inquit, "imperator, in Hispania, talum extorsisse te circa Sucronem ?" Cum Caesar meminisse se dixisset : "Meministi quidem sub quadam arbore minimum umbrae spargente cum velles residere ferventissimo sole et esset asperrimus locus, in quo ex rupibus acutis unica illa
2 arbor eruperat, quendam ex commilitonibus paenulam suam substravisse ?" Cum dixisset Caesar : "Quidni meminerim ? Et quidem siti confectus, quia impeditus ire ad fontem proximum non poteram, repere manibus volebam, nisi commilito,[1] homo fortis ac strenuus, aquam mihi in galea sua adtulisset"—, "Potes ergo," inquit, "imperator, adgnoscere illum hominem aut illam galeam ?" Caesar ait se non posse galeam adgnoscere, hominem pulchre posse,

    [1] nisi commilito *editors* : manibus milito *O*.

What if I have not watched for an opportunity because I was distracted by business and occupied with other interests ? Show me what I can do, what you wish me to do. Why do you lose faith before you put me to the test ? Why are you in a hurry to lose both your benefit and a friend ? How do you know whether I am unwilling, or merely unaware—whether I am lacking in opportunity, or intention ? Give me a chance ! " I shall, therefore, remind him of my benefit, not bitterly, not publicly, not with reproaches, but in such a way that he will think that, instead of being brought back, he himself has come back, to the recollection of it.

One of his veterans, being greatly incensed against his neighbours, was once pleading his case before the deified Julius, and the case was going against him. " Do you remember, general," he said, " the time in Spain when you sprained your ankle near the river Sucro ? " When Caesar replied that he remembered it, he continued : " Do you remember, too, when, because of the powerful heat of the sun, you wanted to rest under a certain tree that cast very little shade, that one of your fellow-soldiers spread out his cloak for you because the ground, in which that solitary tree had sprung up among the sharp stones, was very rough ? " When Caesar replied : " Of course I do ; and, too, when I was perishing with thirst, and wanted to crawl to a nearby spring because, crippled as I was, I could not walk, unless my companion, who was a strong and active man, had brought me some water in his helmet—" " Could you, then, general," interrupted the veteran, " recognize that man, or that helmet ? " Caesar replied that he could not recognize the helmet, but that he could the man,

et adiecit, puto obiratus, quod se a cognitione media
3 ad veterem fabulam abduceret : " Tu utique ille non
es." " Merito," inquit, " Caesar, me non adgnoscis ;
nam cum hoc factum est, integer eram ; postea ad
Mundam in acie oculus mihi effossus est et in capite
lecta ossa. Nec galeam illam, si videris, adgnosces ;
machaera enim Hispana divisa est." Vetuit illi ex-
hiberi negotium Caesar et agellos, in quibus vicinalis
via causa rixae ac litium fuerat, militi suo donavit.

1   25. Quid ergo ? Non repeteret beneficium ab
imperatore, cuius memoriam multitudo rerum con-
fuderat, quem fortuna ingentes exercitus disponen-
tem non patiebatur singulis militibus occurrere ?
Non est hoc repetere beneficium, sed resumere bono
loco positum et paratum, ad quod tamen, ut sumatur,
manus porrigenda est. Repetam itaque, quia hoc
aut ex magna necessitate facturus ero aut illius causa,
a quo repetam.

2   Ti. Caesar inter initia dicenti cuidam : " Meministi—"antequam plures notas familiaritatis veteris
proferret : " Non memini," inquit, " quid fuerim."
Ab hoc quidni non esset repetendum beneficium ?
Optanda erat oblivio ; aversabatur omnium amicorum

perfectly, and, irritated I suppose because he allowed
himself to revert to the old incident in the midst of a
trial, added : " You, at any rate, are not the one."
" You have good reason, Caesar," he replied, " not
to recognize me ; for, when this happened, I was a
whole man ; later, during the battle of Munda, one of
my eyes was torn out, and some bones were taken
from my skull. And you would not recognize that
helmet if you saw it ; for it was split by a Spanish
sword." Caesar gave orders that the man was not
to be troubled, and presented his old soldier with the
bit of ground which, because his neighbours made a
path through it, had been the cause of the quarrel
and the suit.

What, then ? Because his commander's memory
of a benefit he received had been dimmed by a multitude of happenings, and his position as the organizer
of vast armies did not permit him to meet individual
soldiers, should the veteran not have asked him to
return the benefit he had conferred ? This is, not so
much asking for the repayment of a benefit, as taking
repayment when it lies waiting in a convenient place,
although one must stretch forth one's hand in order
to take it. I shall, therefore, ask for repayment,
when either the pressure of great necessity, or the
best interest of him from whom I am asking it shall
urge me to do so.

Tiberius Caesar, when a certain man started to say :
" You remember—," interrupted him before he
could reveal more evidence of an old intimacy with :
" I do not remember what I was." Why should he
not have been asked to repay a benefit ? He had a
reason for desiring forgetfulness ; he was repudiating
the acquaintance of all friends and comrades, and

et aequalium notitiam et illam solam praesentem
fortunam suam adspici, illam solam cogitari ac narrari
volebat. Inquisitorem habebat veterem amicum !

3 Magis tempestive repetendum est beneficium
quam petendum. Adhibenda verborum moderatio,
ut nec gratus possit offendi nec[1] ingratus dissimulare.
Tacendum erat et expectandum, si inter sapientes
viveremus ; et tamen sapientibus quoque indicare
melius fuisset, quid rerum nostrarum status posceret.

4 Deos, quorum notitiam nulla res effugit, rogamus, et
illos vota non exorant, sed admonent. Dis quoque,
inquam, Homericus ille sacerdos adlegat officia et aras
religiose cultas. Moneri velle ac posse secunda virtus

5 est. Equus obsequens facile et parens huc illuc frenis
leniter motis flectendus est. Paucis animus sui rector
optimus ; proximi sunt, qui admoniti in viam redeunt ;

6 his non est dux detrahendus. Opertis oculis inest
acies, sed sine usu ; quam lumen diei iis immissum ad
ministeria sua evocat. Instrumenta cessant, nisi illa
in opus suum artifex movit. Inest interim animis
voluntas bona, sed torpet modo deliciis ac situ, modo
officii inscitia. Hanc utilem facere debemus nec irati
relinquere in vitio, sed ut magistri patienter ferre

gratus possit offendi nec *added by Haase.*

---

[a] Chryses, priest of Apollo, in *Iliad*, i. 39-42.
[b] See Hesiod, *Works and Days*, 293-295 :

Οὗτος μὲν πανάριστος, ὃς αὐτὸς πάντα νοήσῃ
φρασσάμενος, τά κ' ἔπειτα καὶ ἐς τέλος ᾖσιν ἀμείνω·
ἐσθλὸς δ' αὖ κἀκεῖνος, ὃς εὖ εἰπόντι πίθηται.

wished men to behold only the high position he then filled, to think and to talk only of that. He regarded an old friend as an accuser !

It is even more needful to choose the right time for requesting the return of a benefit than for requesting its bestowal. We must be temperate in our language, so that the grateful man may not take offence, nor the ungrateful pretend to do so. If we lived among wise men, it would have been our duty to keep silence and wait ; and yet it would have been better to indicate even to wise men what the condition of our affairs demanded. We petition even the gods, whose knowledge nothing escapes, and, although our prayers do not prevail upon them, they remind them of us. Homer's priest,[a] I say, recounts even to the gods his services and his pious care of their altars. The second best form of virtue is to be willing and able to take advice.[b] The horse that is docile and obedient can easily be turned hither and thither by a gentle movement of the reins. Few men follow reason as their best guide ; next best are those who return to the right path when they are admonished ; these must not be deprived of their guide. The eyes, even when they are closed, still have the power of sight, but do not use it ; but the light of day, when it has been admitted to them, summons their power of sight into service. Tools lie idle unless the workman uses them to perform his task. Our minds all the while possess the virtuous desire, but it lies torpid, now from their softness and disuse, now from their ignorance of duty. We ought to render this desire useful, and, instead of abandoning it in vexation to its weakness, we should bear with it as patiently as schoolmasters bear with the blunders of young pupils

offensationes puerorum discentium memoriae labentis;
quae quemadmodum saepe subiecto uno aut altero
verbo ad contextum reddendae orationis adducta est,
sic ad referendam gratiam admonitione revocanda
est.

when their memory fails ; and, just as one or two words of prompting will bring back to their memory the context of the speech they must deliver, so the virtuous desire needs some reminder to recall it to the repayment of gratitude.

LIBER VI

1. Quaedam, Liberalis, virorum optime, exercendi tantum ingenii causa quaeruntur et semper extra vitam iacent ; quaedam et, dum quaeruntur, oblectamento sunt et quaesita usui. Omnium tibi copiam faciam ; tu illa, utcumque tibi visum erit, aut peragi iubeto aut ad explicandum ludorum ordinem induci. Quin his quoque, si abire protinus iusseris, non nihil actum erit ; nam etiam quae discere supervacuum est, prodest cognoscere. Ex vultu igitur tuo pendebo ; prout ille suaserit mihi, alia detinebo diutius, alia expellam et capite agam.

1 **2.** An beneficium eripi posset, quaesitum est. Quidam negant posse ; non enim res est, sed actio. Quomodo aliud est munus, aliud ipsa donatio, aliud qui navigat, aliud navigatio, et, quamvis in morbo aeger sit, non tamen idem est aeger et morbus, ita aliud est beneficium ipsum, aliud quod ad unum-
2 quemque nostrum beneficio pervenit. Illud incorporale est, irritum non fit ; materia vero eius huc et

BOOK VI

THERE are some matters, my most excellent
Liberalis, that are investigated simply for the sake of
exercising the intellect, and lie altogether outside of
life ; others that are a source of pleasure while the
investigation is in progress, and of profit when it is
finished.   I shall lay the whole store of them before
you ; do you, as you may feel inclined, order me
either to discuss them at length, or merely to present
them in order to show the programme of the enter-
tainment.   But something will be gained even from
those which you may order to be at once dismissed :
for there is some advantage in discovering even what
is not worth learning.   I shall, therefore, watch the
expression of your face, and, according as it guides
me, deal with some questions at greater length, and
pitch others headlong out of court.

The question has been raised whether it is possible
to take away a benefit.   Some say that it is not possible, for a benefit is, not a thing, but an act.   As a gift
is one thing, the act of giving another, as a sailor is
one thing, the act of sailing another, and, as a sick man
and his disease are not the same thing although a sick
man is not without disease, so a benefit is one thing,
and that which anyone receives by means of the
benefit another.   The benefit is incorporeal, and is
never rendered invalid ; the matter of it is passed

365

illuc iactatur et dominum mutat.   Itaque cum eripis,
ipsa rerum natura revocare, quod dedit, non potest.
Beneficia sua interrumpit, non rescindit : qui moritur,
tamen vixit ; qui amisit oculos, tamen vidit.   Quae
ad nos pervenerunt, ne sint, effici potest, ne fuerint,
non potest ; pars autem beneficii et quidem certissima
3 est, quae fuit.   Non numquam usu beneficii longiore
prohibemur, beneficium quidem ipsum non eraditur.
Licet omnes in hoc vires suas natura advocet, retro
illi agere se non licet.   Potest eripi domus et pecunia
et mancipium et quidquid est, in quo haesit beneficii
nomen ; ipsum vero stabile et immotum est ; nulla
vis efficiet, ne hic dederit, ne ille acceperit.

1   3. Egregie mihi videtur M. Antonius apud Rabi-
rium poetam, cum fortunam suam transeuntem alio
videat et sibi nihil relictum praeter ius mortis, id
quoque, si cito occupaverit, exclamare :

<blockquote>Hoc habeo, quodcumque dedi.</blockquote>

O ! quantum habere potuit, si voluisset ! Hae
sunt divitiae certae in quacumque sortis humanae
levitate uno loco permansurae ; quae cum maiores
fuerint, hoc minorem habebunt invidiam.   Quid
2 tamquam tuo parcis ? Procurator es. Omnia ista,
quae vos tumidos et supra humana elatos oblivisci

---

^a *i.e.*, the immaterial benefit.   To relieve the harshness of
the Latin, Gertz posits a loss of the text after *eripis*.
^b A minor Augustan poet.

from hand to hand, and changes its owner. And so, when you take this away, even Nature herself is not able to recall what she has once given.[a] She may break off her benefits, she cannot annul them ; he who dies has nevertheless lived ; he who has lost his eyes has nevertheless seen. Blessings that we have received can cease to be ours, but they can never cease from having been ours ; what has been, too, is part of a benefit, and, indeed, its surest part. Sometimes we are kept from very long enjoyment of a benefit, but the benefit itself is not obliterated. Nature is not allowed to reverse her acts, though she should summon all her powers to the task. A man's house, his money, his property, everything that passes under the name of a benefit, may be taken away from him, but the benefit itself remains fixed and unmoved ; no power can efface the fact that this man has given, and that one received.

Those seem to me noble words, which in the poet Rabirius [b] are ascribed to Mark Antony, when, seeing his fortune deserting him, and nothing left him but the privilege of dying, and even that on the condition of his seizing it promptly, he is made to exclaim :

> Whatever I have given, that I still possess !

O ! how much he might have possessed if he had wished ! These are the riches that will abide, and remain steadfast amid all the fickleness of our human lot ; and, the greater they become, the less envy they will arouse. Why do you spare your wealth as though it were your own ? You are but a steward. All these possessions that force you to swell with pride, and, exalting you above mortals, cause you to

cogunt vestrae fragilitatis, quae ferreis claustris
custoditis armati, quae ex alieno sanguine rapta
vestro defenditis, propter quae classes cruentaturas
maria deducitis, propter quae quassatis urbes ignari,
quantum telorum in aversos fortuna comparet,
propter quae ruptis totiens adfinitatis, amicitiae,
collegii foederibus inter contendentes duos terrarum
orbis elisus est, non sunt vestra. In depositi causa
sunt iam iamque ad alium dominum spectantia ; aut
hostis illa aut hostilis animi successor invadet.
3 Quaeris, quomodo illa tua facias ? Dona dando.
Consule igitur rebus tuis et certam tibi earum atque
inexpugnabilem possessionem para honestiores illas,
4 non solum tutiores facturus. Istud, quod suspicis,
quo te divitem ac potentem putas, quam diu possides,
sub nomine sordido iacet. Domus est, servus est,
nummi sunt ; cum donasti, beneficium est.

1 4. "Fateris," inquit, "nos aliquando beneficium
non debere ei, a quo accepimus ; ergo ereptum est."
Multa sunt, propter quae beneficium debere desini-
mus, non quia ablatum sed quia corruptum est.
Aliquis reum me defendit, sed uxorem meam per
vim stupro violavit ; non abstulit beneficium, sed
opponendo illi parem iniuriam solvit me debito, et,

forget your own frailty; all these that you guard with
iron bars and watch under arms; these that, stolen
from others at the cost of their blood, you defend at
the cost of your own; these for which you launch
fleets to dye the sea with blood; these for which you
shatter cities to destruction, unconscious of how
many arrows Fortune may be preparing for you behind your back; these for which you have so many
times violated the ties of kinship, of friendship, and
of partnership, while the whole world lies crushed
amid the rivalry of two contestants—all these are not
your own. They are committed to your safe keeping,
and at any moment may find another guardian;
your enemy will seize upon them, or the heir who
accounts you an enemy. Do you ask how you can
make them your own? By bestowing them as gifts!
Do you, therefore, make the best of your possessions,
and, by making them, not only safer, but more honourable, render your own claim to them assured and
inviolable. The wealth that you esteem, that, as you
think, makes you rich and powerful, is buried under
an inglorious name so long as you keep it. It is but
house, or slave, or money; when you have given it
away, it is a benefit.

"You admit," says someone, "that there are
times when we are under no obligation to the man
from whom we have received a benefit; it has,
therefore, been taken away." There are many
things that might cause us to cease to feel indebted
for a benefit, not because it has been removed, but
because it has been ruined. Suppose a man defends
me in a lawsuit, but has forced my wife to commit
adultery; he has not removed his benefit, but has
freed me from indebtedness by matching his benefit

si plus laesit, quam ante profuerat, non tantum gratia
extinguitur, sed ulciscendi querendique libertas fit,
ubi in comparatione beneficii praeponderavit iniuria ;
2 ita non aufertur beneficium, sed vincitur. Quid ?
non tam duri quidam et tam scelerati patres sunt,
ut illos aversari et eiurare ius fasque sit ? Numquid
ergo illi abstulerunt, quae dederant ? Minime, sed
impietas sequentium temporum commendationem
omnis prioris officii sustulit. Non beneficium tollitur,
sed beneficii gratia, et efficitur, non ne habeam, sed
ne debeam. Tamquam pecuniam aliquis mihi credidit, sed domum meam incendit. Pensatum est
creditum damno ; nec reddidi illi, nec tamen debeo.
3 Eodem modo et hic, qui aliquid benigne adversus me
fecit, aliquid liberaliter, sed postea multa superbe,
contumeliose, crudeliter, eo me loco posuit, ut proinde
liber adversus eum essem, ac si nihil accepissem ;
4 vim beneficiis suis attulit. Colonum suum non tenet
quamvis tabellis manentibus, qui segetem eius pro-
culcavit, qui succidit arbusta, non quia recepit, quod
pepigerat, sed quia, ne reciperet, effecit. Sic debitori
suo creditor saepe damnatur, ubi plus ex alia causa
5 abstulit, quam ex crediti petit. Non tantum inter
creditorem et debitorem iudex sedet, qui dicat :

with an equally great wrong, and, if he has injured me more than he had previously benefited me, he not only extinguishes my gratitude, but leaves me free to protest and avenge myself whenever, in balancing the two, the wrong outweighs the benefit; thus the benefit is not withdrawn, but is surpassed. Tell me, are not some fathers so harsh and so wicked that it is right and proper to turn away from them and disown them? Have they, then, withdrawn the benefits that they had given? By no means, but their unfeeling conduct in later years has removed the favour that they had won from all their earlier service. It is not the benefit, but gratitude for the benefit, that is removed, and the result is, not that I do not possess it, but that I am under no obligation for it. It is just as if someone should lend me money, and then set fire to my house. The loan has been balanced by my loss; I have made him no return, and yet I owe him nothing. In the same way, too, a man who has acted kindly and generously toward me, yet later has shown himself in many ways haughty, insulting, and cruel, places me in the position of being just as free from any obligation to him as if I had never received anything; he has murdered his benefits. Though the lease remains in force, a landlord has no claim against his tenant if he tramples upon his crops, if he cuts down his orchard; not because he received the payment agreed upon, but because he has made it impossible to receive it. So, too, a creditor is often adjudged to his debtor, when on some other account he has robbed him of more than he claims on account of the loan. It is not merely the creditor and debtor who have a judge to sit between them, and say: "You lent the man

371

" Pecuniam credidisti. Quid ergo est ? Pecus ab-
egisti, servum eius occidisti, argentum, quod non
emeras, possides ; aestimatione facta debitor discede,
qui creditor veneras " ; inter beneficia quoque et
6 iniurias ratio confertur. Saepe, inquam, beneficium
manet nec debetur ; si secuta est dantem paenitentia,
si miserum se dixit, quod dedisset, si, cum daret,
suspiravit, vultum adduxit, perdere se credidit, non
donare, si sua causa aut certe non mea dedit, si non
desiit insultare, gloriari, ubique iactare et acerbum
munus suum facere, manet beneficium, quamvis non
debeatur, sicuti quaedam pecuniae, de quibus ius
creditori non dicitur, debentur, sed non exiguntur.
1 5. Dedisti beneficium, iniuriam postea fecisti ; et
beneficio gratia debebatur et iniuriae ultio ; nec ego
illi gratiam debeo nec ille mihi poenam : alter ab
2 altero absolvitur. Cum dicimus : " Beneficium illi
reddidi," non hoc dicimus illud nos, quod accepera-
mus, reddidisse, sed aliud pro illo. Reddere est enim
rem pro re dare ; quidni ? cum omnis solutio non
idem reddat, sed tantundem. Nam et pecuniam
dicimur reddidisse, quamvis numeraverimus pro
argenteis aureos, quamvis non intervenerint nummi,
sed delegatione et verbis perfecta solutio sit.
3 Videris mihi dicere : " Perdis operam ; quorsus

money. Very well, then! But you drove off his flock, you killed his slave, you have in your possession silver that you did not buy ; having calculated the value of these, you who came into court as a creditor, must leave it as a debtor." So, too, a balance is struck between benefits and injuries. Often, I say, the benefit endures, and yet imposes no obligation. If the giver repents of his gift, if he says that he is sorry that he gave it, if he sighs, or makes a wry face when he gives it, if he thinks that he is, not bestowing, but throwing away, his gift, if he gave it to please himself, or, at any rate, not to please me, if he persists in being offensive, in boasting of his gift, in bragging of it everywhere, and in making it painful to me, the benefit endures, although it imposes no obligation, just as certain sums of money to which a creditor can establish no legal right may be owed to him though he cannot demand them. You have bestowed a benefit upon me, yet afterwards you did me an injury ; the reward of a benefit should be gratitude, of an injury punishment ; but I do not owe you gratitude, nor do you owe me my revenge—the one is absolved by the other. When we say : " I have returned to him his benefit," we mean that we have returned, not the actual gift that we had received, but something else in its place. For to return is to give one thing in return for another ; evidently so, since in every act of repayment we return, not the same object, but the same value. For we are said to have returned money even though we count out gold coins for silver, and, even though no money passes between us, payment may be effected by the assignment of a debt and orally.

I think I hear you saying : " You are wasting your

enim pertinet scire me, an maneat, quod non debetur?
Iuris consultorum istae acutae ineptiae sunt, qui
hereditatem negant usu capi posse sed ea, quae in
hereditate sunt, tamquam quicquam aliud sit here-
4 ditas, quam ea, quae in hereditate sunt. Illud potius
mihi distingue, quod potest ad rem pertinere, cum
idem homo beneficium mihi dedit et postea fecit
iniuriam, utrum et beneficium illi reddere debeam
et me ab illo nihilo minus vindicare ac veluti duobus
nominibus separatim respondere an alterum alteri
contribuere et nihil negotii habere, ut beneficium
iniuria tollatur, beneficio iniuria. Illud enim video
in hoc foro fieri ; quid in vestra schola iuris sit, vos
5 sciatis. Separantur actiones nec de eo, quod agimus,
et de eo, quod nobiscum agitur, confunditur formula.
Si quis apud me pecuniam deposuerit, idem postea
furtum mihi fecerit, et ego cum illo furti agam et ille
mecum depositi.''
1 6. Quae proposuisti, mi Liberalis, exempla certis
legibus continentur, quas necesse est sequi. Lex
legi non miscetur, utraque sua via it. Depositum
habet actionem propriam tam mehercules quam
furtum. Beneficium nulli legi subiectum est, me
arbitro utitur ; licet mihi inter se comparare, quantum profuerit mihi quisque aut quantum nocuerit,

---

a The word-splitting lawyers, presumably, attempted to
distinguish between the abstract and concrete meanings of
" inheritance."

time ; for what is the use of my knowing whether
the benefit that imposes no obligation remains a
benefit. This is like the clever stupidities of lawyers,
who declare that one can take possession, not of
an inheritance, but only of the objects that are included in the inheritance, just as if there were any
difference between an inheritance and the objects
that are included in an inheritance.[a] Do you, instead,
make clear for me this point, which may be of some
practical use. When the same man has bestowed on
me a benefit, and has afterwards done me an injury,
ought I to return to him the benefit, and nevertheless
to avenge myself upon him, and to make reply, as it
were, on two distinct scores, or ought I to combine
the two into one, and take no action at all, leaving the
benefit to be wiped out by the injury, and the injury
be the benefit ? For this is what I see is the practice
of our courts ; you Stoics should know what the law is
in your school. In the courts the processes are kept
separate, and the case that I have against another
and the case that another has against me are not
merged under one formula. If anyone deposits a
sum of money in my safekeeping, and the same man
afterwards steals something from me, I shall proceed
against him for theft, and he will proceed against me
for the money deposited."

The instances that you have set forth, Liberalis,
come under fixed laws, which we are bound to follow.
One law does not merge into another law ; each proceeds along its own way. A particular action deals
with a deposit, and just as clearly another deals with
theft. But a benefit is subject to no law, it makes me
the judge. I have the right to compare the amount
of good or the amount of harm anyone may have

tum pronuntiare, utrum plus debeatur mihi an de-
2 beam. In illis nihil est nostrae potestatis, eundum
est, qua ducimur ; in beneficio tota potestas mea est,
ego iudico. Itaque non separo illa nec diduco, sed
iniurias et beneficia ad eundem iudicem mitto.
Alioqui iubes me eodem tempore et amare et odisse
et queri et gratias agere, quod natura non recipit.
Potius comparatione facta inter se beneficii et iniuriae
3 videbo, an mihi etiam ultro debeatur. Quomodo, si
quis scriptis nostris alios superne imprimit versus,
priores litteras non tollit, sed abscondit, sic beneficium
superveniens iniuria apparere non patitur.

1   7. Vultus tuus, cui regendum me tradidi, colligit
rugas et trahit frontem, quasi longius exeam. Videris
mihi dicere :

> Quo tantum mihi dexter abis ? Huc derige cursum,
> litus ama.

Non possum magis. Itaque, si huic satis factum
existimas, illo transeamus, an ei debeatur aliquid, qui
nobis invitus profuit. Hoc apertius potui dicere, nisi
propositio deberet esse confusior, ut distinctio statim
subsecuta ostenderet utrumque quaeri, et an ei debe-
remus, qui nobis, dum non vult, profuit, et an ei, qui,
2 dum nescit. Nam si quis coactus aliquid boni fecit

         • Virgil, *Aeneid*, v. 162 *sq.*

done me, and then to decide whether he is more indebted to me, or I to him. In legal actions we ourselves have no power, we must follow the path by
which we are led ; in the case of a benefit I have all
the power, I render judgement. And so I make no
separation or distinction between benefits and injuries, but commit them both to the same judge.
Otherwise, you force me to love and to hate, and to
complain and to give thanks, at the same time ; but
this is contrary to nature. Instead, after making a
comparison of benefit and injury, I shall discover
whether there is still any balance in my favour. As,
if anyone imprints other lines of writing upon my
manuscript, he conceals, though he does not remove,
the letters that were there before, so an injury that
comes on top of a benefit does not allow the benefit to
be seen.

Your face, by which I agreed to be guided, is now
puckered and frowning, as though I were straying
too far afield. You seem to me to be saying :

> Whither so far to the right ? Port your helm ;
> Hug the shore.[a]

I cannot more closely. So now, if you think that I
have exhausted this question, let me pass to the next
one—whether anyone who does us a service without
wishing to, imposes any obligation upon us. I might
have expressed this more clearly, but the proposition
had to be stated somewhat obscurely in order that
it might be shown by the distinction immediately
following that two questions are involved—both
whether we are under any obligation to a man who
does us a service against his will, and whether we are
under obligation to one who does us a service without
knowing it. For why a man does not place us under

quin nos non obliget, manifestius est, quam ut ulla
in hoc verba impendenda sint. Et haec quaestio
facile expedietur et si qua similis huic moveri potest,
si totiens illo cogitationem nostram converterimus
beneficium nullum esse, nisi quod ad nos primum
aliqua cogitatio defert, deinde amica et benigna.
3 Itaque nec fluminibus gratias agimus, quamvis aut
magna navigia patiantur et ad subvehendas copias
largo ac perenni alveo currant aut piscosa et amoena
pinguibus arvis interfluant ; nec quisquam Nilo beneficium debere se iudicat, non magis quam odium, si
immodicus superfluxit tardeque decessit ; nec ventus
beneficium dat, licet lenis et secundus adspiret, nec
utilis et salubris cibus. Nam qui beneficium mihi
daturus est, debet non tantum prodesse, sed velle.
Ideo nec mutis animalibus quicquam debetur : et
quam multos e periculo velocitas equi rapuit ! nec
arboribus : et quam multos aestu laborantes ra-
4 morum opacitas texit ! Quid autem interest, utrum
mihi, qui nescit, profuerit, an qui scire non potuit,
cum utrique velle defuerit ? Quid interest, utrum
me iubeas navi aut vehiculo aut lanceae debere beneficium an ei, qui aeque quam ista propositum bene
faciendi nullum habuit, sed profuit casu ?

obligation if he has done us some favour because he was forced to is so clear that no words need to be devoted to it. Both this question and any similar one that can be raised will be easily settled if in every case we direct our attention to the thought that a benefit is always something that is conveyed to us, in the first place, by some intent, in the second place, by some intent that is kind and friendly. Consequently, we do not expend our thanks upon rivers even though they may bear large ships, flow in copious and unfailing stream for the conveyance of merchandise, or wind beauteously and full of fish through the rich farm-lands. And no one conceives of himself as being indebted for a benefit to the Nile, any more than he would owe it a grudge if it overflowed its banks immoderately, and was slow in retiring ; the wind does not bestow a benefit, even though its blast is gentle and friendly, nor does wholesome and serviceable food. For he who would give me a benefit must not only do, but wish to do, me a service. We, therefore, become indebted neither to dumb animals—and yet how many men have been rescued from peril by the speed of a horse ! nor to trees—and yet how many toilers have been sheltered from the summer's heat by the shade of their boughs ! But what difference does it make whether I have received a service from someone who did not know, or from someone who was not able to know, that he was doing it if in both cases the desire to do it was lacking ? What difference is there between expecting me to feel indebted for a benefit to a ship or to a carriage or to a spear, and expecting me to feel indebted to a man who had just as little intention as they of performing a good act, yet chanced to do me a service ?

1 8. Beneficium aliquis nesciens accipit, nemo a nesciente. Quomodo multos fortuita sanant nec ideo
remedia sunt, et in flumen alicui cecidisse frigore
magno causa sanitatis fuit, quomodo quorundam
flagellis quartana discussa est et metus repentinus
animum in aliam curam avertendo suspectas horas
fefellit nec ideo quicquam horum, etiam si saluti fuit,
salutare est, sic quidam nobis prosunt, dum nolunt,
immo quia nolunt ; non tamen ideo illis beneficium
debemus, quod perniciosa illorum consilia fortuna
2 deflexit in melius. An existimas me debere ei quicquam, cuius manus, cum me peteret, percussit hostem
meum, qui nocuisset, nisi errasset ? Saepe testis,
dum aperte peierat, etiam veris testibus abrogavit
fidem et reum velut factione circumventum misera-
3 bilem reddidit. Quosdam ipsa, quae premebat,
potentia eripuit, et iudices, quem damnaturi erant
causae, damnare gratiae noluerunt. Non tamen hi
beneficium reo dederunt, quamvis profuerint, quia,
quo missum sit telum, non quo pervenerit, quaeritur,
et beneficium ab iniuria distinguit non eventus sed
4 animus. Adversarius meus, dum contraria dicit et
iudicem superbia offendit et in unum testem temere

Anyone can receive, but no one can bestow, a benefit without knowing it. Many sick persons are cured by chance happenings that are not for that reason to be counted remedies, and a man's falling into a river in very cold weather has restored him to health ; some have had a quartan fever broken by a flogging, and the dangerous hours passed unnoticed because their sudden fear diverted their attention to another trouble, and yet none of these things are for that reason to be counted salutary, even if they have restored health. In like manner, certain persons do us service while they are unwilling, nay, because they are unwilling ; and yet they do not for that reason make us indebted for a benefit, because it was Fortune that turned their harmful designs into good. Do you think that I am under any obligation to a man whose hand struck my enemy when it was aimed at me, who, unless he had blundered, would have done me an injury ? Often a witness, by openly perjuring himself, causes even truthful witnesses to be disbelieved, and thus arouses compassion for the man under accusation because he seems to be beset by a conspiracy. Some men have been saved by the very power that was exerted to crush them, and judges who were about to convict a man on the score of his case have refused to convict him on the score of influence.[a] Yet, although the great men did him a service, it was not a benefit that they bestowed upon the accused, because it is a question of, not what the dart hits, but what it was aimed at, and it is, not the result, but the intention, that distinguishes a benefit from an injury. My opponent, by contradicting himself, by offending the judge by his arrogance, and by rashly reducing his case

rem[1] demittit, causam meam erexit ; non quaero,
an pro me erraverit : contra me voluit.

1 9. Nempe, ut gratus sim, velle debeo idem facere,
quod ille, ut beneficium daret, debuit.   Num quid est
iniquius homine, qui eum odit, a quo in turba calcatus
aut respersus aut, quo nollet, impulsus est ?   Atqui
quid est aliud, quod illum querellae eximat, cum in
2 re sit iniuria, quam nescisse, quid faceret ?   Eadem
res efficit, ne hic beneficium dederit, ne ille iniuriam
fecerit ;   et amicum et inimicum voluntas facit.
Quam multos militiae morbus eripuit !   Quosdam,
ne ad ruinam domus suae occurrerent, inimicus vadi-
monio tenuit ;   ne in piratarum manus pervenirent,
quidam naufragio consecuti sunt ;   nec his tamen
beneficium debemus, quia extra sensum officii casus
est, nec inimico, cuius nos lis servavit, dum vexat ac
3 detinet.   Non est beneficium, nisi quod a bona
voluntate proficiscitur, nisi illud adcognoscit, qui
dedit.   Profuit aliquis mihi, dum nescit : nihil illi
debeo.   Profuit, cum vellet nocere : imitabor ipsum.

1 10. Ad primum illum revertamur.   Ut gratiam referam, aliquid facere me vis ?   Ipse, ut beneficium
mihi daret, nihil fecit !   Ut ad alterum transeamus,

---

[1] rem *added by Madvig.*

to one witness, advanced my cause ; I do not consider whether his mistake helped me—he meant to do
me harm.

Of course, in order to show gratitude to my
benefactor, I must wish to do the same thing that he
must have wished in order to give a benefit to me.
Can anything be more unjust than to hate a person
who has trodden upon your foot in a crowd, or splashed
you, or shoved you where you did not wish to go ?
Yet, since he actually does us an injury, what besides
the fact that he did not know what he was doing
exempts him from blame ? The same reason keeps
this man from having given us a benefit, and that one
from having done us an injury ; it is the intention
that makes both the friend and the enemy. How
many have escaped military service because of sickness ! Some have escaped from sharing the destruction of their house by being forced by an enemy to
appear in court, some have escaped falling into the
hands of pirates by having met with shipwreck ; yet
such happenings do not impose the obligation of a
benefit, because chance has no sense of the service
rendered, nor does an enemy, whose lawsuit, while it
harassed and detained us, saved our lives. Nothing
can be a benefit that does not proceed from goodwill,
that is not recognized as such by the one who gives
it. Someone did me a service without knowing it—I
am under no obligation to him. Someone did me a
service when he wished to injure me—I will imitate
him !

Let us revert to the first type. Would you have me
do something in order to show my gratitude ? But
he himself did nothing in order to give me a benefit !
Passing to the second type, do you wish me to show

vis me huic gratiam referre, ut, quod a nolente accepi,
volens reddam ? Nam quid de tertio loquar, qui ab

2 iniuria in beneficium delapsus est ? Ut beneficium
tibi debeam, parum est voluisse te dare ; ut non
debeam, satis est noluisse. Beneficium enim voluntas
nuda non efficit, sed, quod beneficium non esset, si
optimae ac plenissimae voluntati fortuna defuisset,
id aeque beneficium non est, nisi fortunam voluntas
antecessit. Non enim profuisse te mihi oportet, ut
ob hoc tibi obliger, sed ex destinato profuisse.

1 11. Cleanthes exemplo eiusmodi utitur : " Ad
quaerendum," inquit, " et accersendum ex Academia
Platonem duos pueros misi. Alter totam porticum
perscrutatus est, alia quoque loca, in quibus illum
inveniri posse sperabat, percucurrit et domum non

2 minus lassus quam irritus redit ; alter apud proximum circulatorem resedit et, dum vagus atque erro
vernaculis congregatur et ludit, transeuntem Platonem, quem non quaesierat, invenit. Illum, inquit,
laudabimus puerum, qui, quantum in se erat, quod
iussus est, fecit ; hunc feliciter inertem castiga-
bimus."

3 Voluntas est, quae apud nos ponit officium ; cuius
vide quae condicio sit, ut me debito obstringat.
Parum est illi velle, nisi profuit ; parum est profuisse,

gratitude to such a man—of my own will to return what I received from him against his will ? And what shall I say of the third type, the man who stumbled into doing a benefit in trying to do an injury ? To render me indebted to you for a benefit, it is not enough that you wished to give ; but, to keep me from being indebted to you, it is enough that you did not wish to give. For a benefit is not accomplished by a mere wish ; but, because the best and most copious wish would not be a benefit if good fortune had been lacking, just as truly good fortune is not a benefit unless the good wish has preceded the good fortune. For in order to place me under obligation to you, you must not merely have done me a service, but have done it intentionally.

Cleanthes makes use of the following example. " I sent," he says, " two lads to look for Plato and bring him to me from the Academy. One of them searched through the whole colonnade, and also hunted through other places in which he thought that he might be found, but returned home alike weary and unsuccessful ; the other sat down to watch a mountebank near by, and, while amusing himself in company with other slaves, the careless vagabond found Plato without looking for him, as he happened to pass by. The first lad, he says, will have our praise, for, to the best of his ability, he did what he had been ordered ; the fortunate idler we shall flog."

It is the desire that, according to us, establishes the service ; and consider what the terms are if you would place me under obligation. It is not enough for a man to have the wish without having done a service ; it is not enough to have done a service

nisi voluit. Puta enim aliquem donare voluisse nec
donasse ; animum quidem eius habeo, sed beneficium
4 non habeo, quod consummat et res et animus. Quemadmodum ei, qui voluit mihi quidem pecuniam
credere, sed non dedit, nihil debeo, ita ei, qui voluit
mihi beneficium dare, sed non potuit, amicus quidem
ero sed non obligatus ; et volam illi aliquid praestare
(nam et ille voluit mihi), ceterum, si benigniore usus
fortuna praestitero, beneficium dedero, non gratiam
rettulero. Ille mihi gratiam referre debebit ; hinc
initium fiet, a me numerabitur.

1   12. Intellego iam, quid velis quaerere ; non opus
est te dicere ; vultus tuus loquitur. " Si quis sua
nobis causa profuit, eine," inquis, " debetur aliquid ?
Hoc enim saepe te conquerentem audio, quod quaedam homines sibi praestant, aliis imputant." Dicam,
mi Liberalis ; sed prius istam quaestiunculam dividam
2 et rem aequam ab iniqua separabo. Multum enim
interest, utrum aliquis beneficium nobis det sua causa
an et sua. Ille, qui totus ad se spectat et nobis prodest, quia aliter prodesse sibi non potest, eo mihi loco
est, quo, qui pecori suo hibernum et aestivum pabulum
prospicit ; eo loco est, quo, qui captivos suos, ut com-
modius veneant, pascit et ut¹ opimos boves saginat

---

¹ ut *added by Rossbach.*

without having had the wish. For suppose that someone wished to make a gift, but did not make it; I have, it is true, the intention, but I do not have the benefit, for its consummation requires both an object and an intention. Just as I owe nothing to a man who wished to lend me money, but did not supply it, so, if a man wished to give me a benefit, but was not able to do so, though I shall remain a friend, I shall be under no obligation to him; and I shall wish to bestow something upon him (for he wished to bestow something on me), but, if, having enjoyed better fortune than he, I shall have succeeded in bestowing it, I shall not be returning gratitude, but shall be giving him a benefit. What he will owe me will be the repayment of gratitude; the favour will begin with me, it will be counted from me.

I already know what you wish to ask; there is no need for you to say anything; your countenance speaks for you. " If anyone has done us a service for his own sake, are we," you ask, " under any obligation to him? For I often hear you complain that there are some things that men bestow upon themselves, but charge them up to others." I will tell you, Liberalis; but first let me break up that question, and separate what is fair from what is unfair. For it makes a great difference whether anyone gives us a benefit for his own sake, or for his own sake and ours. He who looks wholly to his own interest, and does us a service only because he could not otherwise do himself a service, seems to me to be in a class with the man who provides food for his flock summer and winter; in a class with the man who, in order that he may sell his captives to greater advantage, feeds them, stuffs them as fat as oxen, and rubs them down; in a class

ac defricat, quo lanista, qui familiam summa cura
exercet atque ornat. Multum, ut ait Cleanthes, a
beneficio distat negotiatio.

1 13. Rursus non sum tam iniquus, ut ei nihil debeam,
qui, cum mihi utilis esset, fuit et sibi ; non enim exigo,
ut mihi sine respectu sui consulat, immo etiam opto,
ut beneficium mihi datum vel magis danti profuerit,
dum modo id, qui dabat duos intuens dederit et
2 inter me seque diviserit. Licet id ipse ex maiore
parte possideat, si modo me in consortium admisit,
si duos cogitavit, ingratus sum, non solum iniustus,
nisi gaudeo hoc illi profuisse, quod proderat mihi.
Summae malignitatis est non vocare beneficium,
nisi quod dantem aliquo incommodo adfecit.

3 Alteri illi, qui beneficium dat sua causa, respondebo : " Usus me quare potius te mihi profuisse dicas
quam me tibi ? " " Puta," inquit, " aliter fieri non
posse me magistratum, quam si decem captos cives
ex magno captivorum numero redemero ; nihil debebis mihi, cum te servitute ac vinculis liberavero ?
Atqui mea id causa faciam." Adversus hoc respon-
4 deo : " Aliquid istic tua causa facis, aliquid mea :
tua, quod redimis, mea, quod me redimis ; tibi enim
ad utilitatem tuam satis est quoslibet redemisse.

with the fencing-master who takes the greatest pains
in training and equipping his troop of gladiators.
There is a great difference, as Cleanthes says, between
benefaction and trade.

On the other hand, I am not so unjust as to feel
under no obligation to a man who, when he was
profitable to me, was also profitable to himself. For
I do not require that he should consult my interests
without any regard to his own, nay, I am also
desirous that a benefit given to me should be even
more advantageous to the giver, provided that, when
he gave it, he was considering us both, and meant to
divide it between himself and me. Though he should
possess the larger part of it, provided that he allowed
me to share in it, provided that he considered both of
us, I am, not merely unjust, I am ungrateful, if I do
not rejoice that, while he has benefited me, he has
also benefited himself. It is supreme niggardliness
to say that nothing can be a benefit that does not
inflict some hardship upon the giver of it.

To one of the other type, the man who gives a
benefit for his own sake only, I shall reply : " Having
made use of me, why have you any more right to say
that you have been of service to me, than I have to
you ? " " Suppose," he retorts, " that the only way
in which I can obtain a magistracy is to ransom ten
out of a great number of captive citizens ; will you
owe me nothing when I have freed you from bondage
and chains ? Yet I shall do that for my own sake
only." To this I reply : " In this case you are acting
partly for your own sake, partly for mine—for your
own, in paying the ransom, for mine, in paying a
ransom for me. For you would have served your own
interests sufficiently by ransoming any you chose.

Itaque debeo, non quod redimis me, sed quod eligis ;
poteras enim et alterius redemptione idem consequi,
quod mea. Utilitatem rei partiris mecum et me in
beneficium recipis duobus profuturum. Praefers me
5 aliis ; hoc totum mea causa facis. Itaque, si prae-
torem te factura esset decem captivorum redemptio,
decem autem soli captivi essemus, nemo quicquam
tibi deberet ex nobis, quia nihil haberes, quod cuiquam imputares, a tua utilitate seductum. Non sum
invidus beneficii interpres nec desidero illud mihi
tantum dari, sed et mihi.''

1 14. '' Quid ergo ? '' inquit ; '' si in sortem nomina
vestra coici iussissem, et tuum nomen inter redimen-
2 dos exisset, nihil deberes mihi ? '' Immo deberem,
sed exiguum ; quid sit hoc, dicam. Aliquid istic mea
causa facis, quod me ad fortunam redemptionis ad-
mittis ; quod nomen meum exit, sorti debeo, quod
exire potuit, tibi. Aditum mihi ad beneficium tuum
dedisti, cuius maiorem partem fortunae debeo, sed
hoc ipsum tibi, quod fortunae debere potui.

3 Illos ex toto praeteribo, quorum mercennarium
beneficium est, quod qui dat, non computat, cui sed
quanti daturus sit, quod undique in se conversum est.
Vendit mihi aliquis frumentum ; vivere non possum,
4 nisi emero ; sed non debeo vitam, quia emi. Nec,

I am, therefore, indebted to you, not because you ransom me, but because you choose me ; for you might have attained the same thing by ransoming someone else instead of me. You divide the advantage of your act with me, and you permit me to share in a benefit that will be of profit to both of us. You prefer me to others ; all this you do for my sake only. If, therefore, you would be made praetor by ransoming ten captives, and there were only ten of us in captivity, no one of us would owe you anything, for you would have nothing apart from your own advantage which you could charge up to anyone of us. I do not regard a benefit jealously, nor desire that the whole of it should be given to me, but I desire a part."

"What, then," he replies, "if I had committed your names to a choice by lot, and your name had appeared among those to be ransomed, would you owe nothing to me?" Yes, I should owe something, but very little ; just how much, I will tell you. In that case you do something for my sake, in that you admit me to the chance of being ransomed. I owe it to Fortune that my name was drawn ; I owe it to you that my name could be drawn. You gave me the opportunity to share in your benefit, for the greater part of which I am indebted to Fortune ; but I am indebted to you for the fact that I was able to become indebted to Fortune.

I shall wholly omit notice of those who make benefaction mercenary, for he who gives in this spirit takes count of, not to whom, but on what terms, he will give a benefit that is wholly directed to his own interest. Someone sells me grain ; I cannot live unless I buy it ; yet I do not owe my life to him because I bought it. And I consider, not how

quam necessarium fuerit, aestimo, sine quo victurus
non fui, sed quam ingratum, quod non habuissem, nisi
emissem, in quo invehendo mercator non cogitavit,
quantum auxilii adlaturus esset mihi, sed quantum
lucri sibi. Quod emi, non debeo.

1 **15.** "Isto modo," inquit, "nec medico quicquam
debere te nisi mercedulam dicis nec praeceptori, quia
aliquid numeraveris. Atqui omnium horum apud
nos magna caritas, magna reverentia est." Adversus
2 hoc respondetur quaedam pluris esse, quam emuntur.
Emis a medico rem inaestimabilem, vitam ac bonam
valetudinem, a bonarum artium praeceptore studia
liberalia et animi cultum ; itaque his non rei pretium,
sed operae solvitur, quod deserviunt, quod a rebus
suis avocati nobis vacant ; mercedem non meriti, sed
3 occupationis suae ferunt. Aliud tamen dici potest
verius, quod statim ponam, si prius, quomodo istud
refelli possit, ostendero. "Quaedam," inquit, "pluris
sunt, quam venierunt, et ob hoc aliquid mihi extra pro
4 illis quamvis empta sunt, debes." Primum quid
interest, quanti sint, cum de pretio inter ementem
vendentemque convenerit ? Deinde non emi illud
suo pretio, sed tuo. "Pluris est," inquis, "quam
venit" ; sed pluris venire non potuit. Pretium
autem rei cuiusque pro tempore est ; cum bene ista

necessary the thing was without which I could not have lived, but how little gratitude I owe for something that I should not have had unless I had bought it, in the transportation of which the trader thought, not of how much help he would bring to me, but of how much gain he would bring to himself. What I have paid for entails no obligation.

"According to that," you say, "you would claim that you are under no obligation to your physician beyond his paltry fee, nor to your teacher, because you have paid him some money. Yet for all these we have great affection, great respect." The answer to this is that the price paid for some things does not represent their value. You pay a physician for what is invaluable, life and good health, a teacher of the liberal sciences for the training of a gentleman and cultivation of the mind. Consequently the money paid to these is the price, not of their gift, but of their devotion in serving us, in putting aside their own interests and giving their time to us ; they get paid, not for their worth, but for their trouble. Yet I might more truly make another statement, which I shall at once present, having first pointed out how your quibble can be refuted. "If," you say, "the value of some things is greater than the price they cost, then, although you have paid for them, you still owe me something besides." But, in the first place, what difference does it make what they are really worth, since the seller and the buyer have agreed upon their price ? In the second place, I bought the thing, not at its own value, but at your price. "It is," you retort, "worth more than it costs." Yes, but it could not have been sold for more. Besides, the price of everything varies with circumstances ;

laudaveris, tanti sunt, quanto pluris venire non possunt ; propterea nihil venditori debet, qui bene emit.
5 Deinde, etiam si pluris ista sunt, non tamen ullum istic
tuum munus est, ut non ex usu effectuve, sed ex con-
6 suetudine et annona aestimetur. Quod tu pretium
ponis traicienti maria et per medios fluctus, cum terra
e conspectu recessit, certam secanti viam et prospi-
cienti futuras tempestates et securis omnibus subito
iubenti vela substringi, armamenta demitti, paratos
ad incursum procellae et repentinum impetum stare ?
Huic tamen tantae rei praemium vectura persolvit !
7 Quanti aestimas in solitudine hospitium, in imbre
tectum, in frigore balneum aut ignem ? Scio tamen,
quanti ista consecuturus deversorium subeam !
Quantum nobis praestat, qui labentem domum sus-
cipit et agentem ex imo rimas insulam incredibili
arte suspendit ! Certo tamen et levi pretio fultura
8 conducitur. Murus nos ab hostibus tutos et a subitis
latronum incursionibus praestat ; notum est tamen,
illas turres pro securitate publica propugnacula habi-
turas excitaturus faber quid in diem mereat.
1 16. Infinitum erit, si latius exempla conquiram,
quibus appareat parvo magna constare. Quid ergo ?
Quare et medico et praeceptori plus quiddam debeo

though you have well praised your wares, they are worth only the highest price at which they can be sold ; a man, therefore, who buys them cheap, owes nothing more to the seller. Again, even if they are worth more, nevertheless the fact that their price is determined, not by their utility or efficacy, but by the customary rate of the market, does not imply that there is any gift on your part. At what would you value the service of the man who crosses the seas, and, when he has lost sight of the land, traces an unerring course through the midst of the waves, who forecasts coming storms, and suddenly orders the crew, when they have no sense of danger, to furl the sails, to lower the tackle, and to stand ready to meet the assault and sudden fury of the storm ? Yet this man's reward for such great service is paid by the passenger's fare ! What value do you set on finding lodging in a wilderness, a shelter in rain, a warm bath or a fire in cold weather ? Yet I know at what price I can obtain these things when I enter an inn ! How great a service does he do us who props up our tottering house, and with unbelievable skill keeps erect a group of buildings that are showing cracks at the bottom ! Yet a contract for underpinning is made at a fixed and cheap rate. The city wall provides us protection from the enemy and from the sudden attacks of brigands ; yet it is well known how much a workman is paid each day for erecting the towers provided with parapets to assure the public safety.

My task would be endless if I tried to collect more instances to prove that valuable things are sold at a low price. What, then ? Why is it that I owe something more to my physician and my teacher, and yet

nec adversus illos mercede defungor ? Quia ex
medico et praeceptore in amicum transeunt et nos non
arte, quam vendunt, obligant, sed benigna et familiari
2 voluntate. Itaque medico, si nihil amplius quam
manum tangit et me inter eos, quos perambulat, ponit
sine ullo adfectu facienda aut vitanda praecipiens,
nihil amplius debeo, quia me non tamquam amicum
3 videt, sed tamquam imperatorem. Ne praeceptorem
quidem habeo cur venerer, si me in grege discipu-
lorum habuit, si non putavit dignum propria et
peculiari cura, si numquam in me derexit animum, et,
cum in medium effunderet, quae sciebat, non didici,
4 sed excepi. Quid ergo est, quare istis multum debeamus ? Non quia pluris est, quod vendiderunt,
quam emimus, sed quia nobis ipsis aliquid praestiterunt. Ille magis pependit, quam medico necesse est ;
pro me, non pro fama artis extimuit ; non fuit contentus remedia monstrare : et admovit ; inter sol-
licitos adsedit, ad suspecta tempora occurrit ; nullum
5 ministerium illi oneri, nullum fastidio fuit ; gemitus
meos non securus audivit ; in turba multorum invo-
cantium ego illi potissima curatio fui ; tantum aliis
vacavit, quantum mea valetudo permiserat : huic
ego non tamquam medico sed tamquam amico ob-

---

do not complete the payment of what is due to them ?
Because from being physician and teacher they pass
into friends, and we are under obligation to them, not
because of their skill, which they sell, but because of
their kindly and friendly goodwill. If, therefore, a
physician does nothing more than feel my pulse, and
put me on the list of those whom he visits in his
rounds, instructing me what to do or to avoid without
any personal feeling, I owe him nothing more than
his fee, because he views me, not as a friend, but as a
commander.[a] Nor is there any reason why I should
venerate a teacher if he has considered me merely
one of his many pupils, and has not deemed me worthy
of any particular and special consideration, if he has
not directed his attention to me, but has allowed me,
not so much to learn from him, as to pick up any
knowledge that he spilled into our midst. What
reason, then, do we have for being much indebted to
them ? It is, not that what they have sold is worth
more than we paid for it, but that they have contributed something to us personally. Suppose a physician gave me more attention than was professionally
necessary ; that it was, not for his professional reputation, but for me, that he feared ; that he was not
content to indicate remedies, but also applied them ;
that he sat at my bedside among my anxious friends,
that he hurried to me at the crises of my illness ;
that no service was too burdensome, none too distasteful for him to perform ; that he was not indifferent when he heard my moans ; that, though a
host of others called for him, I was always his chief
concern ; that he took time for others only when my
illness had permitted him—such a man has placed me
under obligation, not as a physician, but as a friend.

6 ligatus sum. Alter rursus docendo et laborem et taedium tulit ; praeter illa, quae a praecipientibus in commune dicuntur, aliqua instillavit ac tradidit, hortando bonam indolem erexit et modo laudibus fecit animum, modo admonitionibus discussit de- 7 sidiam ; tum ingenium latens et pigrum iniecta, ut ita dicam, manu extraxit ; nec, quae sciebat, maligne dispensavit, quo diutius esset necessarius, sed cupit, si posset, universa transfundere : ingratus sum, nisi illum inter gratissimas necessitudines diligo.

1   17. Sordidissimorum quoque artificiorum institoribus supra constitutum aliquid adiecimus, si nobis illorum opera enixior visa est ; et gubernatori et opifici vilissimae mercis et in diem locanti manus suas corollarium adspersimus.   In optimis vero artibus, quae vitam aut conservant aut excolunt, qui nihil se plus existimat debere, quam pepigit, ingratus est. 2 Adice, quod talium studiorum traditio miscet animos ; hoc cum factum est, tam medico quam praeceptori pretium operae solvitur, animi debetur.

1   18. Platon cum flumen nave transisset nec ab illo quicquam portitor exegisset, honori hoc suo datum credens dixit positum illi esse apud Platonem officium; deinde paulo post, cum alium atque alium gratis

Suppose, again, that the other endured labour and weariness in teaching me ; that, besides the ordinary sayings of teachers, there are things which he has transmitted and instilled into me ; that by his encouragement he aroused the best that was in me, at one time inspirited me by his praise, at another warned me to put aside sloth ; that, laying hand, so to speak, on my mental powers that then were hidden and inert, he drew them forth into the light ; that, instead of doling out his knowledge grudgingly in order that there might be the longer need of his service, he was eager, if he could, to pour the whole of it into me—if I do not owe to such a man all the love that I give to those to whom I am bound by the most grateful ties, I am indeed ungrateful.

If the hawkers of even the meanest forms of service seem to us to have put forth unusual effort, we give them something besides what we have agreed upon ; we dispense gratuities to a pilot, to a man who works with the commonest material, and to one who hires out his services by the day. Surely, in the case of the noblest professions that either maintain or beautify life, a man is ungrateful if he thinks that he owes no more than he bargained for. Add, too, that in the transmission of such knowledge mind is fused with mind ; therefore, when this happens, to the teacher, and to the physician as well, is paid the price of his service, but the price of his mind is still owed.

Once when Plato had been put across a river in a boat, and found that the ferryman asked for no pay, thinking that he had been shown a special compliment, he said that the ferryman had placed Plato under obligation to him. But a little later, when he saw him just as zealously convey one after another

eadem sedulitate transveheret, negavit illi iam apud
2 Platonem positum officium. Nam ut tibi debeam
aliquid pro eo, quod praestas, debes non tantum mihi
praestare, sed tamquam mihi ; non potes ob id quemquam appellare, quod spargis in populum. Quid
ergo ? Nihil tibi debebitur pro hoc ? Tamquam ab
uno nihil ; cum omnibus solvam, quod cum omnibus
debeo.

1   19. " Negas," inquit, " ullum dare beneficium eum,
qui me gratuita nave per flumen Padum tulit ? "
Nego. Aliquid boni facit, beneficium non dat ; facit
enim aut sua causa aut utique non mea ; ad summam
ne ipse quidem se mihi beneficium iudicat dare, sed
aut rei publicae aut viciniae aut ambitioni suae praestat et pro hoc aliud quoddam commodum expectat,
2 quam quod a singulis recepturus est. " Quid ergo ? "
inquit, " si princeps civitatem dederit omnibus Gallis,
si immunitatem Hispanis, nihil hoc nomine singuli
debebunt ? " Quidni debeant ? debebunt autem
non tamquam proprium beneficium, sed tamquam
3 publici partem. " Nullam," inquit, " habuit cogitationem illo tempore mei, quo universis proderat ;
noluit mihi civitatem proprie dare nec in me direxit
animum ; ita quare ei debeam, qui me sibi non sub-
4 stituit, cum facturus esset, quod fecit ? " Primum,
cum cogitavit Gallis omnibus prodesse, et mihi cogi-

across without any charge, he denied that the ferryman had placed Plato under any obligation to him.
For, if you wish me to feel indebted for something
that you bestow, you must bestow it, not merely upon
me, but because of me ; you cannot dun any man for
the dole that you fling to the crowd. What, then ?
Will no one owe you anything in return for it ? No
one as an individual ; the debt that I owe in company
with all I shall pay in company with all.

"Do you say," you ask, "that a man who has
carried me across the river Po in a boat without
charge gives me no benefit ? " I do. He does me a
good turn, but he does not give me a benefit ; for he
does it for his own sake, or, at any rate, not for mine.
In short, even the man himself does not suppose that
he is giving a benefit to me, but he bestows it for the
sake of the state, or of the neighbourhood, or of
his own ambition, and in return for it he expects
some sort of advantage quite different from that
which he might receive from individual passengers.
"What, then," you say, "if the emperor should
grant citizenship to all the Gauls, and exemption
from taxes to all the Spaniards, would the individual on account of that owe him nothing ? "
Of course he would owe something, but he
would owe it, not because of a personal benefit,
but because of his share in a public benefit. "The
emperor," he says, "had no thought of me at the
time when he benefited us all ; he did not desire to
give citizenship to me personally, nor did he direct
his attention to me ; so why should I feel indebted to
one who did not put me before himself when he was
thinking of doing what he did ? " In the first place,
when he planned to benefit all the Gauls, he planned

tavit prodesse ; eram enim Gallus et me etiam si non
mea, publica tamen nota comprendit.   Deinde ego
quoque illi non tamquam proprium debebo, sed
tamquam commune munus ; unus[1] ex populo non
tamquam pro me solvam, sed tamquam pro patria
5 conferam. Si quis patriae meae pecuniam credat,
non dicam me illius debitorem nec hoc aes alienum
profitebor aut candidatus aut reus ; ad exsolvendum
tamen hoc dabo portionem meam. Sic istius muneris,
quod universis datur, debitorem me nego, quia mihi
quidem dedit sed non propter me, et mihi quidem,
sed nesciens, an mihi daret ; nihilo minus aliquid mihi dependendum sciam, quia ad me quoque
circumitu longo pervenit. Propter me debet factum
esse, quod me obliget.

1 20. " Isto," inquit, " modo nec lunae nec soli quicquam debes ; non enim propter te moventur." Sed
cum in hoc moveantur, ut universa conservent, et pro
me moventur ; universorum enim pars sum. Adice
2 nunc, quod nostra et horum condicio dissimilis est ;
nam qui mihi prodest, ut per me prosit sibi, non
dedit beneficium, quia me instrumentum utilitatis
suae fecit ; sol autem et luna, etiam si nobis
prosunt sua causa, non in hoc tamen prosunt,

---

[1] unus *added by Fickert.*

---

[a] The inference from this unique passage seems to be that
both a candidate for office and the defendant in a suit that
involved money declared their debts, the first, probably, in
order that he might prove his possession of enough property
to satisfy the senatorial requirement (1,000,000 sesterces),
the other, in order that he might give evidence of being
solvent.

to benefit me also ; for I was a Gaul, and under my national, even if not under my personal, designation he included me. In the second place, I shall, in like manner, be indebted to him as having received, not a personal, but a general, gift ; being one of the people, I shall not pay the debt as one incurred by myself, but shall contribute to it as one incurred by my country. If anyone should lend money to my country, I should not call myself his debtor, nor should I declare this as my debt when a candidate for office or a defendant in a suit[a] ; yet I will pay my share toward quashing the indebtedness. So I deny that a gift which is given to an entire people makes me a debtor, because, while it was given to me, it was not given because of me, and, while it was given to me, the giver was not aware that he was giving to me ; nevertheless I shall be aware that I must pay something for the gift, because after a roundabout course it arrived also at me. An act that lays me under obligation must have been done because of me.

" According to that," you say, " you are under no obligation to the sun or to the moon ; for they do not perform their movements solely because of you." But, since the purpose of their movements is to preserve the universe, they perform their movements for my sake also ; for I am a part of the universe. And besides, our position is different from theirs ; for he who does me a service in order that by means of me he may do himself a service, has not given a benefit, because he has made me an instrument for his own advantage. But in the case of the sun and the moon, even if they do us a service for their own sake, yet their purpose in doing the service is not that by

ut per nos prosint sibi ; quid enim nos conferre illis possumus ?

1 21. " Sciam," inquit, "solem ac lunam nobis velle prodesse, si nolle potuerint ; illis autem non licet non moveri. Ad summam consistant et opus suum intermittant." Hoc vide quot modis refellatur. Non 2 ideo minus vult, qui non potest nolle ; immo maximum argumentum est firmae voluntatis ne mutari quidem posse. Vir bonus non potest non facere, quod facit ; non enim erit bonus, nisi fecerit ; ergo nec bonus vir beneficium dat, quia facit, quod debet, non potest autem non facere, quod debet. Praeterea 3 multum interest, utrum dicas : " Non potest hoc non facere," quia cogitur, an : " Non potest nolle." Nam si necesse est illi facere, non debeo ipsi beneficium, sed cogenti ; si necesse est illi velle ob hoc, quia nihil habet melius, quod velit, ipse se cogit ; ita, quod tamquam coacto non deberem, tamquam cogenti debeo.

4 " Desinant," inquit, " velle." Hoc loco tibi illud occurrat : Quis tam demens est, ut eam neget voluntatem esse, cui non est periculum desinendi vertendique se in contrarium, cum ex diverso nemo aeque videri debeat velle, quam cuius voluntas usque eo

---

^a The thought is : Let the sun and moon prove their desire to benefit us by showing their ability to refuse to benefit us.

means of us they may do themselves a service; for what is there that we can possibly bestow on them?

"I should be sure," you say, "that the sun and the moon really wish to do us a service if it was possible for them to be unwilling; but they cannot help being in motion. In short, let them halt and discontinue their work." But see in how many ways this argument may be refuted. It is not true that a man who is unable to refuse is for that reason the less willing to do; nay, the greatest proof of a fixed desire is the impossibility of its being altered. A good man is unable to fail to do what he does; for unless he did it, he would not be a good man. And, therefore, a good man gives a benefit, not because he does what he ought to do, but because it is not possible for him not to do what he ought to do. Besides, it makes a great difference whether you say: "It is not possible for him not to do this," because he is forced to do it, or: "It is not possible for him to be unwilling." For, if he is compelled to do it, I owe my benefit, not to him, but to the one who forces him; if he is compelled to wish to do it for the reason that he finds nothing better that he wishes to do, it is a case of the man forcing himself; so, while, in the one case, I should not be indebted to him on the ground that he was forced, in the other, I am indebted to him on the ground that he forces himself.

"Let them cease wishing," [a] you say. At this point the following question should occur to you. Who is so crazy as to deny that an impulse that is in no danger of ceasing and being changed into the exact opposite can be a desire, when, on the contrary, no one must appear more surely to have desire than one whose desire is so completely fixed as to be

certa est, ut aeterna sit ? An, si is quoque vult, qui
potest statim nolle, is non videbitur velle, in cuius
naturam non cadit nolle ?

22. " Agedum," inquit, " si possunt, resistant."
Hoc dicis : " Omnia ista ingentibus intervallis diducta
et in custodiam universi disposita stationes suas
deserant ; subita confusione rerum sidera sideribus
incurrant, et rupta rerum concordia in ruinam divina
labantur, contextusque velocitatis citatissimae in tot
saecula promissas vices in medio itinere destituat,
et, quae nunc alternis eunt redeuntque opportunis
libramentis mundum ex aequo temperantia, repen-
tino concrementur incendio, et ex tanta varietate
solvantur atque eant in unum omnia ; ignis cuncta
possideat, quem deinde pigra nox occupet, et pro-
funda vorago tot deos sorbeat." Est tanti, ut tu
coarguaris, ista concidere ? Prosunt tibi etiam invito
euntque ista tua causa, etiam si maior illis alia ac
prior causa est.

1 23. Adice nunc, quod non externa cogunt deos, sed
sua illis in lege aeterna voluntas est. Statuerunt,
quae non mutarent ; itaque non possunt videri facturi
aliquid, quamvis nolint, quia, quidquid desinere non

---

^a To paraphrase : What is so crazy as to deny that an
impulse that cannot be altered is a desire, when there is no
clearer proof of desire than the fact that it is unalterable?
^b *i.e.*, the heavenly bodies.

everlasting ? ^a Or, if even he who is able at any moment to change his desire may be said to have desire, shall not he whose nature does not admit his changing a desire appear to have desire ?

" Very well ! let them stop moving if they can," you say. But you really mean this : " Let all the heavenly bodies, separated as they are by vast distances and appointed to the task of guarding the universe, leave their posts ; let sudden confusion arise, let stars clash with stars, let the harmony of the world be destroyed, and the divine creations totter to destruction ; let the heavenly mechanism, moving as it does with the swiftest speed, abandon in the midst of its course the progressions that had been promised for so many ages, and let the heavenly bodies that now, as they alternately advance and retreat, by a timely balancing keep the world in a state of equipoise be suddenly consumed by flames, and, with their infinite variations broken up, let them all pass into one condition ; let fire claim all things, then let sluggish darkness take its place, and let these many gods ^b be swallowed up in the bottomless abyss." Is it worth while to cause all this destruction in order to convince you ? They do you a service even against your will, and for your sake they follow their courses even if these result from some earlier and more important cause.

Remark, too, at this point, that the gods are constrained by no external force, but that their own will is a law to them for all time. What they have determined upon, they do not change, and, consequently, it is impossible that they should appear likely to do something although it is against their will, since they have willed to

possunt, perseverare voluerunt, nec umquam primi
2 consilii deos paenitet. Sine dubio stare illis et de-
sciscere in contrarium non licet, sed non ob aliud,
quam quia vis sua illos in proposito tenet ; nec im-
becillitate permanent, sed quia non libet ab optimis
3 aberrare et sic ire decretum est. In prima autem
illa constitutione, cum universa disponerent, etiam
nostra viderunt rationemque hominis habuerunt ;
itaque non possunt videri sua tantum causa decurrere
et explicare opus suum, quia pars operis et nos sumus.
Debemus ergo et soli et lunae et ceteris caelestibus
beneficium, quia, etiam si potiora illis sunt, in quae
4 oriuntur, nos tamen in maiora ituri iuvant. Adice,
quod ex destinato iuvant, ideoque obligati sumus,
quia non in beneficium ignorantium incidimus, sed
haec, quae accipimus, accepturos scierunt ; et quamquam maius illis propositum sit maiorque actus sui
fructus, quam servare mortalia, tamen in nostras
quoque utilitates a principio rerum praemissa mens
est et is ordo mundo datus, ut appareat curam nostri
5 non inter ultima habitam. Debemus parentibus
nostris pietatem, et multi non, ut gignerent, coierant.

---

a *i.e.*, the heavenly bodies, being gods, will not violate
their own laws, since they once willed to be subject to them.
408

persist in doing whatever it is impossible for them to cease from doing,[a] and the gods never repent of their original decision. Undoubtedly, it is not in their power to halt and to desert to an opposite position, but it is for no other reason than that their own resolution holds them to their purpose ; and they continue in it, not from weakness, but because they have no desire to stray from the best course, and it was decreed that this is the path for them to follow. Moreover, when, at the time of the original creation, they set in order the universe, they had regard also for our interests, and took account of man ; it cannot be thought, therefore that they follow their courses and display their work merely for their own sake, for we also are a part of that work. We are indebted, therefore, to the sun and the moon and the rest of the heavenly host for a benefit, because, even though the purposes for which they rise are in their eyes more important, nevertheless in their progress toward these greater things they do assist us. Besides, too, they assist us in accordance with a set purpose, and, therefore, we are placed under obligation to them, because we do not stumble upon a benefit from those who are unaware of their gift, but they knew that we should receive the gifts that we do ; and, although they may have a greater purpose, and greater reward for their effort than the mere preservation of mortal creatures, yet from the beginning of things their thought has been directed also to our interests, and from the order bestowed upon the world it becomes clear that they did not regard their interest in us as a matter of very small concern. We owe filial duty to our parents, and yet many at the time of their union had no thought of

Di non possunt videri nescisse, quid effecturi essent,
cum omnibus alimenta protinus et auxilia providerint,
nec eos per neclegentiam genuere, quibus tam multa
generabant.

Cogitavit nos ante natura, quam fecit, nec tam leve
6 opus sumus, ut illi potuerimus excidere. Vide, quantum nobis permiserit, quam non intra homines humani
imperii condicio sit; vide, in quantum corporibus
vagari liceat, quae non coercuit fine terrarum, sed in
omnem partem sui misit; vide, animi quantum
audeant, quemadmodum soli aut noverint deos aut
quaerant et mente in altum elata divina comitentur:
scies non esse hominem tumultuarium et incogitatum
7 opus. Inter maxima rerum suarum natura nihil
habet, quo magis glorietur, aut certe, cui glorietur.
Quantus iste furor est controversiam dis muneris sui
facere! Quomodo adversus eos hic erit gratus,
quibus gratia referri sine impendio non potest, qui
negat se ab iis accepisse, a quibus cum maxime
accepit, qui et semper daturi sunt et numquam re-
8 cepturi? Quanta autem perversitas ob hoc alicui
non debere, quia etiam infitianti benignus est, et con-
tinuationem ipsam seriemque beneficiorum argumentum vocare necessario dantis! "Nolo! Sibi habeat!
Quis illum rogat?" et omnes alias impudentis animi
voces his adstrue. Non ideo de te minus meretur is,

begetting us. But it is not possible for us to suppose that the gods did not know what they would accomplish when they promptly supplied to all men food and support, nor were those for whom they produced so many blessings begotten without purpose.

Nature took thought of us before she created us, nor are we such a trifling creation that we could merely have dropped from her hand. See how great privilege she has bestowed upon us, how the terms of man's empire do not restrict him to mankind ; see how widely she allows our bodies to roam, she has not confined them within the limits of the land, but has dispatched them into every part of her domain ; see how great is the audacity of our minds, how they alone either know, or seek, the gods, and, by directing their thought on high, commune with powers divine. You will discover that man is not a hasty and purposeless creation. Among the greatest of her works Nature has none of which she can more boast, or, surely, no other to which she can boast. What madness it is to quarrel with the gods over their gift ! How shall a man show gratitude to those to whom he cannot return gratitude without expenditure, if he denies that he has received anything from beings from whom he has received most of all, from those who are always ready to give and will never expect return ? And how blind men are not to feel indebted to someone for the very reason that he is generous even to one who denies his gift, and to call the very continuance and succession of his benefits a proof that he is forced to give them ! Put in the lips of these such words as : " I don't want it ! ", " Let him keep it ! ", " Who asks him for it ? " and all the other utterances of insolent minds. Yet it is not true that you are under less

411

cuius liberalitas ad te etiam, dum negas, pervenit,
cuiusque beneficiorum vel hoc maximum est, quod
etiam querenti daturus est.

1   24. Non vides, quemadmodum teneram liberorum
infantiam parentes ad salubrium rerum patientiam
cogant ? Flentium corpora ac repugnantium dili-
genti cura fovent et, ne membra libertas immatura
detorqueat, in rectum exitura constringunt et mox
liberalia studia inculcant adhibito timore nolentibus ;
ad ultimum audacem iuventam frugalitati, pudori,
moribus bonis, si parum sequitur, coactam applicant.
2 Adulescentibus quoque ac iam potentibus sui, si
remedia metu aut intemperantia reiciunt, vis adhibe-
tur ac severitas.   Itaque beneficiorum maxima sunt,
quae a parentibus accepimus, dum aut nescimus aut
nolumus.

1   25. His ingratis et repudiantibus beneficia, non quia
nolunt, sed ne debeant, similes sunt ex diverso nimis
grati, qui aliquid incommodi precari solent iis, quibus
obligati sunt, aliquid adversi, in quo adfectum me-
2 morem accepti beneficii approbent.   An hoc recte
faciant et pia voluntate, quaeritur ; quorum animus
simillimus est pravo amore flagrantibus, qui amicae
suae optant exilium, ut desertam fugientemque comi-

obligation to one whose bounty extends to you even while you deny it, whose benefits include even this the greatest of all—a readiness to give to you even while you complain.

Do you not see how parents force their children in the stage of tender infancy to submit to wholesome measures ? Though the infants struggle and cry, they tend their bodies with loving care, and, fearing that their limbs may become crooked from too early liberty, they swathe them in order that they may grow to be straight, and later they force them to take a liberal education, and, if they are unwilling, resort to the incentive of fear ; finally, upon the recklessness of youth they inculcate thrift, decency, and good habits, and use force if it is too unheedful. As they grow up, too, and are now their own masters, if from fear or from insubordination they refuse needed remedies, sternness and force are applied. And so the greatest of all benefits are those that, while we are either unaware or unwilling, we receive from our parents.

Like those who are ungrateful and repudiate benefits, not because they do not wish them, but in order to escape obligation, are those who at the other extreme are too grateful, who pray that some trouble or some misfortune may befall those who have placed them under obligation, in order that they may have a chance to prove how gratefully they remember the benefit they have received. It is debated whether they are right in doing this, and act from a dutiful desire. They are very much in the same state of mind as those who are inflamed with abnormal love, who long for their mistress to be exiled in order that they may accompany her in her loneliness and

413

tentur, optant inopiam, ut magis desideranti donent,
optant morbum, ut adsideant, et, quidquid inimicus
optaret, amantes vovent. Fere idem itaque exitus
3 est odii et amoris insani. Tale quiddam et his accidit,
qui amicis incommoda optant, quae detrahant, et ad
beneficium iniuria veniunt, cum satius sit vel cessare,
4 quam per scelus officio locum quaerere. Quid, si
gubernator a dis tempestates infestissimas et procellas
petat, ut gratior ars sua periculo fiat ? Quid, si imperator deos oret, ut magna vis hostium circumfusa
castris fossas subito impetu compleat et vallum trepi-
dante exercitu vellat et in ipsis portis infesta signa
constituat, quo maiore cum gloria rebus lassis pro-
5 fligatisque succurrat ? Omnes isti beneficia sua de-
testabili via ducunt, qui deos contra eum advocant,
cui ipsi adfuturi sunt, et ante illos sterni quam erigi
volunt. Inhumana ista perverse grati animi natura
est contra eum optare, cui honeste deesse non possis.
1 26. " Non nocet," inquit, "illi votum meum, quia
simul opto et periculum et remedium." Hoc dicis
non nihil te peccare sed minus, quam si sine remedio
periculum optares. Nequitia est ut extrahas mer-

414

flight, who long that she may be poor in order that she may have more need of their gifts, who long that she may be ill in order that they may sit at her bedside, who, though her lovers, pray for all that an enemy might long for her to have. And so the results of hatred and insane love are almost the same. Somewhat similar is the case of those who long for their friends to have troubles in order that they may remove them, and arrive at beneficence by doing an injury, though it would be better for them to do nothing than by a crime to seek an opportunity for doing a duty. What should we think if a pilot should pray to the gods for fierce tempests and storms in order that danger might cause more esteem for his skill ? What, if a general should beg that a vast force of the enemy might surround his camp, fill the trenches by a sudden charge, tear down the rampart around his panic-stricken army, and plant its hostile standards in the very gates—all in order that he might have greater glory in coming to the rescue of his drooping and shattered fortunes ? All those who ask the gods to injure those whom they themselves intend to help use odious means to bring them benefits, and wish them to be laid low before they raise them up. To desire to injure one whom you cannot in all honour fail to help is a sense of gratitude cruelly distorted.

" My prayer," you say, " does him no harm, because at the same time that I wish for his danger I wish for his relief." What you mean is, not that you do no wrong, but that you do less than if you were to wish for his danger without wishing for his relief. But it is wicked to submerge a man in water in order that you may pull him out, to throw him down in order

415

gere, evertere ut suscites, ut emittas includere. Non
est beneficium iniuriae finis, nec umquam id detraxisse
2 meritum est, quod ipse, qui detraxit, intulerat. Non
vulneres me malo quam sanes. Potes inire gratiam,
si, quia vulneratus sum, sanas, non, si vulneras, ut
sanandus sim. Numquam cicatrix nisi conlata vul-
neri placuit, quod ita coisse gaudemus, ut non fuisse
mallemus. Si hoc ei optares, cuius nullum beneficium haberes, inhumanum erat votum ; quanto inhumanius ei optas, cui beneficium debes !

1 27. " Simul," inquit, " ut possim ferre illi opem,
precor." Primum, ut te in media parte voti tui oc-
cupem, iam ingratus es ; nondum audio, quid illi velis
praestare, scio, quid illum velis pati. Sollicitudinem
illi et metum et maius aliquod imprecaris malum.
Optas, ut ope indigeat : hoc contra illum est ; optas,
ut ope tua indigeat : hoc pro te est. Non succurrere
vis illi, sed solvere : qui sic properat, solvi vult, non
2 solvere. Ita, quod unum in voto tuo honestum videri
poterat, ipsum turpe et ingratum est, nolle debere ;
optas enim, non ut tu facultatem habeas referendae
gratiae, sed ut ille necessitatem implorandae.
Superiorem te facis et, quod nefas est, bene meritum

416

that you may raise him up, to imprison him in order
that you may release him. To end an injury is not
a benefit, and there is never any merit in removing a
burden which the one who removes it had himself imposed. I would rather have you not wound me than
cure my wound. You may gain my gratitude, not by
wounding me in order that you may have a chance to
cure me, but by curing me because I have been
wounded. There is never any pleasure in a scar
except in comparison with a wound, for, while we
are glad that this has healed, we would rather not
have had it. If you wished this to be the fortune of
one from whom you received no benefit, your desire
would be cruel ; how much more cruel to wish it for
one to whom you are indebted for a benefit !

" I pray at the same time," you say, " that I may
bring him aid." In the first place—to stop you in
the middle of your prayer—you at once show yourself ungrateful ; what you wish to bestow upon him
I have not yet heard, what you wish him to suffer I
now know. You pray that anxiety and fear and even
some greater evil may befall him. You hope that he
may need help—this is to his disadvantage. You
hope that he may need help from you—this is for
your advantage. You wish, not to aid him, but to
pay him ; but one who shows such eagerness wishes,
not to pay, but to be freed from debt. So the only
part of your prayer that might have seemed to be
honourable is itself the base and ungrateful feeling
of unwillingness to remain under obligation ; for you
hope, not that you may have an opportunity of returning gratitude, but that he may be under the necessity
of imploring your help. You make yourself the
superior, and force one who has done you a service to

ad pedes tuos mittis. Quanto satius est honesta
voluntate debere, quam rationem per malam solvere !
3 Si infitiareris, quod acceperas, minus peccares ; nihil
enim, nisi quod dederat, amitteret. Nunc vis illum
subici tibi, iactura rerum suarum et status mutatione
in id devocari, ut infra beneficia sua iaceat. Gratum
te putabo ? Coram eo, cui prodesse vis, opta !
Votum tu istud vocas, quod inter gratum et inimicum
potest dividi, quod non dubites adversarium et hostem
4 fecisse, si extrema taceantur ? Hostes quoque opta-
verunt capere quasdam urbes, ut servarent, et vincere
quosdam, ut ignoscerent, nec ideo non hostilia vota,
in quibus, quod mitissimum est, post crudelitatem
venit.

5   Denique qualia esse iudicas vota, quae nemo minus
tibi volet, quam is, pro quo fiunt, succedere ? Pessime cum eo agis, cui vis a dis noceri, a te succurri,
inique cum ipsis dis ; illis enim durissimas partes
6 imponis, tibi humanas ; ut tu prosis, di nocebunt. Si
accusatorem submitteres, quem deinde removeres,
si aliqua illum lite implicares, quam subinde dis-
cuteres, nemo de tuo scelere dubitaret. Quid

grovel at your feet, which is wrong. How much better would it be to remain indebted with an honourable intention than to be released by evil means ! You would be less guilty if you were to repudiate what you had received ; for his only loss would be what he had given. But as it is, you wish him to become subservient to you, by loss of his property and change of social position to be reduced to the state of being in a worse plight than his own benefits relieved. Shall I count you grateful ? Make your prayer in the hearing of the man whom you wish to help ! Do you call that a prayer, in which a grateful friend and an enemy might equally share, and which, if the last part were unuttered, you would not doubt that an adversary and foe had made ? Even the enemy will sometimes hope to capture certain cities in order to spare them, and to conquer certain men in order to pardon them, yet these will not for that reason fail to be hostile desires, in which a very great kindness is preceded by cruelty.

Finally, what sort of prayers do you suppose those can be which no one will desire so little to see fulfilled as he in whose behalf they are made ? You treat a man very badly in wishing him to be injured by the gods, and you treat the gods themselves unfairly in wishing him to be rescued by yourself ; for you assign a most cruel rôle to them, and a kindly one to yourself. The gods must do him an injury in order that you may do him a service. If you suborned someone to be his accuser, and then withdrew him, if you entangled him in a lawsuit, and then suddenly quashed it, no one would be in doubt about your baseness. What difference does it make whether you

interest, utrum istuc fraude temptetur an voto, nisi
quod potentiores illi adversarios quaeris ? Non est,
7 quod dicas : " Quam enim illi iniuriam facio ? "
Votum tuum aut supervacuum est aut iniuriosum,
immo iniuriosum, etiam si irritum. Quidquid non
efficis, dei munus est, iniuria vero, quidquid optas.
Sat est ; tibi non aliter debemus irasci, quam si pro-
feceris.

1   28. " Si vota," inquit, " valuissent, et in hoc valuissent, ut tutus esses." Primum certum mihi optas
periculum sub incerto auxilio. Deinde utrumque
2 certum puta : quod nocet, prius est. Praeterea tu
condicionem voti tui nosti, me tempestas occupavit
portus ac praesidii dubium. Quantum tormentum
existimas, etiam si accepero, eguisse ? Etiam si servatus fuero, trepidasse ? Etiam si absolutus fuero,
causam dixisse ? Nullius metus tam gratus est finis,
ut non gratior sit solida et inconcussa securitas.
3 Opta, ut reddere mihi beneficium possis, cum opus
erit, non, ut opus sit. Si esset in tua potestate, quod
optas, ipse fecisses.

1   29. Quanto hoc honestius votum est : " Opto, in
eo statu sit, quo semper beneficia distribuat, numquam desideret ; sequatur illum materia, qua tam
benigne utitur, largiendi iuvandique ; numquam illi
sit dandorum beneficiorum inopia, datorum paeni-

try to accomplish your purpose by chicanery or by prayer, except that by prayer you summon against him adversaries that are more powerful? You have no right to say: "What harm, pray, do I do him?" Your prayer is either futile or harmful, nay, harmful even if it is in vain. God is responsible for all that you fail to accomplish, but all that you pray for is injury. Wishing is enough—we ought to be just as angry with you as if your wish were fulfilled.

"If my prayers," you say, "had had any power, they would also have had power to bring you safety." In the first place, you desire for me certain danger that is subject to uncertain succour. Again, suppose you consider both certain, the injury comes first. Besides, while *you* know the terms of your prayer, I have been caught in a storm, and am doubtful of gaining the protection of a harbour. Do you think what torture it was to have needed help even if I received it? To have been panic-stricken even if I was saved? To have pleaded my cause even if I was acquitted? No matter how welcome the end of any fear may be, firm and un-shaken security is even more welcome. Pray that it may be in your power to repay my benefit when I shall need it, not that I may need it. If it were in your power, you would yourself have done what you pray for.

How much more righteous would have been this prayer! "I pray that he may be in a position al-ways to dispense benefits, and never to need them; that he may be attended by the means which he uses so generously in giving bounty and help to others; that he may never have lack of benefits to bestow

421

tentia; naturam per se pronam ad misericordiam, humanitatem, clementiam irritet ac provocet turba gratorum, quos illi et habere contingat nec experiri necesse sit; ipse nulli implacabilis sit, ipsi nemo placandus; tam aequali in eum fortuna indulgentia perseveret, ut nemo in illum possit esse nisi conscientia gratus."

2 Quanto haec iustiora vota sunt, quae te in nullam occasionem differunt, sed gratum statim faciunt! Quid enim prohibet referre gratiam prosperis rebus? Quam multa sunt, per quae, quidquid debemus, reddere etiam felicibus possumus! Fidele consilium, adsidua conversatio, sermo comis et sine adulatione iucundus, aures, si deliberari velit, diligentes, tutae, si credere, convictus familiaritas. Neminem tam alte secunda posuerunt, ut non illi eo magis amicus desit, quia nihil absit.

1 30. Ista tristis et omni voto submovenda occasio ac procul repellenda. Ut gratus esse possis, iratis dis opus est? Ne ex hoc quidem peccare te intellegis, quod melius cum eo agitur, cui ingratus es? Propone animo tuo carcerem, vincula, sordes, servitutem, bellum, egestatem; haec sunt occasiones voti tui. Si
2 quis tecum contraxit, per ista dimittitur! Quin

nor regret for those bestowed ; may his nature that
of itself is inclined to pity, kindness, and mercy find
stimulus and encouragement from a host of grateful
persons, and may he be fortunate enough to find
them without the necessity of testing them ; may
none find him implacable, and may he have need to
placate none ; may Fortune continue to bestow on
him such unbroken favour that it will be impossible
for anyone to show gratitude to him except by feeling it."

How much more proper are such prayers as these,
which do not make you wait for an opportunity but
show your gratitude at once ! For what is there
prevent your returning gratitude to a benefactor
while his affairs are prosperous ? How many ways
there are by which we may repay whatever we
owe even to the well-to-do !—loyal advice, constant intercourse, polite conversation that pleases
without flattery, attentive ears if he should wish
to ask counsel, safe ears if he should wish to
be confidential, and friendly intimacy. Good fortune has set no one so high that he does not the
more feel the want of a friend because he wants
for nothing.

This waiting for an opportunity is sorry business—
the thought is to be banished and utterly rejected
from every prayer. Must the gods show their anger
before you can show gratitude ? Do you not understand that you are doing wrong from the very fact
that they treat better the one to whom you are ungrateful ? Set before your mind the dungeon, chains,
disgrace, slavery, war, poverty—these are the opportunities for which you pray. If anyone has had
dealings with you, it is through these that he gets his

potius eum potentem esse vis, cui plurimum debes,
et[1] beatum ? Quid enim, ut dixi, vetat te referre
etiam summa felicitate praeditis gratiam ? Cuius
plena tibi occurret et varia materia. Quid ? tu nescis
3 debitum etiam locupletibus solvi ? Nec te invitum
distringam. Omnia sane excluserit opulenta felicitas,
monstrabo tibi, cuius rei inopia laborent magna fa-
stigia, quid omnia possidentibus desit : scilicet ille,
qui verum dicat et hominem inter mentientes stupen-
tem ipsaque consuetudine pro rectis blanda audiendi
ad ignorantiam veri perductum vindicet a consensu
4 concentuque falsorum. Non vides, quemadmodum
illos in praeceps agat extincta libertas et fides in ob-
5 sequium servile submissa ? Dum nemo ex animi sui
sententia suadet dissuadetque, sed adulandi certamen
est et unum amicorum omnium officium, una contentio,
quis blandissime fallat, ignoravere vires suas, et, dum
se tam magnos, quam audiunt, credunt, attraxere
supervacua et in discrimen rerum omnium perventura
bella, utilem et necessariam rupere concordiam,
secuti iram, quam nemo revocabat, multorum san-
6 guinem hauserunt fusuri novissime suum ; dum vin-
dicant inexplorata pro certis flectique non minus
existimant turpe quam vinci et perpetua credunt,

---

[1] et *commonly added.*

discharge ! Why do you not wish, instead, that the man to whom you owe most may be powerful and happy ? For, as I have said, what prevents your returning gratitude even to those who are endowed with the utmost good fortune ? The opportunities for doing this, you will find, are ample and varied. What ! do you not know that one can pay a debt even to a rich man ? Nor shall I censure you if you are unwilling. Yet, granted that a man's wealth and success may shut you off from all gifts, I will show you what the highest in the land stand in need of, what the man who possesses everything lacks—someone, assuredly, who will tell him the truth, who will deliver him from the constant cant and falsehood that so bewilder him with lies that the very habit of listening to flatteries instead of facts has brought him to the point of not knowing what truth really is. Do you not see how such persons are driven to destruction by the absence of frankness and the substitution of cringing obsequiousness for loyalty ? No one is sincere in expressing approval or disapproval, but one person vies with another in flattery, and, while all the man's friends have only one object, a common aim to see who can deceive him most charmingly, he himself remains ignorant of his own powers, and, believing himself to be as great as he hears he is, he brings on wars that are useless and will imperil the world, breaks up a useful and necessary peace, and, led on by a madness that no one checks, sheds the blood of numerous persons, destined at last to spill his own. While without investigation such men claim the undetermined as assured, and think that it is as disgraceful to be diverted from their purpose as to be defeated, and believe that what has already

quae in summum perducta maxime nutant, ingentia
super se ac suos regna fregerunt; nec intellexerunt
in illa scena vanis et cito diffluentibus bonis reful-
gente ex eo tempore ipsos nihil non adversi expectare
debuisse, ex quo nihil veri audire potuerunt.

1   31. Cum bellum Graeciae indiceret Xerxes, animum tumentem oblitumque, quam caducis confideret,
nemo non impulit. Alius aiebat non laturos nun-
tium belli et ad primam adventus famam terga ver-
2 suros; alius nihil esse dubii, quin illa mole non vinci
solum Graecia, sed obrui posset; magis verendum,
ne vacuas desertasque urbes invenirent et profugis
hostibus vastae solitudines relinquerentur non habi-
3 turis, ubi tantas vires exercere possent; alius vix illi
rerum naturam sufficere, angusta esse classibus maria,
militi castra, explicandis equestribus copiis campestria,
vix patere caelum satis ad emittenda omni manu
tela.

4   Cum in hunc modum multa undique iactarentur,
quae hominem nimia aestimatione sui furentem con-
citarent, Demaratus Lacedaemonius solus dixit ipsam
illam, qua sibi placeret, multitudinem indigestam et
gravem metuendam esse ducenti; non enim vires

reached its highest development, and is even then tottering, will last for ever, they cause vast kingdoms to come crashing down upon themselves and their followers. And, living in that gorgeous show of unreal and swiftly passing blessings, they failed to grasp that from the moment when it was impossible for them to hear a word of truth they ought to have expected nothing but misfortune.

When Xerxes declared war on Greece, everyone encouraged his puffed-up mind that had forgotten what slender reasons he had for confidence. One would say that the Greeks could not even endure the announcement of war, and would take to flight at the first rumour of his arrival; another, that there was not the slightest doubt that with that vast force Greece could be, not only conquered, but crushed; that there was more need to fear that his army would find the cities abandoned and empty, and that the headlong flight of the enemy would leave but a vast wilderness in which his forces would have no chance to display their strength. Another would say that the world was scarcely big enough to contain him, that the seas were too narrow for his fleets, the camps for his soldiers, the plains for the manœuvres of his cavalry forces, and that the sky was scarcely wide enough to allow every man to hurl his darts at once.

While much boasting of this sort was going on around him, exciting the man, who had already too high opinion of himself, to a frantic pitch, Demaratus, the Lacedaemonian, alone told him that that very multitude, on which he congratulated himself, disorganized and unwieldy as it was, was in itself a danger to its leader, for that it had, not strength, but

427

habere, sed pondus ; immodica numquam regi posse,
nec diu durare, quidquid regi non potest. " In
5 primo," inquit, " statim monte Lacones obiecti
dabunt sui experimentum. Tot ista gentium milia
trecenti morabuntur ; haerebunt in vestigio fixi et
commissas sibi angustias armis tuebuntur, corporibus
obstruent ; tota illos Asia non movebit loco ; tantas
minas belli et paene totius generis humani ruentis
6 impetum paucissimi sistent. Cum te mutatis legibus
suis natura transmiserit, in semita haerebis et aestimabis futura damna, cum computaveris, quanti
Thermopylarum angusta constiterint ; scies te fugari
7 posse, cum scieris posse retineri. Cedent quidem
tibi pluribus locis velut torrentis modo ablati, cuius
cum magno terrore prima vis defluit ; deinde hinc
atque illinc coorientur et tuis te viribus prement.
8 Verum est, quod dicitur, maiorem belli apparatum
esse, quam qui recipi ab his regionibus possit, quas
oppugnare constituis, sed haec res contra nos est.
Ob hoc ipsum te Graecia vincet, quia non capit ; uti
9 toto te non potes. Praeterea, quae una rebus salus
est, occurrere ad primos rerum impetus et inclinatis
opem ferre non poteris nec fulcire ac firmare labentia ;
multo ante vinceris, quam victum esse te sentias.

ᵃ A prophecy of the event immortalized by Simonides in
the famous epigram :

Ὦ ξεῖν', ἀγγέλλειν Λακεδαιμονίοις ὅτι τῇδε
κείμεθα τοῖς κείνων ῥήμασι πειθόμενοι.

" Stranger, to Lacedaemon go, and tell
    That here, obedient to her words, we fell."

mere weight; that forces that were too large could
never be controlled, and that an army that could not
be controlled did not last long. " The Lacedaemonians," he said, " will meet you on the first mountain,
and immediately give you a foretaste of their quality.
These countless thousands of various nations will be
held in check by three hundred men[a]; they will
stand firmly at their post, they will defend the pass
entrusted to them with their arms, and block the way
with their bodies; all Asia will not drive them from
their position; pitifully few as they are, they will
stop all this threatened invasion and the wild onrush
of almost the whole human race. When Nature,
changing her laws, has allowed you to traverse the sea,
you will be held up on a footpath, and will be able to
estimate your later losses when you have reckoned
the price the pass of Thermopylae cost you; when
you have learned that you can be checked, you will
know that you can be routed. The Greeks will retreat before you in many places as if swept away by
some mountain torrent that in the first onrush de-
scends with great terror; then from this side and
that they will rise against you, and crush you by
the might of your own forces. What is commonly
said is true—your preparations for war are too great
to find room in the country that you mean to attack,
but this fact is to our disadvantage. Greece will
conquer you for the very reason that she has no
room for you; you cannot use the whole of you. Besides, and in this lies your only hope of victory, you
will not be able to rush forward at the first attack,
and bear aid to your men if they yield, or to support
and strengthen their wavering ranks; you will have
lost the victory long before you know that you have

10 Ceterum non est, quod exercitum tuum ob hoc sus-
tineri non putes posse, quia numerus eius duci quoque
ignotus est ; nihil tam magnum est, quod perire non
possit, cui nascitur in perniciem, ut alia quiescant, ex
ipsa magnitudine sua causa.''

11 Acciderunt, quae Demaratus praedixerat. Divina
atque humana impellentem et mutantem, quidquid
obstiterat, trecenti stare iusserunt, stratusque passim
per totam Graeciam Perses intellexit, quantum ab
exercitu turba distaret. Itaque Xerxes pudore quam
damno miserior Demarato gratias egit, quod solus
sibi verum dixisset, et permisit petere, quod vellet.

12 Petit ille, ut Sardis, maximam Asiae civitatem, curru
vectus intraret rectam capite tiaram gerens ; id solis
datum regibus. Dignus fuerat praemio, ante quam
peteret ; sed quam miserabilis gens, in qua nemo
fuit, qui verum diceret regi, nisi qui non dicebat
sibi !

1   32. Divus Augustus filiam ultra impudicitiae maledictum impudicam relegavit et flagitia principalis
domus in publicum emisit : admissos gregatim adul-
teros, pererratam nocturnis comissationibus civitatem,
forum ipsum ac rostra, ex quibus pater legem de
adulteriis tulerat, filiae in stupra placuisse, cotidianum
ad Marsyam concursum, cum ex adultera in quae-

---

a Julia, wife of Tiberius.
b A resort of courtesans in the Forum.

been conquered. However, you may well suppose that your army will be able to hold out for the reason that not even its leader knows its numbers; but there is nothing so large that it cannot perish, and, though there may be no other agents, its very size gives birth to the cause of its destruction."

It all happened as Demaratus had predicted. And to him who assailed the works of man and God, and removed whatever blocked his path, three hundred men cried, "Halt," and, when everywhere throughout the whole of Greece the Persian had been laid low, he understood how great a difference there was between a mob and an army! And so Xerxes, made more unhappy by his shame than by his loss, expressed his thanks to Demaratus because he had been the only one to tell him the truth, and permitted him to ask any reward he pleased. What he asked was that he should be allowed to enter Sardis, the largest city of Asia, riding in a chariot and wearing a tiara erect upon his head, a privilege that was accorded only to kings. He had earned his reward before he asked for it, but how pitiable the nation in which the only man who told the king the truth was one who did not tell it to himself!

The deified Augustus banished his daughter,[a] who was shameless beyond the indictment of shamelessness, and made public the scandals of the imperial house—that she had been accessible to scores of paramours, that in nocturnal revels she had roamed about the city, that the very forum and the rostrum, from which her father had proposed a law against adultery, had been chosen by the daughter for her debaucheries, that she had daily resorted to the statue of Marsyas,[b] and, laying aside the rôle of adulteress,

431

stuariam versa ius omnis licentiae sub ignoto adultero
peteret.

2   Haec tam vindicanda principi quam tacenda, quia
quarundam rerum turpitudo etiam ad vindicantem
redit, parum potens irae publicaverat. Deinde, cum
interposito tempore in locum irae subisset verecundia,
gemens, quod non illa silentio pressisset, quae tam
diu nescierat, donec loqui turpe esset, saepe exclamavit : " Horum mihi nihil accidisset, si aut
Agrippa aut Maecenas vixisset ! "   Adeo tot habenti
3 milia hominum duos reparare difficile est. Caesae
sunt legiones et protinus scriptae ; fracta classis et
intra paucos dies natavit nova ; saevitum est in opera
publica ignibus, surrexerunt meliora consumptis.
Tota vita Agrippae et Maecenatis vacavit locus.
Quid ? Putem defuisse similes, qui adsumerentur,
an ipsius vitium fuisse, quia maluit queri quam
4 quaerere ? Non est, quod existimemus Agrippam et
Maecenatem solitos illi vera dicere ; qui si vixissent,
inter dissimulantes fuissent. Regalis ingenii mos
est in praesentium contumeliam amissa laudare et
his virtutem dare vera dicendi, a quibus iam audiendi
periculum non est.

1   33. Sed ut me ad propositum reducam, vides, quam
facile sit gratiam referre felicibus et in summo hu-

---

^a In a message to the senate which, not having the heart
to read it himself, he committed to the quaestor (Suetonius,
Aug. 65).

there sold her favours, and sought the right to every indulgence with even an unknown paramour.

Carried away by his anger, he divulged *a* all these crimes, which, as emperor, he ought to have punished, and equally to have kept secret, because the foulness of some deeds recoils upon him who punishes them. Afterwards, when with the lapse of time shame took the place of anger, he lamented that he had not veiled with silence matters that he had not known until it was disgraceful to mention them, and often exclaimed : " If either Agrippa or Maecenas had lived, none of this would have happened to me ! " So difficult was it for one who had so many thousands of men to repair the loss of two ! When his legions were slaughtered, others were at once enrolled ; when his fleet was wrecked, within a few days a new one was afloat ; when public buildings were swept away by fire, finer ones than those destroyed rose in their place. But the place of Agrippa and Maecenas remained empty all the rest of his life. What ! Am I to suppose that there were no more like them who could take their place, or that it was the fault of Augustus himself, because he chose rather to sorrow than to search for others ? There is no reason for us to suppose that Agrippa and Maecenas were in the habit of speaking the truth to him ; they would have been among the dissemblers if they had lived. It is a characteristic of the kingly mind to praise what has been lost to the detriment of what is present, and to credit those with the virtue of telling the truth from whom there is no longer any danger of hearing it.

But, to return to my subject, you see how easy it is to return gratitude to the prosperous and those who

manarum opum positis. Dic illis, non quod volunt
audire, sed quod audisse semper volent ; plenas aures
adulationibus aliquando vera vox intret ; da con-
2 silium utile.   Quaeris, quid felici praestare possis ?
Effice, ne felicitati suae credat, ut sciat illam multis
et fidis manibus continendam.   Parum in illum con-
tuleris, si illi stultam fiduciam permansurae semper
potentiae excusseris docuerisque mobilia esse, quae
dedit casus, et maiore cursu fugere, quam veniunt,
nec iis portionibus, quibus ad summa perventum est,
retro iri, sed saepe inter maximam fortunam et ulti-
3 mam nihil interesse ?   Nescis, quantum sit pretium
amicitiae, si non intellegis multum te ei daturum, cui
dederis amicum, rem non domibus tantum, sed saeculis raram, quae non aliubi magis deest, quam ubi
4 creditur abundare.   Quid ?   Istos tu libros, quos vix
nomenclatorum complectitur aut memoria aut manus,
amicorum existimas esse ?   Non sunt isti amici, qui
agmine magno ianuam pulsant, qui in primas et
secundas admissiones digeruntur.

1   34. Consuetudo ista vetus est regibus regesque
simulantibus populum amicorum discribere, et proprium superbiae magno aestimare introitum ac tactum
sui liminis et pro honore dare, ut ostio suo propius
adsideas, ut gradum prior intra domum ponas, in qua

---

a A slave whose business it was to recognize and announce
the guests who attended his master's levees, and arrange the
order of their admission.

have been placed at the summit of human power. Tell them, not what they wish to hear, but what they will wish they had always heard; sometimes let a truthful voice penetrate ears that are filled with flatteries ; give them useful advice. Do you ask what you can bestow on a fortunate man ? Teach him not to trust his felicity, let him know that it must be sustained by hands that are many and faithful. Will you not have conferred enough upon him if you rob him of the foolish belief that his power will endure for ever, and teach him that the gifts of chance soon pass, and depart with greater speed than they come ; that the descent from the summit of fortune is not made by the same stages by which it was reached, but that often it is only a step from the height of good fortune to ruin ? You do not know how great is the value of friendship if you do not understand that you will give much to the man to whom you have given a friend, something rare not only in great houses, but in the ages, something of which there is nowhere a greater dearth than where it is supposed most of all to abound. What ! Do you think that those lists, which a nomenclator [a] can scarcely hold either in his memory or in his hand, are the lists of friends ? Your friends are not those who, in a long line, knock at your door, whom you distribute into the two classes of those to be admitted first, and those to be second !

It is an old trick of kings and those who imitate kings to divide the company of their friends into classes, and but a part of their arrogance to count crossing, even touching, their threshold a great privilege, and as an honour to grant you permission to sit nearer the front door, and to be the first to set

deinceps multa sunt ostia, quae receptos quoque ex-
2 cludant. Apud nos primi omnium C.[1] Gracchus et mox
Livius Drusus instituerunt segregare turbam suam
et alios in secretum recipere, alios cum pluribus, alios
universos. Habuerunt itaque isti amicos primos, ha-
3 buerunt secundos, numquam veros. Amicum vocas,
cuius disponitur salutatio ? Aut potest huius tibi
fides patere, qui per fores maligne apertas non in-
trat, sed illabitur ? Huic pervenire usque ad libertatem destringendam licet, cuius vulgare et publicum verbum et promiscuum ignotis " Have ! " non
4 nisi suo ordine emittitur ? Ad quemcumque itaque
istorum veneris, quorum salutatio urbem concutit,
scito, etiam si animadverteris obsessos ingenti fre-
quentia vicos et commeantium in utramque partem
catervis itinera compressa, tamen venire te in locum
5 hominibus plenum, amicis vacuum. In pectore
amicus, non in atrio quaeritur ; illo recipiendus,
illic retinendus est et in sensus recondendus. Hoc
doce : gratus es.

1   35. Male de te existimas, si inutilis es nisi adflicto,
si rebus bonis supervacuus es. Quemadmodum te et
in dubiis et in adversis et in laetis sapienter geris, ut
dubia prudenter tractes, adversa fortiter, laeta moderate, ita in omnia utilem te exhibere amico potes.

---

[1] C. *added by Muretus.*

foot inside the house, in which, in turn, there are many other doors that will shut out even those who have gained admittance. With us, Gaius Gracchus and, a little later, Livius Drusus were the first to set the fashion of classifying their followers, and of receiving some in privacy, some in company with others, and others *en masse.* These men, consequently, had chief friends, ordinary friends, never true friends. Do you call a man who must stand in line to give you his greeting a friend? Or can anyone possibly reveal loyalty to you who, through doors that are opened grudgingly, does not so much enter as sneak in? Can anyone reach the point of even approaching to frankness when he must take his turn simply to say "How do you do?", the ordinary and common term of greeting universally used by strangers? And so, whenever you go to wait upon any of the men whose receptions upset the whole city, even though you find the streets beset with a huge throng of people, and the ways jammed with the crowds of those passing in both directions, yet you may be sure that you are going to a place full of people, but void of friends. We must look for a friend, not in a reception hall, but in the heart; there must he be admitted, there retained, and enshrined in affection. Teach a man this—and you show gratitude!

You have a poor opinion of yourself if you are useful to a friend only when he is in distress, if you are unnecessary when fortune smiles. As you conduct yourself wisely in doubtful, in adverse, and in happy circumstances by exercising prudence in case of doubt, bravery in adversity, and restraint in good fortune, so under all circumstances you can make yourself useful to a friend. In adversity do

Adversa eius nec deserueris nec optaveris ; multa
nihilo minus, ut non optes, in tanta varietate, quae
tibi materiam exercendae fidei praebeant, incident.
2 Quemadmodum, qui optat divitias alicui in hoc, ut
illarum ipse partem ferat, quamvis pro illo videatur
optare, sibi prospicit, sic, qui optat amico aliquam
necessitatem, quam adiutorio suo fideque discutiat,
quod est ingrati, se illi praefert et tanti existimat
illum miserum esse, ut ipse gratus sit, ob hoc ipsum
ingratus ; exonerare enim se vult et gravi sarcina
3 liberare.   Multum interest, utrum properes referre
gratiam, ut reddas beneficium, an ne debeas.   Qui
reddere vult, illius se commodo aptabit et idoneum
illi venire tempus volet ; qui nihil aliud quam ipse
liberari vult, quomodocumque ad hoc cupiet per-
4 venire, quod est pessimae voluntatis.   " Ista," inquit,
" festinatio nimium grati est ! "   Id apertius ex-
primere non possum, quam si repetivero, quod dixi.
Non vis reddere acceptum beneficium, sed effugere.
Hoc dicere videris : " Quando isto carebo ? Quocumque modo mihi laborandum est, ne isti obligatus
sim."   Si optares, ut illi de suo solveres, multum
abesse videreris a grato.   Hoc, quod optas, iniquius

not abandon him, but do not wish him misfortune ;
none the less, without your wishing it, in the many
and varied incidents of human life, many things will
befall him that will provide you with an opportunity
of displaying your loyalty. As he who prays that
another may have riches in the hope that he may get
a share of them, has an eye to his own interests
although he offers his prayer ostensibly for the benefit
of the other, so he who prays that a friend may have
some dire need from which he may rescue him by his
help and loyalty, which is really the wish of an ingrate,
sets himself before his friend, and deems it worth
while that his friend should be wretched in order that
he may show himself grateful, for this very reason
proves himself ungrateful ; for he wishes to get rid
of a burden, and to free himself from a heavy load.
It makes a great difference whether you hasten to
return gratitude in order that you may repay a
benefit, or in order that you may not be under
obligation. He who wishes to repay a benefit will
adjust himself to the convenience of his friend, and
will hope for the arrival of a suitable opportunity ; he
who only wishes to get rid of a burden will be eager
to accomplish this by any means whatever, which
is the worst sort of wish. "This haste," you say,
"shows that one is exceedingly grateful !" I cannot
express the matter more clearly than by repeating
what I have said. You wish, not to return, but to
escape from, a benefit. You seem to say : "When
shall I be rid of it ? I must strive in every possible
way to avoid being indebted to him." If you wished
to pay a debt to him with money from his own pocket,
you would appear to be very far from being grateful.
This which you do desire is even more unjust ; for

est; exsecraris enim illum et caput sanctum tibi dira
5 precatione defigis. Nemo, ut existimo, de immani-
tate animi tui dubitaret, si aperte illi paupertatem,
si captivitatem, si famem ac metum imprecareris; at
quid interest, utrum vox ista sit voti tui an vis?
Aliquid enim horum optas. I nunc et hoc esse grati
puta, quod ne ingratus quidem faceret, qui modo non
usque in odium, sed tantum usque ad infitiationem
beneficii perveniret!

1   36. Quis pium dicet Aenean, si patriam capi
voluerit, ut captivitati patrem eripiat? Quis Siculos
iuvenes ut bona liberis exempla monstrabit, si opta-
verint, ut Aetna immensam ignium vim super solitum
ardens et incensa praecipitet datura ipsis occasionem
exhibendae pietatis ex medio parentibus incendio
2 raptis? Nihil debet Scipioni Roma, si Punicum
bellum, ut finiret, aluit; nihil Deciis, quod morte
patriam servaverunt, si prius optaverant, ut devotioni
fortissimae locum ultima rerum necessitas faceret.
Gravissima infamia est medici opus quaerere; multi,
quos auxerant morbos et irritaverant, ut gloria maiore
sanarent, non potuerunt discutere aut cum magna
miserorum vexatione vicerunt.

1   37. Callistratum aiunt (ita certe Hecaton auctor
est), cum in exilium iret, in quod multos cum illo

---

a See note, iii. 37. 2.
b Publius Decius Mus sacrificed himself for the safety of
his country in a battle against the Latins in 337 B.C., and
later his son followed his example.
c An Athenian orator, who for political reasons in 361 B.C.
was sentenced to death, but went into exile.
440

you invoke curses upon him, and call down terrible imprecations upon the head of one whom you hold sacred. No one, I suppose, would have any doubt about the cruelty of your intention if you openly invoked upon him poverty, or captivity, or hunger and fear. But what difference does it make whether that is an uttered or a silent prayer? For someone of these things you do desire. But go now and suppose that it is gratitude to do what not even an ungrateful man would do, provided he confined himself to repudiation of the benefit, and stopped short of hatred!

Who will say that Aeneas is righteous if he wished his native city to be captured in order that he might rescue his father from captivity? Who will point to the Sicilian youths [a] as good models for children if they had prayed that Aetna, all aglow and afire, might hurl forth a huge volume of flame with unusual violence in order to give them an opportunity of showing their devotion to their parents by rescuing them from the midst of the conflagration? Rome owes nothing to Scipio if he fostered the Carthaginian War in order that he might end it. She owes nothing to the Decii [b] for saving their city by dying if they prayed beforehand that they might find in some desperate need of the state an opportunity to show their heroic devotion. It is a burning disgrace for a physician to try to make practice. Many who have aggravated and augmented an illness in order that they may win greater fame by curing it have not been able to banish it, or have conquered it at the cost of great suffering on the part of their victims.

It is said (at any rate Hecaton tells this story) that, when Callistratus [c] was going into exile, forced into it

simul seditiosa civitas et intemperanter libera expulerat, optante quodam, ut Atheniensibus necessitas restituendi exules esset, abominatum talem reditum.

2 Rutilius noster animosius, cum quidam illum consolaretur et diceret instare arma civilia, brevi futurum, ut omnes exules reverterentur : " Quid tibi," inquit, " mali feci, ut mihi peiorem reditum quam exitum optares ? Ut malo, patria exilio meo erubescat, quam reditu maereat ! " Non est istud exilium, cuius neminem non magis quam damnatum pudet.

3 Quemadmodum illi servaverunt bonorum civium officium, qui reddi sibi penates suos noluerunt clade communi, quia satius erat duos iniquo malo adfici quam omnes publico, ita non servat grati hominis adfectum, qui bene de se merentem difficultatibus vult opprimi, quas ipse submoveat, quia, etiam si bene cogitat, male precatur. Ne in patrocinium quidem, nedum in gloriam est incendium extinxisse, quod feceris.

1 38. In quibusdam civitatibus impium votum sceleris vicem tenuit. Demades certe Athenis eum, qui necessaria funeribus venditabat, damnavit, cum probasset magnum lucrum optasse, quod contingere illi sine multorum morte non poterat. Quaeri tamen solet, an merito damnatus sit. Fortasse optavit, non ut multis venderet, sed ut care, ut parvo sibi con-

---

^a A stock type of rectitude. He was forced into exile by unscrupulous public enemies in 92 B.C.

^b An Athenian orator, bitter opponent of Demosthenes, put to death in 318 B.C.

along with many others by his factious and outrageously lawless country, and heard someone express the hope that dire necessity might force the Athenians to recall the exiles, he cried : " God forbid such a return ! "

Our countryman Rutilius [a] showed even more spirit. When someone tried to console him by saying that civil war was threatening, and that in a short time all exiles would be brought back, he replied : " What sin have I committed that you should wish me a more unhappy return than departure ? I should much prefer to have my country blush for my exile than weep at my return ! " The exile that causes no one less shame than the victim is not exile at all.

But as these men maintained their duty as good citizens in being unwilling to be restored to their homes at the cost of a public disaster, because it was better that two should suffer from undeserved misfortune than that all should suffer from universal misfortune, so, in like manner, he does not maintain the character of a grateful man who wishes that another, who has done him a service, may be loaded with troubles in order that he himself may remove them, because, even if his purpose is good, his desire is evil. To put out a fire that you yourself have caused does not excuse you—still less do you credit.

In some states an unholy prayer was treated as a crime. At any rate, at Athens Demades [b] won a suit against a man who sold funeral requirements, by proving that he had prayed for great gain, and that he could not have been successful unless many persons had died. Yet the question is often raised whether he was rightly convicted. Perhaps he prayed, not that he might sell to many, but that he might sell at a

2 starent, quae venditurus esset. Cum constet negotiatio eius ex empto et vendito, quare votum eius in
unam partem trahis, cum lucrum ex utraque sit ?
Praeterea omnes licet, qui in ista negotiatione sunt,
damnes ; omnes enim idem volunt, id est, intra se
optant. Magnam partem hominum damnabis ; cui
3 enim non ex alieno incommodo lucrum ? Miles
bellum optat, si gloriam ; agricolam annonae caritas
erigit ; eloquentiae pretium excitat litium numerus ;
medicis gravis annus in quaestu est ; institores de-
licatarum mercium iuventus corrupta locupletat ;
nulla tempestate tecta, nullo igne laedantur : iacebit
opera fabrilis. Unius votum deprensum est, omnium
4 simile est. An tu Arruntium et Haterium et ceteros,
qui captandorum testamentorum artem professi sunt,
non putas eadem habere quae dissignatores et libi-
tinarios vota ? Illi tamen, quorum mortes optent,
nesciunt, hi familiarissimum quemque, ex quo propter
amicitiam spei plurimum est, mori cupiunt. Illorum
damno nemo vivit, hos, quisquis differt, exhaurit ;
optant ergo non tantum, ut accipiant, quod turpi servitute meruerunt, sed etiam, ut tributo gravi libe-
5 rentur. Non est itaque dubium, quin hi magis, quod
damnatum est in uno, optent, quibus, quisquis morte
profuturus est, vita nocet. Omnium tamen istorum

good profit—that what he would naturally sell might
be bought cheaply. Since his business consisted in
buying and selling, why do you restrict his prayer
to one side of the transaction when there was gain
in both ? Besides, you might convict everyone who
followed that business ; for they all wish, that is,
secretly pray for, the same thing. You will have to
convict, too, a great part of the human race, for who
does not derive gain from another's distress ? The
soldier, if he wants glory, prays for war ; the farmer
is cheered by the high price of grain ; a number
of lawsuits raise the price of eloquence ; the doctor
makes money from an unhealthy season ; the vender
of sybaritic wares is enriched by the corruption of
youth ; if no houses should be damaged by storm or
fire, the builder's trade will suffer. One man's prayer
was detected, but all make a similar prayer. Or do
you suppose that Arruntius and Haterius, and all the
rest who have followed the profession of hunting
legacies, do not put up the same prayers that funeral
directors and undertakers make ? Yet these do not
know whose death it is that they are praying for,
while the former long for the death of their most intimate friends, from whom on account of friendship
they have most hope of a legacy. No one's living
causes the latter any loss, while the former are worn
out if a victim is slow in dying ; they pray, therefore,
not only that they may receive what they have earned
by base servitude, but also that they may be released from the burdensome tribute. There is no
doubt, therefore, that these pray more earnestly for
that which convicted the Athenian, for whoever is
likely to profit them by dying injures them by living.
Yet the prayers of all these men, while well known,

tam nota sunt vota quam impunita. Denique se quisque consulat et in secretum pectoris sui redeat et inspiciat, quid tacitus optaverit. Quam multa sunt vota, quae etiam sibi fateri pudet! Quam pauca, quae facere coram teste possimus!

1 39. Sed non, quidquid reprehendendum, etiam damnandum est, sicut hoc votum amici, quod in manibus est, male utentis bona voluntate et in id vitium incidentis, quod devitat; nam dum gratum 2 animum festinat ostendere, ingratus est. Hoc ait: "In potestatem meam recidat, gratiam meam desideret, sine me salvus, honestus, tutus esse non possit, tam miser sit, ut illi beneficii loco sit, quidquid redditur." Haec dis audientibus: "Circumveniant illum domesticae insidiae, quas ego possim solus opprimere, instet potens inimicus et gravis, infesta turba nec inermis, creditor urgueat, accusator."

1 40. Vide, quam sis aecus! Horum optares nihil, si tibi beneficium non dedisset. Ut alia taceam, quae graviora committis pessima pro optimis referendo, hoc certe delinquis, quod non expectas suum cuiusque rei tempus, quod aeque peccat, qui non sequitur, quam qui antecedit. Quomodo beneficium non semper recipiendum est, sic non utique reddendum. 2 Si mihi non desideranti redderes, ingratus esses; quanto ingratior es, qui desiderare me cogis! Expecta! Quare subsidere apud te munus meum non

are unpunished. Lastly, let every man examine himself, let him retire into the secrecy of his heart, and discover what it is that he has silently prayed for. How many prayers there are which he blushes to acknowledge, even to himself! How few that we could make in the hearing of a witness!

But not everything that is blameworthy is to be considered also a crime, as, for instance, this prayer of a friend, which we are considering, for, while his purpose was good, his method was evil, and he fell into the very fault he was trying to avoid. For he is ungrateful while he hurries to show his gratitude. He prays aloud : " May he fall into my power, may he need my influence, may it not be possible for him to find safety, honour, or security without me, may he be so unhappy that whatever I return to him will count as a benefit." What the ears of the gods hear is : " May he be beset by domestic intrigues which I alone shall be able to crush, may he be assailed by a powerful and bitter enemy, by a hostile mob supplied with arms, may he be hard pressed by a creditor, or by an informer." See how just you are ! You would not have prayed for any of these things if he had not given to you a benefit. To say nothing of your other more serious sin in returning the worst for the best, you are certainly at fault in not waiting for the fitting time for each particular action, for it is as wrong to anticipate this as to fall behind it. As a benefit ought not always to be accepted, so it ought not in every case to be returned. If you were to make return to me though I did not need it, you would be ungrateful ; how much more ungrateful you are if you force me to need it ! Wait a while ! Why are you unwilling to allow my gift to linger in

vis ? Quare obligatum moleste te[1] fers ? Quare
quasi cum acerbo feneratore signare rationem parem
properas ? Quid mihi negotium quaeris ? Quid in
me deos immittis ? Quomodo exigeres, qui sic
reddis ?

1   41. Ante omnia ergo, Liberalis, hoc discamus, beneficia debere secure et occasiones reddendorum ob-
servare, non manu facere. Ipsam hanc cupiditatem
primo quoque tempore liberandi se meminerimus
ingrati esse ; nemo enim libenter reddit, quod invitus
debet, et, quod apud se esse non vult, onus iudicat
2 esse, non munus. Quanto melius ac iustius in
promptu habere merita amicorum et offerre, non
ingerere, nec obaeratum se iudicare, quoniam beneficium commune vinculum est et inter se duos adligat !
Dic : " Nihil moror, quominus tuum revertatur ;
opto, hilaris accipias. Si necessitas alterutri nostrum
imminet fatoque quodam datum est, ut aut tu cogaris
beneficium recipere aut ego alterum[2] accipere, det
potius, qui solet. Ego paratus sum :

> Nulla mora in Turno est;[a]

ostendam hunc animum, cum primum tempus ad-
venerit ; interim di testes sunt."

1   42. Soleo, mi Liberalis, notare hunc in te adfectum
et quasi manu prendere verentis et aestuantis, ne in
ullo officio sis tardior. Non decet gratum animum

---

[1] te *added by Gruter.*
[2] alterum *added by Gertz.*

---

[a] *i.e.,* to meet Aeneas in battle (Virgil, *Aen.* xii. 11).

your hands ? Why do you resent being under obligation ? Why, as though you were dealing with a sharp usurer, are you in such a hurry to square and close your account ? Why do you want to make trouble for me ? Why do you turn the gods against me ? If this is your way of making repayment, what would you do if you were exacting repayment ?

Above all, therefore, Liberalis, let us learn this—to rest easy under the obligation from benefits, and to watch for opportunities of returning them, not to manufacture them. Let us remember that this very eagerness to set oneself free at the first possible moment marks one as ungrateful ; for a man is not glad to repay a benefit that he is unwilling to owe, and one that he is not willing to keep he counts, not a gift, but a burden. How much better and more seemly it is for a man to keep in view the services of friends, and to offer, not to obtrude, his own, and not to count himself a mere debtor ; for a benefit is a common bond and binds two persons together. Say : " I make no delay in returning what is yours ; I hope you will gladly accept it. If a cruel fortune threatens either of us, and some fate decrees either that you must accept return of your benefit, or that I must accept a second one, let him give by preference who is used to giving. I am ready :

'Tis not for Turnus to delay.[a]

This is the spirit I shall show whenever the time comes ; meanwhile the gods are my witnesses."

I have often observed in you, Liberalis, and, as it were, " laid hand on " a feeling of nervous fear that you might be remiss in the performance of any duty. Anxiety ill becomes the grateful heart, which, on

sollicitudo, contra summa fiducia sui et ex conscientia
veri amoris dimissa omnis anxietas. Tam convicium
est : " Recipe " quam : " Debes." Hoc primum
beneficii dati sit ius, ut recipiendi tempus eligat,
qui dedit. " At vereor, ne homines de me sequius
loquantur." Male agit, qui famae, non conscientiae
gratus est. Duos istius rei iudices habes, illum,
quem non debes timere, et te,[1] quem non potes.
" Quid ergo ? Si nulla intervenerit occasio, semper
debebo ? " Debebis ; sed palam debebis, sed
libenter debebis, sed cum magna voluptate apud
te depositum intueberis. Paenitet accepti beneficii,
quem nondum redditi piget. Quare, qui tibi dignus
visus est, a quo acciperes, indignus videatur, cui diu
debeas ?

1   43. In magnis erroribus sunt, qui ingentis animi
credunt proferre, donare, plurium sinum ac domum
implere, cum ista interdum non magnus animus
faciat, sed magna fortuna ; nesciunt, quanto interim
maius ac difficilius sit capere, quam fundere. Nam,
ut nihil alteri detraham, quoniam utrumque, ubi
virtute fit, par est, non minoris est animi beneficium
debere quam dare ; eo quidem operosius hoc quam
illud, quo maiore diligentia custodiuntur accepta,
2 quam dantur. Itaque non est trepidandum, quam

---

[1] quem non debes timere, et te *added by Gertz.*

the contrary, should show the utmost self-confidence and that all worry has been banished because of the consciousness of true love. To say " Take back " casts as much reproach as to say " You owe." Let this be the first rule in giving a benefit, that the right to choose the time of having it returned is the giver's. But you say : " I am afraid that men will talk about me later." If a man is grateful, not because of his conscience, but because of his reputation, his motive is wrong. You have in this matter two judges—your benefactor, whom you ought not to fear, and yourself, whom you cannot fear. " What, then," you say, " if no opportunity comes ? Shall I always remain in debt ? " You will remain in debt, but openly in debt, gladly in debt—you will view with great pleasure what has been left in your hands. A man who is irked at not having returned a benefit is sorry that he received it. Why, if you thought a man was worthy to make you his debtor, do you think that he is unworthy of your remaining long in debt ?

Those who think that to proffer and to bestow and to fill many men's pockets and houses with their gifts are proof of a great soul make a great mistake, since sometimes these are due, not so much to a large soul, as to a large fortune ; they do not know how much greater and more difficult it is at times to take, than to lavish, gifts. For, although I would not disparage either act, since both are of equal value when Virtue directs them, to become indebted for a benefit requires no smaller spirit than to give it ; of the two, the former, in fact, is the more laborious, as greater effort is expended in guarding, than in giving, the objects that are received. Therefore we ought not

451

cito reponamus, nec procurrendum intempestive,
quia aeque delinquit, qui ad referendam gratiam suo
tempore cessat, quam qui alieno properat. Positum
est illi apud me ; nec illius nomine nec meo timeo.
Bene illi cautum est ; non potest hoc beneficium perdere nisi mecum, immo ne mecum quidem. Egi illi
3 gratias, id est, rettuli. Qui nimis de reddendo beneficio cogitat, nimis cogitare alterum de recipiendo
putat. Praestet se in utrumque facilem. Si vult
recipere beneficium, referamus reddamusque laeti ;
si illud apud nos custodiri mavult, quid thensaurum
eius eruimus ? Quid custodiam recusamus ? Dignus
est cui, utrum volet, liceat. Opinionem quidem et
famam eo loco habeamus, tamquam non ducere sed
sequi debeat.

to be worried over how soon we can repay, nor should we rush to do so at an unseemly time, for he who hastens to return gratitude at the wrong time is as much at fault as he who is remiss in returning it at the proper time. He has placed his gift in my hands ; I have no fear on his account or on my own. He has good security ; he cannot lose his benefit unless he loses me, nay, not even if he loses me. I have paid him my thanks—that is, I have made return. He who thinks too much about returning a benefit must suppose that the other thinks too much about having it returned. One should lend himself to both points of view. If a man wishes his benefit to be returned, let us repay and return it cheerfully ; if he prefers that it should remain in our custody, why do we dig up his treasure ? Why do we refuse to guard it ? He deserves to be allowed to do whichever he pleases. As for rumour and reputation, let us consider them as matters that must, not guide, but follow, our actions.

LIBER VII

1   **1.** Bonum, mi Liberalis, habeas animum volo :

> In manibus terrae ; non hic te carmine longo
> atque per ambages et longa exorsa tenebo.[a]

Reliqua hic liber cogit, et exhausta materia circum-
spicio, non quid dicam, sed quid non dixerim ; boni
tamen consules, quidquid ibi superest, cum tibi super-
fuerit.

2   Si voluissem lenocinari mihi, debuit paulatim opus
crescere et ea pars in finem reservari, quam quilibet
etiam satiatus appeteret. Sed quidquid maxime
necessarium erat, in primum congessi ; nunc, si quid
effugit, recolligo. Nec mehercules, si me interroges,
nimis ad rem existimo pertinere, ubi dicta sunt, quae
regunt mores, prosequi cetera non in remedium
animi, sed in exercitationem ingenii inventa.

3   Egregie enim hoc dicere Demetrius Cynicus, vir
meo iudicio magnus, etiam si maximis comparetur,
solet plus prodesse, si pauca praecepta sapientiae

---

[a] Virgil, *Georgics*, ii. 45 *sq.*

BOOK VII

Be of good cheer, Liberalis :

> The land is close—I will not keep you long
> By rambling outbursts of a long-drawn song.[a]

This book gathers up the remnants, and, after the subject has been exhausted, I am casting about to discover, not what I shall say, but what I have not said. If there is anything in it that could be omitted, you will take it in good part, since it was for your sake that I did not omit it.

If I had wished to curry favour for myself, I ought to have let my work grow gradually in interest, and to have reserved for the last a part that any reader would be eager for even if he were surfeited. But all that is most essential I have massed together at the beginning ; now I am merely recovering whatever escaped me. Nor, seriously, if you ask me, do I think that, after stating the rules that govern conduct, there is very much point in my pursuing the other questions that have been raised, not to further the health of the mind, but to provide exercise for the intellect.

For Demetrius the Cynic, a great man, in my opinion, even if compared with the greatest, is fond of stating very admirably that it is far better for us to possess only a few maxims of philosophy that are

455

teneas, sed illa in promptu tibi et in usu sint, quam si multa quidem didiceris, sed illa non habeas ad 4 manum. " Quemadmodum," inquit, " magnus luctator est, non qui omnes numeros nexusque perdidicit, quorum usus sub adversario rarus est, sed qui in uno se aut altero bene ac diligenter exercuit et eorum occasiones intentus expectat (neque enim refert, quam multa sciat, si scit, quantum victoriae satis est), sic in hoc studio multa delectant, pauca vincunt. 5 Licet nescias, quae ratio oceanum effundat ac revocet, quare septimus quisque annus aetati signum imprimat, quare latitudo porticus ex remoto spectantibus non servet portionem suam, sed ultima in angustius coeant et columnarum novissime intervalla iungantur, quid sit, quod geminorum conceptum separet, partum iungat, utrum unus concubitus spargatur in duos an totiens concepti sint, cur pariter natis fata diversa sint maximisque rerum spatiis distent, quorum inter ortus minimum interest : non multum tibi nocebit transisse, quae nec licet scire 6 nec prodest. Involuta veritas in alto latet. Nec de malignitate naturae queri possumus, quia nullius rei difficilis inventio est, nisi cuius hic unus inventae fructus est invenisse ; quidquid nos meliores beatosque facturum est, aut in aperto aut in proximo 7 posuit. Si animus fortuita contempsit, si se supra

nevertheless always at our command and in use, than
to acquire vast knowledge that notwithstanding serves
no practical purpose. "Just as," he says, "the best
wrestler is not one who is thoroughly acquainted with
all the postures and grips of the art, which he will
seldom use against an adversary, but he who has well
and carefully trained himself in one or two of them,
and waits eagerly for the opportunity to use them
—for it makes no difference how much he knows if
he knows enough to give him the victory—, so in
this effort of ours there are many points that are interesting, few that are decisive. Though you may
not know what principle causes the ebb and flow of the
ocean tides, why every seventh year leaves its mark
on the life of a man, why the width of a colonnade,
when you look at it from a distance, does not keep its
true proportion, but towards the end grows narrower,
and at last the spaces between the columns disappear,
why it is that twins are conceived separately, but are
born together, whether in coition one act gives birth
to two, or each is born from a separate act, why those
who are born together have different destinies, and,
though their births were very close together, are
very far apart in the differences of their experiences—
it will not do you much harm to pass over matters
which it is neither possible nor advantageous for you
to know. Truth lurks in deep hiding and is wrapped
in mystery. Nor can we complain that Nature is
grudgingly disposed towards us, for there is nothing
that is hard to discover except that which, when
discovered, brings no other reward than the fact of
discovery; all that tends to make us better and
happier has been placed either in plain sight or near by.
The soul that can scorn all the accidents of fortune,

metus sustulit nec avida spe infinita complectitur, sed
didicit a se petere divitias ; si deorum hominumque
formidinem eiecit et scit non multum esse ab homine
timendum, a deo nihil ; si contemptor omnium, quibus
torquetur vita, dum ornatur, eo perductus est, ut illi
liqueat mortem nullius mali materiam esse, multorum
finem ; si animum virtuti consecravit et, quacumque
vocat illa, planum putat ; si sociale animal et in
commune genitus mundum ut unam omnium domum
spectat et conscientiam suam dis aperuit semperque
tamquam in publico vivit se magis veritus quam alios :
subductus ille tempestatibus in solido ac sereno stetit
consummavitque scientiam utilem ac necessariam.
Reliqua oblectamenta otii sunt ; licet enim iam in
tutum retracto animo ad haec quoque excurrere cultum, non robur, ingeniis adferentia."

1   2. Haec Demetrius noster utraque manu tenere
proficientem iubet, haec nusquam dimittere, immo
adfigere et partem sui facere eoque cotidiana medi-
tatione perduci, ut sua sponte occurrant salutaria et
ubique ac statim desiderata praesto sint et sine ulla
2 mora veniat illa turpis honestique distinctio. Sciat
nec malum esse ullum nisi turpe nec bonum nisi
honestum. Hac regula vitae opera distribuat ; ad
hanc legem et agat cuncta et exigat miserrimosque

that can rise superior to fears, that does not greedily covet boundless wealth, but has learned to seek its riches from itself ; the soul that can cast out all dread of men and gods, and knows that it has not much to fear from man and nothing from God ; that, despising all those things which, while they enrich, harass life, can rise to the height of seeing that death is not the source of any evil, but the end of many ; the soul that can dedicate itself to Virtue, and think that every path to which she calls is smooth ; that, social creature that it is and born for the common good, views the world as the universal home of mankind, that can bare its conscience to the gods, and, respecting itself more than all others, always live as if in the sight of men—such a soul, remote from storms, stands on the solid ground beneath a blue sky, and has attained to perfect knowledge of what is useful and essential. All other matters are but the diversions of a leisure hour ; for when the soul has once found this safe retreat, it may also make excursions into things that bring polish, not strength, to its powers."

These are the things that my friend Demetrius says the tiro in philosophy must grasp with both hands, these are the precepts that he must never let go, nay, must cling fast to, and make a part of himself, and by daily meditation reach the point where these wholesome maxims occur to him of their own accord, and are promptly at hand whenever they are desired, and the great distinction between base and honourable action presents itself without any delay. Let him know that there is no evil except what is base, and no good except what is honourable. Let him apply this rule to all the deeds of life ; in accordance with this law let him both order and weigh all his

mortalium iudicet, in quantiscumque opibus refulge-
bunt, ventri ac libidini deditos quorumque animus
inerti otio torpet. Dicat sibi ipse : " Voluptas
fragilis est, brevis, fastidio obiecta, quo avidius hausta
est citius in contrarium recidens, cuius subinde necesse
est aut paeniteat aut pudeat, in qua nihil est magnificum aut quod naturam hominis dis proximi deceat,
res humilis, membrorum turpium aut vilium mini-
3 sterio veniens, exitu foeda. Illa est voluptas et
homine et viro digna non implere corpus nec saginare
nec cupiditates irritare, quarum tutissima est quies,
sed perturbatione carere et ea, quam hominum inter
se rixantium ambitus concutit, et ea, quae intolerabilis
ex alto venit, ubi de dis famae creditum est vitiisque
4 illos nostris aestimavimus." Hanc voluptatem aequa-
lem, intrepidam, numquam sensuram sui taedium
percipit hic, quem deformamus cum maxime, ut ita
dicam, divini iuris atque humani peritus. Hic praesentibus gaudet, ex futuro non pendet ; nihil enim
firmi habet, qui in incerta propensus est. Magnis
itaque curis exemptus et distorquentibus mentem
nihil sperat aut cupit nec se mittit in dubium suo
contentus.

5   Et ne illum existimes parvo esse contentum, omnia
illius sunt, non sic, quemadmodum Alexandri fuerunt,
cui, quamquam in litore rubri maris steterat, plus de-

actions, and those who are given over to gluttony and lust, whose minds are deadened by sluggish inaction, let him judge to be the most wretched of mortals, no matter how great the splendour of their wealth may be. Let him say to himself: " Pleasure is frail, short-lived, and prone to pall ; the more eagerly it is indulged, the more swiftly it changes into the opposite, it forces us straightway either to repentance or to shame, it has in it nothing of nobility, nothing worthy of the nature of man, second as he is to the gods, a lowly thing, produced by subservience to the parts of our body that are either base or vile, and in the end repulsive. True pleasure, worthy either of man or hero, comes, not from filling and gorging the body and from exciting the lusts that are safest when they are quiet, but from freedom from all mental disturbance, both that which is aroused by the ambition of men struggling with one another, and that which comes, insufferably, from on high when we give credence to the stories of the gods, and estimate them by the standard of our own vices." This is the pleasure, constant, serene, always uncloyed, that is experienced by the man we were just now delineating, one skilled, so to speak, in the laws of gods and men. Such a man rejoices in the present, and puts no faith in the future ; for he who leans upon uncertainties can have no sure support. Free, therefore, from the great anxieties that rack the mind, there is nothing which he hopes for or covets, and, content with what he has, he does not plunge into what is doubtful.

And do not suppose that he is content with a little —all things are his, and not in the sense in which they were Alexander's, who, although he stood upon the shore of the Indian Ocean, had need of more territory

erat, quam qua venerat. Illius ne ea quidem erant, quae tenebat aut vicerat, cum in oceano Onesicritus praemissus explorator erraret et bella in ignoto mari

6 quaereret. Non satis apparebat inopem esse, qui extra naturae terminos arma proferret, qui se in profundum inexploratum et immensum aviditate caeca prosus immitteret? Quid interest, quot e- ripuerit regna, quot dederit, quantum terrarum tributo premat? Tantum illi deest, quantum cupit.

1 3. Nec hoc Alexandri tantum vitium fuit, quem per Liberi Herculisque vestigia felix temeritas egit, sed omnium, quos fortuna irritavit implendo. Cyrum et Cambysen et totum regni Persici stemma percense. Quem invenies, cui modum imperii satietas fecerit, qui non vitam in aliqua ulterius procedendi cogitatione finierit? Nec id mirum est; quidquid cupiditati contingit, penitus hauritur et conditur, nec interest, quantum eo, quod inexplebile est, congeras.

2 Unus est sapiens, cuius omnia sunt nec ex difficili tuenda. Non habet mittendos trans maria legatos nec metanda in ripis hostilibus castra, non opportunis castellis disponenda praesidia ; non opus est legione nec equestribus turmis. Quemadmodum di immor- tales regnum inermes regunt et illis rerum suarum ex edito tranquilloque tutela est, ita hic officia sua,

---

[a] A Greek historian, who accompanied Alexander, and by his order investigated, with Nearchus, the sea route from India to the mouths of the Euphrates and Tigris.
[b] Son and successor of Cyrus the Great.

462

than that he had passed through. Nor did he own even the kingdoms that he was holding or had conquered, while Onesicritus,[a] who had been sent ahead to discover new ones, was wandering about the ocean and stirring up war on unknown seas. Was it not quite clear that it was a man in need who pushed his arms beyond the bounds of Nature, who, driven on by reckless greed, plunged headlong into an unexplored and boundless sea? What difference does it make how many kingdoms he seized, how many he bestowed, how many lands submitted to tribute? He still had need of as much as he still coveted.

Nor was this the vice of Alexander alone, whose successful audacity led him to follow in the footsteps of Liber and Hercules, but of all those whom Fortune has goaded on by rich gifts. Consider Cyrus and Cambyses [b] and all the royal line of Persia. Will you find any among them who was satisfied with the bounds of his empire, who did not end his life in some plan of advancing farther? Nor need we wonder; for whatever is gained by covetousness is simply swallowed up and buried, nor does it make any difference how much you pour into a vessel that can never be filled.

It is only the wise man who has all things, and has no difficulty in retaining them. He has no need to send legates across the seas, nor to measure out camps on hostile shores, nor to place garrisons in strategic forts—he has no need of a legion or squadrons of cavalry. Like the immortal gods who govern their realm without recourse to arms, and still from their serene and lofty heights safeguard their own, so the wise man performs his duties, however far-

quamvis latissime pateant, sine tumultu obit et omne
humanum genus potentissimus eius optimusque infra
3 se videt. Derideas licet: ingentis spiritus res est,
cum Orientem Occidentemque lustraveris animo,
quo etiam remota et solitudinibus interclusa pene-
trantur, cum tot animalia, tantam copiam rerum,
quas natura beatissime fundit, adspexeris, emittere
hanc dei vocem: "Haec omnia mea sunt!" Sic
fit, ut nihil cupiat, quia nihil est extra omnia.

1   4. "Hoc ipsum," inquis, "volui! teneo te! Volo
videre, quomodo ex his laqueis, in quos tua sponte
decidisti, expliceris. Dic mihi. Quemadmodum potest aliquis donare sapienti, si omnia sapientis sunt?
Nam id quoque, quod illi donat, ipsius est. Itaque
non potest beneficium dari sapienti, cui, quidquid
datur, de suo datur; atqui dicitis sapienti posse
donari. Idem autem me scito et de amicis interrogare. Omnia dicitis illis esse communia; ergo
nemo quicquam donare amico potest; donat enim
illi communia."

2   Nihil prohibet aliquid et sapientis esse et etiam
eius, qui possidet, cui datum et adsignatum est. Iure
civili omnia regis sunt, et tamen illa, quorum ad regem
pertinet universa possessio, in singulos dominos di-
scripta sunt, et unaquaeque res habet possessorem

reaching they may be, without any turmoil, and, being the most powerful and best of mankind, sees the whole human race beneath him. Smile though you may, yet if you survey the East and the West with your thought, which can penetrate even to lands that are far removed and shut off by vast wastes, if you behold all creatures of earth, all the bounteous store, which Nature so richly pours forth, it is the claim of no mean spirit to be able to utter these words of God : " All these things are mine ! " Thus it comes that he covets nothing because there is nothing outside of the all.

" This," you say, " is the very thing I wanted ; I have caught you ! I want to see how you will release yourself from this trap into which you have fallen of your own accord. Tell me this. If the wise man possesses everything, how can anyone possibly give anything to a wise man ? For even what one gives to him is already his. It is impossible, therefore, to bestow a benefit on a wise man, for whatever is given to him is given out of his own store ; yet you Stoics say that it is possible to give to a wise man. Know, too, that I raise the same question also with reference to friends. You say that they have all things in common ; no one, consequently, can give anything to a friend ; for he gives to him what is common property."

There is nothing to prevent a thing's belonging both to the wise man and to him who actually possesses it as something that was granted and assigned to him. According to civil law everything belongs to the king, and yet property, to which the king lays claim by his universal right, is parcelled out to individual owners, and each separate thing is someone's

465

suum. Itaque dare regi et domum et mancipium et pecuniam possumus nec donare illi de suo dicimur ; ad regem enim potestas omnium pertinet, ad singulos proprietates.

3 Fines Atheniensium aut Campanorum vocamus, quos deinde inter se vicini privata terminatione distinguunt ; et totus ager utique ullius rei publicae est, pars deinde suo domino quaeque censetur ; ideoque donare agros nostros rei publicae possumus, quamvis illius esse dicantur, quia aliter illius sunt, aliter mei.

4 Numquid dubium est, quin servus cum peculio domini sit ? Dat tamen domino suo munus. Non enim ideo nihil habet servus, quia non est habiturus, si dominus illum habere noluerit ; nec ideo non est munus, cum volens dedit, quia potuit eripi, etiam si noluisset.

5 Quemadmodum probemus omnia ? Nunc enim omnia sapientis esse inter duos convenit ; illud, quod quaeritur, colligendum est, quomodo liberalitatis materia adversus eum supersit, cuius universa esse 6 concessimus. Omnia patris sunt, quae in liberorum manu sunt ; quis tamen nescit donare aliquid et filium patri ? Omnia deorum sunt ; tamen et dis donum posuimus et stipem iecimus. Non ideo, quod

---

^a *i.e.*, make donations of money.

personal possession.   And so we are able to give to
a king a house, or a slave, or money, and are not said
to be bestowing upon him a gift of his own property ;
for the right of ownership of all things belongs to the
king, the actual ownership to the individual citizen.

We speak of the territories of the Athenians and
the Campanians, which, in turn, the dwellers divide
among themselves by private agreements ;   and
while the whole land is undoubtedly the property
of any commonwealth, each part of it in turn is
reckoned as the possession of its owner ; and we
are able, therefore, to present our lands to the
state, although they are said to belong to the state,
because, in one way, they are the state's, in another,
mine.

Can there be any doubt that a slave, along with his
private savings, belongs to his master ?   Yet he can
give a present to his master.   For it is not true that
a slave owns nothing for the mere reason that he will
not be able to own it if his master should be unwilling
for him to own it, nor is it true that he does not give
a present, when he gives it willingly, for the mere
reason that it could have been seized from him even
if he had been unwilling.

How can we prove everything ?   For we are now
both agreed that the wise man possesses all things ;
the question that we must settle is how there can
remain any means of showing generosity to one to
whom we have granted all things belong.   All things
that are in the hands of his children belong to the
father ;   yet who does not know that even a son can
make a gift to his father ?   All things belong to the
gods ;   yet we both offer gifts to the gods, and throw
them alms.[a]   It is not necessarily true that what I

habeo, meum non est, si meum tuum est; potest
enim idem meum esse et tuum.

7 " Is," inquit, " cuius prostitutae sunt, leno est;
omnia autem sapientis sunt; inter omnia et prostitutae sunt; ergo prostitutae sapientis sunt. Leno
autem est, cuius prostitutae sunt; ergo sapiens leno
8 est." Sic illum vetant emere, dicunt enim : " Nemo
rem suam emit; omnia autem sapientis sunt; ergo
sapiens nihil emit." Sic vetant mutuum sumere, quia
nemo usuram pro pecunia sua pendat. Innumerabilia sunt, per quae cavillantur, cum pulcherrime,
1 quid a nobis dicatur, intellegant. 5. Etenim sic
omnia sapientis esse dico, ut nihilo minus proprium
quisque in rebus suis dominium habeat, quemadmodum sub optimo rege omnia rex imperio possidet, singuli dominio. Tempus istius probandae rei
veniet; interim hoc huic quaestioni sat est me
id, quod aliter sapientis est, aliter meum est,
2 posse donare sapienti. Nec mirum est aliquid ei,
cuius est totum, posse donari. Conduxi domum
a te; in hac aliquid tuum est, aliquid meum : res
tua est, usus rei tuae meus est. Itaque nec fructus
tanges colono tuo prohibente, quamvis in tua pos-

have is not mine if what is mine is also yours; for it is possible that the same thing may be both mine and yours.

"He to whom courtesans belong," you say, "is a pimp; but all things belong to a wise man, and all things must also include courtesans; therefore courtesans belong to a wise man. But he to whom courtesans belong is a pimp; therefore a wise man is a pimp." In the same way they forbid him to buy anything, for they say: "No one buys his own property; but all things belong to the wise man; therefore the wise man buys nothing." In the same way they forbid him to take a loan, because no one is going to pay interest for the use of his own money. They raise endless quibbles, although they perfectly well understand what we mean. For I mean that, while all things belong to the wise man, each person, nevertheless, has the ownership of his own property, just as under the best sort of king everything belongs to the king by his right of authority, and to his subjects by their individual rights of ownership. The time will come for proving this statement; meanwhile the question in hand will be sufficiently answered if I say that it is possible for me to give to the wise man something that, in one way, belongs to the wise man, and, in another way, belongs to me. Nor is it surprising that it is possible to give something to one who possesses all there is. Suppose I have rented a house from you; you still have some "right" in it, and I have some right—the property is yours, the use of the property is mine. Nor, likewise, will you touch crops, although they may be growing on your own

469

sessione nascantur, et, si annona carior fuerit aut
fames,

Heu ! frustra magnum alterius spectabis acervum

in tuo natum, in tuo positum, in horrea iturum tua.
3 Nec conductum meum, quamquam sis dominus, in-
trabis nec servum tuum, mercennarium meum, ab-
duces et, cum a te raedam conduxero, beneficium
accipies, si tibi in vehiculo tuo sedere permisero.
Vides ergo posse fieri, ut aliquis accipiendo, quod
suum est, munus accipiat.

1   6. In omnibus istis, quae modo rettuli, uterque
eiusdem rei dominus est.   Quo modo ?   Quia alter
rei dominus est, alter usus.   Libros dicimus esse
Ciceronis ;   eosdem Dorus librarius suos vocat, et
utrumque verum est.   Alter illos tamquam auctor
sibi, alter tamquam emptor adserit ; ac recte utriusque dicuntur esse, utriusque enim sunt, sed non
eodem modo.   Sic potest Titus Livius a Doro accipere
2 aut emere libros suos.   Possum donare sapienti, quod
viritim meum est, licet illius sint omnia ; nam cum
regio more cuncta conscientia possideat, singularum
autem rerum in unumquemque proprietas sit sparsa,
et accipere munus et debere et emere et conducere
3 potest.   Caesar omnia habet, fiscus eius privata tan-

---

estate, if your tenant objects ; and if the price of corn becomes too dear, or you are starving, you will

Alas ! in vain another's mighty store behold,[a]

grown upon your own land, lying upon your own land, and about to be stored in your own granary. Nor, although you are the owner, will you set foot on what I have rented, nor will you take away a slave of yours, now a hireling of mine ; and if I have hired a carriage from you, you will be receiving a benefit if I permit you to sit in your own vehicle. You see, therefore, that it becomes possible for someone to receive a present by receiving what is his own.

In all these cases that I have just cited there are two owners of one and the same thing. How is it possible ? Because one is the owner of the thing, the other of the use of the thing. We say that certain books are Cicero's ; Dorus, the bookseller, calls these same books his own, and both statements are true. The one claims them, because he wrote them, the other because he bought them ; and it is correct to say that they belong to both, for they do belong to both, but not in the same way. So it is possible for Titus Livius to receive his own books as a present, or to buy them from Dorus. Although all things belong to a wise man, yet I am able to give to him what is individually mine ; for, although he is conscious of possessing all things in the manner of a king, yet the ownership of the several things is divided among individuals, and it is possible for him to receive a present and to be indebted and to buy and to hire. Everything belongs to Caesar, yet the only private and personal property he has is the

471

tum ac sua ; et universa in imperio eius sunt, in patrimonio propria. Quid eius sit, quid non sit, sine
diminutione imperii quaeritur ; nam id quoque, quod
tamquam alienum abiudicatur, aliter illius est. Sic
sapiens animo universa possidet, iure ac dominio sua.

1   7. Bion modo omnes sacrilegos esse argumentis
colligit, modo neminem. Cum omnes de saxo de-
iecturus est, dicit : " Quisquis id, quod deorum est,
sustulit et consumpsit atque in usum suum vertit,
sacrilegus est ; omnia autem deorum sunt ; quod
quisque ergo tollit, deorum tollit, quorum omnia sunt ;

2 ergo, quisquis tollit aliquid, sacrilegus est." Deinde,
cum effringi templa et expilari impune Capitolium
iubet, dicit nullum sacrilegum esse, quia, quidquid
sublatum est, ex eo loco, qui deorum erat, in eum
transfertur locum, qui deorum est.

3   Hic respondetur omnia quidem deorum esse, sed
non omnia dis dedicata ; in iis observari sacrilegium,
quae religio numini adscripsit. Sic et totum mundum
deorum esse immortalium templum, solum quidem
amplitudine illorum ac magnificentia dignum : tamen
a sacris profana discerni ; non omnia licere in angulo,

---

a A philosophic wit of Borysthenes, near the mouth of the
Dnieper, who taught philosophy at Athens in the first half
of the third century B.C.

imperial treasury; all things are his by right of his authority, but his personal property is acquired by right of inheritance. The question may be raised as to what is his, and what is not his, without assailing his authority; for even that which the court may decide belongs to another, from another point of view belongs to him. So in his mind the wise man possesses all things, by actual right and ownership only his own things.

Bion[a] at one time proves by argument that all men are sacrilegious, at another, that no one is. When he is disposed to hurl all men from the Tarpeian Rock, he says: "Whoever abstracts and consumes and appropriates to his own use what belongs to the gods, commits sacrilege; but all things belong to the gods; that which anyone abstracts, therefore, he abstracts from the gods, to whom all things belong; consequently, whoever abstracts anything commits sacrilege." Again, when he bids men to break into temples and to pillage the Capitol without fear of punishment, he says that no one commits sacrilege, because whatever is abstracted from one place that belongs to the gods is transferred to another place that belongs to the gods.

The answer to this is that, while it is true that all things belong to the gods, all things are not consecrated to the gods, and that only in the case of the things that religion has assigned to a divinity is it possible to discover sacrilege. That thus, also, the whole world is the temple of the gods, and, indeed, the only one worthy of their majesty and grandeur, and yet that there is a distinction between things sacred and profane; that not all things which it is

cui fani nomen impositum est, quae sub caelo et conspectu siderum licent.

Iniuriam sacrilegus deo quidem non potest facere,
quem extra ictum sua divinitas posuit, sed punitur,
quia tamquam deo fecit : opinio illum nostra ac sua
4 obligat poenae. Quomodo ergo sacrilegus videtur,
qui aliquid aufert sacri, etiam si, quocumque transtulit, quod surripuerat, intra terminos mundi est,
sic et sapienti furtum potest fieri ; auferetur enim
illi non ex iis, quae universa habet, sed ex iis, quibus
dominus inscriptus est, quae viritim ei serviunt.
5 Illam alteram possessionem adgnoscet, hanc nolet
habere, si poterit, emittetque illam vocem, quam
Romanus imperator emisit, cum illi ob virtutem et
bene gestam rem publicam tantum agri decerneretur,
quantum arando uno die circumire potuisset : " Non
opus est," inquit, " vobis eo cive, cui plus opus sit
quam uni civi." Quanto maioris viri putas respuisse
hoc munus, quam meruisse ! Multi enim fines aliis
abstulerunt, sibi nemo constituit !

1   8. Ergo cum animum sapientis intuemur potentem
omnium et per universa dimissum, omnia illius esse
dicimus, cum ad hoc ius cotidianum, si ita res tulerit,
capite censebitur. Multum interest, possessio eius

lawful to do under the open sky and in the sight of the stars are lawful to do in the nook to which has been assigned the name of a sanctuary.

The sacrilegious man is not able, indeed, to do any injury to God, whose own divinity has placed him beyond the reach of harm, yet he is punished because he aimed an injury at God—he is subjected to punishment by our feeling and his own. As, therefore, he who carries off something sacred seems to have committed a sacrilege, even if the place to which he has transferred what he had stolen is within the limits of the world, so it is possible for a theft to be committed upon even a wise man. For he will be robbed of something, taken, not from that universe which he possesses, but from the things of which he is the registered owner, and which are at his individual service. He will claim his ownership of the former, ownership of the latter he will be unwilling to have even if he is able, and will give voice to the famous words that a Roman general uttered when, as a reward for his prowess and his good service to the state, he was being awarded as much land as he could have covered in one day's ploughing : " You have no need," said he, " of a citizen who needs to have more than is necessary for one citizen." How much more a hero will you think him for having rejected this gift than for having deserved it ! For many have removed the boundary lines of other men's lands, no one has set limits to his own !

When, therefore, we behold the mind of the wise man, master as it is of all things and a ranger of the universe, we say that all things belong to him, although, according to our every-day law, his only assessment, it may be, will be a head-tax. It makes

2 animo ac magnitudine aestimetur an censu. Haec
universa habere, de quibus loqueris, abominabitur.

Non referam tibi Socraten, Chrysippum, Zenonem
et ceteros magnos quidem viros, maiores quidem,
quia in laudem vetustorum invidia non obstat. Paulo
ante Demetrium rettuli, quem mihi videtur rerum
natura nostris tulisse temporibus, ut ostenderet nec
illum a nobis corrumpi nec nos ab illo corripi posse,
virum exactae, licet neget ipse, sapientiae firmaeque
in iis, quae proposuit, constantiae, eloquentiae vero
eius, quae res fortissimas deceat, non concinnatae nec
in verba sollicitae, sed ingenti animo, prout impetus
3 tulit, res suas prosequentis. Huic non dubito quin
providentia et talem vitam et talem dicendi facultatem dederit, ne aut exemplum saeculo nostro aut
convicium deesset. Demetrio si res nostras aliquis
deorum possidendas velit tradere sub lege certa, ne
liceat donare, adfirmaverim repudiaturum dicturum-
1 que : 9. " Ego vero me ad istud inextricabile pondus
non adligo nec in altam faecem rerum hunc expeditum
hominem demitto. Quid ad me defers populorum
omnium mala ? Quae ne daturus quidem acciperem,
quoniam multa video, quae me donare non deceat.
Volo sub conspectu meo ponere, quae gentium oculos
regumque praestringunt, volo intueri pretia sanguinis
2 animarumque vestrarum. Prima mihi luxuriae spolia

a great difference whether his holdings are estimated by the censor's register, or by the greatness of his mind. He will pray to be delivered from the ownership of all the things of which you speak.

I shall not remind you of Socrates, of Chrysippus, of Zeno, and the others, truly great men—in fact, too great, because envy sets no bounds to our praise of the ancients. But a little while ago I reminded you of Demetrius, whom, it seems to me, Nature produced in these times of ours in order to prove that he could not be corrupted even by us, and that we could not be reproved even by him—a man of consummate wisdom, though he himself disclaimed it, of steadfast firmness in all his purposes, of an eloquence fitted to deal with the mightiest subjects, not given to graces, nor finical about words, but proceeding to its theme with great spirit, as impulse inspired it. I doubt not that this man was endowed by divine providence with such a life, with such power of speech in order that our age might not lack either a model or a reproach. If some god should wish to commit all our wealth to the hands of Demetrius on the fixed condition that he should not be allowed to give it away, I am ready to assert that he would refuse it, and say: "Really, I cannot be bound down by this inextricable burden, nor, unhampered as I now am, do I mean to be dragged down to the dregs of existence. Why do you offer to me what is the bane of all peoples? I would not accept it even if I intended to give it away, for I see many things that are not fit for me to bestow. I wish to set clearly before myself the things that blind the eyes of nations and kings, I wish to behold the recompenses for your life-blood and your lives. Array before me first the trophies of

propone, sive illa vis per ordinem expandere sive, ut
est melius, in unum acervum dare. Video elaboratam
scrupulosa distinctione testudinem et foedissimorum
pigerrimorumque animalium testas ingentibus pretiis
emptas, in quibus ipsa illa, quae placet, varietas
subditis medicamentis in similitudinem veri coloratur.
Video istic mensas et aestimatum lignum senatorio
censu, eo pretiosius, quo illud in plures nodos arboris
3 infelicitas torsit. Video istic crystallina, quorum
accendit fragilitas pretium ; omnium enim rerum
voluptas apud imperitos ipso, quo fugari debet, periculo crescit. Video murrea pocula ; parum scilicet
luxuria magno fuerit, nisi, quod vomant, capacibus
4 gemmis inter se propinaverint. Video uniones non
singulos singulis auribus comparatos ; iam enim exer-
citatae aures oneri ferundo sunt ; iunguntur inter
se et insuper alii binis superponuntur. Non satis
muliebris insania viros superiecerat, nisi bina ac terna
5 patrimonia auribus singulis pependissent. Video
sericas vestes, si vestes vocandae sunt, in quibus nihil
est, quo defendi aut corpus aut denique pudor possit,
quibus sumptis parum liquido nudam se non esse
iurabit. Hae ingenti summa ab ignotis etiam ad
commercium gentibus accersuntur, ut matronae
nostrae ne adulteris quidem plus sui in cubiculo, quam
in publico ostendant.

1 10. " Quid agis, avaritia ? Quot rerum caritate

---

a Cicero is said to have paid 500,000 sesterces (roughly
$25,000) for one, Pollio 1,000,000 sesterces.
b The most prized woods were citrus and maple, which
were enhanced in value by natural curlings and markings.
c Vessels made of *murra*, a gem-like mineral introduced
into Rome from the East, brought enormous prices.
478

Luxury, spreading them out in a row, if you wish, or, as is better, piling them into one heap. I see there the shell of the tortoise, a most ugly and sluggish creature, bought for huge sums and embellished with elaborate markings, and the very variety of their colours, which is their chief attraction, is accentuated by the application of dyes that resemble the natural tint. I see there tables of wood, valued at the price of a senatorial fortune,[a] and the more knotted the contortions of the unhappy tree, the more precious [b] it is. I see there objects of crystal, whose very fragility enhances their price ; for to the ignorant mind, the pleasure of all things is increased by the very risk that ought to drive pleasure away. I see there murrine cups [c]—men, forsooth, would pay too little for their luxury unless, when they toasted each other, they had precious stones to hold the wine they will vomit up ! I see pearls—not single ones designed for each ear, but clusters of them, for the ears have now been trained to carry their load ; they are joined together in pairs, and above each pair still others are fastened ; feminine folly could not sufficiently have overwhelmed men unless two or three fortunes had hung in each ear ! I see there raiments of silk—if that can be called raiment, which provides nothing that could possibly afford protection for the body, or indeed modesty, so that, when a woman wears it, she can scarcely, with a clear conscience, swear that she is not naked. These are imported at vast expense from nations unknown even to trade, in order that our married women may not be able to show more of their persons, even to their paramours, in a bedroom than they do on the street.

" And how, O Avarice, dost thou fare ? How many

aurum tuum victum est! Omnia ista, quae rettuli,
in maiore honore pretioque sunt. Nunc volo tuas
opes recognoscere, lamnas utriusque materiae, ad
2 quam cupiditas nostra caligat. At mehercules terra,
quae, quidquid utile futurum nobis erat, protulit, ista
defodit et mersit et ut noxiosis rebus ac malo gentium
in medium predituris toto pondere incubuit. Video
ferrum ex isdem tenebris esse prolatum, quibus
aurum et argentum, ne aut instrumentum in caedes
3 mutuas deesset aut pretium. Et tamen adhuc ista
aliquam materiam habent; est, in quo errorem ocu-
lorum animus subsequi possit. Video istic diplomata
et syngraphas et cautiones, vacua habendi simulacra,
umbracula avaritiae quaedam laborantis, per quae
decipiat animum inanium opinione gaudentem. Quid
enim ista sunt, quid fenus et calendarium et usura,
nisi humanae cupiditatis extra naturam quaesita
nomina?

4   "Possum de rerum natura queri, quod aurum ar-
gentumque non interius absconderit, quod non illis
maius, quam quod detrahi posset, pondus iniecerit:
quid sunt istae tabellae, quid computationes et venale
tempus et sanguinulentae centesimae? Voluntaria
mala ex constitutione nostra pendentia, in quibus
nihil est, quod subici oculis, quod teneri manu possit,
5 inanis avaritiae somnia. O miserum, si quem delectat

are the things that in costliness have surpassed thy
gold! All those that I have mentioned are more
honoured and valued. Now I wish to review thy
wealth, the plates of gold and silver, for which our
greed gropes in darkness. Yet, in very truth, the
earth, which has revealed everything that was likely
to be of use to us, has hidden these things, and buried
them deep, and weighted them down with all her
mass, regarding them as harmful substances, destined
to be a curse to the nations if brought forth into the
light. I see that iron has been brought forth from
the same dark depths that yielded gold and silver in
order that we might not lack either the instrument
or the reward for slaughtering one another. And
yet the forms of thy wealth, so far, have some actual
substance ; but there is another in which the mind
and the eye alike can be deceived. I see there allot-
ments, bonds, and securities—the empty phantoms
of ownership, the secret haunts of Avarice devising
some means by which she may deceive the mind
that delights in empty fancies. For what are these
things, what are interest and the account-book and
usury, but the names devised for unnatural forms of
human greed ?

"I might make complaint against Nature because
she did not hide gold and silver more deeply, because
she did not lay a weight upon them too heavy to be
removed—but these bills of thine, what are they ?
what the computations and the sale of time and the
blood-thirsty twelve per cent ? Evils that we will,
that originate from our own character, that have in
them nothing which can be put before the eyes,
nothing that can be held in the hand—the mere
dreams of empty Avarice ! Wretched, indeed, is he

patrimonii sui liber magnus et vasta spatia terrarum
colenda per vinctos et immensi greges pecorum per
provincias ac regna pascendi et familia bellicosis
nationibus maior et aedificia privata laxitatem urbium
6 magnarum vincentia ! Cum bene ista, per quae
divitias suas disposuit ac fudit, circumspexerit super-
bumque se fecerit, quidquid habet, ei, quod cupit,
comparet : pauper est. Dimitte me et illis divitiis
meis redde. Ego regnum sapientiae novi, magnum,
securum ; ego sic omnia habeo, ut omnium sint."

1   11. Itaque cum C.[1] Caesar illi ducenta donaret,
ridens reiecit ne dignam quidem summam iudicans,
qua non accepta gloriaretur. Di deaeque, quam
pusillo animo illum aut honorare voluit aut corrum-
2 pere ! Reddendum egregio viro testimonium est ;
ingentem rem ab illo dici audivi, cum miraretur Gai
dementiam, quod se putasset tanti posse mutari.
" Si temptare," inquit, " me constituerat, toto illi fui
experiendus imperio."

1   12. Sapienti ergo donari aliquid potest, etiam si
sapientis omnia sunt. Aeque nihil prohibet, cum
omnia amicis dicamus esse communia, aliquid amico
donari. Non enim mihi sic cum amico communia
omnia sunt, quomodo cum socio, ut pars mea sit, pars
illius, sed quomodo patri matrique communes liberi

[1] C. *added by Pincianus.*

who can take delight in the huge record of his estate, in his vast tracts of land that need to be tilled by men in chains, in huge herds and flocks that need whole provinces and kingdoms to provide them with pasture, and in private palaces that cover more ground than great cities! When he has carefully reviewed all his wealth, in what it is invested and on what it is squandered, and is puffed up with pride, let him compare all that he has with what he still covets, and he is a poor man! Let me go—restore me to the riches that are mine. I know the kingdom of wisdom, a mighty, a secure kingdom— I possess all in the sense that all things belong to all!'"

And so, when Gaius Caesar wanted to give Demetrius two hundred thousand, he laughingly refused it, not even deeming it a sum the refusal of which was worth boasting about! Ye gods and goddesses, what a petty mind Gaius showed in trying either to compliment or to corrupt him! I must here render testimony to the distinction of the man. I heard him say a fine thing when he expressed surprise at the madness of Gaius in supposing that he could have been influenced by such an amount. " If he meant to tempt me," said he, " he ought to have tested me by offering me his whole kingdom."

It is possible, consequently, to bestow a gift on a wise man even if all things belong to the wise man. And, just as truly, there is nothing to prevent my making a gift to a friend, although we say that friends have all things in common. For I have all things in common with my friend, not as I would with a partner, when one share would belong to me, and another to him, but as children are the common possession of

sunt, quibus cum duo sunt, non singuli singulos
habent, sed singuli binos.

2 Primum omnium iam efficiam, ut, quisquis est iste,
qui me in societatem vocat, sciat se nihil mecum
habere commune. Quare ? Quia hoc inter sapientes
solum consortium est, inter quos amicitia est ; ceteri
non magis amici sunt quam socii.

3 Deinde pluribus modis communia sunt. Equestria
omnium equitum Romanorum sunt ; in illis tamen
meus fit proprius locus, quem occupavi ; hoc si cui
cessi, quamvis illi communi re cesserim, tamen aliquid
4 dedisse videor. Quaedam quorundam sub certa con-
dicione sunt. Habeo in equestribus locum, non ut
vendam, non ut locem, non ut habitem, in hoc tantum,
ut spectem ; propterea non mentior, si dico habere
me in equestribus locum. Sed cum in theatrum veni,
si plena sunt equestria, et iure habeo locum illic, quia
sedere mihi licet, et non habeo, quia ab his, cum
quibus mihi ius loci commune est, occupatus est.
5 Idem inter amicos puta fieri. Quidquid habet
amicus, commune est nobis, sed illius proprium est,
qui tenet ; uti iis illo nolente non possum. " Derides
me," inquis ; " si, quod amici est, meum est, liceat
mihi vendere." Non licet ; nam nec equestria, et

---

a The first fourteen rows of the theatre behind the orchestra,
which was reserved for senators.

their father and mother, who, if they have two, do not each claim one, but they each claim two.

First of all, I shall now proceed to show that every man who invites me to enter into partnership with him, knows well that he possesses nothing in common with me. And why ? Because this community of goods can exist between wise men only, who alone are capable of knowing friendship ; the rest are just as little friends as they are partners.

In the second place, there are many ways of owning things in common. The seats reserved [a] for the knights belong to all the Roman knights ; yet of these the seat that I have occupied becomes my own property, and, if I surrender it to anyone, I am supposed to have given him something although I have only surrendered to him what was common property. Certain things belong to certain persons under particular conditions. I have a seat among the knights, not to sell, not to let, not to dwell in, but to use only for the purpose of viewing the spectacle. Therefore I am not speaking an untruth when I say that I have a seat in the equestrian rows. But, if the equestrian rows are full when I enter the theatre, I both have a right to a seat there, because I have the privilege of sitting there, and have not a right, because the seat is occupied by those who have with me a common right to the space. Consider that the same relation exists between friends. Whatever our friend possesses is common to us, but it is the property of the one who holds it ; I cannot use the things against his will. " You are making fun of me," you say ; " if what belongs to my friend is mine, I have a right to sell it." Not so ; for you have no right to sell the equestrians' seats, and yet they belong to you

485

tamen communia tibi cum ceteris equitibus sunt.
6 Non est argumentum ideo aliquid tuum non esse,
quia vendere non potes, quia consumere, quia mutare
in deterius aut melius; tuum enim est etiam, quod
sub lege certa tuum est.

13. * * * accepi, sed certe non minus. Ne traham
longius, beneficium maius esse non potest; ea, per
quae beneficium datur, possunt esse maiora et plura,
in quae se denique benevolentia effundat et sic sibi
indulgeat, quemadmodum amantes solent, quorum
plura oscula et complexus artiores non augent
amorem, sed exercent.

1 14. Haec quoque, quae venit, quaestio profligata
est in prioribus; itaque breviter perstringetur;
possunt enim in hanc, quae aliis data sunt, argu-
menta transferri. Quaeritur, an, qui omnia fecit, ut
2 beneficium redderet, reddiderit. "Ut scias," inquit,
"illum non reddidisse, omnia fecit, ut redderet;
apparet ergo non esse id factum, cuius faciendi occasionem non habuit. Et creditori suo pecuniam non
solvit is, qui, ut solveret, ubique quaesivit nec invenit."

3 Quaedam eius condicionis sunt, ut effectum praestare debeant; quibusdam pro effectu est omnia
temptasse, ut efficerent. Si omnia fecit, ut sanaret,
peregit partes suas medicus; etiam damnato reo

---

^a Something has been lost from the text.

in common with the other knights. The fact that you cannot sell something, or consume it, or alter it for the better or worse is, in itself, no proof that it does not belong to you ; for something that is yours under particular conditions is nevertheless yours.

. . .*ᵃ* I have received, but at any rate not less. Not to prolong the discussion, a benefit cannot be more than a benefit ; but the means employed to convey a benefit may be both greater and more numerous — the things in which, in short, one's benevolence runs riot, and indulges itself as lovers are wont to do, for these by their more numerous kisses and closer embraces do not increase their love, but give it play.

This other question, which now comes up, has been exhausted in the earlier books, and will, therefore, be touched upon briefly ; for the arguments that have been given for other cases may be transferred to this. The question is, whether anyone who has done everything in his power to return a benefit has returned it. "You may be sure," you say, "that he has not returned it, for he did everything in his power to return it ; it is evident, therefore, that he did not accomplish his purpose if he failed to find opportunity for its accomplishment. And a man does not discharge his debt to a creditor if he searches everywhere for money in order to be able to discharge it, and yet has not found it."

Some efforts are of such a character that they are bound to achieve their end ; in the case of others, to have tried in every way to achieve an end takes the place of achievement. If a physician has made every effort to effect a cure, he has performed his part; the

oratori constat eloquentiae officium, si omni vi usus
est ; laus imperatoria etiam victo duci redditur, si
et prudentia et industria et fortitudo muneribus suis
4 functa est. Omnia fecit, ut beneficium redderet,
obstitit illi felicitas tua ; nihil incidit durius, quod
veram amicitiam experiretur ; locupleti donare non
potuit, sano adsidere, felici succurrere : gratiam
rettulit, etiam si tu beneficium non recepisti. Praeterea huic intentus semper et huius rei tempus op-
periens, qui in hoc multum curae, multum sedulitatis
impendit, plus laboravit, quam cui cito referre gratiam
5 contigit. Debitoris exemplum dissimile est, cui
parum est pecuniam quaesisse, nisi solvit ; illic enim
stat acerbus super caput creditor, qui nullum diem
gratis occidere patiatur ; hic benignissimus, qui, te
cum viderit concursantem et sollicitum atque anxium,
dicat :

    " Mitte hanc de pectore curam ;

desine tibi molestus instare. Omnia a te habeo ; iniuriam mihi facis, si me quicquam desiderare amplius
iudicas ; plenissime ad me pervenit animus tuus."
6   " Dic," inquit, " mihi : si reddidisset beneficium,
diceres illum gratiam rettulisse ; eodem ergo loco
est, qui reddidit et qui non reddidit ? "

---

[a] Virgil, *Aeneid*, vi. 85.

pleader, if he has used all the power of his eloquence, fulfils his duty even if his client is convicted; praise for his generalship is bestowed even upon a vanquished commander if he has performed his duties with prudence, with diligence, and with bravery. A man has made every effort to return your benefit, but your good fortune stood in his way; no hardship befell you which could put his true friendship to the test; he could not give to you when you were rich, nor sit at your bedside when you were not sick, nor succour you when you had no misfortune—this man has repaid gratitude even if you have not received the return of your benefit. Moreover, he who is always intent upon this, is on the watch for an opportunity of doing it, and expends upon it much thought and much anxiety, has taken more trouble than one who has had the good fortune to repay his gratitude quickly. Quite different is the case of the debtor, for it is not enough for him to have sought for the money unless he pays it; for in his case a harsh creditor stands over him, who suffers not a single day to pass without charging him interest; in your case there is a very generous friend, who, if he saw you rushing about and troubled and anxious, would say:

" This trouble from thy breast expel [a];

cease to cause yourself concern. I have all that I want from you; you do me an injustice if you suppose that I desire from you anything further; your intention has reached me most fully."

" Tell me," you say: " if he had returned the benefit, you would say that he has shown gratitude; are both, therefore, in the same position—the one who returned it, and the one who did not return it?"

Contra nunc illud pone : si oblitus esset accepti
beneficii, si ne temptasset quidem gratus esse, negares
illum gratiam rettulisse ; at hic se diebus noctibusque
lassavit et omnibus aliis renuntiavit officiis huic uni
imminens et operatus, ne qua se fugeret occasio ;
eodem ergo loco erunt ille, qui curam referendae
gratiae abiecit, et hic, qui numquam ab illa recessit ?
Iniquus es, si rem a me exigis, cum videas animum
non defuisse.

1   15. Ad summam puta, cum captus esses, me
pecuniam mutuatum rebus meis in securitatem
creditoris oppositis navigasse hieme tam saeva per
infesta latrociniis litora, emensum, quidquid periculorum adferre potest etiam pacatum mare ; per-
agratis omnibus solitudinibus, cum, quos nemo non[1]
fugiebat, ego quaererem, tandem ad piratas perveni ;
iam te alius redemerat : negabis me gratiam rettulisse ? Etiamne, si in illa navigatione pecuniam,
quam saluti tuae contraxeram, naufragus perdidi,
etiamne, si in[2] vincula, quae detrahere tibi volui,
2 ipse incidi, negabis me rettulisse gratiam ?   At mehercules Athenienses Harmodium et Aristogitonem
tyrannicidas vocant, et Mucio manus in hostili ara
relicta instar occisi Porsinae fuit, et semper contra
fortunam luctata virtus etiam citra effectum pro-

---

[1] non *commonly added.*
[2] in *added by Gruter.*

---

[a] Killed in 514 B.C. in an attempt to overthrow the
Pisistratidae and immortalized by the Athenians as martyrs
to liberty, they were honoured with bronze statues, which
stood upon the ascent to the Acropolis, and are now shown in
the spirited copies preserved in the National Museum at
Naples.
[b] Called Scaevola, " the Left-Handed," because in the

On the other hand, consider this. If he had forgotten the benefit he had received, if he had not even
tried to be grateful, you would say that he had not
shown gratitude. Yet this other man has worn himself out night and day, and, neglecting all his other
duties, has concentrated on this single one, and has
taken pains not to let any opportunity escape him.
Will, therefore, he who has put aside all concern
about showing gratitude and he who has never
ceased to be concerned be considered in the same
class ? You are unjust if you require me to pay in
fact when you see that I have not failed in intention.

In short, suppose, when you had been taken captive,
that I, having borrowed money, and having made
over my property to my creditor as security, set sail
along shores infested with pirates in the midst of
winter with all its fierceness, and traversed all the
perils that even a peaceful sea can offer ; that,
having wandered through all wildernesses, in search
of men from whom every one else was fleeing, I at
last reached the pirates, and found that someone else
had ransomed you—will you say that I have not repaid gratitude ? Even if, during that voyage, I was
shipwrecked, and lost the money that I had raised to
rescue you, even if I myself have fallen into the chains
which I hoped to remove from you, will you say that I
have not repaid gratitude ? No, by the gods !—the
Athenians call Harmodius and Aristogiton [a] " tyranni-
cides," and the hand that Mucius [b] left on the enemy's
altar was as glorious as if it had killed Porsina, and
the valour that struggles against fortune always wins
lustre even if it fails to accomplish the task set before

enemy's camp he proved his resolution by thrusting his right
hand into the flame.

positi operis enituit. Plus praestitit, qui fugientes occasiones secutus est et alia atque alia captavit, per quae referre gratiam posset, quam quem sine ullo sudore gratum prima fecit occasio.

3   " Duas," inquit, " res ille tibi praestitit, voluntatem et rem ; tu quoque illi duas debes." Merito istud diceres ei, qui tibi reddidit voluntatem otiosam, huic vero, qui et vult et conatur et nihil intemptatum relinquit, id non potes dicere ; utrumque enim prae-
4 stat, quantum in se est. Deinde non semper numero numerus aequandus est, aliquando una res pro duabus valet ; itaque in locum rei succedit tam propensa voluntas et cupida reddendi. Quod si animus sine re ad referendam gratiam non valet, nemo adversus deos gratus est, in quos voluntas sola confertur.
5 " Dis," inquit, " nihil aliud praestare possumus." Sed si huic quoque, cui referre gratiam debeo, nihil aliud praestare possum, quid est, quare non eo adversus hominem gratus sim, quo nihil amplius in deos confero ?

1   16. Si tamen quaeris, quid sentiam, et vis signare responsum, hic beneficium recepisse se iudicet, ille se sciat non reddidisse ; hic illum dimittat, ille se teneat ; hic dicat : " Habeo," ille respondeat :
2 " Debeo." In omni quaestione propositum sit nobis

it. He who pursues opportunities that elude him, and clutches at them one after another in order that he may be able to have the means of showing his gratitude, renders far more than he who without strenuous effort proves himself grateful at the first opportunity.

"But," you say, "your benefactor bestowed on you two things, his property and his goodwill; you, likewise, owe him two." You might say this very properly to one who returns to you goodwill without further effort, but you cannot say it to one who both wishes and makes effort, and leaves nothing untried; for, so far as it is in his power, he bestows on you both. Again, it is not always desirable to pit number against number; sometimes one thing has the value of two; and so such ardent and eager desire to repay takes the place of repayment. And, if the intention without a material offering has no value in repaying gratitude, no one shows himself grateful to the gods, to whom the only contribution that we make is goodwill. "We cannot," you say, "bestow anything else on the gods." But, if I am also unable to bestow anything else on a man to whom I ought to return gratitude, why is it that the only means that I have of showing my gratitude to the gods does not permit me to show myself grateful to a man?

If, however, you ask me what I think, and wish me to set my seal on the reply, I should say that the one should consider that he has received the return of his benefit, while the other should know that he has not returned it; the one should release the other, while the other should feel himself bound; the one should say, "I have received," the other, "I still owe." In the case of every question, let us keep before us the

bonum publicum ; praecludendae sunt excusationes
ingratis, ad quas refugere non possint et sub quibus
infitiationem suam tegere. "Omnia feci." Fac
3 etiamnunc. Quid ? tu tam imprudentes iudicas
maiores nostros fuisse, ut non intellegerent iniquis-
simum esse eodem loco haberi eum, qui pecuniam,
quam a creditore acceperat, libidini aut aleae adsump-
sit, et eum, qui incendio aut latrocinio aut aliquo casu
tristiore aliena cum suis perdidit ? Nullam excusationem receperunt, ut homines scirent fidem utique
praestandam ; satius enim erat a paucis etiam iustam
excusationem non accipi quam ab omnibus aliquam
4 temptari. Omnia fecisti, ut redderes ; hoc illi satis
sit, tibi parum. Nam quemadmodum ille, si enixam
et sedulam operam transire pro irrita patitur, cui
gratia referatur, indignus est, ita tu ingratus es, nisi
ei, qui voluntatem bonam in solutum accipit, eo
libentius debes, quia dimitteris. Non rapias hoc nec
testeris ; occasiones reddendi nihilo minus quaeras.
Redde illi, quia repetit, huic, quia remittit ; illi, quia
bonus est, huic, quia malus.

5 Ideoque hanc quaestionem non est quod ad te
iudices pertinere, an, quod beneficium quis a sapiente
accepit, reddere debeat, si ille desiit esse sapiens et

public good ; the door must be closed to all excuses,
to keep the ungrateful from taking refuge in them
and using them to cover their repudiation of the
debt. " I have done all in my power," says he.
Well, keep on doing so. Tell me, do you suppose that
our forefathers were so foolish as not to understand
that it was most unjust to consider a man who spent
in debauchery or gambling the money he had received from a creditor to be in the same class with
one who lost the borrowed property along with his
own in a fire, or by robbery, or some other major
mishap ? Yet they accepted no excuses in order to
teach men that a promise must be kept at all costs ;
in their eyes it was better that a few should not find
even a good excuse accepted than that all should
resort to excuse. You have done everything in
order to make return ; this should be enough for
your benefactor, it should not be enough for you.
For, just as he is unworthy of being repaid with gratitude if he permits all your earnest and diligent effort
to pass as nothing, so, if anyone accepts your goodwill as full payment, you are ungrateful if you are not
all the more eager to acknowledge your indebtedness
because he has released you. Do not snatch up
your release, nor demand witnesses ; no whit the less
should you seek opportunities for making full return.
Return to one because he demands repayment, to
another because he releases you from the debt ; to
the former, because he is bad, to the latter, because
he is good.

There is, consequently, no reason why you should
suppose that you have any concern with the question
of whether a man ought to return the benefit that
he has received from a wise man if he has ceased to

in malum versus est. Redderes enim et depositum,
quod a sapiente accepisses, etiam malo, redderes
creditum. Quid est, cur non et beneficium? Quia
6 mutatus est, ille te mutet? Quid? Si quid a sano
accepisses, aegro non redderes, cum plus semper
imbecillo amico debeamus? Et hic aeger est animo;
adiuvetur, feratur. Stultitia morbus est animi.

1 17. Distinguendum hoc, quo magis intellegatur,
existimo. Duo sunt beneficia: unum, quod dare
nisi sapiens sapienti non potest; hoc est absolutum
et verum beneficium; alterum vulgare, plebeium,
2 cuius inter nos imperitos commercium est. De hoc
non est dubium, quin illi, qualiscumque est, debeam
reddere, sive homicida sive fur sive adulter evasit.
Habent scelera leges suas; melius istos iudex quam
ingratus emendat. Nemo te malum, quia est, faciat.
Malo beneficium proiciam, bono reddam, huic, quia
debeo, illi, ne debeam.

1 18. De altero beneficii genere dubitatur, quod si
accipere non potui nisi sapiens, ne reddere quidem
nisi sapienti possum. " Puta enim me reddere: ille
496

be wise and has turned into a bad man. For you would return a deposit that you had received from a wise man even if he had become bad, you would return a loan. What reason is there why you should not return a benefit also? Because he has changed, should he change you? Tell me, if you had received anything from a man when he was well, would you not return it to him if he were sick, seeing that a friend's weakness always increases our obligation to him? This other also is sick—but in his mind; we should help him, and bear with him. The mind's illness is folly.

In order that the matter may become more intelligible, I think that here I ought to make a distinction. Benefits are of two kinds—one, the perfect and true benefit, which only a wise man can give to none but a wise man; the other, the everyday, common sort, in which we ignorant men have dealings with each other. With regard to the latter, there is no doubt that I ought to make return to the giver, no matter what sort of a man he may be, whether he has turned out to be a murderer or a thief or an adulterer. Crimes have their appointed laws; let such men be reformed rather by a judge than by the ingrate. Let no man make you bad because he is. To a good man I shall hand back his benefit, to a bad one I shall fling it back; to the former, because I am indebted to him, to the latter, in order that I may no longer be indebted to him.

With regard to the other kind of benefit, a question arises, for, if I could not have received the benefit unless I had been a wise man, neither can I return it to the giver unless he is a wise man. For you say: " Suppose that I do return it—he is not able to take it

non potest recipere, non est iam huius rei capax, scientiam utendi perdidit. Quid, si me remittere manco pilam iubeas ? Stultum est dare alicui, quod accipere non possit."

2 Ut respondere ab ultimo incipiam : non dabo ulli, quod accipere non poterit ; reddam, etiam si recipere non poterit. Obligare enim non possum nisi accipientem ; liberari tantum, si reddidi, possum. Ille uti illo non poterit ? Viderit ; penes illum erit culpa, non penes me.

1 19. " Reddere est," inquit, " accepturo tradidisse. Quid enim ? si cui vinum debeas et hoc ille te infundere reticulo iubeat aut cribro, reddidisse te dices ? Aut reddere voles, quod, dum redditur, inter duos pereat ? "

2 Reddere est id, quod debeas, ei, cuius est, volenti dare. Hoc unum mihi praestandum est. Ut quidem habeat, quod a me accepit, iam ulterioris est curae ; non tutelam illi, sed fidem debeo, multoque satius 3 est illum non habere, quam me non reddere. Et creditori statim in macellum laturo, quod acceperit, reddam ; etiam si mihi adulteram, cui numerem, delegaverit, solvam ; et, si nummos, quos accipiet, in sinum suum discinctus infundet, dabo. Reddendum enim mihi est, non servandum, cum reddidero,

---

a i.e., to show himself a glutton.
b The height of folly, since thus this Roman " pocket " would lack a bottom.

back, he is no longer capable of such an act, he has lost his knowledge of how to use it. Tell me, would you bid me throw back a ball to a player who had maimed his hand? It is foolish to try to give any-one something that he is not able to accept."

To attempt a reply to your last point, I shall not give to any man what he will not be able to accept; but I shall make return even if he will not be able to accept return. For I am able to place a man under obligation only if he accepts; I am able to be freed from obligation only if I make return. He will not be able to use it? Let him look to that; the fault will lie with him, not with me.

" To return," you say, " is to have handed some-thing over to one who will receive it. Come, tell me, if you owe wine to someone, and he should bid you pour it into a net or a sieve, would you say that you had returned it? Or would you be willing to return it if, in the act of returning it, it is lost between the two?"

To return is to give something that you owe to the one to whom it belongs when he wishes it. This is the only act that I need perform. That he should possess what he has received from me is a later con-sideration; I owe him, not tutelage, but good faith, and it is much better that he should fail to possess than that I should fail to return. Likewise, I would repay my creditor even though he intended to spend at once in the meat-market[a] what he received from me; even if he should designate that I am to pay it over to an adulteress, I would pay it; even if he will pour the coins he receives into a fold of his toga with-out being girdled,[b] I shall give them. For my duty is to return, not to protect and safeguard, what I

ac tuendum; beneficii accepti,[1] non redditi, custodiam debeo. Dum apud me est, salvum sit ; ceterum, licet accipientis manibus effluat, dandum est reposcenti. Reddam bono, cum expediet, malo, cum petet.

4 " Tale," inquit, " illi beneficium, quale accepisti, non potes reddere ; accepisti enim a sapiente, stulto reddis." Non ; reddo illi, quale nunc potest recipere, nec per me fit, quod deterius id, quod accepi, reddam, sed per illum, cui, si ad sapientiam redierit, reddam, quale accepi[1] ; dum in malis est, reddam, quale ab illo potest accipi.

5 " Quid ? si," inquit, " non tantum malus factus est, sed ferus, sed immanis, qualis Apollodorus aut Phalaris,[a] et huic beneficium, quod acceperas, reddes ? " Mutationem sapientis tantam natura non patitur. Non in pessima ab optimis lapsus ; necesse est etiam in malo vestigia boni teneat ; numquam tantum virtus extinguitur, ut non certiores animo notas im-
6 primat, quam ut illas eradat ulla mutatio. Ferae inter nos educatae si in silvas eruperunt, aliquid mansuetudinis pristinae retinent tantumque a placidissimis absunt, quantum a veris feris et numquam humanam manum passis. Nemo in summam nequitiam incidit, qui umquam haesit sapientiae ; altius

---

[1] accepi *commonly added.*

---

[a] Types of cruel tyrants, the one in Macedonia, the other in Sicily.

have returned; I owe protection to a benefit that has been received, not to one that has been returned. While it is in my hands, it must be kept safe; but I must give it back when he demands it even if it escapes from his hands as he takes it. To a good man I shall make return when it is convenient; to a bad man, when he asks for it.

"You cannot," you say, "return to him the same sort of benefit that you received; for you received it from a wise man, you are returning it to a fool." No; I am returning to him the sort that he is now able to receive, and it is not my fault if that which I shall return is inferior to what I received, but the fault lies with him, and if he is restored to wisdom, I shall return the sort that I received; while he lingers in evil, I shall return the sort that he is able to receive.

"Tell me," you say, "if he has become, not only bad, but savage, even ferocious, like Apollodorus or Phalaris,[a] will you return even to such a man a benefit that you had received?" Nature does not permit a wise man to suffer so great a change. A man does not fall from the best state into the worst; even a bad man must necessarily retain some traces of good; virtue is never so wholly extinguished as not to leave upon the mind indelible imprints that no change can ever erase. Wild beasts that have been bred in captivity, if they escape into the forests, retain something of their earlier tameness, and are as far removed from the most peaceful beasts as they are from those that have always been wild and have never submitted to the hand of man. No one who has ever adhered to wisdom can fall into the depths of wickedness; its

501

infectus est, quam ut ex toto elui et transire in colorem malum possit.

7 Deinde interrogo, utrum iste ferus sit animo tantum, an et in perniciem publicam excurrat? Proposuisti enim mihi Phalarim et alterum[1] tyrannum, quorum si naturam habet intra se malus, quidni ego isti beneficium suum reddam, ne quid mihi cum illo

8 iuris sit amplius? Si vero sanguine humano non tantum gaudet, sed pascitur, sed et suppliciis omnium aetatium crudelitatem insatiabilem exercet nec ira sed aviditate quadam saeviendi furit, si in ore parentium liberos iugulat, si non contentus simplici morte distorquet nec urit solum perituros, sed excoquit, si arx eius cruore semper recenti madet, parum est huic beneficium non reddere! Quidquid erat, quo mihi cohaereret, intercisa iuris humani societas abscidit.

9 Si praestitisset quidem aliquid mihi, sed arma patriae meae inferret, quidquid meruerat, perdidisset, et referre illi gratiam scelus haberetur. Si non patriam meam impugnat, sed suae gravis est et sepositus a mea gente suam exagitat, abscindit, nihilo minus illum tanta pravitas animi, etiam si non inimicum, invisum mihi efficit, priorque mihi ac potior eius officii ratio est, quod humano generi, quam quod uni homini debeo.

[1] alterum *added by Hosius.*

colour is too deeply fixed to be able to fade altogether from his mind and to take on the hue of evil.

In the second place, I ask you whether the man you are thinking of is ferocious in spirit only, or whether he bursts forth into acts of public violence ? You have cited the cases of Phalaris and another tyrant, but if, while an evil man possesses their nature, he keeps it concealed, why should I not return to him his benefit in order that there may be no further bond between him and me ? If, however, he not only delights in human blood, but feeds upon it ; if also he exercises his insatiable cruelty in the torture of persons of all ages, and his frenzy is the result, not of anger, but of a certain delight in cruelty ; if he butchers children before the eyes of their parents ; if, not content with simply killing his victims, he tortures them, and not only burns, but roasts, them to death ; if his castle is always wet with freshly shed blood—then not to return a benefit to him is too small a thing ! For whatever the tie that bound him to me, it has been severed by his breach of the common bond of humanity. If he had bestowed something upon me, and yet bore arms against my country, he would have lost all claim upon me, and it would be considered a crime to repay him with gratitude. If he does not assail my country, but is the bane of his own, and, while he keeps aloof from my own people, harrows and rends his own, nevertheless, even if such depravity does not make him my personal enemy, it makes him hateful to me, and regard for the duty that I owe to the whole human race is, in my eyes, more primary and more pressing than the duty I owe to a single man.

1 20. Sed quamvis hoc ita sit et ex eo tempore omnia mihi in illum libera sint, ex quo corrumpendo fas omne, ut nihil in eum nefas esset, effecerit, illum mihi servandum modum credam, ut, si beneficium illi meum neque vires maiores daturum est in exitium commune nec confirmaturum, quas habet, id autem erit, quod illi reddi sine pernicie publica possit, red-
2 dam. Servabo filium eius infantem ; quid hoc beneficium obest cuiquam eorum, quos crudelitas eius lacerat ? Pecuniam, quae satellitem stipendio teneat, non subministrabo. Si marmora et vestes desideraverit, nihil oberit cuiquam id, quo luxuria eius in-
3 struitur ; militem et arma non suggeram. Si pro magno petet munere artifices scenae et scorta et quae feritatem eius emolliant, libens offeram. Cui triremes et aeratas non mitterem, lusorias et cubiculatas et alia ludibria regum in mari lascivientium mittam. Et si ex toto desperata eius sanitas fuerit, eadem manu beneficium omnibus dabo, illi reddam ; quoniam ingeniis talibus exitus remedium est optimumque est abire ei, qui ad se numquam rediturus
4 est. Sed haec rara nequitia est semper portenti loco habita, sicut hiatus terrae et e cavernis maris ignium eruptio ; itaque ab illa recedamus, de iis loquamur vitiis, quae detestamur sine horrore.
5 Huic homini malo, quem invenire in quolibet foro possum, quem singuli timent, reddam beneficium,

---

^a *i.e.*, war-ships.
^b Here the means of suicide.

504

But, although this be so, although I am free to act as I please toward him, from the moment when by violating all law he put himself beyond the pale of the law, I shall think that I ought to observe moderation, as follows. If my benefit to him is likely neither to increase his powers to work general harm, nor to strengthen what he already has, if, too, it shall be of such a character that it can be returned to him without being disastrous to the state, then I shall return it. I shall be willing to save the life of his infant son—for what harm can this benefit do to any of those whom he tortures with his cruelty ?—but I shall not supply him with money to maintain his bodyguard. If he desires marbles and raiments, these trappings of his luxury will do nobody any harm ; but I shall not furnish him with soldiers and arms. If, as a great boon, he asks for stage-players and prostitutes and things that will soften his fierce nature, I shall gladly present them. I would not send to him triremes and bronze-beaked ships,[a] but I should send pleasure-boats and yachts and the other playthings of kings who indulge in sport on the sea. And if his sanity should be despaired of, with the hand that returns a benefit [b] to him, I shall bestow one on all men ; since for such characters the only remedy is death, and, if a man will probably never return to his senses, it is best for him to depart. But so rare is such a degree of wickedness that it is always regarded as a portent—as much so as the yawning of the earth and the bursting forth of fires from the caverns of the sea. So let us leave it, and talk of vices that we can detest without shuddering.

As for the type of bad man that I can find in any market-place, who is feared, but only by individuals,

quod accepi. Non oportet mihi nequitiam eius prodesse ; quod meum non est, redeat ad dominum. Bonus sit an malus, quid differt[1] ? Diligenter istud excuterem, si non redderem, sed darem.

1   21. Hic locus fabulam poscit. Pythagoricus quidam emerat a sutore phaecasia, rem magnam, non praesentibus nummis. Post aliquot dies venit ad tabernam redditurus et, cum clusam diu pulsaret, fuit, qui diceret : " Quid perdis operam ? Sutor ille, quem quaeris, elatus, combustus est ; quod nobis fortasse molestum est, qui in aeternum nostros amittimus, tibi minime, qui scis futurum, ut renascatur," 2 iocatus in Pythagoricum. At philosophus noster tres aut quattuor denarios non invita manu domum rettulit subinde concutiens ; deinde, cum reprehendisset hanc suam non reddendi tacitam voluptatem, intellegens arrisisse illud lucellum sibi redit ad eandem tabernam et ait : " Ille tibi vivit ; redde, quod debes." Deinde per clostrum, qua se commissura laxaverat, quattuor denarios in tabernam inseruit ac misit poenas a se exigens improbae cupiditatis, ne alieno adsuesceret.

1   22. Quod debes, quaere, cui reddas, et, si nemo poscet, ipse te appella. Malus an bonus, ad te non pertinet ; redde et accusa. Oblitus es, quem-

---

[1] differt *added by Gertz.*

---

[a] Elegant shoes, sometimes adorned with gold, affected in Alexandria and Athens, notably by priests.
[b] Who believed in the transmigration of souls.

I shall return to him the benefit that I have received.
It is not right that I should profit by his wickedness ;
let me return what is not mine to its owner. What
difference does it make whether he is good or bad ?
But I would sift out that matter most carefully if I
were giving, not returning, a benefit.

This point calls up a story. A certain Pythagorean
once bought some white shoes [a] from a cobbler, a fine
pair, without paying for them in cash. Some days
later he returned to the shop in order to make payment, and, after he had been knocking for a long time
at the closed door, someone appeared, and said :
" Why do you waste your time ? The cobbler you
are looking for passed away, and has been cremated ;
this is, perhaps, a grief to us, who believe that we
lose our friends for ever, but not to you, who know
that they will be reborn," jeering at the Pythagorean.[b]
But our philosopher, not unwillingly, carried his
three or four denarii back home, shaking them now
and then in his hand. Later, after blaming himself
for the secret pleasure he had had from not paying
the money, and perceiving that he had derived
satisfaction from his trifling gain, he returned to the
same shop, saying to himself : " For you the man
is alive, pay him what you owe." Thereupon, he
dropped the four coins into the shop, thrusting them
through the closed door by means of a crack in the
joining, and exacted punishment of himself for his
unconscionable greed in order that he might not
form the habit of being in debt.

Try to find someone to whom you can pay what you
owe, and, if no one demands it, do you dun yourself.
It is no concern of yours whether the man is good or
bad ; first pay, then accuse. You have forgotten how

SENECA

admodum inter vos officia divisa sint : illi oblivio
imperata est, tibi meminisse mandavimus. Errat
tamen, si quis existimat, cum dicimus eum, qui beneficium dedit, oblivisci oportere, excutere nos illi
memoriam rei praesertim honestissimae ; quaedam
praecipimus ultra modum, ut ad verum et suum re-
2 deant. Cum dicimus : " Meminisse non debet,"
hoc volumus intellegi : " Praedicare non debet nec
iactare nec gravis esse." Quidam enim beneficium,
quod dederunt, omnibus circulis narrant ; hoc sobrii
locuntur, hoc ebrii non continent, hoc ignotis in-
gerunt, hoc amicis committunt ; ut haec nimia et
exprobratrix memoria subsideret, oblivisci eum, qui
dedit, iussimus et plus imperando, quam praestari
poterat, silentium suasimus.

1   23. Quotiens parum fiduciae est in iis, quibus im-
peres, amplius exigendum est, quam sat est, ut prae-
stetur, quantum sat est. In hoc omnis hyperbole
extenditur, ut ad verum mendacio veniat. Itaque
ille, cum dixit :

> Qui candore nives anteirent, cursibus auras,

quod non poterat fieri, dixit, ut crederetur, quantum
plurimum posset. Et qui dixit :

> His inmobilior scopulis, violentior amne,

ne hoc quidem se persuasurum putavit aliquem tam
2 immobilem esse quam scopulum. Numquam tantum

---

a Virgil, *Aeneid*, xii. 84.
b Ovid, *Met.* xiii. 801.

508

your several duties have been divided—for him forgetfulness is enjoined, for you we have decreed remembrance. Yet it is a mistake to suppose that, when we say that the man who has given a benefit ought to forget, we would rob him of all memory of his act, especially if it was a very honourable one. We overstate some rules in order that in the end they may reach their true value. When we say : " He must not remember," we really mean : " He must not babble, nor boast, nor give offence." For some men in all gatherings tell of a benefit that they have given ; talk of it when they are sober, make no secret of it when they are drunk, force it upon strangers, confide it to friends. It is to quell this excessive and reproachful consciousness of it that we have said that the man who gives must forget, and, by ordering something more than he is able to accomplish, have commended to him silence.

Whenever you lack confidence in those to whom you are giving orders, you should demand of them more than is necessary in order that they may perform all that is necessary. The set purpose of all hyperbole is to arrive at the truth by falsehood. And so when the poet said :

Whose whiteness shamed the snow, their speed the winds,[a]

he stated what could not possibly be true in order to give credence to all that could be true. And the other who said :

Firmer than a rock, more headlong than the stream,[b]

did not suppose that he could convince anyone by this that any person was as immovable as a rock. Hyperbole never expects to attain all that it

509

sperat hyperbole, quantum audet, sed incredibilia adfirmat, ut ad credibilia perveniat. Cum dicimus: "Qui beneficium dedit, obliviscatur," hoc dicimus: "Similis sit oblito ; memoria eius non appareat nec 3 incurrat." Cum dicimus beneficium repeti non oportere, non ex toto repetitionem tollimus ; saepe enim opus est malis exactore, etiam bonis admonitione. Quid ergo ? Occasionem ignoranti non ostendam ? Necessitates illi meas non detegam ? Quare nescisse se aut mentiatur aut doleat ? Interveniat aliquando admonitio, sed verecunda, quae non poscat nec in ius vocet.

1 24. Socrates amicis audientibus : "Emissem," inquit, "pallium, si nummos haberem." Neminem poposcit, omnes admonuit. A quo acciperet, ambitus fuit ; quidni esset ? Quantulum enim erat, quod Socrates accipiebat ! At multum erat eum fuisse, 2 a quo Socrates acciperet. Num illos castigare mollius potuit ? "Emissem," inquit, "pallium, si nummos haberem." Post hoc quisquis properaverit, sero dat ; iam Socrati defuit. Propter acerbos exactores repetere prohibemus, non, ut numquam fiat, sed ut parce.

1 25. Aristippus aliquando delectatus unguento : "Male," inquit, "istis effeminatis eveniat, qui rem tam bellam infamaverunt." Item dicendum est:

---

[a] Pupil of Socrates and founder of the Hedonistic school of philosophy.

ventures, but asserts the incredible in order to arrive at the credible. When we say : " Let him who gives a benefit forget it," we mean : " Let him seem to have forgotten it ; let not his memory of it appear or obtrude." When we say that we ought not to demand the repayment of a benefit, we do not banish every demand for repayment ; for bad men often need to be dunned, even good men to be reminded. What, then ? Am I not to point out an opportunity to one who is not aware of it ? Am I not to reveal my own wants ? Why should anyone have the chance to deny or be sorry that he did not know of them ? Sometimes we may venture to remind, but modestly, with no air of making a demand or of claiming a legal right.

Socrates once said in the hearing of his friends : " I would have bought a cloak, if I had had the money." He asked from no one, he reminded all. Rivalry sprang up as to who should be allowed to give it to him. Why should there not have been ? For how small a thing it was that Socrates was receiving ! But to have been the one from whom Socrates received was a great thing. Could he have upbraided them more gently ? " I would have bought a cloak," he said, " if I had had the money." After this, whoever made haste to give, gave too late ; he had already failed in duty to Socrates. Because some men are harsh in demanding repayment, we forbid it, not in order that the demand may never be made, but that it may be made sparingly.

Once when Aristippus [a] was enjoying the odour of a perfume, he cried : " Curses upon these effeminate fellows who have cast discredit upon so nice a thing ! " So, too, we should exclaim : " Curses upon these un-

" Male istis improbis et importunis beneficiorum
suorum quadriplatoribus eveniat, qui tam bellam rem,
admonitionem inter amicos, sustulerunt ! " Ego
tamen utar hoc iure amicitiae et beneficium ab eo
repetam, a quo petissem, qui alterius beneficii loco
2 accepturus est potuisse reddere. Numquam ne
querens quidem dicam :

> eiectum litore, egentem
> excepi et regni demens in parte locavi.

Non est ista admonitio, convicium est ; hoc est in
odium beneficia perducere, hoc est efficere, ut ingratum esse aut liceat aut iuvet. Satis abundeque
est submissis et familiaribus verbis memoriam revocare :

> si bene quid de te merui, fuit aut tibi quicquam
> dulce meum.

Ille in vicem dicat : " Quidni merueris ? Eiectum
litore, egentem excepisti."
1   26. Sed nihil," inquit, " proficimus ; dissimulat,
oblitus est : quid facere debeam ? " Quaeris rem
maxime necessariam et in qua hanc materiam con-
summari decet, quemadmodum ingrati ferendi sint.
2 Placido animo, mansueto, magno. Numquam te tam
inhumanus et immemor et ingratus offendat, ut non
tamen dedisse delectet ; numquam in has voces
iniuria impellat : " Vellem, non fecissem." Beneficii
tui tibi etiam infelicitas placeat ; semper illum pae-

---

^a Dido in frenzied despair recounts her services to Aeneas
(Virgil, *Aeneid*, iv. 373 *sq.*).
^b Virgil, *Aeneid*, iv. 317 *sq.*, where Dido still hopes to win
Aeneas from his resolve.

conscionable and importunate magnifiers of their
benefits who have banished so nice a thing as the
right of one friend to remind another ! " I, however,
shall make use of this privilege of friendship, and I
shall ask the return of a benefit from anyone from
whom I would have asked a benefit, who will be
ready to accept as a second benefit the opportunity
of returning the first. Not even when complaining
of him would I ever say :

> Needy I found him, a wretch, cast up on the shore,
> And, fool, the half of my kingdom I made his store.[a]

This is not to remind, but to reproach ; this is to
make a benefit hateful, this is to give a man either the
right, or the pleasure, of being ungrateful. It would
be enough, and more than enough, to refresh his
memory with the gentle and friendly words :

> If I to you by aught have help or pleasure brought—[b]

and he, in turn, would say : " Brought me help ?
' Needy you found me, a wretch, cast up on the
shore ! ' "

" But," you say, " if we gain nothing ; if he dis-
sembles, if he forgets—what ought I to do ? " You
now bring up the very pressing question, which will
fittingly complete our subject, of how we are to deal
with the ungrateful. I answer, deal calmly, gently,
magnanimously. Never let anyone's discourtesy,
forgetfulness, and ingratitude offend you so much
that you will not, after all, be glad that you gave ;
never let the injustice of it drive you into saying :
" I wish that I had not done it." You should find
pleasure even in the mischance of your benefit ; the

nitebit, si te ne nunc quidem paenitet. Non est,
quod indigneris, tamquam aliquid novi acciderit;
3 magis mirari deberes, si non accidisset. Alium labor,
alium impensa deterret, alium periculum, alium
turpis verecundia, ne, dum reddit, fateatur accepisse,
alium ignorantia officii, alium pigritia, alium occupatio.
Adspice, quemadmodum immensae hominum cupiditates hient semper et poscant; non miraberis ibi
4 neminem reddere, ubi nemo satis accepit. Quis est
istorum tam firmae mentis ac solidae, ut tuto apud
eum beneficia deponas? Alius libidine insanit, alius
abdomini servit; alius lucri totus est, cuius summam,
non vias, spectat; alius invidia laborat, alius caeca
ambitione et in gladios irruente. Adice torporem
mentis ac senium et contraria huic inquieti pectoris
agitationem tumultusque perpetuos; adice aestimationem sui nimiam et tumorem, ob quae contem-
nendus est, insolentem. Quid contumaciam dicam[1]
in perversa nitentium, quid levitatem semper aliquo
5 transilientem? Hoc accedat temeritas praeceps et
numquam fidele consilium daturus timor et mille
errores, quibus volvimur: audacia timidissimorum,
discordia familiarissimorum et, publicum malum,
incertissimis fidere, fastidire possessa, quae consequi

---

[1] dicam *added by Gertz.*

ingrate will always regret it if *you* do not even now regret it! There is no reason why you should be exasperated as if something strange had happened; you ought rather to have been surprised if it had not happened. One balks at the trouble, another at the expense, another at the danger, another is deterred by false shame, since returning the benefit would be an admission that he had received it, another by ignorance of his duty, another by laziness, another by the engrossments of business. See how greedy are men's desires and always asking for more! You need not wonder that no one makes return in a world where no one is satisfied. Who of men is of so firm and dependable a mind that you can safely deposit your benefits with him? One is crazed by lust, another is the slave of his belly; another is wholly engrossed with gain, and considers, not the means, but the amount, of it; another suffers from envy, another from blind ambition that drives him to the sword. Consider, too, mental sluggishness and senility, and opposed to them, the perpetual turmoil and commotion of the restless heart. Consider, too, excessive self-esteem and swollen pride in the things for which a man should be despised. And what shall I say of the obstinate persistence in wrongdoing, what of the fickleness that is always leaping from one thing to another? Add to these the headlong rashness, the fear that is never ready to give faithful counsel, and the thousand errors in which we are entangled— the audacity of the greatest of cowards, the discord of the greatest of friends, and the universal evil of trusting in everything that is most uncertain, and of disdaining the possessions that once we had no hope

posse spes non fuit. Inter adfectus inquietissimos rem quietissimam, fidem, quaeris?

1 27. Si tibi vitae nostrae vera imago succurret, videre[1] videberis tibi captae cum maxime civitatis faciem, in qua omisso pudoris rectique respectu vires in concilio sunt velut signo ad permiscenda omnia dato. Non igni, non ferro abstinetur; soluta legibus scelera sunt; ne religio quidem, quae inter arma hostilia supplices texit, ullum impedimentum est 2 ruentium in praedam. Hic ex privato, hic ex publico, hic ex profano, hic ex sacro rapit; hic effringit, hic transilit; hic non contentus angusto itinere ipsa, quibus arcetur, evertit et in lucrum ruina venit; hic sine caede populatur, hic spolia cruenta manu gestat; nemo non fert aliquid ex altero.

In hac aviditate generis humani o ne tu nimis fortunae communis oblitus es, qui quaeris inter 3 rapientes referentem! Si indignaris ingratos esse, indignare luxuriosos, indignare avaros, indignare impudicos, indignare aegros deformes, senes pallidos! Est istuc grave vitium, est intolerabile et quod dissociet homines, quod concordiam, qua imbecillitas nostra fulcitur, scindat ac dissipet, sed usque eo vulgare est, ut illud ne qui queritur quidem effugerit.

1 28. Cogita tecum, an, quibuscumque debuisti,

---

[1] videre *added by Gertz.*

of ever being able to attain. In the company of the most restless passions do you hope to find that calmest of qualities, good faith ?

If a true picture of our life should be flashed before your mind, you would think that you were seeing the representation of a city that had just been stormed, in which all regard for decency and right had been abandoned and only force holds sway, as if the word had gone out to cause universal confusion. Fire is not idle, the sword is not idle ; all crime is free from the law ; not even religion, which has protected its suppliants in the midst of a hostile invasion, affords any check upon those rushing to seize plunder. This one strips a private house, this one a public building, this one a sacred place, this one a place profane ; this one breaks down, this one leaps over ; this one, not content with a narrow path, overthrows the very walls that block his way, and reaches his booty over ruins ; one ravages without murdering, another bears his spoils in a hand stained with blood ; everyone carries off something that belongs to another.

O ! you have too easily forgotten the common lot, if, in this greed of the human race, you seek to find among these plunderers even one who brings back ! If you are indignant that men are ungrateful, be indignant that they are sybaritic, indignant that they are greedy, indignant that they are shameless, indignant that the sick are unsightly, that the old are pale ! This is, indeed, a heinous vice, it is intolerable —one that sets men at variance, that rends and destroys the harmony which props our human weakness, but it is so common that not even he who complains of it escapes it.

Ask your secret soul whether you have always

517

gratiam rettuleris, an nullum umquam apud te
perierit officium, an omnium te beneficiorum memoria
comitetur. Videbis, quae puero data sunt, ante
adulescentiam elapsa, quae in iuvenem conlata sunt,
non perdurasse in senectutem. Quaedam perdi-
dimus, quaedam proiecimus, quaedam e conspectu
nostro paulatim exierunt, a quibusdam oculos aver-
2 timus. Ut excusem tibi imbecillitatem, imprimis vas
fragile est memoria et rerum turbae non sufficit;
necesse est, quantum recipit, emittat et antiquissima
recentissimis obruat. Sic factum est, ut minima
apud te nutricis esset auctoritas, quia beneficium eius
longius aetas sequens posuit; sic factum est, ut
praeceptoris tibi non esset ulla veneratio; sic evenit,
ut circa consularia occupato comitia aut sacerdotiorum
3 candidato quaesturae suffragator excideret. Fortasse vitium, de quo quereris, si te diligenter excusseris, in sinu invenies. Inique publico crimini ira-
sceris, stulte tuo; ut absolvaris, ignosce. Meliorem
illum facies ferendo, utique peiorem exprobrando.
Non est, quod frontem eius indures; sine, si quid est
pudoris residui, servet. Saepe dubiam verecundiam
vox convicantis clarior rupit. Nemo id esse, quod
iam videtur, timet; deprenso pudor demitur.

1 29. "Perdidi beneficium." Numquid, quae con-

repaid gratitude to those to whom you owed it, whether no one's kindness has ever been wasted on you, whether the memory of all your benefits lives ever in you. You will find that those you received as a boy slipped from your memory before you were a youth, those that were bestowed in your early manhood have not survived into old age. Some we have lost, some we have thrown away, some have gradually slipped from our sight, from some we have turned away our eyes. In order to excuse your weakness, I might say that the memory is a very frail vessel, and is not strong enough to hold a mass of things ; it must necessarily lose to the extent that it receives, and the newest impressions crowd out the oldest. Thus it is that your nurse has least influence over you because the passing years have left her benefit in the long ago ; thus it is that you have no longer any veneration for your teacher ; so it happens that now, when you are occupied with your election to the consulship or your candidature for the priesthood, you have lost all memory of the voter who gave you the quaestorship. Perhaps, if you search carefully, you will find in your own bosom the vice of which you complain. It is unfair for you to be angry with a universal failing, foolish to be angry with your own—you must pardon if you would win pardon. You will make a man better by bearing with him, certainly worse by reproaching him. There is no reason why you should harden him in effrontery ; let him keep what little shame he has. Too loud reproaches often hurry wavering probity to its fall. No man shrinks from being what he appears to be ; he loses his sense of shame by being found out.

" I have wasted my benefit," you say. Can we

secravimus, perdidisse nos dicimus? Inter conse-
crata beneficium est, etiam si male respondit, bene
conlatum. Non est ille, qualem speravimus; simus
nos, quales fuimus, ei dissimiles. Damnum non tunc
factum: apparuit. Ingratus non sine nostro pudore
protrahitur, quoniam quidem querella amissi bene-
2 ficii non[1] bene dati signum est. Quantum possumus,
causam eius apud nos agamus: " Fortasse non potuit,
fortasse ignoravit, fortasse facturus est." Quaedam
nomina bona lentus et sapiens creditor fecit, qui sus-
tinuit ac mora fovit. Idem nobis faciundum est;
nutriamus fidem languidam.

1 30. " Perdidi beneficium." Stulte non nosti detri-
menti tui tempora! Perdidisti, sed cum dares; nunc
palam factum est. Etiam in his, quae videntur in
perdito, moderatio plurimum profuit; ut corporum
ita animorum molliter vitia tractanda sunt. Saepe,
quod explicari pertinacia potuit, violentia[2] trahentis
abruptum est. Quid opus est maledictis? Quid
querellis? Quid insectatione? Quare illum liberas?
Quare dimittis? Si ingratus est, iam nihil debet.
2 Quae ratio est exacerbare eum, in quem magna con-
tuleris, ut ex amico dubio fiat non dubius inimicus et
patrocinium sibi nostra infamia quaerat, nec desit

---

[1] non *commonly added.*
[2] potuit violentia *added*, potuit *commonly*, violentia *by
Haupt.*

ever say that we have wasted the things that we have hallowed ? But a benefit that has been well bestowed, even if we have ill return for it, is one of the hallowed things. He is not the kind of man we hoped he was ; unlike him, let us be the kind we have always been. Your loss did not occur at the time of his ingratitude—it then simply became evident. A man is not revealed as ungrateful without bringing shame on us, since, in fact, to complain of the loss of a benefit is proof that it was not well bestowed. As far as we can, we ought to plead his case before our own bar : " Perhaps he was not able, perhaps he was unaware, perhaps he will still do so." Some accounts have been made good by a long-suffering and wise creditor who has kept them alive and nursed them by waiting. We ought to do the same ; let us strengthen a weak sense of good faith.

" I have wasted my benefit," you say. You fool, you do not understand when your loss took place ! You wasted it, but at the time you gave it ; the fact has only now been revealed. Even in the case of those which seem to have been wasted, forbearance is often most valuable ; the cankers of the mind, as of the body, must be handled tenderly. The string that might have been untied by patience is often snapped by a violent pull. What need is there of abuse ? Of complaints ? Of reproaches ? Why do you free him from obligation ? Why do you let him go ? Even if he is ungrateful, he owes you nothing after this. What sense is there in exasperating one upon whom you have bestowed great favours, with the result that from being a doubtful friend he will become an undoubted enemy, and will seek to protect himself by defaming you, nor will gossip fail to

521

vox[1] : " Nescio quid est, quod eum, cui tantum debuit, ferre non potuit ; subest aliquid " ? Nemo non
superioris dignitatem querendo, etiam si non in-
quinavit, adspersit ; nec quisquam fingere contentus
est levia, cum magnitudine mendacii fidem quaerat.

1 31. Quanto illa melior via, qua servatur illi species
amicitiae et, si reverti ad sanitatem velit, etiam amicitia ! Vincit malos pertinax bonitas, nec quisquam
tam duri infestique adversus diligenda animi est, ut
etiam in[2] iniuria bonos non amet, quibus hoc quoque
coepit debere, quod impune non solvit. Ad illa

2 itaque cogitationes tuas flecte : " Non est relata mihi
gratia ; quid faciam ? Quod di, omnium rerum
optimi auctores, qui beneficia ignoranti dare incipiunt,

3 ingratis perseverant. Alius illis obicit neclegentiam
nostri, alius iniquitatem ; alius illos extra mundum
suum proicit et ignavos hebetesque sine luce, sine
ullo opere destituit ; alius solem, cui debemus, quod
inter laborem quietemque tempus divisimus, quod
non tenebris mersi confusionem aeternae noctis
effugimus, qui annum cursu suo temperat et corpora
alit, sata evocat, percoquit fructus, saxum aliquod
aut fortuitorum ignium globum et quidvis potius

4 quam deum appellat. Nihilo minus tamen more
optimorum parentium, qui maledictis suorum in-
fantium arrident, non cessant di beneficia congerere

---

[1] desit vox *Rossbach* : desit *O* : dicere *Madvig, Hosius.*
    [2] in *added by Lipsius.*

---

[a] *i.e.*, the Epicureans.

say : " I do not know why he could not put up with one to whom he owed so much ; there is something at the bottom of it " ? Any man, even if he does not stain, asperses the reputation of a superior by complaining of him ; and no one is content to trump up light accusations, since he seeks to win belief by the very magnitude of his lie.

How much better the course that will preserve a semblance of friendship with him, and, if he returns to his senses, even friendship ! Persistent goodness wins over bad men, and no one of them is so hard-hearted and hostile to kindly treatment as not to love a good man even while they wrong him, when even the fact that they can fail to pay with impunity is made an additional source of indebtedness to him. And so let your thoughts follow this trend : " He has not repaid me with gratitude ; what shall I do ? Do as the gods, those glorious authors of all things, do ; they begin to give benefits to him who knows them not, and persist in giving them to those who are ungrateful. Some reproach them with indifference to us, others with injustice ; some [a] place them outside of their world, and abandon them to sloth and languor, leaving them without light, without any task ; others call the sun, to whom we owe the division of our hours of work and rest, and our escape from being plunged into darkness and the chaos of eternal night, who by his course regulates the seasons, nourishes our bodies, calls forth the crops, and ripens the fruits, merely a mass of stone or a fortuitous collection of fiery particles—anything rather than a god. Yet, none the less, like the best of parents, who only smile at the spiteful words of their children, the gods do not cease to heap their benefits upon those

de beneficiorum auctore dubitantibus, sed aequali
tenore bona sua per gentes populosque distribuunt;
unam potentiam, prodesse, sortiti spargunt opportunis imbribus terras, maria flatu movent, siderum
cursu notant tempora, hiemes aestatesque interventu
lenioris spiritus molliunt, errorem labentium ani-
5 marum placidi ac propitii ferunt. Imitemur illos;
demus, etiam si multa in irritum data sunt; demus
nihilo minus aliis, demus ipsis, apud quos facta iactura
est. Neminem ad excitandas domos ruina deterruit,
et, cum penates ignis absumpsit, fundamenta tepente
adhuc area ponimus et urbes haustas saepius eidem
solo credimus; adeo ad bonas spes pertinax animus
est. Terra marique humana opera cessarent, nisi
male temptata retemptare[1] libuisset.

32. "Ingratus est: non mihi fecit iniuriam, sed sibi;
ego beneficio meo, cum darem, usus sum. Nec ideo
pigrius dabo, sed diligentius; quod in hoc perdidi,
ab aliis recipiam. Sed huic ipsi beneficium dabo
iterum et tamquam bonus agricola cura cultuque
sterilitatem soli vincam; perit mihi beneficium, iste
hominibus. Non est magni animi beneficium dare
et perdere; hoc est magni animi perdere et dare."

[1] retemptare *Madvig*: temptare *MSS*.

who are doubtful about the source of benefits, but distribute their blessings among the nations and peoples with unbroken uniformity. Possessing only the power of doing good, they sprinkle the lands with timely rains, they stir the seas with their blasts, they mark off the seasons by the course of the stars, they modify the extremes of summer and winter by interposing periods of milder temperature, and, ever gentle and kindly, bear with the errors of our feeble spirits. Let us imitate them ; let us give, even if many of our gifts have been given in vain ; none the less, let us give to still others, nay, even to those at whose hands we have suffered loss. The destruction of one house deters no one from erecting another, and, when fire has swept away our household gods, we lay new foundations while the ground is still hot, and over and over we entrust new cities to the same spot that has swallowed up others ; so persistently does the mind foster fair hopes. Men would cease their operations on land and sea unless they had been willing to renew the attempts that had failed.

" If a man is ungrateful, he has done, not me, but himself, an injury ; I had the fruit of my benefit when I gave it. And the experience will make me, not slower to give, but more careful in giving ; what I have lost in the case of one man, I shall recover from others. But even to him I shall give a second benefit, and, even as a good farmer overcomes the sterility of his ground by care and cultivation, I shall be victor ; my benefit is lost to me, he is lost to mankind. It is no proof of a fine spirit to give a benefit and lose it ; the proof of a fine spirit is to lose and still to give ! "

INDEX OF NAMES

(The references are to the pages of the English translation.)

Academy (the grove and school in the suburbs of Athens where Plato taught), 385

Achaeans, immunity of the, 337

Achilles, bravery of, 259

Aeneas, nobility of, 199, 441

Aeschines (Athenian philosopher, pupil of Socrates), poverty of, 27

Aetna, fury of, 201, 441

Aglaia (one of the Graces), 15

Agrippa, Marcus Vipsanius (see note, p. 188), greatness of, 189; mourned by Augustus, 433

Alcibiades (Athenian politician, pupil and friend of Socrates, noted for his beauty, talents, and wealth), wealth of, 27

Alexander (the Great, king of Macedonia, 356-323 B.C.), victorious over the East, 41; pride of, 79; scorned by Diogenes, 299; boastfulness of, 303; covetousness of, 461, 463

Allobroges (a people of Gaul), enemies of Rome, 333

Allobrogicus (see note *b*, p. 266), 267

Alps, 333

Annaeus (see note *c*, p. 218), name of Seneca, 219

Annals of Claudius Quadrigarius, 169

Antigonus (probably the "One-Eyed," one of Alexander's generals, king of Asia), a story about, 81

Antony, Mark (triumvir with Octavian and Lepidus), rivalry of, 101; ingratitude of, 337; utterance of, 367

Apollodorus (see note, p. 500), 501

Arcesilaus (Greek sceptical philosopher, born about 316 B.C., founder of the second Academy), tact of, 65; refuses money, 95

Archelaus (king of Macedonia, 413-399 B.C.), scorned by Socrates, 303, 305, 307

Aristides (Athenian statesman surnamed "the Just," rival of Themistocles), 259

Aristippus (see note, p. 510), 511

Aristo (father of Plato), 189

Aristogiton (see note *a*, p. 490), praise of, 491

Arrhidaeus (see note *a*, p. 268), censure of, 269

Arruntius (a Roman legacy-hunter), 445

Asia, place of exile, 339; army of Xerxes, 429; Sardis, city of, 431

Athenian (undertaker), 445

Athenians, commonwealth of, 443, 491; territory of, 467

Athens, Demades at, 443

Augustus (Caesar, first emperor of Rome, 27 B.C.-A.D. 14), praise of, 47; generosity of, 101; blamed by Lentulus, 105; moderation of, 175; greater than his father, 191; banished his daughter, 431; sorrow of, 433

Bacchus, the benefactor, 41

Benacus (Lago di Garda), 213

Bion (see note, p. 472), 473

Brutus, Marcus Iunius (85-42 B.C., nephew of the younger Cato, one

527

INDEX OF NAMES

of the assassins of Caesar), his debt to Caesar, 93

Caesar, C. Iulius (the dictator), assassination of, 93; at siege of Corfinium, 171; a veteran recalls his service to, 357, 359; reward of, 359

Caesar (title of the Roman emperors), 67, 471; Augustus, 101, 175, 177; Tiberius, 61, 173, 175, 359; Caligula, 71

Callistratus (see note c, p. 440), 441

Cambyses (see note b, p. 462), 463

Camillus (recalled from voluntary exile, he became the saviour of Rome after the invasion of the Gauls about 390 B.C.), praise of, 259; exile of, 337

Campanians (people of western Italy), territory of, 467

Capitol (temple on the Capitoline, sacred to Jupiter, Juno, and Minerva), 473

Carians (people of south-western Asia Minor), 303

Carthaginians, Regulus captured by, 297

Carthaginian War (Second Punic, 218–202 B.C.), Scipio and the, 441

Catiline, Lucius Sergius (Roman conspirator, put down by Cicero in 63 B.C.), 333, 339

Cato, Marcus Porcius (the Censor, 234–149 B.C.), noted for austerity), saying of, 311

Cato, Marcus Porcius (the Younger, an ardent and high-minded Stoic, supporter of Pompey's cause, who committed suicide after Caesar's victory at Thapsus in 46 B.C.), denied the praetorship and consulship, 339

Charis (see note b, p. 16), 17

Chrysippus (Stoic philosopher of Soli in Cilicia, successor of Cleanthes and third head of the Stoic School), puerilities of, 17; acumen of, 19; an illustration of cited, 83, 103; his definition of a slave, 167; greatness of, 477

Cicero, Marcus Tullius (the famous orator, 106–43 B.C.), debt of his

son to, 267; exiled, 339; books of, 471

Cimbrians, slaughtered by Marius, 335

Cinna, Gnaeus (see note a, p. 266), 267

Circus Flaminius (in the Campus Martius), Caesar's camp in, 337

Civil War, 173, 191

Claudius (Caesar, fourth emperor of Rome, A.D. 41–54), bounty of, 47

Cleanthes (Stoic philosopher, successor of Zeno as head of the Stoic School), saying of, 329, 389; story of cited, 385

Colline Gate (one of the gates of Rome, on the Quirinal Hill), Sulla at the, 335

Corfinium (chief town of Samnium), besieged by Caesar, 171

Corinthians, their embassy to Alexander, 41

Coriolanus (Roman legendary hero, who, yielding to the entreaties of his wife and mother, withdrew his hostile army from an attack upon Rome), 333

Crispus Passienus (a famous orator, consul in A.D. 42, and step-father of the emperor Nero), saying of, 47

Cynic (adherent of the Cynic school of philosophy, which favoured austerity and self-abnegation), Antigonus and the, 81; Demetrius the, 455

Cyprus, sovereignty of, 201

Cyrus (the Great, founder of the Persian empire, died 529 B.C.), covetousness of, 463

Decii (see note b, p. 440), 441

Decius (Mus, Publius; see Decii), 259

Demades (Athenian orator, bitter enemy of Demosthenes), 443

Demaratus (deposed Spartan king, who found refuge at the court of Xerxes), advice of, 427, 431

Demetrius (Cynic philosopher, who taught at Rome during the reign of Caligula), statement of, 455,

INDEX OF NAMES

459; greatness of, 477; scorns gift of Caligula, 483

Diogenes (celebrated Cynic philosopher of Sinope, died 323 B.C.), his scorn of wealth, 299; greater than Alexander, 303

Domitius (Ahenobarbus, Lucius, supporter of the aristocratical party against Caesar, consul 54 B.C.), attempts suicide, 171, 173

Dorus (bookseller), 471

Drusus, Livius (the Elder, who as tribune in 122 B.C. opposed the reforms of Gaius Gracchus), classified his friends, 437

Epicureans, effeminacy of, 207

Epicurus (founder of the Epicurean school of philosophy, 341–270 B.C.), complaint of, 133; doctrine of, 211, 243

Euphrates, 181

Euphrosyne, one of the Graces, 15

Eurynome, mother of the Graces, 17

Fabii (see note c, p. 266), bravery of the, 297

Fabius (Q. Maximus, Cunctator, who, appointed dictator after the battle of Trasumenus, harassed Hannibal by his dilatory policy), 259

Fabius Persicus, Paullus (see note b, p. 266), bad reputation of, 97, 267

Fabius Verrucosus (see note b, p. 266), saying of, 61

Furnius, Gaius (consul 17 B.C.), reconciled Augustus to his father, 101

Gaius Caesar (Caligula, emperor of Rome, A.D. 37–41), arrogance of, 71; cruelty of, 97, 269; madness of, 483

Gallic (tombs), 335

Gaul, 337

Gauls, 401; (a Gaul), 403

Germanicus (15 B.C.–A.D. 19, son of Drusus, adopted by his uncle Tiberius; died in the East, according to rumour, from poison), father of Caligula, 269

Germany, 337

Gracchus, Gaius (Sempronius, early agrarian reformer, killed in 121 B.C.), classified his friends, 437

Graces, the (three in number), 13; (names of), 15; (daughters of Jupiter), 17, 19

Graecinus, Iulius, put to death by Caligula, 97

Greece, Xerxes' invasion of, 427, 429, 431

Greeks, 15, 303, 427, 429; (a Greek), 19

Grumentum (city of Lucania, besieged by the Romans during the Social War, 90–88 B.C.), 169

Gryllus (father of Xenophon), 189

Harmodius (see note a, p. 490), 491

Haterius (probably Quintus, a servile senator and rhetorician under Augustus and Tiberius, a legacy-hunter, 445

Hecaton (Stoic philosopher, a native of Rhodes), copies from Chrysippus, 17; teaching of, 87; citation from, 95, 441; query of, 159

Hercules, the benefactor, 41, 43, 463; a god, 219

Hesiod (early Greek poet), his names for the Graces, 15, 17

Homer, changes the name of a Grace, 15, 17

Hours, the (goddesses who preside over the changes of the seasons), 17

Indian Ocean, reached by Alexander, 461

Julius, see Caesar

Jupiter, father of the Graces, 17 19; epithets of, 219

Lacedaemonians, discipline of the, 295, 297; money of the, 331; their opposition to Xerxes, 429; the Lacedaemonian (Demaratus), 427

Larius (Lago di Como), 213

Lentulus, Gnaeus (Cornelius, see note, p. 102), wealth of, 103

529

INDEX OF NAMES

Liber (identified with Bacchus), the All-father, 219; the benefactor, 463

Liberalis, Aebutius (a native of Lyons, friend of Seneca, to whom are addressed the seven books *De Beneficiis*), 3, 51, 61, 111, 127, 133, 205, 209, 269, 291, 365, 375, 387, 449, 455

Livius, Titus (the most popular of Roman historians, 59 B.C.–A.D. 17), books of, 471

Lucius (see note *c*, p. 218), praenomen of Seneca, 219

Lynceus (see note *b*, p. 258), keen sight of, 259

Macedonia (district north of Greece), Alexander king of, 41; people of, 137

Macedonians, Philip king of the, 281; treasures of the, 299; Alexander king of the, 303; Macedonian (a certain), 281

Maecenas, Gaius Cilnius (Roman statesman, courtier, and patron of literature under Augustus), saying of, 279; mourned by Augustus, 433

Manlius (Titus Torquatus, twice dictator, thrice consul, last time in 340 B.C., a favourite hero of Roman story), rescues his father, 201

Marius, Gaius (Roman statesman and general, opponent of Sulla, died 86 B.C.), butchers his countrymen, 335

Maro, notorious informer, 175

Marsians (a people of Latium), 171

Marsyas (in myth, a rival of Apollo with the flute, flayed alive for his presumption), statue of in the Forum, 431

Mercury, companion of the Graces, 15; identified with God, 219

Mucius (Scaevola, C., hero of the Roman-Etruscan wars; see note *b*, p. 490), 259, 491

Munda (town in southern Spain, where Caesar gained a victory over the sons of Pompey, 45 B.C.), battle of, 359

Muse (Thalia), 17

Nepos, Marius (expelled from the senate by Tiberius on account of his extravagance), aided by Tiberius, 61

Nile, overflow of the, 379

Octavius, Gaius (father of Augustus), fame of his son, 191

Onesicritus (see note *a*, p. 462), 463

Ovid (P. Ovidius Naso, a fashionable poet of the Augustan age), saying of, 233

Pasithea, one of the Graces, 15

Paulus (a praetorian), befriended by his slave, 173

Pausanias (see note *a*, p. 282), 283

Peripatetics (the Aristotelian school of philosophers), teaching of the, 327

Persia, servitude of, 71; royal line of, 463

Persians, in Xerxes' army, 303; the Persian (Xerxes), 431

Persicus, Paulus Fabius (consul A.D. 34), bad reputation of, 97

Phalaris (tyrant of Agrigentum in Sicily), ferocity of, 501, 503

Phidias (a celebrated Greek sculptor of the fifth century B.C.), art of, 117

Philip (the Second, king of Macedonia and father of Alexander the Great), punishes ingratitude, 281, 283, 285

Phryxian (wool), 15

Plato (Athenian philosopher, 428–347 B.C.), father of, 189; saving of, 273; sought by Cleanthes, 385; a story of, 399, 401

Po (river in northern Italy), 401

Pollio, Annius (accused of treason under Tiberius, later an intimate friend of Nero, but finally banished), insulted by Scaurus, 269

Pompeii (the descendants of Pompey), 267

Pompeius Magnus, Gnaeus (leader of the senatorial party in opposition to Caesar, defeated at Pharsalus in 48 B.C., and murdered shortly afterwards in Egypt), ingratitude of, 335; conqueror of, 337

INDEX OF NAMES

Pompeius Pennus, insulted by Caligula, 71

Pompeius, Sextus (probably the consul of A.D. 14), a descendant of Pompey, 267

Porsina (Lars Porsena, in Roman legend, the Etruscan king who gave aid to the deposed Tarquin), 337, 491

Praeneste (an ancient city in Latium), 335

Pythagorean, story of a, 507

Quadrigarius, Q. Claudius (a Roman historian who flourished about 100 B.C.), *Annals* of, 169

Rabirius (see note *a*, p. 366), quotation from, 367

Rebilus, bad reputation of, 97

Regulus, M. Atilius (hero of the First Punic War, captured by the Carthaginians), 297

Rhine, 181

Rhodians, immunity of, 337

Roman (general), 171, 475; (citizens), 173, 335; (empire), 193, 201; (battle-line), 219; (leaders), 335; (lives), 335; (kings), 337; (people), 337, 339; (knights), 485

Romans, conduct of, 169

Rome, 337, 441

Rufus (probably Plautius Rufus, who conspired against Augustus), rash utterance of, 175

Rutilius (Rufus, P., Roman statesman; see note *a*, p. 338), 339, 442

Sallust (Gaius Sallustius Crispus, a Roman historian, 86–35 B.C.), quoted, 205

Sardis (capital of Lydia, Asia Minor), 431

Scaurus, Mamercus Aemilius (see note *b*, p. 268), character of, 269

Scaurus, Marcus Aemilius (see note *c*, p. 268), character of, 269

Scipio (Africanus Maior, conqueror of Hannibal at Zama in 202 B.C.), saved the life of his father, 191, 193; voluntary exile of, 337; ended Carthaginian War, 441

Seneca, Lucius Annaeus (see note *c*, p. 218), 219

Sicilians (Sicilian youths; see note *b*, p. 200), 201, 441

Socrates (Athenian philosopher, 469–399 B.C.), Aeschines' gift to, 27, 29; father of, 189; greatness of, 299, 303, 477; scorned invitation of Archelaus, 303, 305, 307; Plato's gratitude to, 309, 311; poverty of, 511

Sophroniscus (father of Socrates), 189

Spain, Caesar in, 357

Spaniards, exempt from taxation, 401

Spanish (sword), 359

Stoic (teaching), 93; (school), 113; (mint), 195

Stoics, 47, 113, 121, 207, 257, 259, 307, 323, 325, 331, 375, 465

Sucro (a river of Spain, now the Xucar), 357

Sulla, Lucius (Roman dictator, rival of Marius, died 78 B.C.), ingratitude of, 335

Tarpeian Rock (a cliff on the Capitoline, from which criminals were hurled), 473

Tarquin (Tarquinius Superbus, in Roman legendary history, the seventh and last king of Rome), 93

Thalia, a Grace, 15; a Muse, 17

Thermopylae (a pass in Thessaly, where, in 480 B.C., Xerxes was halted by a small band of Greeks), 429

Thrace (a district north of Greece), 303

Tiberius Caesar (emperor of Rome, A.D. 14–37), aids Nepos, 61, 63; cruel reign of, 173, 175; character of, 359

Tiberius, see Tiberius Caesar

Tibur (ancient name of Tivoli), a villa at, 229

Turnus (king of the Rutulians, a hero of the *Aeneid*, opponent of Aeneas in Italy), 449

Tusculum (a town in the Alban Mountains), a villa at, 229

Venus, the Graces companions of, 17

531

INDEX OF NAMES

Verrucosus (see note *b*, p. 266), 267

Vestals, 15

Vettius, praetor of the Marsians, 171

Xenophon (celebrated Greek commander and historian, pupil of Socrates), father of, 189

Xerxes (king of Persia, 485-465 B.C.), counselled by Demaratus, 427, 431

Zeno (founder of the Stoic School at Athens; flourished about 300 B.C.), good faith of, 285; greatness of, 477

Printed in Great Britain by R. & R. CLARK, LIMITED, *Edinburgh*

THE LOEB CLASSICAL LIBRARY

VOLUMES ALREADY PUBLISHED

LATIN AUTHORS

AMMIANUS MARCELLINUS. J. C. Rolfe. 3 Vols.

APULEIUS : THE GOLDEN ASS (METAMORPHOSES). W. Adlington (1566). Revised by S. Gaselee.

ST. AUGUSTINE : CITY OF GOD. 7 Vols. Vol. I. G. E. McCracken. Vol. II. W. M. Green. Vol. III. D. Wiesen. Vol. IV. P. Levine. Vol. V. E. M. Sanford and W. M. Green. Vol. VI. W. C. Greene. Vol. VII. W. M. Green.

ST. AUGUSTINE, CONFESSIONS OF. W. Watts (1631). 2 Vols.

ST. AUGUSTINE : SELECT LETTERS. J. H. Baxter.

AUSONIUS. H. G. Evelyn White. 2 Vols.

BEDE. J. E. King. 2 Vols.

BOETHIUS : TRACTS AND DE CONSOLATIONE PHILOSOPHIAE. Rev. H. F. Stewart and E. K. Rand. Revised by S. J. Tester.

CAESAR : ALEXANDRIAN, AFRICAN AND SPANISH WARS. A. G. Way.

CAESAR : CIVIL WARS. A. G. Peskett.

CAESAR : GALLIC WAR. H. J. Edwards.

CATO AND VARRO : DE RE RUSTICA. H. B. Ash and W. D. Hooper.

CATULLUS. F. W. Cornish ; TIBULLUS. J. B. Postgate ; and PERVIGILIUM VENERIS. J. W. Mackail.

CELSUS : DE MEDICINA. W. G. Spencer. 3 Vols.

CICERO : BRUTUS AND ORATOR. G. L. Hendrickson and H. M. Hubbell.

CICERO : DE FINIBUS. H. Rackham.

CICERO : DE INVENTIONE, etc. H. M. Hubbell.

CICERO : DE NATURA DEORUM AND ACADEMICA. H. Rackham.

CICERO : DE OFFICIIS. Walter Miller.

CICERO : DE ORATORE, etc. 2 Vols. Vol. I : DE ORATORE, Books I and II. E. W. Sutton and H. Rackham. Vol. II : DE ORATORE, Book III ; DE FATO ; PARADOXA STOICORUM ; DE PARTITIONE ORATORIA. H. Rackham.

CICERO : DE REPUBLICA, DE LEGIBUS, SOMNIUM SCIPIONIS. Clinton W. Keyes.

THE LOEB CLASSICAL LIBRARY

CICERO: DE SENECTUTE, DE AMICITIA, DE DIVINATIONE. W. A. Falconer.

CICERO: IN CATILINAM, PRO MURENA, PRO SULLA, PRO FLACCO. Louis E. Lord.

CICERO: LETTERS TO ATTICUS. E. O. Winstedt. 3 Vols.

CICERO: LETTERS TO HIS FRIENDS. W. Glynn Williams, M. Cary, M. Henderson. 4 Vols.

CICERO: PHILIPPICS. W. C. A. Ker.

CICERO: PRO ARCHIA, POST REDITUM, DE DOMO, DE HARUSPICUM RESPONSIS, PRO PLANCIO. N. H. Watts.

CICERO: PRO CAECINA, PRO LEGE MANILIA, PRO CLUENTIO, PRO RABIRIO. H. Grose Hodge.

CICERO: PRO CAELIO, DE PROVINCIIS CONSULARIBUS, PRO BALBO. R. Gardner.

CICERO: PRO MILONE, IN PISONEM, PRO SCAURO, PRO FONTEIO, PRO RABIRIO POSTUMO, PRO MARCELLO, PRO LIGARIO, PRO REGE DEIOTARO. N. H. Watts.

CICERO: PRO QUINCTIO, PRO ROSCIO AMERINO, PRO ROSCIO COMOEDO, CONTRA RULLUM. J. H. Freese.

CICERO: PRO SESTIO, IN VATINIUM. R. Gardner.

[CICERO]: RHETORICA AD HERENNIUM. H. Caplan.

CICERO: TUSCULAN DISPUTATIONS. J. E. King.

CICERO: VERRINE ORATIONS. L. H. G. Greenwood. 2 Vols.

CLAUDIAN. M. Platnauer. 2 Vols.

COLUMELLA: DE RE RUSTICA, DE ARBORIBUS. H. B. Ash, E. S. Forster, E. Heffner. 3 Vols.

CURTIUS, Q.: HISTORY OF ALEXANDER. J. C. Rolfe. 2 Vols.

FLORUS. E. S. Forster; and CORNELIUS NEPOS. J. C. Rolfe.

FRONTINUS: STRATAGEMS AND AQUEDUCTS. C. E. Bennett and M. B. McElwain.

FRONTO: CORRESPONDENCE. C. R. Haines. 2 Vols.

GELLIUS. J. C. Rolfe. 3 Vols.

HORACE: ODES AND EPODES. C. E. Bennett.

HORACE: SATIRES, EPISTLES, ARS POETICA. H. R. Fairclough.

JEROME: SELECT LETTERS. F. A. Wright.

JUVENAL AND PERSIUS. G. G. Ramsay.

LIVY. B. O. Foster, F. G. Moore, Evan T. Sage, A. C. Schlesinger and R. M. Geer (General Index). 14 Vols.

LUCAN. J. D. Duff.

LUCRETIUS. W. H. D. Rouse. Revised by M. F. Smith.

MARTIAL. W. C. A. Ker. 2 Vols.

MINOR LATIN POETS: from PUBLILIUS SYRUS to RUTILIUS NAMATIANUS, including GRATTIUS, CALPURNIUS SICULUS, NEMESIANUS, AVIANUS, with "Aetna," "Phoenix" and other poems. J. Wight Duff and Arnold M. Duff.

2

THE LOEB CLASSICAL LIBRARY

OVID : THE ART OF LOVE AND OTHER POEMS. J. H. Mozley.

OVID : FASTI. Sir James G. Frazer.

OVID : HEROIDES AND AMORES. Grant Showerman.

OVID : METAMORPHOSES. F. J. Miller. 2 Vols.

OVID : TRISTIA AND EX PONTO. A. L. Wheeler.

PETRONIUS. M. Heseltine ; SENECA : APOCOLOCYNTOSIS. W. H. D. Rouse.

PHAEDRUS AND BABRIUS (Greek). B. E. Perry.

PLAUTUS. Paul Nixon. 5 Vols.

PLINY : LETTERS, PANEGYRICUS. B. Radice. 2 Vols.

PLINY : NATURAL HISTORY. 10 Vols. Vols. I-V. H. Rackham. Vols. VI-VIII. W. H. S. Jones. Vol. IX. H. Rackham. Vol. X. D. E. Eichholz.

PROPERTIUS. H. E. Butler.

PRUDENTIUS. H. J. Thomson. 2 Vols.

QUINTILIAN. H. E. Butler. 4 Vols.

REMAINS OF OLD LATIN. E. H. Warmington. 4 Vols. Vol. I (Ennius and Caecilius). Vol. II (Livius, Naevius, Pacuvius, Accius). Vol. III (Lucilius, Laws of the XII Tables). Vol. IV (Archaic Inscriptions).

SALLUST. J. C. Rolfe.

SCRIPTORES HISTORIAE AUGUSTAE. D. Magie. 3 Vols.

SENECA : APOCOLOCYNTOSIS. *Cf.* PETRONIUS.

SENECA : EPISTULAE MORALES. R. M. Gummere. 3 Vols.

SENECA : MORAL ESSAYS. J. W. Basore. 3 Vols.

SENECA : NATURALES QUAESTIONES. T. H. Corcoran. 2 Vols.

SENECA : TRAGEDIES. F. J. Miller. 2 Vols.

SENECA THE ELDER : CONTROVERSIAE SUASORIAE. M. Winterbottom. 2 Vols.

SIDONIUS : POEMS AND LETTERS. W. B. Anderson. 2 Vols.

SILIUS ITALICUS. J. D. Duff. 2 Vols.

STATIUS. J. H. Mozley. 2 Vols.

SUETONIUS. J. C. Rolfe. 2 Vols.

TACITUS : AGRICOLA AND GERMANIA. M. Hutton ; DIALOGUS. Sir Wm. Peterson. Revised by R. M. Ogilvie, E. H. Warmington, M. Winterbottom.

TACITUS : HISTORIES AND ANNALS. C. H. Moore and J. Jackson. 4 Vols.

TERENCE. John Sargeaunt. 2 Vols.

TERTULLIAN : APOLOGIA AND DE SPECTACULIS. T. R. Glover ; MINUCIUS FELIX. G. H. Rendall.

VALERIUS FLACCUS. J. H. Mozley.

VARRO : DE LINGUA LATINA. R. G. Kent. 2 Vols.

VELLEIUS PATERCULUS AND RES GESTAE DIVI AUGUSTI. F. W. Shipley.

THE LOEB CLASSICAL LIBRARY

VIRGIL. H. R. Fairclough. 2 Vols.
VITRUVIUS: DE ARCHITECTURA. F. Granger. 2 Vols.

GREEK AUTHORS

ACHILLES TATIUS. S. Gaselee.
AELIAN: ON THE NATURE OF ANIMALS. A. F. Scholfield. 3 Vols.
AENEAS TACTICUS, ASCLEPIODOTUS AND ONASANDER. The Illinois Greek Club.
AESCHINES. C. D. Adams.
AESCHYLUS. H. Weir Smyth. 2 Vols.
ALICIPHRON, AELIAN AND PHILOSTRATUS: LETTERS. A. R. Benner and F. H. Fobes.
APOLLODORUS. Sir James G. Frazer. 2 Vols.
APOLLONIUS RHODIUS. R. C. Seaton.
THE APOSTOLIC FATHERS. Kirsopp Lake. 2 Vols.
APPIAN'S ROMAN HISTORY. Horace White. 4 Vols.
ARATUS. *Cf.* CALLIMACHUS: HYMNS AND EPIGRAMS.
ARISTIDES. C. A. Behr. 4 Vols. Vol. I.
ARISTOPHANES. Benjamin Bickley Rogers. 3 Vols. Verse trans.
ARISTOTLE: ART OF RHETORIC. J. H. Freese.
ARISTOTLE: ATHENIAN CONSTITUTION, EUDEMIAN ETHICS, VIRTUES AND VICES. H. Rackham.
ARISTOTLE: THE CATEGORIES. ON INTERPRETATION. H. P. Cooke; PRIOR ANALYTICS. H. Tredennick.
ARISTOTLE: GENERATION OF ANIMALS. A. L. Peck.
ARISTOTLE: HISTORIA ANIMALIUM. A. L. Peck. 3 Vols. Vols. I and II.
ARISTOTLE: METAPHYSICS. H. Tredennick. 2 Vols.
ARISTOTLE: METEOROLOGICA. H. D. P. Lee.
ARISTOTLE: MINOR WORKS. W. S. Hett. "On Colours," "On Things Heard," "Physiognomics," "On Plants," "On Marvellous Things Heard," "Mechanical Problems," "On Invisible Lines," "Situations and Names of Winds," "On Melissus, Xenophanes, and Gorgias."
ARISTOTLE: NICOMACHEAN ETHICS. H. Rackham.
ARISTOTLE: OECONOMICA AND MAGNA MORALIA. G. C. Armstrong. (With METAPHYSICS, Vol. II.)
ARISTOTLE: ON THE HEAVENS. W. K. C. Guthrie.
ARISTOTLE: ON THE SOUL, PARVA NATURALIA, ON BREATH. W. S. Hett.

4

THE LOEB CLASSICAL LIBRARY

ARISTOTLE: PARTS OF ANIMALS. A. L. Peck; MOVEMENT AND PROGRESSION OF ANIMALS. E. S. Forster.

ARISTOTLE: PHYSICS. Rev. P. Wicksteed and F. M. Cornford. 2 Vols.

ARISTOTLE: POETICS; LONGINUS ON THE SUBLIME. W. Hamilton Fyfe; DEMETRIUS ON STYLE. W. Rhys Roberts.

ARISTOTLE: POLITICS. H. Rackham.

ARISTOTLE: POSTERIOR ANALYTICS. H. Tredennick; TOPICS. E. S. Forster.

ARISTOTLE: PROBLEMS. W. S. Hett. 2 Vols.

ARISTOTLE: RHETORICA AD ALEXANDRUM. H. Rackham. (With PROBLEMS, Vol. II.)

ARISTOTLE: SOPHISTICAL REFUTATIONS. COMING-TO-BE AND PASSING-AWAY. E. S. Forster; ON THE COSMOS. D. J. Furley.

ARRIAN: HISTORY OF ALEXANDER AND INDICA. Rev. E. Iliffe Robson. 2 Vols.

ATHENAEUS: DEIPNOSOPHISTAE. C. B. Gulick. 7 Vols.

BABRIUS AND PHAEDRUS (Latin). B. E. Perry.

ST. BASIL: LETTERS. R. J. Deferrari. 4 Vols.

CALLIMACHUS: FRAGMENTS. C. A. Trypanis; MUSAEUS: HERO AND LEANDER. T. Gelzer and C. Whitman.

CALLIMACHUS: HYMNS AND EPIGRAMS, AND LYCOPHRON. A. W. Mair; ARATUS. G. R. Mair.

CLEMENT OF ALEXANDRIA. Rev. G. W. Butterworth.

COLLUTHUS. *Cf.* OPPIAN.

DAPHNIS AND CHLOE. *Cf.* LONGUS.

DEMOSTHENES I: OLYNTHIACS, PHILIPPICS AND MINOR ORATIONS: I-XVII AND XX. J. H. Vince.

DEMOSTHENES II: DE CORONA AND DE FALSA LEGATIONE. C. A. Vince and J. H. Vince.

DEMOSTHENES III: MEIDIAS, ANDROTION, ARISTOCRATES, TIMOCRATES, ARISTOGEITON. J. H. Vince.

DEMOSTHENES IV-VI: PRIVATE ORATIONS AND IN NEAERAM. A. T. Murray.

DEMOSTHENES VII: FUNERAL SPEECH, EROTIC ESSAY, EXORDIA AND LETTERS. N. W. and N. J. DeWitt.

DIO CASSIUS: ROMAN HISTORY. E. Cary. 9 Vols.

DIO CHRYSOSTOM. 5 Vols. Vols. I and II. J. W. Cohoon. Vol. III. J. W. Cohoon and H. Lamar Crosby. Vols. IV and V. H. Lamar Crosby.

DIODORUS SICULUS. 12 Vols. Vols. I-VI. C. H. Oldfather. Vol. VII. C. L. Sherman. Vol. VIII. C. B. Welles. Vols. IX and X. Russel M. Geer. Vols. XI and XII. F. R. Walton. General Index. Russel M. Geer.

DIOGENES LAERTIUS. R. D. Hicks. 2 Vols. New Introduction by H. S. Long.

DIONYSIUS OF HALICARNASSUS : CRITICAL ESSAYS. S. Usher. 2 Vols.

DIONYSIUS OF HALICARNASSUS : ROMAN ANTIQUITIES. Spelman's translation revised by E. Cary. 7 Vols.

EPICTETUS. W. A. Oldfather. 2 Vols.

EURIPIDES. A. S. Way. 4 Vols. Verse trans.

EUSEBIUS : ECCLESIASTICAL HISTORY. Kirsopp Lake and J. E. L. Oulton. 2 Vols.

GALEN : ON THE NATURAL FACULTIES. A. J. Brock.

THE GREEK ANTHOLOGY. W. R. Paton. 5 Vols.

THE GREEK BUCOLIC POETS (THEOCRITUS, BION, MOSCHUS). J. M. Edmonds.

GREEK ELEGY AND IAMBUS WITH THE ANACREONTEA. J. M. Edmonds. 2 Vols.

GREEK MATHEMATICAL WORKS. Ivor Thomas. 2 Vols.

HERODES. Cf. THEOPHRASTUS : CHARACTERS.

HERODIAN. C. R. Whittaker. 2 Vols.

HERODOTUS. A. D. Godley. 4 Vols.

HESIOD AND THE HOMERIC HYMNS. H. G. Evelyn White.

HIPPOCRATES AND THE FRAGMENTS OF HERACLEITUS. W. H. S. Jones and E. T. Withington. 4 Vols.

HOMER : ILIAD. A. T. Murray. 2 Vols.

HOMER : ODYSSEY. A. T. Murray. 2 Vols.

ISAEUS. E. S. Forster.

ISOCRATES. George Norlin and LaRue Van Hook. 3 Vols.

[ST. JOHN DAMASCENE] : BARLAAM AND IOASAPH. Rev. G. R. Woodward, Harold Mattingly and D. M. Lang.

JOSEPHUS. 9 Vols. Vols. I-IV. H. St. J. Thackeray. Vol. V. H. St. J. Thackeray and Ralph Marcus. Vols. VI and VII. Ralph Marcus. Vol. VIII. Ralph Marcus and Allen Wikgren. Vol. IX. L. H. Feldman.

JULIAN. Wilmer Cave Wright. 3 Vols.

LIBANIUS : SELECTED WORKS. A. F. Norman. 3 Vols. Vol. I.

LONGUS : DAPHNIS AND CHLOE. Thornley's translation revised by J. M. Edmonds ; and PARTHENIUS. S. Gaselee.

LUCIAN. 8 Vols. Vols. I-V. A. M. Harmon. Vol. VI. K. Kilburn. Vols. VII and VIII. M. D. Macleod.

LYCOPHRON. Cf. CALLIMACHUS : HYMNS AND EPIGRAMS.

LYRA GRAECA. J. M. Edmonds. 3 Vols.

LYSIAS. W. R. M. Lamb.

MANETHO. W. G. Waddell ; PTOLEMY : TETRABIBLOS. F. E. Robbins.

THE LOEB CLASSICAL LIBRARY

MARCUS AURELIUS. C. R. Haines.

MENANDER. F. G. Allinson.

MINOR ATTIC ORATORS. 2 Vols. K. J. Maidment and J. O. Burtt.

MUSAEUS: HERO AND LEANDER. *Cf.* CALLIMACHUS: FRAGMENTS.

NONNOS: DIONYSIACA. W. H. D. Rouse. 3 Vols.

OPPIAN, COLLUTHUS, TRYPHIODORUS. A. W. Mair.

PAPYRI. NON-LITERARY SELECTIONS. A. S. Hunt and C. C. Edgar. 2 Vols. LITERARY SELECTIONS (Poetry). D. L. Page.

PARTHENIUS. *Cf.* LONGUS.

PAUSANIAS: DESCRIPTION OF GREECE. W. H. S. Jones. 4 Vols. and Companion Vol. arranged by R. E. Wycherley.

PHILO. 10 Vols. Vols. I-V. F. H. Colson and Rev. G. H. Whitaker. Vols. VI-X. F. H. Colson. General Index. Rev. J. W. Earp.
Two Supplementary Vols. Translation only from an Armenian Text. Ralph Marcus.

PHILOSTRATUS: THE LIFE OF APOLLONIUS OF TYANA. F. C. Conybeare. 2 Vols.

PHILOSTRATUS: IMAGINES; CALLISTRATUS: DESCRIPTIONS. A. Fairbanks.

PHILOSTRATUS AND EUNAPIUS: LIVES OF THE SOPHISTS. Wilmer Cave Wright.

PINDAR. Sir J. E. Sandys.

PLATO: CHARMIDES, ALCIBIADES, HIPPARCHUS, THE LOVERS, THEAGES, MINOS AND EPINOMIS. W. R. M. Lamb.

PLATO: CRATYLUS, PARMENIDES, GREATER HIPPIAS, LESSER HIPPIAS. H. N. Fowler.

PLATO: EUTHYPHRO, APOLOGY, CRITO, PHAEDO, PHAEDRUS. H. N. Fowler.

PLATO: LACHES, PROTAGORAS, MENO, EUTHYDEMUS. W. R. M. Lamb.

PLATO: LAWS. Rev. R. G. Bury. 2 Vols.

PLATO: LYSIS, SYMPOSIUM, GORGIAS. W. R. M. Lamb.

PLATO: REPUBLIC. Paul Shorey. 2 Vols.

PLATO: STATESMAN, PHILEBUS. H. N. Fowler; ION. W. R. M. Lamb.

PLATO: THEAETETUS AND SOPHIST. H. N. Fowler.

PLATO: TIMAEUS, CRITIAS, CLITOPHO, MENEXENUS, EPISTULAE. Rev. R. G. Bury.

PLOTINUS. A. H. Armstrong. 6 Vols. Vols. I-III.

PLUTARCH: MORALIA. 16 Vols. Vols. I-V. F. C. Babbitt. Vol. VI. W. C. Helmbold. Vol. VII. P. H. De Lacy and

THE LOEB CLASSICAL LIBRARY

B. Einarson. Vol. VIII. P. A. Clement, H. B. Hoffleit.
Vol. IX. E. L. Minar, Jr., F. H. Sandbach, W. C.
Helmbold. Vol. X. H. N. Fowler. Vol. XI. L. Pearson,
F. H. Sandbach. Vol. XII. H. Cherniss, W. C. Helmbold.
Vol. XIV. P. H. De Lacy and B. Einarson. Vol. XV.
F. H. Sandbach.
PLUTARCH: THE PARALLEL LIVES. B. Perrin. 11 Vols.
POLYBIUS. W. R. Paton. 6 Vols.
PROCOPIUS: HISTORY OF THE WARS. H. B. Dewing. 7 Vols.
PTOLEMY: TETRABIBLOS. *Cf.* MANETHO.
QUINTUS SMYRNAEUS. A. S. Way. Verse trans.
SEXTUS EMPIRICUS. Rev. R. G. Bury. 4 Vols.
SOPHOCLES. F. Storr. 2 Vols. Verse trans.
STRABO: GEOGRAPHY. Horace L. Jones. 8 Vols.
THEOPHRASTUS: CHARACTERS. J. M. Edmonds; HERODES,
etc. A. D. Knox.
THEOPHRASTUS: ENQUIRY INTO PLANTS. Sir Arthur Hort.
2 Vols.
THUCYDIDES. C. F. Smith. 4 Vols.
TRYPHIODORUS. *Cf.* OPPIAN.
XENOPHON: ANABASIS. C. L. Brownson.
XENOPHON: CYROPAEDIA. Walter Miller. 2 Vols.
XENOPHON: HELLENICA. C. L. Brownson.
XENOPHON: MEMORABILIA AND OECONOMICUS. E. C. Mar-
chant; SYMPOSIUM AND APOLOGY. O. J. Todd.
XENOPHON: SCRIPTA MINORA. E. C. Marchant and G. W.
Bowersock.

VOLUMES IN PREPARATION

GREEK AUTHORS

THEOPHRASTUS: DE CAUSIS PLANTARUM. G. K. K. Link and
B. Einarson.

LATIN AUTHORS

MANILIUS. G. P. Goold.

DESCRIPTIVE PROSPECTUS ON APPLICATION

CAMBRIDGE, MASS.   LONDON
HARVARD UNIV. PRESS   WILLIAM HEINEMANN LTD

8